19

19

THE OFFICIAL HISTORY
OF OUR LEAGUE CHAMPIONS

www.reachsport.com

I would like to dedicate this book to my wife Nati, children Carlos and Nati, mum Lynn, brother and sister-in-law Adrian and Alex and my best friend Rob. Without the support of my close-knit loving family, nothing would be possible. I therefore thank you for allowing me to dedicate so much of my time, which is also your time without me, to Liverpool Football Club.

Carl Clemente, September 2020

Written by Carl Clemente

First published in Great Britain in 2020 by
Reach Sport, 5 St Paul's Square, Liverpool, L3 9SJ.

www.reachsport.com
@reach_sport

Reach Sport is a part of Reach plc.
One Canada Square, Canary Wharf, London, E15 5AP.

ISBN: 978-1-911613-76-3
Ebook ISBN: 978-1-911613-92-3

Edited by Chris Brereton

Photographic acknowledgements:
Liverpool Football Club, Getty Images, PA.

Printed and bound by CPI Group (UK) Ltd,
Croydon, CR0 4YY.

19

19 INTRODUCTION
SETTING THE SCENE

O N JUNE 25, 2020, LIVERPOOL FOOTBALL CLUB were confirmed top-flight league champions for the 19th time since their birth in 1892. Jürgen Klopp's imperious team, who were also the reigning UEFA Champions League and FIFA Club World Cup holders, won their first English Premier League title with seven games to spare, ending an agonising 30-year wait since Kenny Dalglish's team last won the First Division in 1990.

Until then, Liverpool supporters under the age of around 40 were yet to fully appreciate or experience Liverpool winning a League Championship. Some fans would have been educated by older generations on past Liverpool title-winning seasons, whilst others used historical video footage to watch how previous leagues were won.

We have moved from a generation of Liverpool supporters who took winning the league for granted to a three-decade-long rollercoaster ride in which performances on the pitch and decisions off it ultimately prevented the club from achieving English football's top prize.

We all know how number 19 was won, but how does it compare to the other 18 times the Reds were crowned champions? This book aims to take you on a detailed and historical journey through all 19

League Championship-winning seasons. Each have their own unique story involving ups, downs, twists and turns but they all end with the same triumph; the Reds becoming the champions of England.

With the help of the excellent *LFChistory.net*, I have been able to produce the first ever in-depth story of every League Championship-winning season, bringing insights, statistics and analysis into the stand-out games, goals and major incidents.

I have delved into the archives, starting 120 years ago in September 1900, to find out what was written and said during each title-winning season and I have included the thoughts and opinions of the major protagonists from each league victory.

The contemporaneous reports of matches and events involving Liverpool Football Club offer an interesting insight into how the press judged the club. Of course, journalistic styles and methods have evolved with time but we have left newspaper reports as they were written, with some occasionally weird and wonderful phrasing, spelling and grammar.

Interviewed shortly after the 1973 League & UEFA Cup 'double', Bill Shankly pointed proudly to the glistening First Division championship trophy and described it as the club's "bread and butter".

He said that being successful in Europe had been good for the club and good for the country, but that winning the league was what the club wanted to do "all the time". In 1901, Liverpool were crowned league champions for the first time, under the guidance of their longest-ever serving manager, Tom Watson, who also added a second title five years later in 1906.

During the early 1920s, with the legendary Elisha Scott in goal, Liverpool won back-to-back titles. A Liverpool team which featured the legendary Billy Liddell were the first team to win the First Division upon its restart after the conclusion of World War II.

Liverpool teams strode majestically to one honour after another, rewriting the record books as the championship titles rolled in. In 1964, Liverpool won the first of three league titles of the Bill Shankly era, which was the start of a quarter of a century of unsurpassed supremacy. Bob Paisley won an incredible six league titles in nine seasons before he passed on the baton to his trusted lieutenant Joe Fagan, who won a treble in this first season in the hotseat. In 1985, Kenny Dalglish was appointed player-manager to ride the wave of success and after his magnificent 'double' in 1986, two more league titles followed.

During the club's golden years, from 1973 to 1990, no less than 11 league titles were won. They weren't won by just one team, or by a handful of outstanding players, they were won by an entire football club and one that implemented the main principles of stability and continuity.

The only thing that would change was the introduction of a couple of new players per season, who usually came from the reserves where they were nurtured by the famous Boot Room. Everything else stayed the same and was carried out in a simple but effective way – 'the Liverpool Way'.

Every employee of Liverpool Football Club was treated equally, from the manager to the ground staff and from the chairman to the turnstile operators.

After Dalglish resigned in 1990, subsequent managers couldn't emulate the league success of their predecessors and dominance of the English top tier was consequently enjoyed by others although the Reds were runners-up on five occasions until the 2019/2020 season, when Jürgen Klopp's team finally ended the long wait.

The arrival of Klopp on October 8, 2015, coupled with the backing of the clubs' owners, FSG, contributed to significant change at Anfield.

Self-named, 'The Normal One', Klopp instilled new belief into the club.

He stated in his first press conference that arriving at Liverpool was the "biggest honour" that he could have ever imagined and that everyone surrounding the club had to change from "doubters to believers" – a statement of intent that is already regarded as one of the greatest made by any Liverpool manager.

Although Klopp needed time to establish his team and to embed his ideologies into his players and staff, within five years, on July 22, 2020, Kenny Dalglish presented Liverpool's current captain Jordan Henderson with the Premier League trophy; league title number 19.

How that was achieved, and how it followed 18 other seasons to remember, is precisely what this book is about.

Finally, I'd like to acknowledge the efforts and work of Arnie Baldursson and Gudmundur Magnusson. At *LFChistory.net* they have produced the most extensive statistical and historical record imaginable and that has been a wonderful source of information and help.

I'd also like to thank publishers Reach Sport and editor Chris Brereton who have been extremely diligent and supportive throughout the entire process.

The following Liverpool fans also deserve thanks and my gratitude for their invaluable input: Adrian Killen, George Scott, Billy Howard, Ray Hughes, Ed Harris, John Swift, Kjell Hanssen, Michael Burgess, Chetan Muraji, Martin Gander, Paul Moran, Steve Hunter and Antony Murray.

Carl Clemente

1 · UP AND RUNNING

1900/01

AFTER FINISHING RUNNERS-UP BY A MERE TWO points to Aston Villa during the 1898/99 season and achieving their record top-flight league position to date, it was expected that Tom Watson's Liverpool would go one step further the following campaign. However, that was far from the case as Liverpool had an abysmal start to the 1899/1900 season, losing their first eight games in a row which finished their season in October.

The local journalists at the time were at a loss at Liverpool's form: "The question now agitating most minds is whether Liverpool intend scoring any points in this season's league tourney. On present form they are not likely to do so. Whatever other failings may be placed to the account of the present Liverpool team, they cannot be charged with inconsistency for they continue to lose match after match, whether at home or abroad, with surprising regularity. If this be the true form of the players there is only one remedy. The reserve team couldn't fare worse; but it seems astonishing that they can have lost all their skill in a few months' summer vacation."

The tragedy of striker George Allan overshadowed Liverpool's eight successive defeats.

Allan, Liverpool's greatest goalscorer throughout the previous years, had been reported ill for 1899/1900 pre-season training and in September 1899 manager Tom Watson said: "Diseased lungs are not cured in a day. Allan's absence is now beginning to be felt, and we are able to estimate him at his worth. Poor old George!" It had become apparent that Allan would not play league football again but his death from tuberculosis at the age of 24 on October 16, 1899 at his mother's home in Fife was still unexpected and described as a "thunderclap" for Liverpool fans.

Allan scored 56 goals in 96 games for Liverpool and he needed to be replaced if Watson's team were to start to climb the table. 'The Anfielders' made a key signing in Sam Raybould in January 1900. The forward arrived from New Brighton Tower in the Second Division where he had scored 10 goals in 13 games. He made his debut against West Bromwich Albion but despite creating great goalscoring opportunities for himself, he failed to find the net.

However, Liverpool improved from that day forward and Raybould endeared himself to the Liverpool faithful in his second game when he scored in the first minute of the Merseyside derby at Goodison Park. Everton, however, responded with three.

Raybould showed straight away that he might be an important signing for the club as well as left winger Charles Satterthwaite, signed from Burton Swifts, who scored a hat-trick in only his second appearance against Glossop FC at Anfield on December 23, 1899. Liverpool were on their way up the table.

Liverpool finished the season on a high after winning eight out of their last 10 games, but 10th place in the league was a massive disappointment compared to second place the previous year. Yet the club's greatest ever campaign awaited their supporters.

Tom Watson was now entering into his fifth season as manager since his arrival in the summer of 1896, when Liverpool made the most successful manager in the country an offer he couldn't refuse: an annual salary of £300, doubling what he had been receiving at Sunderland. Previous Liverpool manager John McKenna retired to the boardroom after just 36 games in charge and Watson moved across the country from Wearside to Merseyside.

Watson, only 37 at the time of this move, was still a relatively young man, certainly for a secretary. It was Watson's job to arrange fixtures, keep records, and submit match details to local papers. At the time, there was no such thing as a football manager, but Watson went beyond the remit of club secretary, and got involved in team selection, tactics and player recruitment – becoming a manager in all but name. This was a radical change to Liverpool's set-up, the *Cricket and Football Field* reported: "The team have never had a 'boss' off the field, and there have been too many on, so that a central figure, and one that commands respect, should work wonders in this direction." Watson implemented a strict diet and a new coaching regime at Anfield that had served him so well at Sunderland. The players' day started with a 30-minute stroll at 7.30am, breakfast at 8.30am ideally consisted of weak tea, chops, eggs, dry toast or stale bread. Butter, sugar, potatoes and milk were not held in high regard. Training was at 9.45am and again at 3.30pm. A glass of beer or claret was recommended at dinner and tobacco was to be "sparingly used". The day finished with a one hour stroll at 7.30pm.

Tom Watson was immensely popular throughout the game and seemed quite a character. Victor Hall wrote in the *Liverpool Echo*: "Many years ago I met in Glasgow a journalist who wanted to know if I had ever met Tom Watson, the Sunderland Club secretary. I told him I had seen Mr. Watson frequently acting as linesman for the Sunderland Club when they played Everton. 'Well', said he, 'if you ever get him in the humour in Liverpool, get him to sing "Bricks and Mortar". You will never have better fun as long as you live. He sang it here for us at our dinner last night and man I am laughing yet.'

"Well, a few years after that conversation the unexpected happened, and in the process of time Tom had become the Secretary of the Liverpool Football Club and speedily became the most popular club secretary within twenty miles of Liverpool. I heard 'Bricks and Mortar' in due course and like any Glasgow friend, enjoyed the hilarious rendering of the rollicking song, as have no doubt hundreds, if not thousands, of people still living, for there was not a more welcome guest in Liverpool at any function relating to sport than dear 'Old Tom'.

"Whether it was football, bowling, billiards, cycling, cricket or baseball, his name was the first to be written when invitations were being drawn up. When called upon for a song, as always, he was faithful to his old favourite. 'Bricks and Mortar' had a joyous chorus, for the words were simple, the melody easy, and the sentiment, irreproachable!"

Liverpool started the 1900/01 season with a convincing 3-0 home win over Blackburn on September 1, 1900 and the *Liverpool Mercury* reported: "There was the same rousing cheer as the familiar red figures emerged on the green sward, which was in splendid condition. Liverpool are undoubtedly a well-balanced side, and as at present constituted will compare in physique and ability very favourably with any team they may be called upon to meet in the league tourney. They have opened well, and it is to be hoped they will continue likewise."

A capacity crowd of 20,000 turned up at Anfield that afternoon to watch their team's first game of the new campaign. Liverpool's home was, of course, rather different from the present day. Anfield was largely uncovered with few seats and the groundsman used to graze his goats on the grass-covered terraces. The average home attendance was around 15,000, with many spectators not arriving until half-time. Floodlights and sponsorship were unknown, as were aeroplanes and cars, the players travelled to away games by train and horse-drawn wagonette, and changed for home matches at the Sandon public house.

Alex Raisbeck, the newly-named captain for the 1900/01 season, was commanding on the pitch and had a military air in the way he carried himself. This was certainly not out of place as he was one of seven brothers who either became soldiers or footballers and only a select few players in Liverpool's history have commanded so much respect and admiration.

Raisbeck always led by example on and off the pitch. Despite being 'only' 5ft 10ins (178 cm) in height, his timing and athleticism enabled him to reach the ball before taller opponents. He was an energetic centre-half, a position more similar to a modern day midfielder rather than a defender. He was at the forefront of Liverpool's defence and also the instigator of Liverpool's attacks as he possessed impressive stamina on the pitch. Raisbeck was here, there and everywhere. Now initiating an attack, now breaking up another. He dominated the whole field, and was, without question, the one superlative player. The scribe for Everton's programme captured Raisbeck's essence as a player when previewing a Merseyside derby at Goodison Park: "I am never inclined to over-elaborate praise, but truly, Alec Raisbeck was a giant among pigmies."

Liverpool Echo writer Victor Hall also sung Raisbeck's praise in an article called: 'ALEC RAISBECK, WHO RAISED LIVERPOOL'S PRESTIGE'. Hall wrote: "What a trier he was! Who that ever saw him play can forget the unmatchable enthusiasm he displayed in the sheer love of the game. He not only put body and dash into individual games he played, but more importantly he helped to create the soul, that inward sacred fire of zeal without which no club can thrive and live. Let us recall his characteristics. Tall, lithe, sinuous, and yet gifted with muscular and physical development beyond the ordinary. Active to a degree, speed either on the turn or in flight, and with niche, at the addition of resourcefulness and judgement that would have been all sufficient in a other player, without those added gifts, methodical in training, painstaking in preparation, genial with his players and considerate with his committee. With a perfect blending of the qualities that to make a really great player!"

When a survey was conducted among Liverpool supporters in 1939 to name the most famous players Liverpool had ever had in their ranks, Raisbeck – who had left the club three decades earlier – came second behind the incredibly popular Elisha Scott.

Raisbeck is a member of Liverpool's Official Hall of Fame and certainly deserves to be mentioned in the same breath as Kenny Dalglish, Billy Liddell and Steven Gerrard. In later life, after retiring from his managerial career, Raisbeck resumed his links with Liverpool by scouting for them up to the time of his death, at the age of 71, in 1949.

After that opening 3-0 win against Blackburn, Watson and his team were confident for the rest of the season and the Reds scored 10 goals and conceded one in their first three games, with Sam Raybould and Tom Robertson netting four and three goals respectively. Raybould was a future legend at the club and became the first player to score 100 league goals for Liverpool, a feat he achieved in 162 matches between January 20, 1900 and December 9, 1905.

After winning those first three matches, next up was the Merseyside derby.

The "local lions", as they were called, met at Goodison Park on September 22 and drew 1-1 in an entertaining game. The *Liverpool Mercury* wrote: "Both commenced the campaign in glorious fashion, and had secured the full maximum of points for the matches played.

"The first of the league engagements between these clubs brought together over 45,000 spectators at Goodison Park and the sides were at full strength. Everton won the toss, and at once tested the Liverpool defence. Settle was only a trifle wide of the mark with a swift shot and from a free-kick against Raisbeck, Sharp sent in a terrific shot to which Perkins cleverly attended. The pace was highly strong, the home side being slightly more successful with their movements, but eventually Cox was afforded an opening but could not get the better of Wolstenholme.

"Gradually the play became open, and both sides, particularly the half-backs, who covered the rearguard so ably that neither custodian was called upon for a considerable period, showed some very fine football. Proudfoot lost a chance of scoring by failing to take a pass from Turner, and directly following the Everton goal had a marvellous escape from a capital centre by Robertson, both Cox and Satterthwaite being at fault when but a few yards from Muir. Attacking again, Raisbeck conceded a corner, which was well taken, and from a return, McDonald headed into the net, play having been in progress 30 minutes. Play continued fast and interesting up to the interval, without further scoring.

"The second half opened in sensational fashion. The ball had no sooner been put into play, when Cox lifted it over Wolstenholme, and Raybould, racing up, slipped between the backs and scored in the first minute. This success put new life into the play of the Liverpool forwards, but there was no defeating the backs, of whom Balmer stood out conspicuously in sound defence.

"Abbott attempted to score from long range, and for some time afterwards neither side could claim any advantage. Free-kicks were now frequent, and from one of them, Perkins saved splendidly from Settle, while shortly afterwards Booth just skimmed the upright with a fast, low shot. Towards the close, Sharp had the better of a tussle with Dunlop, and shot in, apparently out of Perkins reach, but the custodian cleverly yet luckily met the ball with his foot and prevented a certain score. Everton pressed severely, and the keeper had again to save from a corner kick, but no further score was forthcoming and the game ended in a draw of 1 goal each."

In the next six league games, Liverpool won three and lost three and then faced their old foes Aston Villa, who had won the championship two seasons in a row. Liverpool took Villa to the cleaners with a 5-1 win on November 10, 1900 at Anfield. The *Liverpool Mercury* reported: "The secret of their decisive victory was due to the excellent methods adopted by the forwards, which completely non-plussed the Villa defenders. No sooner did they gain possession of the ball than they were away with it without the slightest hesitation, and the passing, which was delightfully executed, was always forward, so that the Villa backs were often caught napping by the speed with which the movement was developed and brought to a successful climax.

"Sam Raybould scored after five minutes play and his second goal was the pick of the bunch. But the tit-bit of the afternoon was the fourth point which Raybould touched up at the finish. It came from a return almost on the home goal line, and Tommy Robertson tricking Noon in his old style, flashed along the touch-line to near the corner flag. Here he sent across to Raybould, who was coming along with a wet sail, and without the slightest check in his speed the home centre reached the ball just as it touched the ground, and George could only feel the waft of air as the ball crashed past him." Liverpool struggled to impress following this outstanding win, inconsistency not worthy of champions elect. On New Year's Day 1901, the team were in sixth place, but only three points behind Nottingham Forest at the top and with a game in hand. Liverpool and Everton clashed at Anfield on January 19, 1901. A record attendance had seen the derby at Goodison Park but a continuous downpour kept fans away from Anfield, which resembled a quagmire.

The decision to start the game at 2.45pm instead of 3pm – to get the game over with as soon as possible because of the worsening conditions – already caused controversy because the fans who arrived around 3pm had already missed the first 15 minutes. Everton had the best of the play for most of the time in difficult conditions and eventually took the lead after 20 minutes as Jack Taylor managed to drive the ball past Bill Perkins.

Liverpool managed to equalise against the run of play in the 37th minute as John Cox pounced like a greyhound to beat William Muir in the Everton goal. Liverpool scored another goal just before half-time but it was disallowed after John Walker handballed Jack Robertson's goalbound shot.

When the teams came out for the second half, they were both wearing clean, dry costumes and seemed ready for action, but the crowd noticed that team captains, Raisbeck and Jimmy Settle, were in heavy discussion about abandoning the match due to the conditions. However, they were dissuaded from doing so as the crowd loudly exclaimed, "Play the game!"

The churned mud and water made the conditions nearly impossible before Jack Taylor scored his second of the game after 62 minutes to win the contest for Everton.

It was painful enough to lose to their neighbours and matters were then made worse when Liverpool lost their next two games – to Notts County in the first round of the FA Cup and then Bolton in the league.

Liverpool's title charge seemed to be fading. However, Tom Watson's current team beat his former team high-flying Sunderland 1-0 on February 22 and didn't look back after that.

The *Sunderland Daily Echo* reported: "Sunderland were distinctly unfortunate in not at least dividing the points. They had more of the game than their opponents, and had they been more accurate in their shooting the result would have been vastly different. Both sides played capital football, and a more interesting game has not been seen at the ground for a long while. It was full of rapid changes, and there was very little roughness. The visiting right wing were the most prominent on the Liverpool front line, Robertson being a particularly fine players. Raisbeck was the fluest half on the field by a long way, and the defence was of the best. They are a good all-round team are Liverpool, and have so far only lost a point more than Sunderland."

The scorer of the game's only goal was Liverpudlian, Jack Cox. Cox was the only Liverpool-born player to feature prominently during the 1900/1901 season. He was brought up in Robson Street in Everton, only a five-minute walk to Anfield. A joint Everton/Liverpool programme at the time described Cox's abilities: "A brilliant, but erratic genius. His great weakness can be a tendency to over-elaboration when in possession of the ball, but when the mood is on him, there is no hesitation; no finessing to discover the way towards goal. This is Cox, in his international humour, and when such is the case, the opposing defence know about it. On his day there is no cleverer outside-left in the kingdom than Cox."

Liverpool's victory at Roker Park was without doubt the turning point of their season as from March to late April they went on to win five league games out of eight, drawing the other three, scoring 13 goals and conceding four. Tom Robertson, Sam Raybould and Jack Cox were looking sharper up front while Raisbeck marshalled the defence.

There were now just three games to go and Liverpool were sat in fourth position in the table. Four points were separating the top six teams and Liverpool would need nine points from nine to be in contention to be crowned First Division champions for the first time.

On April 22, Liverpool travelled to Bramall Lane, where Raybould and Satterthwaite scored one each as Liverpool beat Sheffield United 2-0. The Reds then faced Nottingham Forest at Anfield in the penultimate game of the season in what was considered to be the decider for the league.

Sunderland had already played all their 34 league games and had 43 points to Liverpool's 41 but the Reds still had two games to play. The weather was fine and so was Liverpool's performance against Forest. Jack Cox gave the home fans something to shout about.

The *Liverpool Echo* reported: "When the game had been in progress for twenty-five minutes the home right wingers worked the ball up towards the Notts goal, and at the proper moment Robertson shot hard, and struck one of the goal posts, it rebounded to Cox, who promptly fastened on and placed the ball past Linacre. Liverpool's goal, being cheered to the echo."

William Goldie's second-half strike sealed Liverpool's win and the *Liverpool Echo* said: "Liverpool had a plethora of free-kicks to commence with, and from one which had an important result, as events will show, the estimable linesman aforesaid again made himself conspicuous. He objected to Robertson sneaking three inches of ground and pointed out the precise spot for the kick. As the result of the kick turned out all right, he was freely forgiven. The ball came to Goldie, who had it past Linacre in a jiffy, so that Liverpool were two goals up, and the ultimate result a long way towards settlement."

As an impartial observer put it: "Raisbeck was Raisbeck" versus Nottingham Forest, which indicates no one was surprised anymore by the brilliant displays of Liverpool's first superstar at the heart of the Anfielders' defence.

Liverpool's last game of the season was against relegation-doomed West Bromwich Albion. Liverpool had to get a draw to be sure of league success as Sunderland were equal on points with superior goal average, but had already played all their games. The *Sporting Life* reported on what happened next: "A considerable amount of importance attached to this conflict, which was decided last Monday evening, at West Bromwich, before 5,000 spectators. Both teams were at full strength. The Albion kicked off, and at once the play became of a fast and exciting character, the visitors testing the home defence severely, Amos Adams cleared, and soon Bill Perkins was called upon, but he managed to save cleverly. After twenty minutes, John Walker scored for Liverpool. After this the Throstles played up with great dash, and repeatedly had hard lines. At half-time the score was: Liverpool, one goal; Albion, nothing.

"The Albion forwards played remarkably well on resuming, but Alex Raisbeck, Billy Dunlop and Tom J. Robertson defied all attempts to score. Sam Raybould and Walker repeatedly tested Joe Reader, but the home goalkeeper managed to keep his charge secure. Fifteen minutes from time the score was still unaltered. Both sides strove desperately hard, the game ending: Liverpool, one goal; Albion, nothing. Liverpool have now secured the championship of the league."

Liverpool captain Raisbeck later told the *Weekly News* his memories of that historic day: "It was a momentous match as a visit to Brum was not lightly taken by any club in those days. But we simply had to win. All the boys were out for it. I remember I said to Willie Goldie on the train when we made for Brum on the day of the match, 'Do you think we'll manage it, Bill?' I think I can see the look on his face as he replied, 'Think we will manage it did ye say? Of course we're going to manage it'. As it turned out we didn't manage it in that confident sort of way as Willie Goldie's answer would have made believe. Time was wearing on and we still wanted that goal. At last! A goa- a goa- not yet. The ball was lying on the goal-line. Johnny Walker and the Throstles' goalkeeper had got mixed up some way and were lying near the back of the net, and there was no friendly foot to put the ball through. I know I stopped dead. I was fascinated, I suppose, by the sight of both goalkeeper and Walker starting to wrestle towards the ball at the same instant. Which would reach it first? There was such a deathly stillness. I fancied I heard the tick of the referee's watch, although he was twenty yards from me, and it seemed as though half an hour had passed. But it must have lasted only a second or two.

"The goalie was on his hands and knees crawling towards the ball, when Walker, with a cat-like movement, wriggled his body along the ground and just tipped the ball over the line and the goal and the championship was ours.

"Our team at that time was a heavy lot. I should say there was an average of twelve stone all over in the team. And the value of height and weight on the field is incalculable. It's a true saying 'a guid big ane is better than a guid wee ane ony day'.

"What a night after the match! We got a great send-off at Snowhill Station by the Brummagen folks who were good enough sports to cheer us off as league champions, but we were unprepared for what was waiting us at Liverpool. I should imagine there was a crowd of between 50-60,000 packed in front of the Central Station, and right along nearly as far as Lime Street. The street was literally black with people, and in the time-honoured way the horses were dispensed with and our brake practically carried along by willing hands to our headquarters at the Sandon Hotel. As we went along, the crowd yelled for me to make a speech from the brake. I was not to be found, however, as I found it convenient to lie low behind some of the others. Speechmaking was never in my line."

A fife and drum band playing 'The Conquering Hero' welcomed the Liverpool team on its return from The Hawthorns. The plan was to lift secretary Tom Watson shoulder-high in celebration, but as the *Liverpool Echo* put it: "No arms were long enough to grip his girth."

The Daily Telegraph summed up Liverpool's title win: "After nearly a decade of ups and downs between the divisions, Liverpool have finally won the league title. Their 1-0 victory over relegated-doomed West Bromwich at the Hawthorns was enough to put them two points clear of Sunderland. With only 59 goals, Liverpool have far from broken the First Division scoring dominance of Aston Villa, who finished well down the table with 45. But their real strength has been in defence, with Scottish international centre-half Alec Raisbeck outstanding in the middle."

The *Liverpool Echo* congratulated Watson's team on their league win: "The league tournament has finished for another season, and Liverpool enthusiasts are proud that the Anfield Road contingent have honoured the city by bringing the League trophy to the banks of the Mersey. Liverpool have fully made up for a moderate season, and from a poor tenth (their position last year) they have now to be hailed as league champions for 1900/01. It was a tussle between Liverpool and Sunderland until the last day of the season, but the Anfield men never faltered. Since the beginning of the year they have only twice gone under. The Liverpool men are the only team to have scored more away goals than they conceded on opponents' grounds (23 to 22). This is a great achievement.

"In away games they won seven times and drew five times, which secured them 19 points out of 34, more than half on opponents' territory. Their goals at home were nearly 3-1 against the opposition, when they won 12 times and drew twice. The facts mentioned point to the all-round excellence of the Liverpool team, their defence having the best record of the whole division. Liverpool are also credited with the most goals in the tourney, 59 to Sunderland's 57." And that, of course, was from only 34 league matches.

Sam Raybould, who was signed to lead the Liverpool attack in wake of the death of previous marksman George Allan, proved his worth by finishing the club's top scorer with 17 league goals.

In nine seasons of league football since the club was formed in 1892, Liverpool had now won the three league competitions they had taken part in. The Lancashire League was won during their very first season in 1893 and they were crowned Division 2 champions the following season in 1894 and for a second time in 1896.

The 1901 championship had been won by two points from, ironically enough, Watson's former employees Sunderland and seemed to herald a new and exciting era.

Interestingly, Liverpool only topped the table on two occasions during the entire season, after the very first game and more importantly the very last game of the season. In short, it was a tremendous performance by a club who were still building the foundations for a host of great teams to follow.

1900/01: Facts and Statistics

Final league table

		P	W	D	L	F	A	W	D	L	F	A	PTS
1	Liverpool FC	34	12	2	3	36	13	7	5	5	23	22	45
2	Sunderland	34	12	3	2	43	11	3	10	4	14	15	43
3	Notts County	34	13	2	2	39	18	5	2	10	15	28	40
4	Nottingham Forest	34	10	4	3	32	14	6	3	8	21	22	39
5	Bury	34	11	3	3	31	10	5	4	8	22	27	39
6	Newcastle United	34	10	5	2	27	13	4	5	8	15	24	38
7	Everton	34	10	4	3	37	17	6	1	10	18	25	37
8	The Wednesday	34	13	2	2	38	16	0	8	9	14	26	36
9	Blackburn Rovers	34	9	4	4	24	18	3	5	9	15	29	33
10	Bolton Wanderers	34	10	5	2	21	12	3	2	12	18	43	33
11	Manchester City	34	12	3	2	32	16	1	3	13	16	42	32
12	Derby	34	10	4	3	43	18	2	3	12	12	24	31
13	Wolves	34	6	10	1	21	15	3	3	11	18	40	31
14	Sheffield United	34	8	4	5	22	23	4	3	10	13	29	31
15	Aston Villa	34	8	5	4	32	18	2	5	10	13	33	30
16	Stoke	34	8	3	6	23	15	3	2	12	23	42	27
17	Preston North End	34	6	4	7	29	30	3	3	11	20	45	25
18	WBA	34	4	4	9	21	27	3	4	10	14	35	22

Games for the 1900/1901 season

(The number after date is league position after the game).

01.09.1900	1	W	3-0	Blackburn Rovers, Anfield, 1st Division
08.09.1900	4	W	2-1	Stoke, Victoria Ground, 1st Division
15.09.1900	2	W	5-0	West Bromwich Albion, Anfield, 1st Division
22.09.1900	2	D	1-1	Everton, Goodison Park, 1st Division
29.09.1900	4	L	1-2	Sunderland, Anfield, 1st Division
06.10.1900	4	W	3-2	Derby County, Baseball Ground, 1st Division
13.10.1900	2	W	2-1	Bolton Wanderers, Anfield, 1st Division
20.10.1900	5	L	0-3	Notts County, Trent Bridge, 1st Division
27.10.1900	4	W	3-2	Preston North End, Anfield, 1st Division
03.11.1900	4	L	1-2	Wolves, Molineux, 1st Division
10.11.1900	3	W	5-1	Aston Villa, Anfield, 1st Division
17.11.1900	5	L	2-3	The Wednesday, Owlerton, 1st Division
24.11.1900	5	D	1-1	Newcastle United, St. James' Park, 1st Division
01.12.1900	6	L	1-2	Sheffield United, Anfield, 1st Division

08.12.1900	6	W	4-3	Manchester City, Hyde Road, 1st Division
15.12.1900	4	W	1-0	Bury, Anfield, 1st Division
22.12.1900	5	D	0-0	Nottingham Forest, City Ground, 1st Division
25.12.1900	2	D	0-0	Derby County, Anfield, 1st Division
29.12.1900	7	L	1-3	Blackburn Rovers, Ewood Park, 1st Division
01.01.1901	6	W	3-1	Stoke, Anfield, 1st Division
05.01.1901		W	1-0	West Ham Utd, Memorial Recreation Ground, FAC SR*
19.01.1901	8	L	1-2	Everton, Anfield, 1st Division
09.02.1901		L	0-2	Notts County, Trent Bridge, FAC 1st round
16.02.1901	8	L	0-1	Bolton Wanderers, Burnden Park, 1st Division
23.02.1901	7	W	1-0	Sunderland, Roker Park, 1st Division
02.03.1901	7	D	2-2	Preston North End, Deepdale, 1st Division
09.03.1901	6	W	1-0	Wolves, Anfield, 1st Division
16.03.1901	6	W	2-0	Aston Villa, Villa Park, 1st Division
23.03.1901	4	D	1-1	The Wednesday, Anfield, 1st Division
30.03.1901	3	W	3-0	Newcastle United, Anfield, 1st Division
08.04.1901	4	W	1-0	Notts County, Anfield, 1st Division
13.04.1901	3	W	3-1	Manchester City, Anfield, 1st Division
20.04.1901	4	D	0-0	Bury, Gigg Lane, 1st Division
22.04.1901	2	W	2-0	Sheffield United, Bramall Lane, 1st Division
27.04.1901	2	W	2-0	Nottingham Forest, Anfield, 1st Division
29.04.1901	1	W	1-0	West Bromwich Albion, The Hawthorns, 1st Division

*Supplementary round of the Football Association Challenge Cup, where the ten finalists in the various divisions were drawn against the ten clubs excused before the first round of the competition proper takes place.

Friendlies

17.09.1900	W	2-1	Stoke, Anfield
01.10.1900	L	0-2	Burnley, Anfield, Lancashire Senior Cup
26.12.1900	L	2-5	West Bromwich Albion, The Hawthorns
19.02.1901	W	8-0	Manchester City, Hyde Road, Testimonial*
05.04.1901	W	2-1	Everton, Anfield
06.04.1901	L	2-3	Manchester City, Hyde Road
09.04.1901	W	4-3	Cumberland, Borough Park

* Testimonial for Manchester City player, Thomas Herbert 'Bert' Read.

Appearances for the 1900/1901 season

Name	League	FA Cup	Total
Bill Goldie	34	2	36
Bill Perkins	34	2	36
Tommy Robertson	34	2	36
Billy Dunlop	33	2	35
Jack Cox	32	2	34
Alex Raisbeck	31	2	33
Sam Raybould	31	2	33
Johnny Walker	29	1	30
Charlie Wilson	26	2	28
Tom Robertson	25	2	27
Charlie Satterthwaite	21	0	21
Andy McGuigan	14	2	16
John Glover	10	0	10
John Hunter	8	1	9
Maurice Parry	8	0	8
Rab Howell	2	0	2
Thomas John Hunter	1	0	1
John Davies	1	0	1

Goalscorers for the 1900/1901 season

Name	League	FA Cup	Total
Sam Raybould	17	1	18
Jack Cox	10	0	10
Tommy Robertson	9	0	9
Johnny Walker	6	0	6
Charlie Satterthwaite	5	0	5
Andy McGuigan	5	0	5
John Hunter	3	0	3
Bill Goldie	2	0	2
Alex Raisbeck	1	0	1
Charlie Wilson	1	0	1

The squad during the 1900/1901 season

Bill Perkins, Goalkeeper.
Billy Dunlop, Defender.
Maurice Parry, Defender.
Alex Raisbeck, Defender.
Charlie Wilson, Defender.
Bill Goldie, Defender.
John Glover, Defender.
Tom Robertson, Defender.
Thomas John Hunter, Defender.
Rab Howell, Defender.
Jack Cox, Midfielder.
Sam Raybould, Striker.
Andy McGuigan, Striker.
Johnny Walker, Striker.
John Hunter, Striker.
Charlie Satterthwaite, Striker.
John Davies, Striker.
Tommy Robertson, Right-winger.

Transfers for the 1900/1901 season

In:
Tom Robertson – Stoke, £400, 26 April 1900
Andy McGuigan – Hibernian, Unknown, May 1900
John Glover – Blackburn Rovers, £350 *, 9 May 1900
Maurice Parry – Brighton United, Free, 13 August 1900

Out:
John Parkinson – Blackpool, Unknown, May 1900
Archie Goldie – New Brighton Tower, Unknown, May 1900
Peter Kyle – Leicester Fosse, Unknown, 9 May 1900
Hugh Morgan – Blackburn Rovers, Unknown, June 1900
General Stevenson – Barnsley, Unknown, 30 June 1900
David Wilson – Airdrieonians, Unknown, 20 July 1900

A collection of statistics for the 1900-1901 season

The season in numbers
Total games: 36
Games won: 20
Games drawn: 7
Games lost: 9
Clean sheets – League: 14
Clean sheets – Overall: 15
Total goals: 60
Average attendance at home – League: 15,647
Average attendance at home – Overall: 15,647
Average goals per game – League: 2.12
Average goals per game – Overall: 2.12

Goals split down to competitions:
League – 59
FA Cup – 1

Player debuts:
Tom Robertson against Blackburn Rovers on 01.09.1900
Andy McGuigan against Derby on 06.10.1900
Maurice Parry against Bolton Wanderers on 13.10.1900
John Glover against Notts County on 20.10.1900
John Davies against Wolves on 09.03.1901

Statistics and information provided by LFChistory.net

2 ONWARDS AND UPWARDS

1905/06

ON APRIL 1, 1901 THE FOOTBALL LEAGUE RULED that players' salaries be capped at £4 a week and signing on fees limited to £10. Liverpool had offered better wages than most and suffered because of this ruling. They failed to attract new additions to the team but, at the same time, they did manage to keep all their key players.

The club tried to get around the new ruling by giving players other jobs at the club which they of course got extra money for. Alex Raisbeck, for example, worked as a bill inspector for the club, supposedly responsible for checking public notice boards advertising the club's matches.

Liverpool struggled to follow up their first league title success and finished 11th in the 1901/02 season. What irritated Liverpool supporters to no end was that for the first time in several years, Everton were considerably stronger in the league, grabbing second place and trailing Sunderland by just three points.

One event overshadowed Liverpool's 1901/02 season. Hardly a year had passed since John Houlding saw his dream finally come true when Liverpool won the league title but Liverpool Football

Club now mourned the death of the club's founder and president, who died at a hotel in Nice, France, on March 1, 1902. Houlding, who was born in 1832 in Liverpool, was a Conservative councillor for Everton and Kirkdale from 1884 and on the extension of the city's boundaries in 1895 he was raised to the bench of aldermen.

He was an Orangeman and Grand Master, second in Freemason seniority only to the King himself and Lord Mayor of Liverpool from 1897/98 where he served "in a way that was above criticism and gained for him much esteem". Houlding always had a keen interest in sports of various kinds. He had been the erstwhile Everton and latter day Liverpool bankroller, second President of The Anfield Bicycle Club and president of the English Baseball Association.

Liverpool needed a boost in the following 1902/03 season and it was provided by Sam Raybould who was absolutely on fire, scoring 32 goals in 34 appearances becoming Liverpool's first ever 30 goals a season striker and the First Division's top scorer.

Raybould scored four goals in a 9-2 win over Grimsby on December 6 and when Liverpool then scored nine more and conceded just three in their next three games, a correspondent of *The Penny Illustrated Paper and Illustrated Times* commented that: "I have a big idea of the powers of Liverpool; their forwards are a very smart line, and if Tom Watson's men don't bring their club bang in the front of the league before the end of the season I shall be more than surprised."

Raybould's goalscoring exploits were, however, not enough for a top spot and Liverpool had to make do with being fifth with 38 points, four points behind champions The Wednesday, who won the title by one point from Aston Villa and Sunderland.

What happened next season in 1903/04 astounded the club's fans. Liverpool completely collapsed in the league, losing their opening five games, a situation compounded when Sam Raybould, John

Glover and William Goldie were banned for seven months after accepting 'financial inducements' to move to the Southern League's Portsmouth. It was ruled that they were not allowed to play football until after December 31, 1903 and could never join Portsmouth.

The Football League, since its inception in 1888, had been based predominantly in the North and Midlands whereas the Southern League was the dominant competition in Southern and central England. Portsmouth tried to use the lack of transfer regulations between the leagues to their advantage but their approach was deemed illegal.

Liverpool had relied on Raybould's goals, Goldie had been an ever present in the league the previous season and left-back Glover had also played 30 out of 34 league games but now the club slumped from fifth place to surprising relegation candidates.

When the suspension was over, Goldie joined Fulham in January 1904 whereas Glover had already left Liverpool in October 1903 for First Division Small Heath. Raybould was expected to save Liverpool from their slump on his return on January 1, but he only scored four goals in 15 games.

The Everton/Liverpool joint programme was sympathetic towards Raybould: "Only one man in a thousand can rise to the height asked of Raybould. It was assumed that when he returned goals would come and victory follow as a natural sequence. They didn't and of course the centre was blamed."

Since the number of teams in the First Division had been increased to 18 a few years before, the two bottom teams were automatically relegated and this cost Liverpool dearly. The Reds only won nine games compared to 17 the year before and finished second from bottom, meaning Liverpool were back in the Second Division just three years after winning the First Division.

Liverpool started slowly in the Second Division, winning unconvincingly 2-0 in the opening game and then drawing two in a row which was way below expectation and the club programme expressed its concern: "It must be confessed the followers of the club are not quite at ease. The three opening matches were fully expected to realise six points, instead of only four have accrued. We are waiting patiently. I hope our waiting will not be too long deferred. At all events, the men are absolutely determined to show the populace that they can still play the game."

However, Liverpool then went on a rampage, scoring 29 goals and conceding only five as they won 10 games in a row remaining undefeated until December when they lost two out of five.

Raybould took a while to get going, having been moved from centre forward to the left wing. He scored only two goals in the opening eight matches but managed two in a 5-0 win over Grimsby Town on October 29, which silenced his critics for the time being, as the club programme noted: "Parkinson missed, but the ball came to Raybould who scored with a beautifully judged shot – the best goal of the day. His success was cordially received, and perhaps the crowd will now give him fair play and encouragement instead of barracking him."

Raybould ended up with 19 goals and Robbie Robinson scored 24 but the scoring sensation of the team proved to be Bootle boy Jack Parkinson who was unstoppable in the Second Division, scoring 20 goals in 21 games.

Liverpool's defence, with Raisbeck in the centre, was also in great form, only conceding 28 goals in 36 games. Sunderland's legendary goalkeeper Ned Doig was also an excellent addition to the squad, keeping 16 clean sheets.

Doig had teamed up with his old boss, Tom Watson, in the summer and became the oldest debutant in Liverpool's history when featuring against Burton United on September 1; two months shy of his 38th birthday.

Three teams – Liverpool, Bolton Wanderers and Manchester United – were in a class of their own in the Second Division. Liverpool drew with Bolton 1-1 at Anfield with six games to go and then brushed aside Manchester United 4-0 at home in the penultimate game of the season, winning the league two points ahead of Bolton.

First Division football would again be witnessed at Anfield next season.

Reporters at the *Liverpool Echo* were clearly optimistic for the battle ahead in the First Division in the 1905/06 season: "The Anfielders have trained loyally and well during the past few weeks, and at the present time they could not be in finer fettle or condition. As will be seen 'the old brigade' of last season are being relied upon to do the battle for the honour of Liverpool, and if the form that lifted them from second-class company can only be maintained they should occupy a high place in the league ladder before the winter is over."

Liverpool's opening game of the 1905/06 season was a complete disaster. Besides losing 3-1 to Woolwich Arsenal, Jack Parkinson broke his wrist and didn't play again until mid-March. Moreover, Watson's team were forced to finish the game with only nine men after Billy Dunlop twisted his knee during the second half. Liverpool had to do without influential Dunlop for their next two matches which were equally disastrous as the opening one.

The directors were fully alive to their need of players. This became especially evident when they had Jack Parkinson smashed up in the first match at Woolwich. However they were judicious in their desperation, and, as their excellent chairman Edwin Berry said at the social gathering at which the medals were presented to the players in commemoration of their winning the Second Division championship: "We don't want to sign on any but absolutely class men. It is useless our filling our books with their names if we are not sure that they will be men of value."

On September 9, 1905 Blackburn Rovers took away a 3-1 victory from rain-soaked Anfield. Referee Fred Kirkham took the players off the pitch after 25 minutes because of torrential rain. During the 13-minute break before play resumed many spectators left the open terracing, jumped onto the pitch and then forced their way into the reserved stand to find shelter from the rain. Liverpool's third consecutive defeat of the season came two days later at Villa Park in a 5-0 thrashing and they now found themselves rock bottom of the First Division.

Tom Watson's former captain Scottish-born left-back Billy Dunlop was a prominent member of the squad which won Liverpool's first ever First Division title in 1901, missing just one of the 34 league games.

According to Liverpool's matchday programme: "Dunlop plays a characteristic full-back game, and the familiar cry of on the Anfield ground 'Boot it, Dunlop' is fairly suggestive of his method of defence. There can be no two opinions of his ability to kick the ball from almost any position. Always keen and watchful on the field, he betrays his over-anxiety to repel the invader by his terrific lunges, and on his day, there is no more brilliant player than this same Dunlop. A better servant no club ever possessed, and though we may occasionally differ from him as to the methods he employs on the field, on one point we must all agree, that for downright single-mindedness of purpose Dunlop's tactics have never been questioned."

Despite their "melancholy experiences" in the league, the Liverpool players were in good spirits for their next game away at Sunderland, not a favourite hunting ground for the Reds throughout the years. Liverpool spent the evening prior to the game at one of the music halls in town and whether that did the trick or not the Anfielders finally registered a win with the enigmatic Sam Raybould scoring twice in a 2-1 win.

A fox terrier who ran onto the pitch and "showed the liveliest interest in football" stole the show according to the *Liverpool Echo*. "He raced for the leather amid roars of Homeric laughter, and Mr. Adams had to suspend hostilities until the little creature was forcibly ejected." Raybould's second goal was simply brilliant, controlling a good pass, taking the ball down the wing, tricking his opponent and shooting well out of the keeper's reach. A second consecutive win a week later was recorded against Birmingham as Watson's men had seemed to put their disastrous start behind them.

Everton, who were one point from the title the previous season, were Liverpool's next opponents on September 30 at Goodison Park. F.E. Hughes wrote in the *Liverpool Echo* that: "Time was when the feelings between adherents of Reds and Blues ran high as twixt Capulet and Montague, but now the vendetta is nothing more serious than a mental reservation on the part of each follower that, come what may, their own side may win."

History was not on Liverpool's side for this eagerly awaited clash. The Merseyside teams had played each other nine times in the league on Everton's ground. Everton had scored 25 goals in their seven wins and only allowed Liverpool eight goals and one win. Liverpool showed much more gusto in the opening exchanges, Cox hitting the upright and Goddard scoring, but judged offside. However, Everton took the lead against run of play in the 15th minute with a goal from Settle and ran out 4-2 winners.

The top two sides were next, second-placed Derby and 1903 and

1904 league champions The Wednesday (they did not change their name to Sheffield Wednesday until 1929). Jack Cox was in impeccable form as Liverpool beat Derby 4-1 but Cox and Raybould were sorely missed when Liverpool were beaten 3-2 by The Wednesday. Liverpool were in 16th place after eight games with only six points.

A 22-year-old Sam Hardy made his debut replacing Doig in the next game against Nottingham Forest as Doig was suffering from rheumatism.

Hardy was one of the outstanding English goalkeepers of his time. He joined from Chesterfield in May 1905 and remained first-choice at Anfield for another six years before moving on to further success with Aston Villa. Liverpool beat Forest 4-1 and went on a great run beating Middlesbrough 5-1 where Joe Hewitt grabbed a hat-trick.

Getting a result against champions Newcastle at St. James' Park was no mean feat, but Liverpool beat the Geordies 3-2. First-placed Aston Villa came to Anfield and were buried 3-0, Sam Hardy saved a penalty from William Garratty in the game which also served as Sam Raybould's benefit match.

After winning 11 out of their last 14 games, Liverpool were top of the table on New Year's Day with a three-point lead on Aston Villa and The Wednesday.

The first game of 1906 was a 3-1 win against Stoke at Anfield. Liverpool started the match with 10 men because Billy Dunlop arrived late at the ground. The full-back then had to leave the pitch with an injury but was able to resume after treatment. Liverpool were forced to play in white, even though they were the home team, because the visitors turned up in red jerseys.

Second Division Leicester Fosse were Liverpool's opponents in the first round of the FA Cup at Anfield and Alf West no doubt never forgot this game as he missed two penalties, one in each half.

West had become Liverpool's first-choice right-back since his £500 move from Barnsley in the autumn of 1903 and his playing style was described in March, 1905 in the matchday programme: "West is an ideal full-back, reliable in tackling, and always cool and collected under the severest pressure. His methods are such as commend themselves to all who desire to see football played with a maximum of skill and a minimum of physical force. West does not rely upon the latter quality; he calmly awaits the oncoming forward and judges the precise moment for intervention with admirable facility."

In all fairness, West was fortunate to be alive after a shooting accident in 1904, an event which was also reported in the programme at the time: "West had been training for a 120 yards handicap and finished his preparation with a week at Lytham. Everything was complete, and he, accompanied by his trainer, went to take the final spin before leaving for Keswick where was due to run the following day. Not having had much practice at starting with the pistol, it was decided to adopt this method. Whilst the trainer was handling the weapon, it accidentally went off and West received a bullet under his right shoulder. He walked away some 200 yards, and then, staggering, fell into his trainer's arms. Fortunately the bullet did not penetrate the lungs, but spent itself by travelling along the outside of the ribs to the front part of the chest." West was in critical condition as he had been actually been shot with two bullets just above the heart by trainer William Norman "who was naturally much upset".

Luckily for Liverpool, Leicester Fosse fared no better from the spot and Billy Bannister missed his spotkick. Three penalty misses and three goals, Liverpool scoring two of them and progressing to the next round against Barnsley. Liverpool were drawn to play away but the tie was switched to Anfield by arrangement with the Yorkshire club. Alf West scored the winning goal.

Liverpool were next drawn versus Western League's runners-up Brentford who had done well reaching this far in the cup. The Reds proved too much of an obstacle and Brentford lost 2-0. Southern League's Southampton awaited in the quarter-finals, who after having disposed of Liverpool 4-1 in 1902, lost in a cup final replay against Sheffield United.

The Saints were ripped apart 3-0 at Anfield this time around by Sam Raybould, who netted a hat-trick, and an exciting tie was on the horizon for the Reds against Everton at Villa Park in the semi-finals. That game was however a major disappointment for the Reds who lost 2-0 in front of a 37,000-strong crowd.

In between their exploits in the cup, Liverpool had held their own in the league, winning three from four games. On March 17, Liverpool slaughtered Middlesbrough 6-1 at Anfield, which became the Reds' biggest win of the season. Jack Parkinson scored on his return from the wrist injury he sustained during the first fixture of the season and which had kept him sidelined for over six months.

After a 0-0 draw versus Bury on April 2, Liverpool had a four-point lead on Preston, but North End had a game in hand. Liverpool were top thanks to 12 wins at home from 16, but the Reds had lost seven away games out of 17.

Champions Newcastle were beaten 3-0 at Anfield, but the scoreline flattered Liverpool with Sam Hardy in impeccable form. Another home game against Everton was next on the agenda. Everton took the lead when Hardy dropped the ball after what should have been an easy save and Jack Taylor capitalised. The game was on occasions held up by the dense crowds lined up around the pitch but Liverpool finally got a breakthrough when Taylor fouled Parkinson in the penalty area and West converted the penalty. Final score: Liverpool 1-1 Everton.

The games came thick and fast and, incredibly, the following day Liverpool faced Wolves away. Preston were breathing down Liverpool's necks, only three points behind with a game in hand, and Liverpool could not afford the slightest slip.

Liverpool proved sharper than Wolves on the day and scored two goals without response. To boost Liverpool's spirits, Preston lost to Stoke and the gap at the top had been widened to five points. Preston had three league games left compared to Liverpool's two and the Reds only needed two more points to secure the title.

Liverpool faced Bolton away and more than 1,000 supporters followed the team to Burnden Park. Liverpool dominated the opening exchanges and Arthur Goddard and Joe Hewitt rattled the posts of the goal. Against the run of play, just before half-time, Shepherd opened the scoring for Bolton after Hardy had failed to clear effectively after a corner. In the early second half, Shepherd increased Bolton's lead with a brilliant goal. Jack Parkinson reduced the advantage, but Bolton got their third goal and despite Parkinson's second, Bolton ran out 3-2 winners.

The result, however, did not matter as Preston lost 2-0 at Sunderland. Liverpool's five-point lead was intact and as Preston could only get a maximum of four points from their last two remaining games Liverpool were champions for the second time in their history.

The League Championship success was particularly impressive as Liverpool had given other teams a headstart by losing their opening three games but they then didn't let go of the top spot once they captured it in the middle of December and Liverpool became the first club to achieve the double feat of winning the Second and First Division championships in successive seasons.

Liverpool's final league game of the season came five days later against Sheffield United at Anfield. Heavy rain in the hour before the scheduled kick-off kept the crowd down to a much lower figure than might have been expected to greet the newly-crowned English champions.

The club programme reported: "The encounter with the Cutlers was spoilt by the elements. Instead of a mammoth gate there was for Anfield Road, but a handful of spectators. Those who did turn up had a run for their money, although the vital interest had gone, as Liverpool were already champions, and Sheffield United had nothing at stake. The home team's victory was sufficiently pronounced, however 3-1 being the verdict in their favour."

Another reason for the low gate at Anfield to welcome the champions, was almost certainly due to the fact that the game clashed with the FA Cup final, in which Everton defeated Newcastle 1-0 at Crystal Palace. It was indeed a notable double for the city.

Arthur Goddard was Liverpool's only ever-present in the team, playing all 38 league games. Goddard was described in the *Lancashire Evening Post* as a "clever dribbler, beats a half-back very smartly, and centres with excellent judgment. He is also a good shot, and plays the game most intelligently. At first he does not look fast, but his long strides take him over the ground quickly, and as an all-round player he has large possibilities".

Liverpool finished the season by winning certainly the largest trophy in the history of football, The Sheriff of London Charity Shield, also known as the Dewar Shield, which was over six feet high. The competition originated from 1898 and was an annual game between the best professional and amateur side in England. The amateurs, Corinthians, were easily defeated 5-1 by Liverpool. A year later the competition was cancelled.

The Sports Spectator saluted the champions: "Perkins had vacated the goal area which was shared by the evergreen James Doig and silent

Sam Hardy. The backs were West, Dunlop, Murray and Chorlton, a capital quartet. The half-backs usually on duty were Parry, Raisbeck and Bradley; the Reds have never had a better line, if one so good, and George Lathom and Fleming occasionally rendered excellent service. In the forward line Goddard, Robinson, Hewitt, Raybould, Cox, Garside and Carlin knew the way to goal, as a tally of 79 goals scored in 38 games testified."

After enjoying league success, the end-of-season meeting between the directors and shareholders of Liverpool was without doubt a pleasant one as the *Cricket and Football Field* reported in June, 1906: "The season had been one of unruffled prosperity, and for the second successive year they met as members of a club that had carried off a championship.

"They had also made history, the team being the first to pose as champions of the two sections of the league in consecutive seasons. That feat may not be rivalled for a generation, was able to point with pardonable pride to three splendid trophies – the league championship, the Liverpool Cup, and the Dewar Shield – a trio never previously held by any one club.

"On top of this came the declaration of a five percent dividend and the prospect of a vastly improved ground by the time another season opens. Tom Watson's reference to the players who had had a share in the brilliant victories was made in his usual happy vein, apt his generous allusion to Everton as the winners of the Football Association Cup awoke a very hearty response. But nothing went down better than his reminder that Alex Raisbeck had been the captain of the team that defeated England.

"Really there seems to be no limit to the honour that came the way of Liverpool during the memorable season of 1905/06. Mr. Watson hit the nail on the head when he drew attention to the fact that the club was noted for its up and downs, and his hearers appreciated his wish that they should take 'Upwards' as their motto of the future. But the puzzle is how much higher can they go. Well, the only thing left for them do is to win the English Cup and keep their grip on the championship. And why should they not do it? We shall see in the sweet by and bye."

Although the 1905/06 season ended on April 21, 1906, Liverpool didn't receive their medals until December 17, 1906 after 17 games of the 1906/07 season were played. The *Cricket and Football Field* reported: "Liverpool's league team of footballers were presented on Monday evening with handsome gold medals to commemorate the club's success in carrying off the league's First Division championship last season. The Chairman of the club (Councillor Edwin Berry) made the presentation, and the occasion was taken advantage of to hold a splendid smoking concert at the Exchange Station Hotel on Tithebarn Street, Liverpool.

"There was a large and enthusiastic attendance of directors, shareholders and privileged friends. The musical part of the programme – in the able hands of Directors William Robert Williams and Albert Worgan, and Secretary Tom Watson – was of the best description, the artists being of first-class quality.

"Mr. Berry explained that the delay in holding the gathering was due to the FA's sanction having to be first received before the medals could be presented. All the players who had participated in five or more schedule engagements last season were awarded medals, the full list thus qualified being Alex Raisbeck, Billy Dunlop, Ned Doig, Tom Chorlton, Maurice Parry, James Bradley, George Latham, Arthur Goddard, Robert Robinson, Jack Parkinson, Joe Hewitt, John Carlin, John Cox, Sam Hardy, Alf West and Sam Raybould.

"The four last named were not presented to receive their medals, but the others had a flattering reception upon stepping forward, especially skipper Raisbeck. Trainer William Connell was also honoured with a medal, and, last but by no means least, Mr. Tom Watson.

"Of course, the popular Secretary made an able speech. He loved Liverpool, its club, and its players, he said. The medal just received constituted his fifth top-flight championship medal, three with Sunderland and two with Liverpool. He complimented the players on their daring and their originality in marching off with the championship of the two divisions in successive years. Nor were Everton forgotten, Mr. Watson congratulating Everton on their FA Cup achievement. He hoped Liverpool would also qualify as holders in the near future; also that in the course of a few years they, too, like Everton, might became wealthy and the owners outright of their ground."

1905/06: Facts and Statistics

Final league table

	P	W	D	L	F	A	W	D	L	F	A	PTS
Liverpool FC	38	14	3	2	49	15	9	2	8	30	31	51
Preston North End	38	12	5	2	36	15	5	8	6	18	24	47
The Wednesday	38	12	5	2	40	20	6	3	10	23	32	44
Newcastle United	38	12	4	3	49	23	6	3	10	25	25	43
Manchester City	38	11	2	6	46	23	8	3	8	27	31	43
Bolton Wanderers	38	13	1	5	51	22	4	6	9	30	45	41
Birmingham	38	14	2	3	49	20	3	5	11	16	39	41
Aston Villa	38	13	2	4	51	19	4	4	11	21	37	40
Blackburn Rovers	38	10	5	4	34	18	6	3	10	20	34	40
Stoke	38	12	5	2	41	15	4	2	13	13	40	39
Everton	38	12	1	6	44	30	3	6	10	26	36	37
Woolwich Arsenal	38	12	4	3	43	21	3	3	13	19	43	37
Sheffield United	38	10	4	5	33	23	5	2	12	24	39	36
Sunderland	38	13	2	4	40	21	2	3	14	21	49	35
Derby	38	10	5	4	27	16	4	2	13	12	42	35
Notts County	38	8	9	2	34	21	3	3	13	21	50	34
Bury	38	8	5	6	30	26	3	5	11	27	48	32
Middlesbrough	38	10	4	5	41	23	0	7	12	15	48	31
Nottingham Forest	38	11	2	6	40	27	2	3	14	18	52	31
Wolves	38	7	5	7	38	28	1	2	16	20	71	23

Games for the 1905-1906 season

(The number after date is league position after the game)

02.09.1905	15	L	1-3	Woolwich Arsenal, Manor Ground, 1st Division
09.09.1905	19	L	1-3	Blackburn Rovers, Anfield, 1st Division
11.09.1905	20	L	0-5	Aston Villa, Villa Park, 1st Division
16.09.1905	18	W	2-1	Sunderland, Roker Park, 1st Division
23.09.1905	14	W	2-0	Birmingham, Anfield, 1st Division
30.09.1905	16	L	2-4	Everton, Goodison Park, 1st Division
07.10.1905	13	W	4-1	Derby County, Anfield, 1st Division
14.10.1905	16	L	2-3	The Wednesday, Owlerton, 1st Division
21.10.1905	14	W	4-1	Nottingham Forest, Anfield, 1st Division
28.10.1905	10	W	1-0	Manchester City, Hyde Road, 1st Division
04.11.1905	9	W	3-1	Bury, Anfield, 1st Division
11.11.1905	8	W	5-1	Middlesbrough, Ayresome Park, 1st Division
18.11.1905	7	D	1-1	Preston North End, Anfield, 1st Division

25.11.1905	6	W	3-2	Newcastle United, St. James' Park, 1st Division
02.12.1905	3	W	3-0	Aston Villa, Anfield, 1st Division
09.12.1905	2	W	4-0	Wolves, Anfield, 1st Division
16.12.1905	1	W	2-1	Sheffield United, Bramall Lane, 1st Division
23.12.1905	1	W	2-0	Notts County, Anfield, 1st Division
25.12.1905	1	D	2-2	Bolton Wanderers, Anfield, 1st Division
26.12.1905	1	L	1-2	Stoke, Victoria Ground, 1st Division
30.12.1905	1	W	3-0	Woolwich Arsenal, Anfield, 1st Division
01.01.1906	1	W	3-1	Stoke, Anfield, 1st Division
06.01.1906	1	D	0-0	Blackburn Rovers, Ewood Park, 1st Division
13.01.1906		W	2-1	Leicester Fosse, Anfield, FA Cup 1st round
20.01.1906	1	W	2-0	Sunderland, Anfield, 1st Division
27.01.1906	1	L	0-1	Birmingham, Muntz Street, 1st Division
03.02.1906		W	1-0	Barnsley, Anfield, FA Cup 2nd round
10.02.1906	1	W	3-0	Derby County, Baseball Ground, 1st Division
17.02.1906	1	W	2-1	The Wednesday, Anfield, 1st Division
24.02.1906		W	2-0	Brentford, Anfield, FA Cup 3rd round
03.03.1906	1	L	0-1	Manchester City, Anfield, 1st Division
10.03.1906		W	3-0	Southampton, Anfield, FA Cup 4th round
14.03.1906	1	W	2-1	Nottingham Forest, City Ground, 1st Division
17.03.1906	1	W	6-1	Middlesbrough, Anfield, 1st Division
21.03.1906	1	L	0-3	Notts County, Trent Bridge, 1st Division
24.03.1906	1	W	2-1	Preston North End, Deepdale, 1st Division
31.03.1906		L	0-2	Everton, Villa Park, FA Cup Semi-final
02.04.1906	1	D	0-0	Bury, Gigg Lane, 1st Division
09.04.1906	1	W	3-0	Newcastle United, Anfield, 1st Division
13.04.1906	1	D	1-1	Everton, Anfield, 1st Division
14.04.1906	1	W	2-0	Wolves, Molineux, 1st Division
16.04.1906	1	L	2-3	Bolton Wanderers, Burnden Park, 1st Division
21.04.1906	1	W	3-1	Sheffield United, Anfield, 1st Division
28.04.1906		W	5-1	Corinthians, Craven Cottage, Sheriff of London Charity Shield

Friendlies

04.09.1905	L	0-4	Chelsea, Stamford Bridge
18.09.1905	L	0-2	Bury, Anfield, Lancashire Senior Cup

Appearances for the 1905/1906 season

Name	League	FA Cup	Total
Arthur Goddard	38	5	43
Joe Hewitt	37	5	42
Alf West	37	5	42
Maurice Parry	36	5	41
Alex Raisbeck	36	4	40
Bobby Robinson	34	4	38
James Bradley	32	5	37
Billy Dunlop	31	5	36
Sam Hardy	30	5	35
Jack Cox	28	4	32
Sam Raybould	25	4	29
John Carlin	14	2	16
Jack Parkinson	9	1	10
Ned Doig	8	0	8
Tom Chorlton	6	0	6
George Latham	5	1	6
James Garside	4	0	4
David Murray	3	0	3
George Fleming	3	0	3
James Gorman	1	0	1
Harry Griffiths	1	0	1

Goalscorers for the 1905/1906 season

Name	League	FA Cup	Total
Joe Hewitt	24	1	28
Sam Raybould	11	4	16
Bobby Robinson	10	0	10
Jack Cox	8	0	8
Arthur Goddard	6	2	8
Jack Parkinson	7	0	7
John Carlin	6	0	6
Alf West	3	1	4
Own goals	1	0	2
Tom Chorlton	1	0	1
Maurice Parry	1	0	1
Alex Raisbeck	1	0	1

The squad during the 1905/1906 season

Sam Hardy, Goalkeeper.
Ned Doig, Goalkeeper.
James Bradley, Defender.
Alf West, Defender.
Billy Dunlop, Defender.
Maurice Parry, Defender.
Alex Raisbeck, Defender.
Tom Chorlton, Defender.
James Gorman, Defender.
George Latham, Defender.
Harry Griffiths, Defender.
David Murray, Defender.
George Fleming, Defender.
James Hughes, Defender.
Arthur Goddard, Midfielder.
Jack Cox, Midfielder.
Jack Parkinson, Striker.
Joe Hewitt, Striker.
Sam Raybould, Striker.
Bobby Robinson, Striker.
John Carlin, Striker.
James Garside, Striker.

Transfers for the 1905/1906 season

In:
Sam Hardy – Chesterfield, £340, May 1905
James Bradley – Stoke, Unknown, September 1905
Bob Blanthorne – Birkenhead, Unknown, 2 November 1905
James Gorman – Darlington St Augustine's, Unknown, March 1906

Out:
Richard Morris – Leeds City, Unknown, 9 May 1905
David Murray – Leeds City, £130, 7 December 1905

A collection of statistics for the 1905/1906 season

The season in numbers:
Total games: 44
Games won: 28
Games drawn: 5
Games lost: 11
Clean sheets – League: 12
Clean sheets – Overall: 15
Total goals: 92
Average attendance at home – League: 17,736
Average attendance at home – Overall: 17,347
Average goals per game – League: 2.58
Average goals per game – Overall: 2.48

Goals split down to competitions:
League – 79
FA Cup – 8
Sheriff of London Charity Shield – 5

Player debuts:
James Bradley against Birmingham on 23.09.1905
Harry Griffiths against The Wednesday on 14.10.1905
Sam Hardy against Nottingham Forest on 21.10.1905
James Gorman against Sheffield United on 21.04.1906

Statistics and information provided by LFChistory.net

3 : HAIL THE CHAMPIONS!

1921/22

SINCE 1906, LEAGUE RESULTS IN THE FOLLOWING years had been erratic and only in 1910 when finishing runners-up to Aston Villa did Liverpool come seriously close to taking another championship. In 1914 Tom Watson at last managed to overcome his semi-final jinx as Liverpool progressed to the FA Cup final at Aston Villa's expense but the big day at London's Crystal Palace ground was to end in disappointment with a 1-0 defeat to Burnley.

As World War I broke out, Watson was preparing for his 19th season in charge at Anfield. It was to be his last. He had visited his native Newcastle for his 56th birthday on April 9. Three weeks later he was back at work when he was seized with a severe chill. A few days later it had developed into a fatal attack of pneumonia and Watson died on May 6, 1915.

Watson had been a popular and successful manager and that was reflected in the turnout for his funeral, where many of the players he signed acted as pall-bearers on his final journey. Alex Raisbeck, Ned Doig, Arthur Goddard, Charlie Wilson, Maurice Parry, George Fleming and Robbie Robinson as well as the club trainer William

Connell carried his coffin. Watson is buried at Anfield Cemetery. Few men take two different clubs to the biggest domestic prize, even in the sport's early days, and the gentleman who would become Liverpool's longest serving manager was the first man to achieve such a feat. Even fewer win the league as many as five times during their managerial lives. Tom Watson did and he was also the man responsible for Liverpool making the big breakthrough by taking them to their first two league titles in 1901 and 1906.

After World War I, the league fixtures were played in a different format, where two clubs faced each other home and away in the space of eight days. Liverpool had finished both the 1919/20 and 1920/1921 seasons in fourth place and the Liverpool team under the management of David Ashworth was ready to blossom.

Pipe-smoking Ashworth, from Poulton-le-Fylde near Blackpool, agreed to become Liverpool's manager in December 1919 from Stockport County. Results had been poor under previous manager George Patterson in the period leading up to Ashworth's appointment.

Ashworth's only significant signing before the 1921/22 season was outside-left Fred Hopkin, who was signed for £2,800 from Manchester United. *The Sports Spectator* commented on Liverpool's transfer dealings: "The players cost very little in transfer fees, only Longworth and Hopkin being anything like expensive, the remainder being locals who were secured at bargain prices."

Liverpool captain Ephraim Longworth was signed by Liverpool on June 9, 1910 even though he had refused to move from Leyton a month earlier. Liverpool are said to have paid a club record fee for his services. Had World War I not taken away so much of his professional career, he would certainly have played in over 500 Football League and FA Cup matches for the club he served so loyally. His playing abilities were described by the *Birmingham Daily Gazette*: "A

Lancashire lad whose abilities were not recognised until he went south. Born in Bolton, Liverpool secured him from Leyton three seasons ago. A consistent and reliable back, who never plays a bad game, and takes his football very seriously. A fearless tackler and a sure kick, and rare judge of the correct time to rush in."

In July, 1921, the *Liverpool Echo* reported that the club was in a healthy position on and off the pitch: "The annual meeting of the shareholders and members of Liverpool Football Club was held at the Law Association Rooms, Cook Street, last evening. Mr. William Robert Williams presided, and there was large attendance of shareholders.

"The speaker mentioned that in finishing fourth in the league competition, they were naturally disappointed, but they were taking all possible steps to strengthen their forces. It was a matter for congratulation to think that the Liverpool team was one of the cleanest in the country.

"No penalty had been given against them throughout the season. With regard to the financial position, the last liability of the club vanished last season. They now had £16,500 in hand. It is proposed to run a third team next season, in which both amateurs and professionals would take part. This team would play on a ground which had been secured in the Wavertree district. The club had taken this step with the object of 'nursing' young players."

The night before the opening fixture of the 1921/22 season against Sunderland at Roker Park, *Liverpool Echo* sports editor Ernest Edwards, who wrote under the famous pseudonym 'Bee', assessed the impending campaign: "The season should be an improvement on last year when there was much variety and generally much poor play. The clubs have got their houses in order and on Merseyside we look like having one of the best seasons in the history of the city.

Liverpool, up north can beat Sunderland if they settle down to their work quickly. Their strength lies in their half-backs (men like Tommy Bromilow and Jock McNab), the solidity of the defence (goalkeeper Elisha Scott, Tommy Lucas, Ephraim Longworth, Donald Mackinlay and Walter Wadsworth) and the excellence of the left-wing (Fred Hopkin and Harry Chambers). Maybe there will be weaknesses at centre-forward and on the right-wing, but on what I have seen the team will have a more balanced appearance than for some years. They are big enough and able enough to carry the day at Sunderland."

The respected *Echo* sports editor – and the man responsible for giving the world famous Spion Kop its name – struck gold with his long-term analysis of the Anfield scene, but he was left eating humble pie over his pre-match prediction concerning the Sunderland clash as Liverpool suffered a 3-0 loss.

The Football Echo the following night summed up a frustrating day: 'LIVERPOOL'S FIRST TEST: SEVERE GAME AT ROKER: F.E.H TELLS OF THE STRIFE: DISASTER TO THE REDS'. The traditional multi-deck headline topped a colourful account of the proceedings. F.E.H wrote: "The afternoon broke out in full summery mood and as I ambled to the scene of operations, shopkeepers were lowering their window shades to keep out the blinding glare of the sun. The day, in fact, suggested cricket and not football and indeed the playing patch looked like a bowling green. Everything looked merry and bright before the ball was started in front of 40,000 people and there was keen anticipation in the air as Liverpool kicked off." Ninety minutes later the Merseysiders were trudging off, heads bowed after Buchan (2) and Martin had inspired a determined home victory. On the Monday, F.E.H's poetic introduction to his match analysis managed to cheer players and fans alike. In his report, he said: "The left wing pair of Hopkin and Chambers certainly justified their selection, as both played with consummate skill. New signing Hopkin's debut was also described in the *Liverpool Echo*: "Hopkins tried hard and put in some excellent centres, but he was well watched."

Seven days later, Liverpool had the chance to revenge their loss versus Sunderland at Anfield. However, Liverpool's defence would have to be at their best to contain Sunderland's Charlie Buchan, who scored two of the three Sunderland goals the previous week.

Donald Mackinlay and his fellow defenders tried to keep Buchan quiet, but still he managed to score once, but that wasn't enough as Liverpool netted twice through Billy Matthews and Dick Forshaw.

Although Liverpool's next six games came without defeat, four of the six ended in a 1-1 draw and the other two 1-0. Liverpool had clearly trouble in scoring goals which seemed to come to an end with a 4-0 win against Preston on October 15. The highlight from this game was a controversial goal scored by Harry Chambers after a goalless first half. The *Liverpool Echo* reported: "Lacey hit the ball so hard that the goalkeeper Fox, appeared stunned. Play went on and one wondered how long the referee would allow before he stopped play. Doolan went into goal and actually saved a shot, having to jump over the body of the true keeper, who in his dazed condition stood up and looked about him in bewildered fashion. Liverpool went on with the game and Chambers headed into the net, which was warmly debated by the Preston players but warmly welcomed by the home support. While Liverpool lined up for the kick off, Preston players were still debating the decision with the referee, somewhat reminiscent of a Debating Society I used to frequent as a youth in college.

"Today's game was a very physical game played in the best tradition of top-flight football. Liverpool won the game through grit, determination and a refusal to go down. Preston would do very well to learn from this lesson conducted by the Anfielders."

Liverpool scored four goals in 12 minutes against Preston and moved up to second in the league table with five wins, four draws and one loss after 10 games. The Reds were on equal on points with Newcastle, but two points behind leaders Burnley.

Burnley finally gave up first place to Liverpool five games later when Liverpool captured first place for the first time during the 1921/22 season, after a convincing 4-0 win over Middlesbrough at Anfield on November 19, despite having drawn 1-1 the previous three league games, among them the two Merseyside derbies of the season. No team seemed to breakaway with a few points lead on the rest. Although Ashworth's team were league leaders, Burnley and Sunderland were only a point behind.

Liverpool's hero that afternoon against Middlesbrough was 22-year-old Liverpudlian Danny Shone who scored three goals in 36 minutes, prompting the *Liverpool Echo* headline: 'THE SUN DID NOT SHINE AT ANFIELD BUT SHONE!'

Shone, from West Derby, joined Liverpool from local amateur side Grayson's of Garston, a representative team from a well-known local shipping company. Shone was officially employed by the firm, but did very little physical labour as he was more of interest to them as a footballer.

After dropping points at Ayresome Park and Villa Park, Liverpool went unbeaten without conceding a single goal through a busy Christmas schedule and muddy pitches, ill-fitting boots and hard leather footballs didn't prevent these troops playing on two consecutive days during this period. Liverpool drew against Manchester United on December 24 (0-0), beat Newcastle on Boxing Day (1-0), beat Huddersfield the following day on December 27 (2-0) and ended 1921 by drawing at Bradford on the 31st (0-0). *The York-shire Post and Leeds Intelligencer* reported on Liverpool's New Year's Eve stalemate: "The first half of this game at Valley Parade, before 22,000 spectators, produced attractive play from both teams. Arthur Rigby was soon in evidence, and came near to charging the ball into the net. Then Algernon Wilkinson, who was in goal for City, displayed splendid form in thwarting Dick Forshaw and George Harold Beadles, whilst John McNab and Harry Chambers both fired just over the crossbar. When Bradford pressed, John Carruthers, the new home centre forward, from Pigton Colliery, North Shields, contributed good work, though his shooting was at fault. Once Elisha Scott was fortunate to thwart him when he turned the ball from a dangerous centre by Dickie Bond. Don Duckett also had shots charged out. Play was not for long at one end of the field, and near half-time Beadles missed an easy chance of scoring when Fred Hopkin gave him an open goal. At half-time there had been no scoring. The second half was in favour of the home team. They were for the most part in the visitors' territory, but Carruthers failed badly when Rigby put him in possession in front of goal, Bond, who had not done well before the interval, was now a more important factor, and when he centred Beadles came near to putting the ball into his own goal. David Pratt fired point blank, but Ephraim Longworth kicked the ball out, Then Wilkinson had to save from Longworth, but soon the visitors were again busy defending, and Scott had to make good saves from Peter Logan and Tom Robb. Final score: Bradford City 0-0 Liverpool."

Liverpool's opponents that afternoon lost their cool on more than one occasion, mainly because they were up against Liverpool's legendary goalkeeper, the mighty Elisha Scott.

Scott is quite possibly the greatest goalkeeper in Liverpool's history, his Anfield career spanned an astonishing 22 years from his arrival in 1912 until he left in 1934. Had World War I not taken away four years of his professional career, Scott would undoubtedly have made many more than the 468 first-team appearances for his one and only English club. Although Scott was as hard working as the rest as his teammates he often trained alone with the punchbag in the Anfield gym to improve his speed and reflexes. He was a superstar before the word was invented and his contribution to the Liverpool cause will never be forgotten.

Scott initially had a trial at Everton after being recommended to the Blues by his older brother William, who was Everton's goalkeeper from 1904-1912 and also played 27 games for Liverpool in the 1918/19 wartime season. Liverpool saw potential in the young Scott and snapped him up.

The Ulsterman's made his debut for Liverpool on January 1, 1913 in a goalless draw against Newcastle at St. James' Park and the *Liverpool Echo* gave him a good review: "Hats off to Scott, Liverpool's youthful guardian. His debut was brilliant and a pleasing augury." Newcastle's board was so impressed with Scott that they made an offer of £1000 for his services.

Ten months passed before the 20-year-old got a second chance between the sticks when Liverpool faced Bolton at Anfield and the *Liverpool Echo* reported: "Campbell's excellence has kept Scott back from senior football, but today Scott made his first appearance at Anfield for the first team, and was accorded a hearty welcome. Very much like Hardy in appearance and in his method of clearing Elisha Scott is described by one critic as 'more promising at his age than even Hardy was.'"

Scott's good form throughout the years for Liverpool prompted Everton to bring him across to Goodison when he was at the height of his powers. Amazingly enough Liverpool's board had agreed to the sale, but such was Scott's popularity, Liverpool fans launched a newspaper campaign, flooding the local paper with letters of protest, which thankfully changed the club's mind.

Although relatively small for a goalkeeper at 5ft 9 1/2 ins (175 cm) Scott's agility and courage were never in question, nor was his loyalty to the club he served so well for so long.

He was adored by Liverpool fans. In one game against Blackburn Rovers he made a miracle save from a played called McClury who had blasted a shot goalwards from just three yards out. The *Liverpool Echo* reported: "One excited fan rushed onto the field and kissed Scott!"

The same newspaper summed up Scott abilities perfectly: "He was a great football personality with the eye of an eagle, the swift movement of a panther when flinging himself at a shot and the clutch of a vice when gripping the ball. In every sense he was a goalkeeper extraordinary."

At the end of 1921, Liverpool and Burnley were still equal with 32 points apiece from 23 games played, Liverpool only edging it with a goal average of 1.78 compared to Burnley's 1.72 and the 1921/22 campaign looked to be warming up nicely for a prolific second part of the season.

Liverpool drew to Newcastle 1-1 in the first game of 1922 at St. James' Park. Club captain Ephraim Longworth had lost his place to Tommy Lucas and resigned as captain contrary to the wishes of the Board and teammates. A scribe at the *Daily Telegraph* fully understood his reasons: "When a captain is left out of the side more often than he plays what can a man do?" Left-back Donald Mackinlay was appointed captain in his place in January 1922.

Five days later, Liverpool travelled to Roker Park to face Sunderland in the first round of the FA Cup. The game finished 1-1 and a replay was needed at Anfield, where Liverpool sensationally beat the Wearsiders 5-0, Chambers and Forshaw grabbing a brace each.

Harry Chambers was now finding his goalscoring form of previous seasons, when he finished the club's top scorer during the 1919/20 and 1920/21 campaigns. After scoring two against Sunderland in the FA Cup, his total for the current season now stood at 10 goals in 18 games. Liverpool needed their main scorer to keep on firing them in and Chambers remained a vital part of Liverpool's side.

Henry "Harry" Chambers was the last player Tom Watson ever signed for Liverpool before he passed away. Chambers only played a couple of reserve games for Liverpool before league football was suspended due to World War I. He became a soldier but was soon invalided out of the Army and while convalescing in Ulster he guested for Belfast Distillery and Glentoran.

Chambers was the greatest personality in this current Liverpool side. He was one of the smartest inside-lefts of his time. The fans called him 'Smiler' while his team mates dubbed him 'Sharky'. Harry had a ferocious shot and won over the fans from the start. He once hit the ball so hard against Sunderland that it finished up deflated in the back of the net! With his bow legs, pigeon toes, toothless grin, jutting chin and a thoroughly likeable personality, Smiler was a man you just couldn't ignore, on and off the field. There was even a period when he got into a bit of bad company and would turn up at Anfield at 2pm a bit the worse for drink. The trainers would stick him under a cold shower and he'd go out and play a blinder.

At the age of 52, Chambers was still playing for Shropshire outfit Oakengates where he operated as player-manager.

Three consecutive league wins followed but West Bromich Albion ended Liverpool's FA Cup hopes in the second round. The league table on February 4 showed Liverpool had temporarily shaken off Burnley and Bolton were now their closest rivals second five points behind Liverpool.

Following their cup exit, the Reds' defence was immense, not conceding a goal in five consecutive games. This included the 4-0 demolition of Arsenal at Anfield, with Dick Forshaw recording a hat-trick. The following day, a *Liverpool Echo* headline was declaring: 'LIVERPOOL'S HAND ON THE HANDLE OF THE CHAMPIONSHIP'. Forshaw not only scored a hat-trick, but also "joined" the crowd at one stage. The *Liverpool Echo* reported: "It was a startling circus trick. He tried to reach an elongated pass from Lacey, but the ball beat the man. Forshaw ran on towards the spectators, finally leaping over the cement wall and pitching headlong into the crowd. He was 'posted missing' for some seconds before coming out of his shell accompanied by the cheer of the supporters."

Inside-left forward Forshaw joined Liverpool after serving for four years in Ceylon [Sri Lanka] with the Royal Garrison Artillery. Forshaw was portrayed by the *Daily Telegraph* as: "One of the most versatile players in the game is this Widnes-born man, who graduated with Gateshead St. Vincent and just missed by Middlesbrough after the war. Was then an inside right, but he can play anywhere in attack of at half. Cool, calm, and methodical, he never appears to be all out, but in front of goal is deadly accurate. He relies on position work and real ball craft for his success. A brainy, unorthodox lad, who does the unexpected thing, but that has been his secret of success. An opponent never knows what Forshaw will do. He never forgets his partner, but is not bound hand and foot to him. Has a powerful shot in either foot."

By mid-March, Burnley had crept up back to second place, but Liverpool had a five-point lead with a game in hand, 46 to Burnley's

41 points. Everything was going well, but then Liverpool's title challenge was put in jeopardy after two consecutive defeats. Firstly, Liverpool lost 2-0 to Bolton at Anfield, where Liverpool had to do without the services of Harry Chambers, Tom Bromilow and Tommy Lucas. Three of Ashworth's usual starting XI were curiously playing for the English League versus the Scottish League on the same day.

The Athletic reported on Liverpool's first home league defeat of the season: "This match at Anfield was too grotesque to capture the imagination or stir the pulse. As Bolton Wanderers earned the distinction of being the first club to win a league match on Liverpool's ground this season the result had its compensations. The speculative instinct of sportsmen are aroused. The championship is not won yet. Liverpool have to visit Bolton, and, judging them on this display, there is still room for an adventurous climax. I do not aim at discouraging the leaders. They sacrificed the services of three lustrous players for the national weal, which is a big thing for a club fighting for honours, whose downfall is sought by all clubs."

The absent trio returned for Liverpool's game in hand the following Wednesday at Highbury. However, Liverpool embarrassed themselves by losing 1-0 to bottom club, Arsenal. Fortunately, for Liverpool, Burnley only drew their game and the gap was now four points and both teams now had nine games each to play.

Liverpool played Bolton at Burnden Park on March 25 and were in search of revenge. Jock McNab let his fighting spirit get the better of him, incapacitating Ted Vizard in the first half and then getting sent off for retaliation against Vizard in the second half after being heckled by the crowd throughout the game. Thankfully, Liverpool survived to win 3-1.

John McNab was more commonly known as 'Jock' because of his Scottish ancestry. He arrived on Merseyside in November 1919 from Scottish club, Bellshill Athletic. Jock McNab was described in the *Liverpool Echo*: "McNab's physique is tremendous. He has height, weight and determination, and never knows when he is beaten. In addition he has a very strong shot. McNab was a real hard nut, whose idea of getting ready for a match was to have a couple of pints of Guinness. In one match against Newcastle, which got a bit out of hand, McNab was sent off for throwing a handful of mud at another player and he was followed to the dressing room by teammate Walter Wadsworth a few minutes later for punching Newcastle's Tommy Urwin in the face in retaliation for also having mud thrown at him."

The following year McNab's Liverpool career – and life – was nearly ended in a traffic accident. The *Daily Telegraph* reported: "John McNab, the well-known Liverpool half-back, and a Scottish International, was on Thursday night injured in a car crash in Bootle. He was thrown through the windscreen, and was taken to Bootle Hospital, where he had sixteen stitches put into his face."

Nineteenth place Oldham Athletic proved no obstacle at Anfield, as they were beaten 2-0. However, a week later the teams met at Oldham's Boundary Park in Liverpool's one thousandth milestone game. The Anfielders suffered an astounding 4-0 defeat which suffice to say was their biggest loss of the season. Despite the heavy loss Liverpool still remained top of the league, six points ahead of second place Tottenham Hotspur.

Liverpool recovered to draw 1-1 with last season's champions Burnley at Turf Moor where Tom Bromilow missed a penalty. The following day Cardiff City visited Anfield and were beaten 5-1 with Harry Chambers scoring a hat-trick and Jock McNab netting his first for the club.

With four games to go the scene was set for a potential league decider against champions Burnley on April 17 at Anfield. Prior to the match Liverpool were top with 53 points, followed by Tottenham with 48 and Burnley with 47 points. Anfield was packed to its rafters witnessing a lively game. Chambers put Liverpool ahead in the 22nd minute when he "shot the ball like lightning into the far bottom corner of the net." George Richardson equalised in the second half, but in the 78th minute, right-back Ephraim Longworth decided to venture up the field as described by the *Evening Express*: "He suddenly took it into his head to retain possession and dribble down the field. Veering into the centre he looked for a likely opening. The full-back was brought down, however, and as he lay on the ground he managed to push the ball to Forshaw." Inside forward Forshaw made no mistake and he and Longworth were "promptly mobbed by their colleagues."

Forshaw's goal clinched a 2-1 Liverpool win. Tottenham lost 1-0 to Oldham Athletic and the Reds now had a seven-point lead on Spurs with only three games left which could produce a maximum of six points in those days.

Liverpool were First Division champions for the third time.

The *Liverpool Echo* commented that Liverpool had won the title: "In the main through brilliance of defence, yet all-round the team has played good-class football, and the honours have gone to a good side – from stern to stern."

On Wednesday, May 10 league champions Liverpool faced FA Cup winners Huddersfield Town at Old Trafford in the Charity Shield. For the last time, the match was played at the end of the season in which the participating teams won their honours. In addition, this was the first occasion both competing clubs were from the north and so the venue moved out of London to Manchester for the first time.

Despite losing the game 1-0, Liverpool were presented with the league trophy at Old Trafford by Football League chairman and former Liverpool chairman John McKenna. On Liverpool's return from Manchester, captain Mackinlay was picked up and carried in triumph out of the station and after the league title was brought back to Liverpool, the club held a gathering to celebrate the occasion with all the former players that they could get together.

Liverpool had last won the championship in 1906 and the champions from that season were invited to celebrate along with the current championships. The 1906 and 1922 champions competed in a tug of war and Alf West, James Bradley and Sam Raybould were given 50 pounds each by the Liverpool board as they had fallen on hard times owing to the present trade depression – a socialist outlook that still exists within the club today.

The Athletic also congratulated the club on becoming first division champions for the third time in the club's history: "This is the third time since this century dawned that Liverpool have been league champions, as they gained this distinction in 1900-01 and in 1905-06, but it is doubtful if they ever had such an evenly-balanced and consistent set of players as at present. We congratulate them on their triumph, on their team spirit, on their unity fore and aft, on the armour-plate character of their defence, and on the cleanliness of their style. The team manager, David Ashworth, has every reason to be proud of the 22 men who have worn the club's red jersey. He has helped them with the fruits of his experience, and they have responded to is advice. The position of Liverpool to-day suggests that money is not indispensable in building a team and that there is material in local areas if it is sought and taught."

Liverpool had won the title for the first time in 16 years and were longing for more success. Few could have predicted the astonishing developments of the coming season...

1921/22: Facts and Statistics

Final league table

		P	W	D	L	F	A	W	D	L	F	A	PTS
1	Liverpool FC	42	15	4	2	43	15	7	9	5	20	21	57
2	Tottenham	42	15	3	3	43	17	6	6	9	22	22	51
3	Burnley	42	16	3	2	49	18	6	2	13	23	36	49
4	Cardiff City	42	13	2	6	40	26	6	8	7	21	27	48
5	Aston Villa	42	16	3	2	50	19	6	0	15	24	36	47
6	Bolton Wanderers	42	12	4	5	40	24	8	3	10	28	35	47
7	Newcastle United	42	11	5	5	36	19	7	5	9	23	26	46
8	Middlesbrough	42	12	6	3	46	19	4	8	9	33	50	46
9	Chelsea	42	9	6	6	17	16	8	6	7	23	27	46
10	Manchester City	42	13	7	1	44	21	5	2	14	21	49	45
11	Sheffield United	42	11	3	7	32	17	4	7	10	27	37	40
12	Sunderland	42	13	4	4	46	23	3	4	14	14	39	40
13	WBA	42	8	6	7	26	23	7	4	10	25	40	40
14	Huddersfield Town	42	12	3	6	33	14	3	6	12	20	40	39
15	Blackburn Rovers	42	7	6	8	35	31	6	6	9	19	26	38
16	Preston North End	42	12	7	2	33	20	1	5	15	9	45	38
17	Arsenal	42	10	6	5	27	19	5	1	15	20	37	37
18	Birmingham	42	9	2	10	25	29	6	5	10	23	31	37
19	Oldham Athletic	42	8	7	6	21	15	5	4	12	17	35	37
20	Everton	42	10	7	4	42	22	2	5	14	15	33	36
21	Bradford City	42	8	5	8	28	30	3	5	13	20	42	32
22	Manchester United	42	7	7	7	25	26	1	5	15	16	47	28

Games for the 1921/1922 season

(The number after date is league position after the game)

1	27.08.1921	20	L	0-3	Sunderland, Roker Park, 1st Division
2	31.08.1921	17	W	3-2	Manchester City, Anfield, 1st Division
3	03.09.1921	10	W	2-1	Sunderland, Anfield, 1st Division
4	07.09.1921	8	D	1-1	Manchester City, Hyde Road, 1st Division
5	10.09.1921	4	W	1-0	Sheffield United, Bramall Lane, 1st Division
6	17.09.1921	5	D	1-1	Sheffield United, Anfield, 1st Division
7	24.09.1921	2	W	1-0	Chelsea, Stamford Bridge, 1st Division
8	01.10.1921	4	D	1-1	Chelsea, Anfield, 1st Division
9	08.10.1921	5	D	1-1	Preston North End, Deepdale, 1st Division
10	15.10.1921	2	W	4-0	Preston North End, Anfield, 1st Division

11	22.10.1921	2	W	1-0	Tottenham Hotspur, White Hart Lane, 1st Division
12	29.10.1921	2	D	1-1	Tottenham Hotspur, Anfield, 1st Division
13	05.11.1921	3	D	1-1	Everton, Goodison Park, 1st Division
14	12.11.1921	2	D	1-1	Everton, Anfield, 1st Division
15	19.11.1921	1	W	4-0	Middlesbrough, Anfield, 1st Division
16	26.11.1921	2	L	1-3	Middlesbrough, Ayresome Park, 1st Division
17	03.12.1921	3	D	1-1	Aston Villa, Villa Park, 1st Division
18	10.12.1921	2	W	2-0	Aston Villa, Anfield, 1st Division
19	17.12.1921	1	W	2-1	Manchester United, Anfield, 1st Division
20	24.12.1921	1	D	0-0	Manchester United, Old Trafford, 1st Division
21	26.12.1921	1	W	1-0	Newcastle United, Anfield, 1st Division
22	27.12.1921	1	W	2-0	Huddersfield Town, Anfield, 1st Division
23	31.12.1921	1	D	0-0	Bradford City, Valley Parade, 1st Division
24	02.01.1922	1	D	1-1	Newcastle United, St. James' Park, 1st Division
25	07.01.1922		D	1-1	Sunderland, Roker Park, FA Cup 1st round
26	11.01.1922		W	5-0	Sunderland, Anfield, FA Cup 1st round replay
27	14.01.1922	1	W	2-1	Bradford City, Anfield, 1st Division
28	21.01.1922	1	W	1-0	Huddersfield Town, Leeds Road, 1st Division
29	28.01.1922		L	0-1	West Bromwich Albion, Anfield, FA Cup 2nd round
30	04.02.1922	1	W	2-0	Birmingham, St. Andrew's, 1st Division
31	11.02.1922	1	W	1-0	Birmingham, Anfield, 1st Division
32	25.02.1922	1	W	4-0	Arsenal, Anfield, 1st Division
33	04.03.1922	1	D	0-0	Blackburn Rovers, Ewood Park, 1st Division
34	11.03.1922	1	W	2-0	Blackburn Rovers, Anfield, 1st Division
35	18.03.1922	1	L	0-2	Bolton Wanderers, Anfield, 1st Division
36	22.03.1922	1	L	0-1	Arsenal, Highbury, 1st Division
37	25.03.1922	1	W	3-1	Bolton Wanderers, Burnden Park, 1st Division
38	01.04.1922	1	W	2-0	Oldham Athletic, Anfield, 1st Division
39	08.04.1922	1	L	0-4	Oldham Athletic, Boundary Park, 1st Division
40	14.04.1922	1	D	1-1	Burnley, Turf Moor, 1st Division
41	15.04.1922	1	W	5-1	Cardiff City, Anfield, 1st Division
42	17.04.1922	1	W	2-1	Burnley, Anfield, 1st Division
43	22.04.1922	1	L	0-2	Cardiff City, Ninian Park, 1st Division
44	29.04.1922	1	L	1-2	West Bromwich Albion, Anfield, 1st Division
45	06.05.1922	1	W	4-1	West Bromwich Albion, The Hawthorns, 1st Division
46	10.05.1922		L	0-1	Huddersfield Town, Old Trafford, Charity Shield

Friendlies

	03.05.1922		L	1-3	Bolton Wanderers, Unknown, Lancashire Senior Cup

Appearances for the 1921/1922 season

Name	League	FA Cup	CS	Total
Dick Forshaw	42	3	1	46
Fred Hopkin	42	3	1	46
Tom Bromilow	40	3	1	44
Bill Lacey	39	3	1	43
Elisha Scott	39	3	1	43
Walter Wadsworth	38	3	1	42
Harry Chambers	32	3	1	36
Jock McNab	29	3	1	33
Donald Mackinlay	29	3	1	33
Tommy Lucas	27	3	0	30
Ephraim Longworth	26	0	1	27
Harry Lewis	19	3	0	22
Danny Shone	15	0	0	15
Harry Beadles	11	0	1	12
John Bamber	8	0	0	8
Billy Matthews	7	0	0	7
Ted Parry	7	0	0	7
Francis Checkland	5	0	0	5
Frank Mitchell	3	0	0	3
Cyril Gilhespy	2	0	0	2
Bill Cunningham	1	0	0	1
Harold Wadsworth	1	0	0	1

Goalscorers for the 1921/1922 season

Name	League	FA Cup	Total
Harry Chambers	19	2	21
Dick Forshaw	17	3	20
Harry Beadles	6	0	6
Danny Shone	6	0	6
Billy Matthews	4	0	4
Jock McNab	2	0	2
Tom Bromilow	2	0	2
Tommy Lucas	2	0	2
Own goals	1	0	1
Cyril Gilhespy	1	0	1
Bill Lacey	1	0	1
Harry Lewis	1	0	1
Walter Wadsworth	0	1	1
Donald Mackinlay	1	0	1

The squad during the 1921/1922 season

Elisha Scott, Goalkeeper
Frank Mitchell, Goalkeeper
Tom Bromilow, Defender
Tommy Lucas, Defender
Donald Mackinlay, Defender
Jock McNab, Defender
Ephraim Longworth, Defender
Walter Wadsworth, Defender
Ted Parry, Defender
Francis Checkland, Defender
John Bamber, Midfielder
Harold Wadsworth, Midfielder
Bill Lacey, Midfielder
Cyril Gilhespy, Midfielder
Bill Cunningham, Midfielder
Harry Beadles, Striker
Harry Chambers, Striker
Dick Forshaw, Striker
Danny Shone, Striker
Dick Johnson, Striker
Harry Lewis, Striker
Billy Matthews, Striker
Fred Hopkin, Left-winger

Transfers for the 1921/1922 season

In:
Fred Hopkin – Manchester United, £2,800, May 1921
Harry Beadles – Grayson's of Garston, Unknown, 12 May 1921
Cyril Gilhespy – Sunderland,£250, August 1921

Out:
Albert Pearson – Port Vale, Unknown, 1921
William Jenkinson – Wigan Borough, Unknown, June 1921
John Miller – Aberdeen, Unknown, 8 June 1921

A collection of statistics for the 1921/1922 season

The season in numbers:
Total games: 46
Games won: 23
Games drawn: 14
Games lost: 9
Clean sheets – League: 17
Clean sheets – Overall: 18
Total goals: 69
Average attendance at home – League: 37,142
Average attendance at home – Overall: 38,086
Average goals per game – League: 2.05
Average goals per game – Overall: 2.09
Average goals per game – Overall: 2.48

Goals split down to competitions:
League – 79
FA Cup – 8
Sheriff of London Charity Shield – 5

Player debuts:
Fred Hopkin against Sunderland on 27.08.1921
Danny Shone against Sunderland on 27.08.1921
Francis Checkland against Sheffield United on 10.09.1921
Harry Beadles against Chelsea on 24.09.1921
Cyril Gilhespy against Blackburn Rovers on 04.03.1922

Statistics and information provided by LFChistory.net

4 | REDS RETAIN THE TITLE

1922/23

DAVID ASHWORTH TREATED HIS CHAMPIONS TO an all-expenses paid pre-season tour to Italy, leaving Lime Street station on May 17, a week after losing the Charity Shield at Old Trafford.

Liverpool travelled for two days through London, Dover, Calais and Paris to get to their base in Milan. The team relaxed for a couple of days taking in the sights of the islands in Lago Maggiore, the second biggest prealpine lake in Italy and went by cableway up Monte Mottarone which has breathtaking views over the Alps.

Eight days after departing for Italy, Liverpool faced travelling companions and 1921/22 third-place team Burnley, who they lost 1-0 to in Milan. Over the following two weeks Liverpool went on to play four Italian sides, winning two and drawing two. Tom Bromilow wrote a column for the local press unimpressed by the tactics of one of their opponents, the Liguria and Toscana select XI: "I have never played in such a game where in so much hacking, kicking and pushing was tolerated. In fact, the home side indulged in everything except biting."

There were no major personnel changes during the summer

of 1922 and manager David Ashworth was optimistic about the upcoming season: "We ought to have a very good season. There is perfect harmony from the boardroom to the dressing-room and that goes a long way." Chairman Mr. William Robert Williams added: "I believe the art is blending players, not in buying players."

Mr. Williams also announced that: "Considerable improvements have been made on the ground. Cinder tracks, both in the approaches and on the ground itself, have given place to concrete, and on Spion Kop entrances have been concreted, with distributing passages and railed insides that should add to the comforts of the spectators. The rising generations have not been overlooked, as one-half of the paddock in front of the Kemlyn Road stand has been railed off and terraced. This Boys' Pen will accommodate 4,500, with separate entrances direct from the road."

These were exciting times for Liverpool, however not everything was plain sailing in the football world. At the start of the 1922/23 season the *Liverpool Echo* headlined a story: 'FOOTBALL SALARIES: PAY ACCORDING TO PLAY' and reported: "There is trouble brewing in the football world over the proposal to reduce the players' wages. Several clubs are suffering depleted gates and cannot afford to pay the maximum wage and bonus to those entitled to it. In a desperate effort to make ends meet, the directors rush with the scissors to the chief item of expenditure, the players' wages. Let us examine the proposal in detail. Not all clubs are in financial straits. Nearly all the Northern Third Division clubs are hard-put financially, but rich clubs like Liverpool, Chelsea and Aston Villa are as safe as the Bank of England. Then because of a few 'poor relations' are handicapped for want of money, why should the wages of the international be cut down?" The writer revealed that the rules regarding benefits, wages and transfers were precisely the same for all four divisions. He declared: "It is ridiculous to couple teams like Tottenham, Cardiff, Everton and those already mentioned with a cry that they cannot afford to pay their men NINE POUNDS a week." The answer? The scribe declared: "It is futile to argue that the fleet-footed international winger is worth no more than a moderate Third Division player. Charges for admission to games should be graduated according to the quality of play, one shilling for First Division, ninepence for Second Division, sixpence for Third. Players' maximum wages should be ten pounds, eight pounds and six pounds a week. An extra pound a week might be granted to every man who is selected to play in an international, but this is a comparatively unimportant point."

The *Liverpool Echo's* Ernest Edwards, 'Bee', suggested that another glittering campaign was on the cards. He wrote: "Where Liverpool are undoubtedly strong is in their excellent duplicating of position." Strength in depth was clearly an Anfield watchword even then. Liverpool's season kicked off on August 26 against Arsenal at Anfield, winning 5-2.

Striker Dick Johnson, who missed the entirety of the previous season due to injury, scored a hat-trick. *The Athletic* reported on Johnson's long-awaited return to action: "The league champions opened their season at Anfield in brilliant fashion and a crowd of over 40,000 spectators had the felicity of seeing quite a big crop of goals in the match with The Arsenal. The team, unchanged from last season except for the welcome return of Johnson, almost from the outset bounded into brilliant form, and for the greater portion of the game completely overwhelmed their visitors from Highbury."

After a bright start to the season, Liverpool then travelled to Sunderland and Arsenal, but disappointingly lost both games 1-0 so after three games, the current champions were 16th in the league. A week later Sunderland played at Anfield where Liverpool avenged their loss at Roker Park in impressive fashion, beating the Wearsiders 5-1. Liverpool scored five after Sunderland took the lead, the pick of the bunch being Harry Chambers' thunderous shot that literally burst the ball en route to goal and Mackinlay's solo effort after picking up the ball from the halfway line, finishing with an unstoppable shot.

The Reds also ran rampant against Preston, winning 3-1 at Deepdale and 5-2 at Anfield a week later. Dick Forshaw scored a hat-trick and all five Liverpool goals were scored in 15 minutes.

Liverpool then showed their strength by beating last season's title rivals Burnley 3-0 but lost 2-0 in the return match at Turf Moor the following Saturday.

Prior to the match at Turf Moor, three Liverpool players had each been offered £10 to lose the game. The honest trio reported the attempted bribe to the Liverpool board. *The Western Times* reported on the incident: "Three famous players of the Liverpool Football League Club received anonymous letters offering them bribes of £10 each to let Burnley win the match at Liverpool on September 23. The game resulted in a win for the home team by three clear goals. The players reported the matter to the club secretary, who gave the letters to his directors, and these gentlemen, after consultation, decided to forward them to the police. The players concerned are Elisha Scott, the goalkeeper; Dick Johnson, the centre-forward; and Walter Wadsworth, the centre-back. Football authorities in Liverpool are inclined to think that the affair is in the nature of a hoax. The letters bore the Liverpool postmark, but no address, or anything to give a clue as to the identity of the sender."

The 51st Merseyside derby was attended by 54,368 spectators at Anfield on October 7, 1922. The weather was ideal and the Kop full to its brim as the *Liverpool Echo* reported: "The day was gloriously fine, but all assembled knew this was the calm before the storm.

The Anfield pitch was looking as good as it ever has before kick-off, but I would think it would have as many scars as the players at full time. As usual there was a big early raid on the Kemlyn Road stand, which offers so good and close a view as one can get anywhere in the country. The crowd had plenty to keep them interested before the battle commenced. There were the boys who ignored the barbed wire to get in. There was the Postal band playing a merry jingle and there was also the latest method adopted for removing young boys from the top to the bottom of the Kop. The assembled Dockers had formed their own umbrella method, by passing the lads over the top of heads, so the wee lads could reach their final destination by the wall at the front. Liverpool won the toss, thus ensuring they attacked their beloved Kop in the second half and also left Fern to be blinded by the mid afternoon sun, which was dazzling today."

The *Liverpool Echo* reporting at the time was colourful on occasions and very humorous: "Liverpool were right on the doorstep of success, thanks to a successful feint from Forshaw. He hammered the ball across to the middle and Johnson looked sure to score until Fern and he collided with a mighty crunch. McDonald walloped the ball clear over the stands into Mrs Molyneux's back garden in Kemlyn Road. She would return the ball later, while complaining that it had scared one of her rabbits half to death. No stew tonight then."

Everton took the lead in the 17th minute when Mackinlay misplaced his back pass. Later in the game he made sure his back pass was not so weak. The *Liverpool Echo* reported: "At this time the Liverpool defence started to take liberties, all saw themselves as attackers and often left MacKinlay alone at the back. On one of these occasions Mackinlay passed back to Scott with such venom, it brought a magnificent save out of Elisha. Scott was not amused by the accompanying wink and nod... Mackinlay's back pass to Scott in the second half was probably the most powerful shot of the match, but I suppose you could forgive him after his earlier lightweight pass that led to Everton's first goal."

Chambers' first goal in the match would hardly be credited to him these days by the dubious goals committee: "Hopkin placed the corner and quickly crossed to the near post where Chambers was waiting. Chambers' flick on header hits the bar. The ball comes off the bar, but in trying to catch it, Fern punched the ball into his own net. In his joy at equalising, Chambers swung on to one of the uprights and hung on to it in a manner of a music hall horizontal bar performer. After witnessing this, I would suggest footballers leave acts like that on the circus circuit."

Liverpool enjoyed playing their old rivals and Chambers was not the only one who celebrated a goal in style: "Two Chambers headers both came close, before a third cross was back headed by Forshaw into the path of McNab. He had all along been running ahead to make a sixth forward and now he found himself with a cross-grained shot and quite a good angle on goal. He fired in a ferocious shot, that hit the back of the net before Ferns had moved an inch. He celebrated his goal by leaping for joy and completing a Scottish Hornpipe."

Chambers completed his hat-trick by scoring two goals in two minutes, including the goal of the game: "Lacey played a ball up to Johnson, who headed to Chambers. Chambers pushed the ball wide for the advancing Lacey. Lacey controlled the ball and played it back into the path of Chambers. 'Smiler' Chambers thumped the ball home. His grin was as big as a Cheshire cat."

Birthday boy Bromilow tapped in Liverpool's fifth from close range. The *Liverpool Echo* reported that: "The crowd, following up on the suggestion in BEE's comments a fortnight ago, started the new chant of the Kop: 'One Two, Three Four Five, One Two Three Four, FIVE-Nil.'"

Incredibly, after the first five home games of the season the Anfield crowd had witnessed no fewer than 23 goals from their team, scoring an incredible five goals in four of the five encounters.

Following their derby triumph, Liverpool went on to win five out of their next seven games and by the end of November, after 16 out of 42 rounds had been played, they were top of the league with 23 points. Sunderland were second with 21 with Burnley and Middlesbrough following on 20. On December 2, Liverpool suffered their first home defeat of the season against Newcastle United, but soon redeemed themselves by beating Newcastle 1-0 at St. James' Park and going on to beat Nottingham Forest 2-1 at Anfield on December 16, 1922.

Liverpool were heading for the title again under Ashworth's wise guidance. However, suddenly a rumour emerged that manager Ashworth would be in charge of Oldham rather than Liverpool come Christmas Day. The *Liverpool Echo* asked Ashworth if these rumours were true, but as the *Echo's* Bee's Sports Notes reported on December 19: "Mr. Ashworth, manager of the Liverpool Football Club, asks me to deny the story that is all over Oldham that he is about to become their manager."

The following day, it was evident that David Ashworth had lied to the newspaper: "The Echo learns today that there was smoke where there was fire. It will be remembered that we stated yesterday that the Liverpool Football Club manager, Mr. David Ashworth, denied that he was to be made the successor of Charlie Roberts, the ex-Manchester United captain, who has been acting as manager for Oldham Athletic for two years. To-day we learn by special wire that Mr. Ashworth has signed as manager for Oldham, a side that he spent so many years with and with which he was connected when they finished second in the Football League in 1915.

"Mr. Ashworth's earliest managerial work was with Stockport County and he joined Liverpool three years ago. These have been Liverpool's most successful years, financially and in a playing sense, therefore it will come as a severe shock to all football supporters that Mr. Ashworth has seen fit to leave Liverpool at their zenith and join Oldham in the depths. At any rate all Liverpool will be surprised that a change has been made, for there had been no suggestion of any movement in connection with the Liverpool Football Club for some time."

Few could understand why Ashworth had decided to leave a team in first place with almost twice as many points as Oldham in 21st position out of a league of 22 teams with 14 points. Ashworth had evidently moved for family reasons as he wanted to live with his wife and daughter, who were both ill, in their home in Stockport which was only 11 miles away from Oldham compared to 43 miles from Liverpool. For the record, Oldham got relegated in the 1922-23 season.

On December 23, Liverpool travelled to Nottingham Forest without a manager. The Anfielders left Liverpool for Nottingham the previous day, arrived in time to dine and then enjoyed a couple of hours' amusement at one of the local variety theatres. The following day at the match, Liverpool didn't look distracted by the loss of their manager as they beat Forest 3-1.

Liverpool were then to play Ashworth's new club, Oldham, home and away on December 25 and 26. Needless to say Liverpool didn't lack encouragement when faced with Ashworth's Oldham side on Christmas Day as Liverpool won 2-0 at Boundary Park. The *Liverpool Echo* reported on the Reds triumph: "In defeating Oldham Athletic at Boundary Park on Christmas Day, Liverpool accomplished a smart performance, and fully deserved the victory, as they were much the superior side, both fore and aft. All the scoring took place in the first half, Mackinlay getting the first, a hard drive of his cannoning off Freeman into the net. Five minutes from the interval Johnson met a low centre from Hopkin, and found the net from two yards' range. Gilhespy was hardly up to form, but the inside men were in excellent fettle, Wadsworth stood out in a strong half-line, while the men behind were equal to all demands."

On Boxing Day, Oldham suffered from "frequent hesitancy and bad tactics" and Liverpool again came out on top, winning 2-1 at Anfield. The *Liverpool Echo* reported: "Anfield was packed to-day, and was in merry mood; first because it was Elisha Scott's benefit (and he captained the side), and secondly because a silly rumour that Chambers had broken his leg was proved to be utterly false. The formation of the team was rather startling; it was a surprise to find Bamber at half-back, and still more of a surprise to find McNab at centre forward. As a matter of fact, many a correspondent has written to me suggesting McNab as a centre forward, but this is the first time the hardy Scot has made his bow in a new position. William Lacey had been picked to play centre forward, but had not turned up."

Chelsea were Liverpool's opponents for the final game of 1922 and the first game of 1923 and the Reds' five-match winning run came to an end as the game at Stamford Bridge ended in a 0-0 draw. However, Liverpool returned to winning ways as they beat Chelsea 1-0 back in Anfield in their next fixture, the only goal of the game coming from Bill Lacey. According to the *Liverpool Echo*, Liverpool's winning goal was dubious to say the least: "Bromilow made a huge lobbing centre, and before the goalkeeper touched the ball he was distinctly charged by two Liverpool men, and when Lacey fired in a shot a free-kick should have been the verdict, but was not, and so

Liverpool took a most lucky lead through a point that was all against the football law.

"As for kicking Lacey as a hobby, I can assure you it's a waste of time; the boy is made from Solid Rock. Dynamite could not shift him off the ball." The match report captured Billy Lacey perfectly. Lacey, an Irishman, was signed from neighbours Everton in 1912. After featuring regularly in the 1910/11 season for Everton, Lacey rarely got a look in, only playing 37 league games in three-and-a-half seasons. During the summer of 1912, Liverpool made one of their shrewdest transfer deals ever when they paid £300 for Lacey and Tom Gracie as well as letting Harold Uren go in exchange.

The *Liverpool Echo* wrote in September 1923 of Lacey's capture: "Was there ever a transfer that turned out so profitable to the Livers!" Lacey immediately went into the first team, making his debut in a 1-1 draw against Middlesbrough on March 2, 1912. The scribe at the club programme was impressed: "I have always had an idea that Lacey would make a better man for Liverpool than Everton. He has, it is true, been more than useful to the Blues, but he is the type of player that has always been associated with Liverpool more than Everton. We as a rule play more robust football, due to the fact that our forwards have been bigger men. And Lacey, while he is capable of clever work, is also a dashing, fearless forward. He was distinctly the personality on the home side against Middlesbrough, and had there been another of equal calibre I am sure we must have won."

David Ashworth's departure failed to knock Liverpool out of their stride. From December 30 to February 10, managerless Liverpool didn't concede a single goal in seven league games, winning five. Liverpool's well established back five consisted of Elisha Scott in goal, Ephraim Longworth, Jock McNab, Walter Wadsworth and their commanding Scottish captain, Donald Mackinlay.

Few came tougher than Mackinlay who was Liverpool's captain from 1922-1928. He made his debut for Liverpool aged 19 on April 20, 1910 when Liverpool defeated Nottingham Forest 7-3. He started to make a name for himself at the end of the 1912/1913 season and suffered his first real big disappointment when he was in the Liverpool XI that lost to Burnley in the FA Cup final in 1914.

World War I then disrupted his progress as the league was effectively shut down for four years. Two years after the league programme resumed, when Mackinlay was 30, he was made captain and was so until he left the club seven years later.

Mackinlay was a Red through and through, evident in his interview with the *Evening Express*: "Red is my colour. I'll play for Liverpool as long as they will have me. I don't want to play for anybody else and when I pull off the red shirt for the last time I expect I will finish with football, at any rate as a player."

Liverpool also beat Arsenal 4-1 at Highbury in a first round FA Cup replay where Harry Chambers netted two and Elisha Scott saved a penalty from Turnbull. Liverpool's third goal scored by Dick Johnson came about in bizarre circumstances as Arsenal's keeper Jock Robson was chased by a stray dog while carrying the ball and kicked it straight to Johnson who scored!

The *Liverpool Echo* had guessed that Liverpool wouldn't search far for David Ashworth's successor: "Who will get the job? I don't want to guess, but I think I am right in forecasting that, as usual, the club will not go out of the region of its former players." As predicted on February 14, 1923 the *Liverpool Echo* reported: "Last night Mr. Matt McQueen was officially appointed team manager of Liverpool Football Club. Many names have been bandied about as to who would fill the position of team manager to the Liverpool club, vacated by Mr. Ashworth. The vacancy attracted many applicants, which included quite a number of former Liverpool players. It is gratifying to know that an old and trusted servant of the club has secured the position.

"'Mattie' as he is known by all, is a popular figure out Anfield way, and he can be relied upon to give of his best in his new post. Mr. McQueen, it is rather strange to say, figured in the four drawn games with Sheffield United in the Cup semi-final in 1899, so it is only fitting that he should have a hand in the next meeting with the Blades."

Matt, along with his brother Hugh, arrived at Liverpool from Leith Athletic in Scotland only two months into the club's first season. Matthew, so named after his grandfather, had eight siblings in total, three brothers and five sisters. They lived in Harthill in North Lanarkshire, a small village of only a couple of hundred inhabitants that made their living in the coalmines. Matt's father, Peter, was a roadman at the pit, preparing and repairing underground passageways. He later became a Coal Oversman, supervising the safety of the working conditions in the pit. Unavoidably the boys were put to work at the Benhar Colliery. William and Hugh were pony drivers and Matt was a coalminer earning about 4 shillings per day (20 pence in today's money). Matt had already been capped by Scotland as a winger, while at Leith Athletic, before moving south to Merseyside.

He and Hugh made their debuts in a 9-0 win over Newtown in an FA Cup qualifier on October 29, 1892 and the local press was pleased with the new additions: "At Anfield, the Liverpool Club management are not allowing the grass to grow under their feet, and are kneading together a team which will take more beating than most elevens will be able to give them. The latest captures have been very quietly effected, and in the brothers McQueen they have secured a couple of players far above the average. The debut of the

McQueens must be regarded as a decided success, to judge from the lavish applause extended to them." Matt featured regularly in his first four seasons at the club, making history as he was certainly the only man in English football to win two league medals, albeit in the Second Division, as both an outfield player and a goalkeeper. He featured on 45 occasions in Liverpool's goal and his skills were praised in a *Liverpool Mercury* report after a home 3-3 draw against Wolves on December 1, 1894: "His clean, sharp and adroit work placing him in the highest rank as a cool custodian."

McQueen was probably the most versatile footballer of his day. He had a lengthy spell as a goalkeeper, about two years as a full-back, and then went into the half-back line. In one match, owing to the poor display of his full-back, he changed positions, leaving his goal to the care of McLean and went to full-back. He also refereed many First Division matches.

Liverpool and Sunderland had created quite a gap on the rest of the teams at the top. The Reds had a three-point lead on the Wearsiders, although having played one more game, when Matt McQueen took charge of his first Liverpool game against Blackburn on February 17, 1923. The *Liverpool Echo* reported on McQueen's debut match: "Welcome to sunny Anfield, hope you've brought your bucket and spade. Today there was a league battle at Anfield and the game was once again blessed with good weather, so there was another enormous gathering around all quarters of the ground.

"Today was the first occasion that MR MATT McQUEEN had been officiating as player's manager and he received a warm welcome from board, players and fans alike. I would like to join in, in wishing him a cordial welcome and good luck."

McQueen was to enjoy his first occasion as Liverpool's manager as his new team again showed their attacking prowess as they beat

Blackburn 3-0. McQueen was now held responsible for having the brains behind the Liverpool team off the pitch while Liverpudlian Tom Bromilow was widely seen as the brains behind the Liverpool team on it.

Born in West Derby, left half-back Bromilow was picked up by his home club after turning up at Anfield to ask for a trial following his time in the army. He made his debut in the 1919/20 season against Burnley at Turf Moor, and played a number of matches for England. George Patterson, Liverpool's secretary at the time, recalls how he signed Bromilow in 1919: "His signature was obtained in the strangest manner. He came to the ground in uniform during the war and asked for a game. I asked George Fleming, who was in charge of the second team then, how he was fixed and he said he could do with another player; Bromilow played at outside right and was an instant success. When the war ended he signed as a professional. Eventually he took his place in the first team when Lacey was playing an international match for Ireland. I should think that it is one of the luckiest signings I have made."

Strong interest was shown in Liverpool's next game against Sheffield United in the third round of the FA Cup on February 24, 1923. Thousands arrived by the train load from Sheffield and as Everton were not playing, the locals' interest was solely focused on the Reds. The average attendance for Anfield that season was 34,790, but no less than 51,859 spectators were in attendance.

The queues in Kemlyn Road had started forming early that morning and some fans had even tried to hide under the director's stand the night before to gain a useful advantage. Harry Chambers gave Liverpool a perfect start by scoring after just 10 minutes of play. Salmon-red-shirted Liverpool were playing brilliantly in the first half, but United equalised before half-time. United's grit proved the deciding factor and, as in 1899 and 1915, Sheffield United knocked Liverpool out of the FA Cup.

Liverpool tried to put their cup disappointment behind them in the league versus Bolton at Anfield on March 2. Dick Forshaw and Dick Johnson put Liverpool 2-0 up in the first half, but following Liverpool's third and Fred Hopkin's first Liverpool goal in 78 games for the club, the Anfield Road stand caught fire!

The *Liverpool Echo* reported on this dramatic moment: "At first it seemed a mere nothing, but later on the smoke threatened to stop the game. The spectators at the bottom end could see little of what was going on, and through my field glasses I could see the police ordering the spectators about and clearing them into the stand. There was a general stampede into the stand, and quite an uncommon sight was witnessed of the spectators being more interested in the fire than the game. The Bolton goalkeeper was badly situated, as he was in a mass of smoke. A massive smoke-screen obscured the field of play, but thankfully the Westminster-Road fire brigade put the fire out and this eventful game finished with a 3-0 win for Liverpool."

Liverpool were defeated by Blackburn in the following game on March 12 at Ewood Park conceding their first league goal since Boxing Day. Five days later, McQueen's team travelled to Hyde Road, the home of Manchester City, and lost by the same 1-0 score-line. It was the first time since September that Liverpool had lost two games in a row. Regardless of failing to add to their points total over the last two fixtures, Liverpool still maintained their place at the summit of the First Division as second-place Sunderland failed to gain advantage.

Liverpool got back on track with three consecutive wins, against Manchester City, Sheffield United and Birmingham. However, on April 2, the Reds suffered their biggest defeat of the season at

Bramall Lane, 4-1. Three draws then followed and only three points were taken from four games. This was far from ideal and this dip in form could have cost them the championship. However, yet again, Sunderland couldn't capitalise and Liverpool stayed top with a four-point lead with three rounds to be played.

Liverpool faced third-place Huddersfield at Anfield on April 21. At half-time the game at Anfield was goalless, but the spectators had every reason to cheer as they learnt that Sunderland were losing 2-0 at Burnley. Huddersfield took the lead at Anfield but it ended 1-1 while Sunderland lost at Burnley. Liverpool's lead had increased to five points with only four points to be played for so the Reds retained the title.

The Anfielders became the fifth side since the league was formed in 1888 to win the championship in two consecutive seasons joining Preston North End's "Invincibles", Sunderland, Aston Villa (twice) and The Wednesday in the history books.

Although Liverpool were crowned champions, the Reds hadn't won a single game in their six previous outings and were desperate to win the last league game in front of their home fans, who had gathered to see Liverpool lift the league trophy. Harry Chambers scored the only goal in the 52nd minute versus Stoke. Liverpool had to play with one less player for a part of the game as goalkeeper Elisha Scott injured his thigh after stretching for an overambitious pass by his own defender, Jock McNab. Scott was carried off the field on the back of one of the ground assistants. Bill Lacey took his place in goal and did marvellously well, keeping a clean sheet.

John McKenna, former chairman of Liverpool, and current president of the league, presented the cup to Walter Williams, Liverpool's chairman, at the end of the game. Liverpool paraded the cup around Anfield and "players and directors received a rallying shout of praise". In fact, the directors' and players' rooms "were stormed by those desiring to offer congratulations". The chairman was overjoyed: "The team have done wonders. You ask the reason of their success, and I reply that they won because they are a good side, and have proved themselves a good side. It is one of happiest days of my life."

Liverpool's proud captain Donald Mackinlay choked back tears of emotion to tell the *Liverpool Echo*: "It was touch and go now and again, and one could see that the boys felt the keenness of the position. We are grateful to all who have helped us to our top position, and we hope the public realise that we have won again, in spite of being on top early on, a big barrier to success in most cases, as teams come along with the avowed intention of making the league game a cup-tie business. However, it is all over now, and I want to thank all the players sincerely for their splendid service in the second championship win in succession."

One jocularly asked: "If we win it for the third time does it become our own property?" Walter Wadsworth presented former and current captains, Ephraim Longworth and Donald Mackinlay, with miniature cups on behalf of the players and board as a tribute for their leadership.

The *Liverpool Echo* congratulated Liverpool on their splendid season: "Undoubtedly the feat is an unusual one in that the league, though won twice in succession before, has not been won in successive years when there was the severe competition that obtains to-day. The Anfield side has won through by its all-round skill, and through its determined, as well as good class standard of play. Every man deserves praise, and the club realises, as well as anyone, that much of the success of the side has been due to immunity from accident. Only 19 players have been called in to service."

1922/23: Facts and Statistics

Final league table

		P	W	D	L	F	A	W	D	L	F	A	PTS
1	Liverpool FC	42	17	3	1	50	13	9	5	7	20	18	60
2	Sunderland	42	15	5	1	50	25	7	5	9	22	29	54
3	Huddersfield Town	42	14	2	5	35	15	7	9	5	25	17	53
4	Newcastle United	42	13	6	2	31	11	5	6	10	14	26	48
5	Everton	42	14	4	3	41	20	6	3	12	22	39	47
6	Aston Villa	42	15	3	3	42	11	3	7	11	22	40	46
7	WBA	42	12	7	2	38	10	5	4	12	20	39	45
8	Manchester City	42	14	6	1	38	16	3	5	13	12	33	45
9	Cardiff City	42	15	2	4	51	18	3	5	13	22	41	43
10	Sheffield United	42	11	7	3	41	20	5	3	13	27	44	42
11	Arsenal	42	13	4	4	38	16	3	6	12	23	46	42
12	Tottenham	42	11	3	7	34	22	6	4	11	16	28	41
13	Bolton Wanderers	42	11	8	2	36	17	3	4	14	14	41	40
14	Blackburn Rovers	42	12	7	2	32	19	2	5	14	15	43	40
15	Burnley	42	12	3	6	39	24	4	3	14	19	35	38
16	Preston North End	42	12	3	6	41	26	1	8	12	19	38	37
17	Birmingham	42	10	4	7	25	19	3	7	11	16	38	37
18	Middlesbrough	42	11	4	6	41	25	2	6	13	16	38	36
19	Chelsea	42	5	13	3	29	20	4	5	12	16	33	36
20	Nottingham Forest	42	12	2	7	25	23	1	6	14	16	47	34
21	Stoke	42	7	9	5	28	19	3	1	17	19	48	30
22	Oldham Athletic	42	9	6	6	21	20	1	4	16	14	45	30

Games for the 1922/1923 season

(The number after date is league position after the game)

1	26.08.1922	8	W	5-2	Arsenal, Anfield, 1st Division
2	30.08.1922	9	L	0-1	Sunderland, Roker Park, 1st Division
3	02.09.1922	16	L	0-1	Arsenal, Highbury, 1st Division
4	06.09.1922	9	W	5-1	Sunderland, Anfield, 1st Division
5	09.09.1922	6	W	3-1	Preston North End, Deepdale, 1st Division
6	16.09.1922	1	W	5-2	Preston North End, Anfield, 1st Division
7	23.09.1922	1	W	3-0	Burnley, Anfield, 1st Division
8	30.09.1922	1	L	0-2	Burnley, Turf Moor, 1st Division
9	07.10.1922	1	W	5-1	Everton, Anfield, 1st Division
10	14.10.1922	1	W	1-0	Everton, Goodison Park, 1st Division

11	21.10.1922	1	W	3-1	Cardiff City, Anfield, 1st Division
12	28.10.1922	1	L	0-3	Cardiff City, Ninian Park, 1st Division
13	04.11.1922	1	W	4-2	Tottenham Hotspur, White Hart Lane, 1st Division
14	11.11.1922	1	D	0-0	Tottenham Hotspur, Anfield, 1st Division
15	18.11.1922	1	W	3-0	Aston Villa, Anfield, 1st Division
16	25.11.1922	1	W	1-0	Aston Villa, Villa Park, 1st Division
17	02.12.1922	1	L	0-2	Newcastle United, Anfield, 1st Division
18	09.12.1922	1	W	1-0	Newcastle United, St. James' Park, 1st Division
19	16.12.1922	1	W	2-1	Nottingham Forest, Anfield, 1st Division
20	23.12.1922	1	W	3-1	Nottingham Forest, City Ground, 1st Division
21	25.12.1922	1	W	2-0	Oldham Athletic, Boundary Park, 1st Division
22	26.12.1922	1	W	2-1	Oldham Athletic, Anfield, 1st Division
23	30.12.1922	1	D	0-0	Chelsea, Stamford Bridge, 1st Division
24	06.01.1923	1	W	1-0	Chelsea, Anfield, 1st Division
25	13.01.1923		D	0-0	Arsenal, Anfield, FA Cup 1st round
26	17.01.1923		W	4-1	Arsenal, Highbury, FA Cup 1st round replay
27	20.01.1923	1	W	2-0	Middlesbrough, Ayresome Park, 1st Division
28	27.01.1923	1	W	2-0	Middlesbrough, Anfield, 1st Division
29	03.02.1923		W	2-0	Wolves, Molineux, FA Cup 2nd round
30	07.02.1923	1	W	2-0	West Bromwich Albion, Anfield, 1st Division
31	10.02.1923	1	D	0-0	West Bromwich Albion, The Hawthorns, 1st Division
32	17.02.1923	1	W	3-0	Blackburn Rovers, Anfield, 1st Division
33	24.02.1923		L	1-2	Sheffield United, Anfield, FA Cup 3rd round
34	03.03.1923	1	W	3-0	Bolton Wanderers, Anfield, 1st Division
35	12.03.1923	1	L	0-1	Blackburn Rovers, Ewood Park, 1st Division
36	17.03.1923	1	L	0-1	Manchester City, Hyde Road, 1st Division
37	24.03.1923	1	W	2-0	Manchester City, Anfield, 1st Division
38	30.03.1923	1	W	2-1	Sheffield United, Anfield, 1st Division
39	31.03.1923	1	W	1-0	Birmingham, St. Andrew's, 1st Division
40	02.04.1923	1	L	1-4	Sheffield United, Bramall Lane, 1st Division
41	07.04.1923	1	D	0-0	Birmingham, Anfield, 1st Division
42	14.04.1923	1	D	0-0	Huddersfield Town, Leeds Road, 1st Division
43	18.04.1923	1	D	1-1	Bolton Wanderers, Burnden Park, 1st Division
44	21.04.1923	1	D	1-1	Huddersfield Town, Anfield, 1st Division
45	28.04.1923	1	D	0-0	Stoke, Victoria Ground, 1st Division
46	05.05.1923	1	W	1-0	Stoke, Anfield, 1st Division

Friendlies

1	25.05.1922		L	0-1	Burnley, Campo di Viale Lombardia, Friendly
2	28.05.1922		W	6-1	Emilia Select, Modena, Friendly
3	01.06.1922		D	2-2	Liguria & Toscana Select, Pisa, Friendly
4	05.06.1922		D	0-0	Pro Vercelli, Vercelli, Friendly

5	07.06.1922	W	4-1	Genoa, Stadio Marassi, Friendly
6	15.11.1922	W	3-1	Derby County, Anfield, Testimonial*
7	07.05.1923	W	2-0	Blackpool, Bloomfield Road, Lancashire Senior Cup
8	12.05.1923	L	0-1	Manchester City, Burnden Park, Lancashire Senior Cup

Appearances for the 1922/1923 season

Name	League	FA Cup	Total
Dick Forshaw	42	4	46
Elisha Scott	42	4	46
Donald Mackinlay	42	4	46
Ephraim Longworth	41	4	45
Tom Bromilow	41	4	45
Fred Hopkin	40	4	44
Harry Chambers	39	4	43
Jock McNab	39	4	43
Walter Wadsworth	37	4	41
Dick Johnson	37	4	41
Bill Lacey	30	4	34
Cyril Gilhespy	10	0	10
David Pratt	7	0	7
John Bamber	4	0	4
Harry Beadles	4	0	4
Harold Wadsworth	3	0	3
Jack Sambrook	2	0	2
Tommy Lucas	1	0	1
Danny Shone	1	0	1

Goalscorers for the 1922/1923 season

Name	League	FA Cup	Total
Harry Chambers	22	3	25
Dick Forshaw	19	1	20
Dick Johnson	14	2	16
Donald Mackinlay	5	1	6
Tom Bromilow	3	0	3
Walter Wadsworth	2	0	2
Cyril Gilhespy	2	0	2
Fred Hopkin	1	0	1
Bill Lacey	1	0	1
Jock McNab	1	0	1

The squad during the 1922/1923 season

Elisha Scott, Goalkeeper
Tom Bromilow, Defender
Tommy Lucas, Defender
Donald Mackinlay, Defender
Jock McNab, Defender
Ephraim Longworth, Defender
David Pratt, Defender
Walter Wadsworth, Defender
Ted Parry, Defender
John Bamber, Midfielder
Harold Wadsworth, Midfielder
Bill Lacey, Midfielder
Cyril Gilhespy, Midfielder
Harry Beadles, Striker
Harry Chambers, Striker
Dick Forshaw, Striker
Danny Shone, Striker
Dick Johnson, Striker
Jack Sambrook, Striker
Fred Hopkin, Left-winger

Transfers for the 1922/1923 season

In:
Jimmy Walsh, Stockport County, Free, 20 May 1922
Jack Sambrook, Wolves, Unknown, August 1922
David Pratt, Bradford City, Unknown, January 1923

Out:
Billy Matthews, Bristol City, £750, 2 March 1922

A collection of statistics for the 1922/1923 season

The season in numbers:
Total games: 46
Games won: 23
Games drawn: 14
Games lost: 9
Clean sheets – League: 17
Clean sheets – Overall: 18
Total goals: 69
Average attendance at home – League: 37,142
Average attendance at home – Overall: 38,086
Average goals per game – League: 2.05
Average goals per game – Overall: 2.09
Average goals per game – Overall: 2.48

Goals split down to competitions:
League – 70
FA Cup – 7

Player debuts:
Jack Sambrook against Chelsea on 30.12.1922
David Pratt against Blackburn Rovers on 17.02.1923

Statistics and information provided by LFChistory.net

5 : BACK TO WINNING WAYS

1946/47

AFTER THE SUCCESSIVE CHAMPIONSHIPS OF 1922 and 1923, the club's fortunes declined somewhat with finishes of 12th, fourth, seventh and ninth. The team started the 1927/28 season in far from convincing form. There were just six victories from 17 matches before Manchester United's visit to Anfield on Christmas Eve. Liverpool eventually finished in what appeared to be a comfortable 16th place out of 22 but that doesn't tell the whole story.

The fight to avoid relegation that year was extraordinary. Middlesbrough finished bottom with 37 points and Tottenham joined them in the Second Division with 38 points. But no fewer than SEVEN clubs, with Liverpool among them, escaped by finishing on 39 points. However, before that end-of-season drama took place, Matt McQueen had stood down as manager. He had tragically lost a leg in a road accident in the early 1920s and his health had deteriorated further by the end of the decade. The joint Everton and Liverpool Programme from March 15, 1924 reported on the devastating news for Liverpool's manager: "It will be remembered in 1923 that in November Mr. McQueen went to Barnsley on a scouting expedition, and when returning from the match with a colleague of mine he was knocked down by a taxi and was found to have a broken leg. He was taken to the Sheffield Royal Hospital after rather considerable delay, the delay arising through the fact that Mr. McQueen waited to see the Liverpool chairman, Mr. William Robert Williams, who was that day at Sheffield.

"In fact, Mr. George Patterson, the secretary of the club, says that Mr. McQueen must have gone through agony when he went to meet the chairman in a two-seater car. Mr. McQueen has been in hospital ever since, and this week it was found necessary to amputate the leg above the knee, as a consequence of septic poisoning arising in the region of the silver plate that had been inserted."

Having already worked at Anfield for 20 years, Matt McQueen decided to retire. It was no surprise that George Patterson was asked to take over the reins with the title of secretary-manager, thus becoming the first man in Liverpool's history to manage the team in two separate eras (Patterson previously managed Liverpool for the first 18 games of the 1919/20 season).

As things turned out, the eight full seasons during which Patterson was in charge were some of the quietest years in the club's history, quiet in that nothing really sensational happened, either good or bad. They retained their place in the top division but never finished higher than fifth; they twice finished low enough to cause concern but not enough concern for relegation to be a serious possibility.

Yet after finishing seventh in 1935, there was an alarming slump the following season with the team being victorious in only three of the last 20 league games. They eventually escaped relegation by three points but it had been a close call. The pressure of managing a First Division club where results were not good when added to a serious illness forced Patterson to resign from the managerial side of his double post, although he continued as the club's secretary. It was another George (Kay) who was persuaded to leave his post at Southampton and head north to take over at Anfield in August, 1936.

Kay had only been at Anfield a couple of years when another world war broke out, a conflict that would interrupt and in some cases end the careers of many a fine footballer. The league was on hiatus but regional competitions took their place.

Many of the club's players served their country and Kay was hard at work to find men to represent Liverpool's XI. Billy Liddell noted that: "With players in the forces stationed all over the country, Mr. Kay wrote thousands of letters and must have spent many hours on the phone to Commanding Officers. Such was his personality that his own players and guest players would willingly make long journeys to play for the Reds." One of those men was a certain Bill Shankly who was impressed by Kay: "I played for Liverpool against Everton during the war in the Liverpool Senior Cup, as a guest from Preston. All the players were in the passageway including Billy Liddell and myself. But George Kay, the Liverpool manager, didn't speak. He just went round touching people on the shoulder. If he touched you then you were playing."

Future Liverpool manager Bob Paisley was equally full of praise for Kay, who gave Paisley his official Liverpool debut, after serving with Montgomery's Eighth Army, the 'Desert Rats' as an anti-tank gunner: "He took Liverpool through the War to come out a bit like West Ham did after the First War. He was one of the people who laid the ground for the way Liverpool teams would play in the future... keeping the ball on the ground and passing it well, but being strong on the ball as well."

Although the League Championship didn't restart until August 1946, Liverpool's official games got under way on January 5 of the same year, by means of a trip to Sealand Road to face Chester in the FA Cup third round first leg. On this day, eight players made their official Liverpool debut including future club legends Billy Liddell and Bob Paisley. Liverpool's cup run was shortened in the following round by Bolton Wanderers.

One of Liverpool's eight debutants that afternoon in Chester was full-back Ray Lambert, who made his official first appearance after being at the club for 10 years. Lambert joined Liverpool as an amateur at the age of 13 in January 1936, becoming the youngest-ever player to join a league club at that time. The Welshman had signed amateur forms for Liverpool before World War II but he didn't get an opportunity to represent his club in a competitive fixture until January 1946. Although regional leagues were still operating in the immediate aftermath of the war, by the time the Reds visited Chester for the FA Cup tie Lambert was now 23. He was a reliable full-back who became an integral member of the team for the next decade, averaging over 30 matches per season during that period. He was able to play on either flank and was a fans' favourite.

With the war now over, the club took the unusual step of deciding to tour North America and Canada. It is quite likely that George Kay was the instigator of this trip; certainly he was fully in favour of it because he felt that the climate and diet in a part of the world that hadn't been affected by food rationing the way European countries had would be extremely beneficial.

The schedule was punishing; 10 matches at various venues between May 12 and June 11 1946, but it benefited the Reds who started the first post-war season in far better physical shape than many of their competitors as Kay claimed himself in a note to the *Liverpool Echo* while in America: "The players are 25 per cent above par in football, due to, in my opinion, the quality, quantity and variety of food."

After an 11-1 victory over Toronto's Ulster United, the *Toronto Globe and Mail* wrote: "Perhaps the finer art of soccer was never better displayed in this country than was the case last night at Maple Leaf Stadium." The *New York Times* also hailed the British visitors: "Liverpool came to the States for a crack at our teams and our vitamins. It was a clean sweep. The Britons swept all ten of their matches and, like Jack Sprat and his wife; they also swept the platter clean. Away from the British austerity program, they plunged zestfully into our steaks, eggs, milk and other vittles. Not only was there a perceptible gain in strength on the playing field, but the squad averaged a gain in weight of seven pounds a man."

Excitement was at fever pitch throughout the land as the season approached, though the Players' Union sent shock waves through club managements by demanding a substantial increase in wages. In those days maximum payments were still enforced, and when the dispute was eventually resolved, top players were delighted to end up with payments of £12 a week during the season and £10 during the summer, which made them feel like embryo millionaires.

The League Championship carried with it total prize money of £550, with £440 for the runners-up and £330 for the side finishing third, while winners of the FA Cup final, which last season had generated net receipts after tax of £23,538, were entitled to receive £20 a head.

The composition of the first post-war First Division was based on pre-war performance and there were some names that were soon to look rather out of place. Brentford, Grimsby Town and Leeds United were clearly ill-equipped to make much of an impression, while the Second Division contained teams like Manchester United, Nottingham Forest and Tottenham Hotspur who were soon to prove themselves capable of greater things.

Liverpool fans had no special reason to believe they would take over the League Championship from Everton at the end of the seven-year gap caused by World War II. They had finished a modest 10th in the interim Football League North, organised the moment the guns stopped firing, and had said farewell to many familiar figures, including former skipper Matt Busby, who had accepted an offer to try his hand at managing Manchester United.

Liverpool's first game of the resurrected Football League was played at Bramall Lane against Sheffield United on August 31, 1946. Liverpool got off to a great start by beating the Blades 1-0. Leonard Carney's late header and only goal for the club was enough to give the Anfielders the two points.

Liverpool's first official league home game after the war was nothing to write home about. On Wednesday, September 4, due to the lack of floodlights at Anfield, the match kicked off early in the evening and more than 30,000 fans took time off work to see Liverpool beaten 1-0 by Middlesbrough. Laurie Hughes scored an own goal after only 11 minutes of play. Hughes was a classy centre-back who had great heading ability and his positional sense and overall reading of the game was second to none. He was a late developer physically and when he asked for a trial at Liverpool's two biggest teams, according to himself: "Liverpool and Everton didn't want to know me!"

Hughes later became Liverpool's first ever player to feature in the World Cup finals representing England three times in the 1950 World Cup in Brazil. He played against Chile, United States and Spain but those were his only 'full' caps. England's 1-0 loss to the USA is still considered one of the most unexpected results in the country's proud football history.

The real fireworks did not begin at Anfield until the following

Saturday, Liverpool's first post-war home match at a weekend. The Reds' third game of the season was played at a sun-drenched Anfield against Chelsea on September 7, 1946. It turned out to be one of the most thrilling matches in memory and Bob Paisley and Billy Liddell finally made their league debuts seven years after signing professional forms for the Reds. Liverpool lined up as follows: Charlie Ashcroft, Jim Harley, Bernard Ramsden, Phil Taylor, Laurie Hughes, Bob Paisley, Berry Nieuwenhuys, Jack Balmer, Bill Jones, Willie Fagan and Billy Liddell.

The Reds made a bright start as reported in the *Liverpool Echo*: "Success came in exactly two minutes. And Paisley was the man who went forward to get the corner kick which produced a direct goal for Liddell. The corner swung in, and Robinson, trying to punch away, put the ball on the inside of an upright whence it turned into the net. Bill Jones scored two in six minutes and Willie Fagan netted Liverpool's fourth. Chelsea looked down and out, losing 4-0 at half-time. An official total of 49,995 people were watching inside Anfield but as the game went on, the total went easily over 50,000 as young supporters were allowed to go pitch side to prevent crushing as some fans from outside the ground were allowed in. When the gates shut shortly before half-time, an estimated 5,000 were still left outside. Liverpool were insatiable for goals and Balmer added the fifth only a couple of minutes after the restart. Liddell added one more in the fiftieth minute when he weaved his way through and went on coura-geously to shoot a sixth.

"When the ball was travelling to goal he was taking a full-length dive to avoid colliding with Danny Winter. Chelsea finally got on the scoresheet after fifty-five minutes and astonishingly the score was suddenly 6-4 after seventy-two minutes of play and still time for the Londoners to get on equal terms. Willie Fagan's goal in the eighty-seventh minute sealed Liverpool's win and when the final whistle was blown the police were powerless to keep the youngsters from invading the pitch and mobbing the players as they left the field. Final score: Liverpool 7-4 Chelsea."

Despite the 24-year-old Liddell having never turned out in the league, he was already viewed as a key player for the side having featured for Liverpool in 152 games, scoring 82 goals in the regional divisions of wartime football.

William Beveridge Liddell first came to Liverpool in July 1938 and nine months later signed a professional contract. Had it not been for a certain Sir Matt Busby, Liverpool's former captain and later Manchester United's manager, Billy might never have been a Liverpool player. Busby found out that representatives of Manchester City had been to see Billy's parents with a view to getting their son to join the club. After learning that Billy had turned down the invitation to go to City, Busby rang Liverpool manager George Kay and suggested that, "this Liddell lad might be worth an enquiry" and indeed he was.

Before Liddell went to Liverpool, he was hired as an accountant at Simon Jude & West in Liverpool. His parents had it put into the contract that Billy would be allowed to continue his studies because they wanted him to have something to fall back on if things didn't work out. Liddell trained full-time in pre-season, but trained only twice a week, on a Tuesday and Thursday morning, when the season started. Liddell went on to become a model gentleman both on and off the park and was admired by everybody in the city, Red and Blue alike.

Apart from playing for his beloved Reds and working as an accountant in Liverpool city centre, he became a member of Court Hey Methodist Church, where he was a local preacher, a Sunday school teacher and a youth leader. In addition to his already hectic weekly schedule, on the last Thursday evening of every month Billy was a DJ in the local children's hospital, Alder Hey. After playing his set, he would walk around the wards and talk to the sick children. As you can imagine, these were both sad and happy times, for Billy and the young patients, but he would never leave the hospital until he had seen all the children.

The Kop idolised Liddell and he went on to be known as 'King Billy', 'The Emperor of Merseyside' and 'Liddellpool' and he went on to score 228 goals in 534 first-team appearances for the Reds.

But what was it that frightened the defenders he played against? Was it the power or guile of his left foot? Was it the power or guile of his right foot? Was it the power with which he headed the ball? Was it his lightning pace? Was it the awesome presence he demanded on the pitch? Was it the adoration of everyone who watched him? Was it his reputation? Was it because he would never quit and continued to push forward for 90 minutes?

The answer was: all of the above, as confirmed by defender – and future World Cup winning manager – Alf Ramsey. Ramsey once said that: "Playing against Billy was an absolute nightmare, because I knew I was going to get run ragged for the whole game." Ramsey once even asked Billy mid-match to go and play on the other wing because he was "knackered". Billy just gave him a look that confirmed he would be staying put.

Teammate and friend Bob Paisley later showed his admiration for Liddell: "Oh, what power! Opponents were frightened to death of the gentlest man on earth. Bill was so strong it was unbelievable. You couldn't shake him off the ball. It didn't matter where he was playing, though I suppose his best position was outside-left. He could go round you, or past you, or even straight through you sometimes!"

Paisley himself had fewer opportunities to play for Liverpool during the war (58 games – 12 goals), but he was important to Liddell's success as former Spurs captain, Danny Blanchflower, once pointed out: "My first match at Anfield was at right-back for Aston Villa. The roar from the Kop was awesome as Billy Liddell waltzed down the wing making us look like idiots. Then I began to recognise the source of Liddell's magic. He was Liverpool's inconspicuous craftsman at left-half, Bob Paisley."

Despite the brilliance of the Chelsea victory, any optimism following the big win was crushed four days later, when Liverpool lost 5-0 to Manchester United at Maine Road, managed by former Liverpool captain Matt Busby. After the war Manchester United played their "home" games at Maine Road, the home of their cross-town rivals, Manchester City, due to the wartime bombing of Old Trafford.

The following day, Liverpool made their record signing to date, when they paid Newcastle United £13,000 for striker Albert Stubbins. Stubbins was already vastly experienced and a prolific marksman when he signed from Newcastle where he scored a record 244 goals during wartime football that included 23 hat-tricks.

Everton and Liverpool were both interested in his services and had both offered a £1,000 less than the record transfer figure, £14,000, paid by Arsenal to Wolverhampton for Bryn Jones in 1938. Stubbins was at the Newcastle News Theatre when there came a notice on the cinema screen: 'Would Albert Stubbins please report to St. James' Park'. Stubbins recalled: "This was about six o'clock and I went up there to meet Mr George Kay and Mr Theo Kelly, representing Everton. Stan Seymour, the Newcastle director said, 'Which representative would you like to see first?' I said, 'Let's flip a coin. Heads Liverpool. Tails Everton'. It came down heads – Liverpool.

"Bill McConnell, the Liverpool chairman, and George Kay and

myself discussed matters and I was impressed with them both, and with the possibilities of the Liverpool team. So I said I would go to Anfield. I also knew several of the Liverpool players at the time like Willie Fagan and Jack Balmer. That probably gave Liverpool the slight edge and in the end I never spoke to Everton because I had been so impressed with Liverpool's offer."

Two days later, on September 14, Stubbins scored on his Reds debut at Burnden Park against Bolton Wanderers, as Liverpool went on a great run, winning eight and drawing four. One draw came against Everton in the highly anticipated first post-war Merseyside derby, which failed to live up to its billing, ending 0-0.

Another draw during this period came against Charlton Athletic at Anfield. An interesting anecdote from this game is future Liverpool manager Don Welsh scores the second of the two goals he scored against Liverpool for Charlton Athletic. The first, also at Anfield, had come just over nine years earlier. Welsh must be one of only a handful of men to have scored against Liverpool in official Football League matches both before and after World War II.

Liverpool's good form lifted the Reds from 12th to the top spot, owing mainly to Jack Balmer's unbelievable feat of scoring three hat-tricks in successive games. He scored three against Portsmouth on November 9, four against Derby County on the 16th and a week later he completed a hat-trick of hat-tricks against Arsenal at Anfield. When he scored his third against Arsenal to complete his third consecutive hat-trick, he was mobbed by his delighted teammates and the biggest cheer Anfield has ever known in its long history was heard.

Balmer became the third player to achieve the feat of a hat-trick of hat-tricks in the top division; first to do so was Tottenham's South African Tom Jennings in 1925 with Frank Osborne at Leeds following in his footsteps in 1926. Incidentally, Liverpool were involved in both of their scoring runs, Osborne scoring three against the Reds on October 24, 1925 at White Hart Lane and Jennings four at Anfield on October 2, 1926. Since Balmer joined this select group of men, no one has managed the incredible feat.

Balmer, from West Derby in Liverpool, was spotted by Everton when playing for Collegiate Old Boys, an amateur club that was founded to provide a football facility for former pupils of the Liverpool Collegiate School. The Blues gave Balmer a trial and he played for them as an amateur for two seasons. The Balmer name was already well known at the club as Jack's uncles, Bill and Bob Balmer, had both been popular players at Everton in the early part of the century. Everton decided not to keep him for a third season and Liverpool snapped Jack up when he was only 19 in May 1935.

He signed professional forms three months later and he came back to haunt Everton in the Merseyside derby on February 16, 1938 at Goodison Park when he scored inside 30 seconds in a 3-1 win!

As well as Balmer's scoring heroics, Billy Liddell, Albert Stubbins and Cyril Done were also chipping in with goals. Bill Jones, who started the 1946-47 season as a centre forward, was consequently moved back to reinforce Liverpool's defence.

Jones, who was born in Whaley Bridge, Derbyshire, joined Liverpool as a teenager in 1938, but his career and life was soon put on hold as World War II immediately deprived him of several years of competitive football. Bill was the grandfather of former Liverpool right-back Rob Jones and he followed his grandson's career closely. "We are very proud of Rob's achievements and I have to admit he is a better player than I was. He is a lot faster for a start," Bill commented on his grandson.

Rob spoke to *LFChistory.net* about his grandad in 2017: "My grandad Bill didn't speak much about his past and was a natural quiet, reserved person. Nevertheless, I loved being in his company as his presence was magical. My grandad was always a man of few words, very modest and very humble. For instance I would ask him what it was like to play with Billy Liddell and he would just say, 'A great man, a wonderful player and a bit of a joker in the dressing room,' and that would be it."

After retiring as a player, Bill later returned to Liverpool as a scout for the club. Rob recalls: "Grandad used to take me to the matches where he used to do his scouting. He first spotted Sir Roger Hunt playing for Stockton Heath, so he wasn't bad at that role either, was he? I still see Roger every now and again and he always speaks fondly of my grandad which is so pleasing. Grandad was also involved in the signings of Ian Rush and John Toshack and told me I attended some of their games, but I was far too young to remember."

When former Liverpool captain and legend Donald Mackinlay was asked in 1955 about the best Liverpool players he had witnessed, he singled out Bill: "One of the finest centre-halves I have ever seen. I would have loved to have played behind him. What a tragedy it was he was moved about such a lot." All in all, grandad and grandson played 520 games for Liverpool Football Club.

At the end of November 1946, Liverpool had taken 24 points from a possible 32 and were sitting at the top of the First Division. However, the Reds had two massive games coming up against fourth-place Blackpool and second-place Wolves. Balmer couldn't stop scoring, but his goal didn't prevent Liverpool from losing 3-2 at Blackpool and his penalty against Wolves mattered little as Dennis Westcott scored four for the visitors in a 5-1 win at Anfield. Westcott's feat of scoring four in the league against Liverpool at Anfield was not repeated until 63 years later by Andrey Arshavin for Arsenal.

In mid-December Liverpool responded with two 4-1 wins, in

which Balmer added three goals. By then he had scored 15 goals over seven successive games.

His prolific run eventually came to an end and from December 25, Liverpool went on to lose five out of the next six league games, which allowed Wolves to build up a healthy lead at the top of the table. Liverpool were sat in sixth place in the league seven points adrift and their recent results were far from championship form.

Things started to go from bad to worse for Kay's men. Not only did they only manage a mere two points from 12, their ninth defeat of the season came on January 29 at Goodison Park. Despite being disputed in far from ideal atmospheric conditions, the supporters weren't disappointed in the standard of football on show.

The *Liverpool Daily Post and Mercury* reported: "30,612 people went to Goodison Park yesterday hoping to see football. The cold was arctic, the wind whistled through half-empty stands, and half-empty spectators, and everyone knew that expecting good football on a brick-hard ground covered by snow was crazy optimism...yet, astonishingly, this proved to be one of the most notable of Liverpool-Everton conflicts, beautifully played and handled, clean, never lacking in interest and generally measuring up to, if not beyond, standards produced with the ground in perfect conditions."

Nothing would go right for Liverpool, who slipped into fourth place, before regaining their momentum with a somewhat fortunate 2-1 victory over relegation-threatened Leeds on a snow-covered surface at Elland Road. Stubbins, by now widely known as 'Ginger' on account of his red hair, and Fagan, put the Reds 2-0 in front against the run of play, and although Leeds got a goal back, that was two more vital points in the bag.

The Liverpool captaincy was split during the 1946/47 season between Jack Balmer and Willie Fagan and Balmer wrote an interesting piece for the 1947 official Liverpool handbook, highlighting the main roles and duties of a Liverpool captain: "Two to three minutes to kick-off. A strange air of expectancy settles over the whole ground and then from out of 'the hole' trot eleven men trained and trusted to carry the tradition and honour at playing in a 'Red' shirt. What are the duties of the man chosen to lead the team onto the field of play, who even now is walking to the middle in answer to the whistle? All important both to spectators and management alike is what takes place on the field of play. If on spinning the coin he has the good fortune to win the 'toss' choice at ends will, in all probability, be a matter for the state of the weather to decide and also the knowledge that kicking into the 'Kop' for the second '45' may well mean pulling the game out of the fire. A few words with the men around him and the game is 'on'.

"Play the game in a true sporting spirit to the best of his ability even when the ball runs unkindly will always be uppermost in his mind. Knowing he is giving of his best will ensure that the men around him will do likewise and pull out that little extra for the man who is temporarily off form. He will call 'to' and not 'at' any of his team mates who are in difficulty with the ball as he would expect them to do to him knowing always that good calling to one another brings good team work and through this, not individualism, he will skipper a successful team. Responsibility for any team changes during the playing time rests with him and is always upheld by the management.

"Team changes unless through injury will always be made with one idea, 'The Reds must win.' Behind the scenes and during every week meetings will he held when he will discuss with the management and players any improvements to benefit both club and players, on and off the field, so that when Saturday comes around everyone is happy.

Directors, manager and trainers are all 'Playing the game' with him and the team. In conclusion – he would say when a team is playing well a captain's "lot" is a happy one. When things go wrong his "lot" is not a happy one."

Scottish inside-left forward Fagan joined Liverpool from Preston North End in October 1937 for £8,000. After World War II, Fagan was young enough to re-establish himself at Anfield when official football resumed in 1946. He was named club captain and led Liverpool's short lived cup run in January 1946.

Fagan was described by the *Liverpool Echo* as: "A ball player of the crafty Scottish type, an effective connecting link between the attack and the half-back line, and a man who can sum up the needs of a situation in the twinkling of an eye. There are few better creators of scoring opportunities for others than Fagan. He can hold the ball, juggle with it if needs be, and then slip it through to the right spot at the psychological moment. He is strong in his tackling, and equally strong to withstand the challenge of opposing defenders."

From February 1 to April 4, Liverpool were on a roll again, gaining 12 points out of a possible 14. The stand-out game from this period was Liverpool's 5-0 demolition of Grimsby Town, when Bootle-born Cyril Done scored a hat-trick. Done was referred to at Anfield as 'Gordon Hodgson the second' as the two strikers were similar in style, exceptionally strong on the ball and possessing a terrific shot with either foot. Done didn't cost Liverpool a penny as they found him playing in his native Bootle with Bootle Grammar School Old Boys, and he was signed on amateur forms. He impressed so much that he was made a professional as soon as he reached the age of 17 in 1937.

In addition, during Liverpool's magnificent run during this time, goalkeeper Cyril Sidlow only conceded five goals in 10 league and cup games. The Welshman appeared for Wolves during the war but was deemed surplus to requirements as the league resumed due to the emergence of future England goalkeeper Bert Williams. As a result, the 30-year-old jumped straight into George Kay's team as his first-choice goalkeeper.

Sidlow became known for throwing the ball to his teammates rather than kicking it aimlessly upfield. Teammate Paisley spoke highly of Liverpool's goalkeeper at the time: "Cyril was another in the long school of accomplished goalkeepers to be at the club. Reading the game was one of his major strengths and while sometimes that isn't quite as flashy as the goalkeeper who is diving about all the time, I know which style most outfield players prefer in their side. Maybe it was that ability which explained why he was never hailed as being as good as he was by supporters. A goalkeeper who is flinging himself about all over the place catches the eye and people will say, 'He's brilliant'. In fact, they are making it hard work for themselves whereas goalkeeping was an easy art for the big Welshman."

Liverpool's good run came to a halt when they were leading 2-0 against Blackpool with less than an hour to go but let the lead slip and lost 3-2. Liverpool were now fifth, with 42 points from 34 games. Wolves were second with 46 points from 33 games and Blackpool were top with 47 points but had played 38 games as they had not been troubled by the frosty weather.

Future Liverpool captain and manager Phil Taylor played in 35 of the 42 league matches during the 1946/47 season and later commented on life as a footballer during the mid-1940s: "It was a very different world back then for a player. When I first played for Liverpool we didn't even have our own training ground because the club didn't buy Melwood from St. Francis Xavier School until the early Fifties. Most of our training on Tuesday, Wednesday and

Thursday consisted of running with virtually no work on individual skills or team tactics at all. I think a modern player would have 10 fits wearing the kind of boots we wore. Ours were so heavy, with solid toecaps that could murder you if you were kicked. I can remember sitting with my boots in a tub of water, so they would shrink to fit my feet."

Liverpool reached the semi-finals of the FA Cup after beating Birmingham 4-1 on March 1, 1947 and Albert Stubbins scored one of the most famous goals in Anfield's history. Billy Liddell, who set it up, recalled: "When I put the ball over it was going a bit off course, but Stubbins literally threw himself through the air to meet it with his head when parallel with the ground, about two feet above the turf. It went in like a rocket, giving Gil Merrick absolutely no chance, and Albert slid on his stomach for several yards on the frozen pitch before coming to a stop."

Liverpool met old foes, Second Division Burnley, in the FA Cup semi-final. Liverpool had a score to settle after losing to Burnley in the 1914 final. Albert Stubbins and Jack Balmer used to sing the popular folk-blues song "Sitting on the Top of the World" before each cup round but forgot to do so before both matches against Burnley. Players − being a superstitious lot − believed that it might have jinxed the side, who lost 1-0 in a replay. Burnley's goalkeeper was in excellent form and was considered the main reason why Liverpool were beaten on the day.

The team recovered from this disappointment and went on to win four out of their next five league games, before travelling to Highbury to take on Arsenal in the penultimate round of the season. Just one point separated the top four and nothing else than four points from their remaining two games would give them a chance of being crowned league champions for the first time in 24 years.

Liverpool found themselves a goal down after an hour's play, which prompted the club's directors to hold a meeting in the Highbury stand. The outcome of the meeting is said to have had a great significance on the final result. The *Liverpool Daily Express* reported: "An inspired thought by the Liverpool directors helped the club overcome Arsenal at Highbury on Saturday. That is the story behind this latest Anfield triumph. It is the players who win matches not directors, but hand it to the directors this time for contributing to the success. After 61 minutes Liverpool found themselves down to a McPherson goal which Liverpool thought was offside, and the side was giving few signs apart from wing and down the centre thrust of ever retrieving the position. Then came the master idea which turned the whole trend of the game and sent the Arsenal home rather unfortunate losers. Directors Messrs. S. Ronnie Williams, W. Harvey Webb, George Richards and Ralph K. Milne were in the director's box, and five minutes before the interval Mr. R. Lawson Martindale, who had been held up by traffic, arrived.

"At half-time Mr. Martindale suggested that if there were no immediate improvement in the side that switches should be made in keeping with Liverpool's pre-war ideas. Well, that leading goal to Arsenal which so dimmed the prospects brought action. Vice-Chairman Ronnie Williams called an informal meeting in the stand and a switch of Jones and Fagan affecting inside left and right half was proposed. The vote was "yes," and off went Mr. Williams through the Highbury corridors to trainer Albert Shelley at the touch line. From Albert the change order was passed to Bobby Priday and on to skipper Fagan, and the switch became a fact. The change was made at the 68th minute and so well did it work − the effect on the side as a whole rather than the actual change − that at the 77th minute had headed a peach of a goal from inside left from Watkinson's corner, and at the 81st minute Balmer had set the seal on Liverpool's victory. Two goals were scored in the space of four minutes. About the winning goal, definitely it was scored by Balmer although at the time there was doubt because of the goalmouth scramble. Priday was the maker and the man to whom chief credit goes, for he bore inside to shake off Male and Sloan and drive in low. Balmer just got his leg to the ball and it turned over the line as Barnes tried to kick clear but instead turned the ball farther into the net. All the Liverpool players assert that the ball was over the line before Barnes touched it and so Balmer gets the credit and once again becomes Liverpool's leading goal-getter, one ahead of Stubbins with a match to go. This victory can be attributed directly to the brilliance of Liverpool's defence – a complete ensemble of men who were masters of position, tackling, intervention and kicking. The attack was rather a disjointed affair enlivened only when Bill Jones went in to add his height, weight, skill and endeavour. The real effect came from Watkinson and Priday, with Priday as the best forward on the field. That is no reflection on Bill Watkinson, who now he has come through extended trials is, in my opinion, a better proposition than many players for whom the club would have to pay out thousands of pounds. Watkinson may easily be the answer to the prayer for a star outside right. Watkinson has now played in five matches out of which the Reds have collected nine points. Priday's tally is three games, five points. Nice pickings on the bonus market. This was not a good game, but it thrilled because Liverpool rose to the occasion so nobly at the vital moment and stayed much better."

Liverpool had one last crucial game left against Wolves on May 31 at Molineux. Both Phil Taylor and Bob Paisley were missing through injury, but the great Liddell, who had missed the previous three games, returned. Eddie Spicer, later to have his career terminated prematurely through a serious leg fracture, played in midfield, instead of his favourite full-back position, but the star men were again Liddell and Stubbins. Wolves were top of the league with 56 points from 41 games, Manchester United were second with 56 points but had played all their 42 games, Stoke third with 55 points after 41 played and Liverpool fourth equal on points with Stoke but with an inferior goal average. Manager George Kay was curiously absent at the vital match as he couldn't miss out on a pre-arranged five-day scouting mission in Ireland! Billy Liddell cherished the memory of this historic game, recalling that it: "Was more suitable for cricket than football. It was extremely hot, with the thermometer somewhere in the Eighties, and I remember remarking to Albert Stubbins about the vast number of spectators in short-sleeves or summer frocks. We were the first to score when Jackie Balmer steered one into the net and when Albert Stubbins got a second we thought the game was safely in the bag."

Stubbins later recalled the moment that he put the Reds 2-0 up: "I had a word with Bob Paisley and told him if he received the ball in a deep midfield position, to knock it straight down the middle for me to chase. The first opportunity he got, he did just that and it took Wolves by surprise. I'd already set off and I left Stan Cullis and Billy Wright trailing in my wake. As I closed in on goal the keeper Bert Williams came rushing off his line, but I just managed to get my toe to the ball and poke it past him. We were already leading 1-0 and that goal put us in the driving seat. Wolves, however, were never a team to give up without a struggle. Their captain, Stan Cullis, was a wonderful inspiration, urging his players on and making them fight as though their lives depended on it. Jimmy Dunn, a Liverpool fan, reduced the lead, but that was all Wolves could achieve, largely because our defence gave one of the finest exhibitions seen at Molineux for many a long day. It was ironic that the man who did most to keep Wolves from the draw, which would, as things turned out, have given them the championship, was their former goalkeeper Sidlow. Cyril made save after save when it seemed certain that he must be beaten. We were a happy party returning from Wolverhampton, but still had to wait a fortnight before knowing whether we were champions."

Stan Cullis, Wolves' captain, widely considered the best defender of his generation, was heartbroken. It was his last ever game and he felt he may have done better when Stubbins scored: "I had no idea Stubbins was so near, and then I saw his red head flash past. He's got amazing speed." The severe weather and the government's ban on midweek games forced the league to extend the season so Stoke's only remaining game, against Sheffield United at Bramall Lane, could not take place until June 14. Liverpool were two points ahead of Stoke but the Potters' superior goal average meant a win would bring them the Championship. Fate would so have it that Liverpool and Everton were playing in the Liverpool Senior Cup final when the game in Sheffield kicked off 15 minutes prior to the game at Anfield. Liddell and his teammates tried their best to keep their focus: "Though our minds were more on what was taking place at Bramall Lane than at Anfield, we defeated Everton 2-1. But the last ten minutes were a mere formality, for the news had been given over the loud-speakers that Stoke had been defeated and the title was ours. The crowd didn't care two straws what happened after that. All they wanted was the final whistle, so they could come swarming over the ground from the Kop and Kemlyn Road and carry us off the field. It was a scene of amazing enthusiasm."

Liverpool had officially been crowned First Division champions for the fifth time in 55 seasons of football. It had been a remarkable achievement, greatly helped by 24 goals from both Stubbins and

Balmer, 10 from Done, and seven each from Fagan and Liddell. Post-war Liverpool had been relaunched in style, and the reward was not only the First Division title, but a profit of just over £17,000.

In retrospect, the turning point can be seen to have been the signing of Stubbins, who provided just the punch that was needed, but Balmer's fabulous autumn scoring spell, and Liddell's winging, were other major factors. Teamwork was also of a high order, with a score of players used at different times. Ray Lambert, Eddie Spicer, Jim Harley and Barney Ramsden all did yeoman service at full-back at various times; Bill Jones played wherever required, and the half-back line of Taylor, Hughes and Paisley was a model of consistency. Nieuwenhuys, generally known as 'Nivvy', alternated with Harry Eastham (uncle of George, whose test case forced the abandonment of football's maximum wage) on the right wing, while Done and Fagan competed to partner Balmer at inside forward. All played their part, and it is likely that Bob Paisley learned much from this marvellously exciting season, knowledge he would put to excellent use to help his own teams achieve so many major successes in later years.

Liverpool director George Richards was the one who delivered the good news over the tannoy to everyone's delight: "The roar which greeted this announcement made the Hampden Park one sound almost like a childish whisper. The crowd threw their hands in the air; many lost their hats and did not bother to look for them after they had tossed them high up in a burst of joyful celebration."

George Kay's post-war heroes had made their supporters proud as the First Division trophy returned to Anfield for the first time in twenty-four years.

Popular Liverpool chairman Billy McConnell had been sick in hospital but had received discharge to watch the crucial Wolves match. He spoke about his pride in the players: "We have had some wonderful players in the club's history but never have we had a finer lot of gentlemen, sportsmen, and 100 per cent triers than we have today. That, plus the good work of the manager and trainer, has put us where we are." McConnell passed away a couple of months later – a huge shock for Liverpool – its ramifications becoming apparent in the disappointing seasons that followed.

1946/47: Facts and Statistics

Final league table

		P	W	D	L	F	A	W	D	L	F	A	PTS
1	Liverpool FC	42	13	3	5	42	24	12	4	5	42	28	57
2	Manchester United	42	17	3	1	61	19	5	9	7	34	35	56
3	Wolves	42	15	1	5	66	31	10	5	6	32	25	56
4	Stoke City	42	14	5	2	52	21	10	2	9	38	32	55
5	Blackpool	42	14	1	6	38	32	8	5	8	33	38	50
6	Sheffield United	42	12	4	5	51	32	9	3	9	38	43	49
7	Preston North End	42	10	7	4	45	27	8	4	9	31	47	47
8	Aston Villa	42	9	6	6	39	24	9	3	9	28	29	45
9	Sunderland	42	11	3	7	33	27	7	5	9	32	39	44
10	Everton	42	13	5	3	40	24	4	4	13	22	43	43
11	Middlesbrough	42	11	3	7	46	32	6	5	10	27	36	42
12	Portsmouth	42	11	3	7	42	27	5	6	10	24	33	41
13	Arsenal	42	9	5	7	43	33	7	4	10	29	37	41
14	Derby	42	13	2	6	44	28	5	3	13	29	51	41
15	Chelsea	42	9	3	9	33	39	7	4	10	36	45	39
16	Grimsby Town	42	9	6	6	37	35	4	6	11	24	47	38
17	Blackburn Rovers	42	6	5	10	23	27	8	3	10	22	26	36
18	Bolton Wanderers	42	8	5	8	30	28	5	3	13	27	41	34
19	Charlton Athletic	42	6	6	9	34	32	5	6	10	23	39	34
20	Huddersfield Town	42	11	4	6	34	24	2	3	16	19	55	33
21	Brentford	42	5	5	11	19	35	4	2	15	26	53	25
22	Leeds United	42	6	5	10	30	30	0	1	20	15	60	18

Games for the 1946/1947 season

(The number after date is league position after the game)

1	31.08.1946	1	W	1-0	Sheffield United, Bramall Lane, 1st Division
2	04.09.1946	8	L	0-1	Middlesbrough, Anfield, 1st Division
3	07.09.1946	5	W	7-4	Chelsea, Anfield, 1st Division
4	11.09.1946	12	L	0-5	Manchester United, Maine Road, 1st Division
5	14.09.1946	8	W	3-1	Bolton Wanderers, Burnden Park, 1st Division
6	21.09.1946	9	D	0-0	Everton, Anfield, 1st Division
7	28.09.1946	7	W	2-0	Leeds United, Anfield, 1st Division
8	05.10.1946	4	W	6-1	Grimsby Town, Blundell Park, 1st Division
9	09.10.1946	3	D	2-2	Middlesbrough, Ayresome Park, 1st Division
10	12.10.1946	6	D	1-1	Charlton Athletic, Anfield, 1st Division

11	19.10.1946	4	W	4-1	Huddersfield Town, Leeds Road, 1st Division
12	26.10.1946	3	W	1-0	Brentford, Anfield, 1st Division
13	02.11.1946	2	D	0-0	Blackburn Rovers, Ewood Park, 1st Division
14	09.11.1946	2	W	3-0	Portsmouth, Anfield, 1st Division
15	16.11.1946	1	W	4-1	Derby County, Baseball Ground, 1st Division
16	23.11.1946	1	W	4-2	Arsenal, Anfield, 1st Division
17	30.11.1946	1	L	2-3	Blackpool, Bloomfield Road, 1st Division
18	07.12.1946	2	L	1-5	Wolves, Anfield, 1st Division
19	14.12.1946	2	W	4-1	Sunderland, Roker Park, 1st Division
20	21.12.1946	2	W	4-1	Aston Villa, Anfield, 1st Division
21	25.12.1946	2	L	1-2	Stoke City, Victoria Ground, 1st Division
22	26.12.1946	2	W	2-0	Stoke City, Anfield, 1st Division
23	28.12.1946	2	L	1-2	Sheffield United, Anfield, 1st Division
24	04.01.1947	4	L	1-3	Chelsea, Stamford Bridge, 1st Division
25	11.01.1947		W	5-2	Walsall, Fellows Park, FA Cup 3rd round
26	18.01.1947	5	L	0-3	Bolton Wanderers, Anfield, 1st Division
27	25.01.1947		W	2-0	Grimsby Town, Anfield, FA Cup 4th round
28	29.01.1947	6	L	0-1	Everton, Goodison Park, 1st Division
29	01.02.1947	6	W	2-1	Leeds United, Elland Road, 1st Division
30	08.02.1947		W	1-0	Derby County, Anfield, FA Cup 5th round
31	12.02.1947	2	W	5-0	Grimsby Town, Anfield, 1st Division
32	22.02.1947	4	W	1-0	Huddersfield Town, Anfield, 1st Division
33	01.03.1947		W	4-1	Birmingham City, Anfield, FA Cup 6th round
34	08.03.1947	2	W	2-1	Blackburn Rovers, Anfield, 1st Division
35	15.03.1947	2	W	2-1	Portsmouth, Fratton Park, 1st Division
36	22.03.1947	3	D	1-1	Derby County, Anfield, 1st Division
37	29.03.1947		D	0-0	Burnley, Ewood Park, FA Cup Semi-final
38	04.04.1947	3	D	0-0	Preston North End, Deepdale, 1st Division
39	05.04.1947	5	L	2-3	Blackpool, Anfield, 1st Division
40	07.04.1947	5	W	3-0	Preston North End, Anfield, 1st Division
41	12.04.1947		L	0-1	Burnley, Maine Road, FA Cup Semi-final replay
42	19.04.1947	5	W	1-0	Sunderland, Anfield, 1st Division
43	26.04.1947	5	W	2-1	Aston Villa, Villa Park, 1st Division
44	03.05.1947	4	W	1-0	Manchester United, Anfield, 1st Division
45	10.05.1947	4	W	3-1	Charlton Athletic, The Valley, 1st Division
46	17.05.1947	4	D	1-1	Brentford, Griffin Park, 1st Division
47	24.05.1947	1	W	2-1	Arsenal, Highbury, 1st Division
48	31.05.1947	1	W	2-1	Wolves, Molineux, 1st Division

Friendlies

1	12.05.1946	W	3-1	New York All Stars, Triborough Stadium, Friendly
2	15.05.1946	W	9-0	Baltimore All Stars, Municipal Stadium, Friendly
3	19.05.1946	W	5-0	American League Select, Triborough Stadium Friendly
4	22.05.1946	W	3-2	New England Select, Fall River, Friendly
5	26.05.1946	W	12-0	Philadelphia Select, Yellow Jacket Field, Friendly
6	31.05.1946	W	5-1	St. Louis All Stars, Walsh Stadium, Friendly
7	02.06.1946	W	9-3	Chicago Maroons, Soldier Field, Friendly
8	05.06.1946	W	11-1	Ulster Select Maple, Leaf Stadium Friendly,
9	09.06.1946	W	3-1	Kearny Celtic Scots, Kearny High School Stadium, Friendly
10	11.06.1946	W	10-1	American League Select, Ebbets Field, Friendly
11	02.10.1946	D	2-2	Blackpool, Bloomfield Road, Lancashire Senior Cup
12	30.10.1946	W	2-1	Blackpool, Anfield, Lancashire Senior Cup
13	20.11.1946	D	3-3	Oldham Athletic, Anfield, Lancashire Senior Cup
14	26.11.1946	W	3-1	Oldham, Athletic Boundary Park, Lancashire Senior Cup
15	21.05.1947	W	1-0	Burnley, Anfield, Lancashire Senior Cup
16	07.06.1947	W	2-1	Bury, Anfield, Lancashire Senior Cup
17	14.06.1947	W	2-1	Everton, Anfield, Liverpool Senior Cup

Appearances for the 1946/1947 season

Name	League	FA Cup	Total
Jack Balmer	39	6	45
Ray Lambert	36	6	42
Albert Stubbins	36	6	42
Phil Taylor	35	6	41
Cyril Sidlow	34	6	40
Billy Liddell	34	6	40
Bob Paisley	33	6	39
Bill Jones	26	6	32
Laurie Hughes	30	1	31
Bernard Ramsden	23	1	24
Cyril Done	17	6	23
Willie Fagan	18	4	22
Jim Harley	17	4	21
Harry Eastham	19	2	21
Berry Nieuwenhuys	15	0	15
Eddie Spicer	10	0	10
Bob Priday	9	0	9
Billy Watkinson	6	0	6
Stan Palk	6	0	6
Ray Minshull	6	0	6
Tommy McLeod	3	0	3
Tom Bush	3	0	3
Len Carney	2	0	2
Charlie Ashcroft	2	0	2
John Easdale	2	0	2
Harry Kaye	1	0	1

Goalscorers for the 1946/1947 season

Name	League	FA Cup	Total
Jack Balmer	24	4	28
Albert Stubbins	24	4	28
Cyril Done	10	2	12
Billy Liddell	7	1	8
Willie Fagan	7	0	7
Berry Nieuwenhuys	5	0	5
Bill Jones	2	0	2
Own goals	1	1	2
Len Carney	1	0	1
Bob Priday	1	0	1
Phil Taylor	1	0	1
Billy Watkinson	1	0	1

The squad during the 1946/1947 season

Charlie Ashcroft, Goalkeeper
Cyril Sidlow, Goalkeeper
Ray Minshull, Goalkeeper
Laurie Hughes, Defender
Ray Lambert, Defender
Bill Jones, Defender
Eddie Spicer, Defender
Bob Paisley, Defender
Phil Taylor, Defender
Jim Harley, Defender
Bernard Ramsden, Defender
Tom Bush, Defender
John Easdale, Defender
Harry Kaye, Defender
Stan Palk, Defender
Billy Liddell, Midfielder
Tommy McLeod, Midfielder
Bob Priday, Midfielder
Harry Eastham, Midfielder
Berry Nieuwenhuys, Midfielder
Billy Watkinson, Midfielder
Jack Balmer, Striker
Kevin Baron, Striker
Albert Stubbins, Striker
Cyril Done, Striker
Willie Fagan, Striker
Len Carney, Striker

Transfers for the 1946/1947 season

In:
Albert Stubbins, Newcastle United, £13,000, 12 September 1946
Doug McAvoy, Kilmarnock, £7,000, 11 December 1947

Out:
George Paterson, Swindon Town, Unknown, 19 October 1946

A collection of statistics for the 1946/1947 season

The season in numbers:
Total games: 48
Games won: 29
Games drawn: 8
Games lost: 11
Clean sheets – League: 13
Clean sheets – Overall: 16
Total goals: 96
Average attendance at home – League: 45,731
Average attendance at home – Overall: 45,917
Average goals per game – League: 2.00
Average goals per game – Overall: 2.04

Goals split down to competitions:
League – 84
FA Cup – 12

Player debuts:

Len Carney against Sheffield United on 31.08.1946
Bill Jones against Sheffield United on 31.08.1946
Cyril Sidlow against Sheffield United on 31.08.1946
Charlie Ashcroft against Chelsea on 07.09.1946
Albert Stubbins against Bolton Wanderers on 14.09.1946
Cyril Done against Charlton Athletic on 12.10.1946
Ray Minshull against Huddersfield Town on 19.10.1946
John Easdale against Stoke City on 25.12.1946
Stan Palk against Grimsby Town on 12.02.1947
Tommy McLeod against Preston North End on 04.04.1947
Billy Watkinson against Aston Villa on 26.04.1947

Statistics and information provided by LFChistory.net

6 A CERTAIN MR SHANKLY

1963/1964

ALTHOUGH LIVERPOOL MAINTAINED THEIR First Division status for a further seven seasons, their best placed finish was a modest eighth. The team wasn't showing any signs of improvement and on April 24, 1954, Don Welsh's team were relegated to the Second Division for the first time in 50 years. Liverpool were relegated after finishing the 1953/54 season bottom from 22 teams, chalking up a mere 28 points and leaking an incredible 97 goals, the worst tally in all four divisions.

Former Liverpool captain Phil Taylor succeeded Don Welsh at the end of the 1955/56 season and did his best to improve the side that he had inherited from Welsh, but somehow the club were unable to take that necessary step that would have got them back into the top division. A cry for another managerial change was needed and Liverpool's next manager was to become the club's most historic appointment to date.

William Shankly arrived from Huddersfield Town in December 1959 and took over a club that was going nowhere.

The training ground, Melwood, was a shambles, Anfield not a pretty sight and Liverpool's starting XI was overburdened with average players while many quality footballers languished in the reserves. Nessie, Bill's wife, later recalled him saying: "Oh Nessie! have I made a terrible mistake leaving Huddersfield?" He thought that coming to Liverpool was a grave error because of the conditions at the training ground. The shack that was the changing rooms were worse than that on many parks for Sunday League teams and the pitches were full of bricks, stones and broken glass. Together with Bob Paisley, Reuben Bennett, Joe Fagan and the groundsman Eli Wass, the five men set about their task. They walked abreast and picked up every stone and foreign object from the playing surface. After walking up and down the pitch 12 times, Bill decided that that was enough for the first day's improvements, but would return again and again until it was like a bowling green.

Shankly's thoughts at the time must have been grave; how can anyone expect a club to improve if they couldn't provide facilities to equal a Sunday League side? But this is what welcomed Bill on his arrival.

Despite the below-par facilities on offer, Shankly immediately felt at home in Liverpool as he sensed in the huge crowds a kinship with the supporters. They were his kind of people.

With the backing of Bennett, Paisley and Fagan – and the enthusiasm of the fans behind him – he set about rebuilding the team.

Shankly's next task was to convince the directors at the club that Liverpool should spare no expense in strengthening the team and finally, 18 months after Shankly took over, in came Ron Yeats and Ian St John, the two players he had wanted at Huddersfield.

Shankly was quite confident that they would prove key signings: "St John and Yeats were both 23, and I said to Mr. Sawyer (Liverpool's financial director), 'You can sack me if they can't play. I'm telling you now, I'll stake my life on it'."

On April 21, 1962 Liverpool's eight-year exile from the top-flight came to an end as promotion from the Second Division was won on a damp afternoon at Anfield with five matches to go with a 2-0 win over Southampton. Liverpool captain Yeats told *LFChistory.net* that the 1961/62 season was the most important triumph in his and arguably Shankly's career: "The most successful thing we did, and I'll say this always, was winning the Second Division. Without that nothing else would have happened, because we couldn't progress without winning it. It was the best season I remember at Liverpool Football Club."

A season of consolidation followed in which Liverpool finished eighth in their return to the top-flight and as the 1963/64 season approached, 16 years had now passed since Liverpool's post-war heroes had last won the First Division.

Bill Shankly, who vowed he would never tie himself to any club, signed a five-year contract with Liverpool less than a week before the new season began. Shankly never had a contract with his previous club, Carlisle United, Grimsby Town or Huddersfield Town, and this was the first contact he had signed since his arrival at Liverpool.

Shankly's speech to his players on July 25, the first day they reported to Melwood for pre-season, reiterated his desire for imminent success as he set out on making the 1963/64 season the most memorable Liverpool had known for a very long time. "I feel much better now than I felt at the start of the previous two seasons," he told the players.

"Two seasons ago we started off in the Second Division – and we won the Championship. Last season we were in the First Division. Both seasons were started in an apprehensive state of mind. To me all that apprehension has gone. We can now feel confident that we can beat any team in the league."

Bill Shankly led Liverpool into the 1963/64 season like a prophet preaching the gospel of power, passion and supreme confidence.

Anfield was going to become a football Mecca, Shanks was convinced of it.

Peter Thompson was the club's only addition to the playing staff during the summer of 1963. Shankly had been impressed by the speed and trickery of the young winger during a marathon fifth round FA Cup tie between Liverpool and Preston in February 1962 which went to a second replay at Old Trafford. After two goalless draws the deadlock was finally broken by Thompson when the ball fell invitingly for him and he hit it straight back past Liverpool keeper Bert Slater to claim a famous win. Thompson was a regular for three seasons for Preston and following relegation from their only top-flight season during his spell there the 20-year-old moved to Liverpool for £37,000. He almost messed up his transfer to the Reds with an inappropriate request, as he told *LFChistory.net*: "I went to Anfield from Preston and there were thousands of people outside. I got my way through to the front door and Shankly is there. 'What are all these here for?' I asked. 'You!' Shankly thundered, 'You!' 'Me?' I gasped. He took me all around Melwood. He showed me Anfield. Took me to the office. The chairman came in, 'Could you sign here?' 'Actually Mr. Shankly, I would like a signing-on fee'. 'You what? I am giving you the chance to play in the greatest city in the greatest team that is going to be in the world and you want illegal money. Get out!' 'Give me the pen,' I said. So I signed. Best thing I ever did."

The Preston lad was an amazing right-footed left winger, who tormented full-backs having spent countless hours on the training ground perfecting crossing with his left on the right side. Which way was Tommo going to go? His opponents didn't have a clue and most of the time his teammates didn't know what to expect either. Liverpool was envied by other teams for possessing such a powerful pairing on opposing flanks as Thompson and Ian Callaghan. Thompson recalls how Shankly drummed into him his winning mentality from day one: "When I arrived Shankly used to prod me, 'Are you a winner? I'm talking to you! Are you a winner?' 'Yes, Mr Shankly'. 'I want winners. Second is no good to me. If you're second, I'll get rid of you. Simple as that'."

Thompson was to become one of the game's great entertainers, his class being recognised at international level in the shape of 16 England caps. Shankly knew he had captured a very special performer, thrusting Thompson straight into his starting line-up to make this debut on the opening fixture of the 1963/64 season at Ewood Park.

The team in full that Shankly picked for the big kick-off at Blackburn was: Tommy Lawrence, Gerry Byrne, Ronnie Moran, Gordon Milne, Ron Yeats (c), Willie Stevenson, Ian Callaghan, Roger Hunt, Ian St John, Jimmy Melia and Peter Thompson.

It was predicted that over half of the 34,390 crowd at Ewood Park was composed of Liverpool supporters who made it more like a home match in different surroundings. The *Liverpool Echo* reported: "Railway police rushed to the Exchange Station as thousands of Liverpool supporters were waiting for football excursion trains to take them to Blackburn. The chaos followed an announcement made over the station's loudspeaker system at 12.15pm that no more tickets were available for the two remaining excursion trains. Others left the station in an attempt to find seats on the coaches which were scheduled to leave the city centre to get to Blackburn by road. Others gave up the attempt. Many said that their opening game of the season would be, of all places, at Goodison Park."

Although Liverpool found themselves 1-0 down at half-time, Ronnie Moran, a man who has since become as much a part of Anfield as the Kop itself, scored on the rebound after goalkeeper Fred Else saved his 65th-minute penalty. The effort wiped out a surprise Blackburn opener scored by Mike Harrison on the stroke of half-time. Ian Callaghan flashed home the winner with 15 minutes left. Shankly's men looked to be on their way.

Next up for the Reds was Nottingham Forest's visit to Anfield four days later but Liverpool could not build on the Blackburn win as Forest won the contest 2-1. Liverpool captain, Ron Yeats, shared his post-match thoughts on the game with the *Liverpool Echo*: "We had looked forward enormously to our game against Nottingham Forest and now we are looking back at it with regret. We felt that we had the beating of this side and were more than anxious to avenge the double which they pulled off last year. On the night, we certainly did not deserve to win, because rarely have things gone more wrong for us. I cannot remember an occasion when so many of us have had poor games."

In recent seasons, Anfield had become a bastion of invincibility and defeats were few and far between. However, three days later on August 31, Liverpool suffered their second consecutive 2-1 home defeat; this time the visiting side was Blackpool.

Thankfully, in the three away games that followed, two ended in victory and the other in a draw, which during these early weeks helped to balance things up a little. The *Liverpool Echo* reported on Liverpool's trip to Stamford Bridge on September 7: "This was essentially a team victory. An Ian St John goal with the last kick of the match in injury time gave the gap comfortable proportions. To make it so, Liverpool had to fight like tigers and strike with deadly efficiency when chances were created. They faced fast, speedy opponents, who might easily have run riot against a less determined defence."

Despite the promising away displays, Liverpool's home form didn't improve as Shankly's team suffered their third home defeat in a row, this time at the hands of Ron Greenwood's West Ham United and yet again by the same 2-1 scoreline. Following his team's third straight home defeat, Shankly declared to the board: "I assure you, gentlemen, that before the end of the season we will win a home game!"

Liverpool faced Wolves at Anfield just two days later on a Monday evening. 44,050 fans turned up to see anything but a fourth straight Liverpool home defeat. The scribe for the *Liverpool Echo*, Horace Yates, wrote: "The Anfield hoodoo lay in fragments last night, smashed to smithereens by the eager forward combination, in which Alf Arrowsmith was included in place of the injured St John, and celebrated his first game of the season with a goal in the first minute, his debut goal in senior football, which put the Kop in gold heart for the rest of the match. Liverpool went on to score four more and with the score at 5-0 the Kop chanted: 'We want six' and their favourites duly obliged with three minutes left when Hunt hit his second of the game. Final score: Liverpool 6-0 Wolves. Bill Shankly's assurance of winning a home game before the end of the season was achieved in tremendous fashion."

Liverpool were unable to use the thrashing of Wolves to kick-start their season against Sheffield United five days later as the Reds disappointingly lost 3-0 at Bramall Lane. After nine league games played, Liverpool found themselves in 10th position with only nine points.

Shankly's team needed to find some consistency if his desires for the 1963/64 were going to be reality.

Liverpool's next game was against neighbours Everton at Anfield and Shankly was boosted by the news that St John had shrugged off an ankle injury which had kept him out of action for the previous two games. Ian Callaghan scored both goals in a 2-1 victory.

This was the turning point in Liverpool's season.

Callaghan, just 21, was now in his fifth season playing for Liverpool's first team. Cally went on to end the 1963/64 season as one of the three ever-presents in the league for Liverpool, along with Gordon

Milne and new signing Peter Thompson. Liverpool legend Billy Liddell was asked in 1961 if there was any player who could replace him in the Liverpool team. Billy said: "There is always someone to follow on. They have one at Anfield already, a youngster named Ian Callaghan. I played with him twice, watched his progress and I believe he'll be a credit to his club, the game and to his country."

Liddell wasn't wrong. Toxteth-born Callaghan went on to achieve remarkable feats at Liverpool and in an interview with *Lfchistory.net*, Cally revealed what it was like playing back in the 1960s under Shankly: "Shanks thought of me as a model professional. I was fit as I used to love training, but Shanks often used to come up to me in training and sort of say, 'You don't train today. You just go through the motions. Just do what you've got to do'. I never had a cross word with him. Training was different back then, Shankly had created the infamous Melwood 'sweat box'. It was just like boards and you had to run. They timed you. You were only in there for one minute or two minutes. You had to run as quick as you can. All the lads were along the touchline and Shanks, Bob and Reuben Bennett were shouting all the time – you had to hit the ball against the board, control it and run to the other boards. It was really hard work. The sweat box became quite famous, you would come out and your legs would be like jelly."

Callaghan also talked about how the diet and lifestyle of players in the 1960s were far removed from today's footballers: "We used to eat a steak before a match and now they reckon it's the worst thing you can eat as it's hard to digest. It wasn't until later we moved to beans on toast or scrambled eggs. I used to love to have a drink with the boys after the match. There were rules that you didn't drink after Wednesday, which I didn't. If you were playing in midweek away somewhere they did allow you to go out and have a beer. You had to be back by 12 o'clock at the hotel. There would be a curfew because you were flying back the next day and then you would be playing again on the Saturday."

Four consecutive victories followed Liverpool's derby win, which propelled the Reds up the table so much that by the end of October they were in fourth position, only two points behind leaders Sheffield United and with a game in hand.

Liverpool's next league game was against Leicester City at Anfield. Leicester's goalkeeper Gordon Banks held firm against Liverpool's front line to enable the Foxes to sneak away with a 1-0 victory as Liverpool slumped to their fourth home defeat of the season and moved down to sixth in the league.

This game on November 2, 1963 had an added significance as it was the first time 'You'll Never Walk Alone' was played at Anfield as part of UK's Top 10 chart. The song had reached number seven a couple of weeks before, but this was the first match at Anfield that had taken place since then. Moreover, the song had just reached the number one spot, so when Anfield DJ Stuart Bateman did his rundown of the Top 10, 'You'll Never Walk Alone' was the final song played before kick-off.

Gerry and the Pacemakers' latest hit stayed at number one for four weeks before the Beatles' 'She Loves You' regained the top spot. YNWA remained in the Top 10 for a further four weeks and when the song had disappeared off the track list at Christmas time, the crowd demanded that it would still be featured. Gerry Marsden said: "When it went out of the Top 10, the Kop were singing, 'Where's our song? Where's our song?'" As a result a tradition was born and Liverpool fans have embraced it ever since.

On the pitch, Liverpool were soon back to winning ways after the Leicester loss, beating Bolton Wanderers 2-1 at Burnden Park the following week. The *Liverpool Echo* reported on a strange incident that happened towards the end of the encounter involving Liverpool full-back Phil Ferns: "Liverpool right-back Phil Ferns became the man in the middle of a Burnden Park soccer mystery after being knocked out in the final minutes of his side's game against Bolton Wanderers on Saturday. Forty minutes after the game Liverpool manager Bill Shankly had to call in a doctor to Ferns, who said he had been punched in the face by a Bolton forward. Most of the 23,824 spectators were mystified when Ferns crumpled up on the pitch with play at the other end."

Referee W.J Downey of Jarrow consulted his linesmen but none of the officials had seen any blow struck. Mr Downey said: "When I saw Ferns in the dressing room, he had a gash on his top lip. He told me, 'I was punched in the face by a Bolton player and I can't remember a thing after that'."

Another run of four consecutive victories, including an away win against Manchester United and a creditable draw away to Arsenal, saw Liverpool top the league at the start of December for the first time since 1947! The attendance at Old Trafford was lower than expected, especially as United had attracted nearly 63,000 for Everton's visit earlier in the season. Although there was no direct link to the event, the assassination of American President John F Kennedy the day before the match might have affected the attendance. Ron Yeats' second-half header was the only goal of the game and proved enough to give Shankly's team the edge over Manchester United's Matt Busby.

Liverpool's victory was helped by the fact that Manchester United's goalkeeper Harry Gregg was stretchered off shortly before the half-time interval after a collision with Yeats as the two of them went up for a corner. Consequently forward David Herd replaced Gregg in goal. As there were no substitutes allowed until the 1965/66 season,

Gregg returned for the final 10 minutes and played outside-right with an arm strapped to his chest. It turned out that he had broken his collarbone.

Not only did captain Yeats score the winner at Old Trafford that afternoon, it was also his first Liverpool goal for the club since his arrival on Merseyside in 1961 from Dundee United. After the game Shankly told the press that Yeats was: "The greatest centre-half in the world today."

Despite Blackburn Rovers inflicting a fifth home defeat on Liverpool and drawing 1-1 at Highbury, Shankly's team won all three of their Christmas and New Year's fixtures, scoring 12 goals and conceding just one. This included the 6-1 demolition of Stoke City at Anfield on December 26 – a Boxing Day fixture list that saw 66 goals scored in 10 First Division matches.

Roger Hunt scored four of Liverpool's six goals that afternoon, which was the sixth time he had scored three or more goals in a match for the Reds. The *Liverpool Echo* reported: "Liverpool were beginning to motor, Roger Hunt plundered four goals in a 6-1 win over Stoke. Remarkably, it was 1-1 at the interval. No wonder the perspiring Kop went home happy. No wonder they cottoned on to a Beatles theme song 'We Love You, Yeh, Yeh, Yeh,' which is much better than marching saints. No wonder Stoke City, minus Stanley Matthews, looked as though they scarcely knew what hit them."

Roger Hunt's goals were paramount to Liverpool's success. Prior to the 1963/64 season, Hunt had scored 110 goals in 168 games and was the club's top scorer for three of the previous four seasons. Goalscoring was not the only attribute of Hunt's game and Bill Shankly's admiration for Hunt didn't stop at his goalscoring prowess. Shankly explained: "When I went to Liverpool in December, 1959, Roger was already there and had been in the first team for two or three months.

After seeing him in only one game I knew he could play. His style and his control, not only in scoring, but in killing the dead ball, stamped him as a player. As he developed his scoring technique he became an even greater player. Goalscoring is an art and a very difficult thing to do. What made Roger Hunt so good at it was: (1) His all-round ability. (2) His willingness to succeed. (3) His perfect temperament. (4) His willingness to train and go through the tough schedule designed specifically for Liverpool. (5) His willingness to go through it to its fullest."

Roger Hunt had thrived on Thompson and Callaghan's service the whole season and the trio were unstoppable up front. Hunt might have even scored more goals if Thompson had been more of a team player. One Friday, the day before a league match, Liverpool had a team meeting. "Roger (Hunt) never said anything," Thompson recalls. "Shankly said, 'Meeting finished', but Roger said, 'Actually, Peter beats his full-back about four or five times and we don't know where to run'. Roger turned to me, 'Why don't you just beat your man and cross it?' Shankly said, 'That is a good idea'. We played against West Brom at Anfield, I pushed it past the full-back, crossed it, Roger smashed it into the net. Roger said, 'That's what I want' and I said, 'That's boring. Let Ian Callaghan do that'. Ian and I were completely different. Ian was straightforward. The problem was when I got the ball I got my head down and off I went. We complemented each other perfectly. Some games one of us would be struggling, the defender facing Cally may have been faster than him or the right-back could handle a dribbler like myself, so we'd simply switch flanks and it'd work."

Having disposed of Derby County 5-0 in the third round of the FA Cup and then being drawn against Third Division Port Vale at home in the fourth round, there were stirrings amongst the fans that this might be Liverpool's year for FA Cup success. Incredibly, Alf Arrowsmith scored four of Liverpool's five goals against Derby, which meant, after Hunt's four goals against Stoke City the previous week, it was the only time in Liverpool's history that four goals were scored by the same player in consecutive games.

Arrowsmith was described as a born goalscorer by Shankly, who arrived at Anfield as a fresh-faced 17-year-old in August 1960 having scored a massive 96 goals for Derbyshire club Tintwistle Villa in the 1959/60 season, a club record that has never been broken. He had just had four months at Ashton United, where he scored nine goals in seven matches, when Liverpool made their move.

A year after his arrival his name was on everybody's lips at Anfield because the lad scored no less than 81 goals from 1961-1963 for the reserves.

The Liverpool faithful didn't really think that the prospect of becoming league champions was a realistic proposition, particularly owing to the team's erratic home form and their FA Cup dreams were dashed in the sixth round at the end of February when the Reds crashed out at Anfield 1-2 against Swansea Town. With the score at 2-1 to Swansea with 10 minutes to go, Liverpool were handed a lifeline when they were awarded a penalty in the 80th minute. Ronnie Moran stepped up and unfortunately made it four penalty misses in a row by blasting the ball wide. This was a harrowing experience for Moran who despaired: "That miss against Swansea was the most terrible moment of my life. I felt I had let Liverpool down." Tommy Lawrence remembers walking off the field with Ronnie after his infamous penalty miss: "I could tell Ron was devastated. As well as hating losing, he felt responsible for Liverpool's cup exit. I remember him saying to me: 'I think that's finished my contract!'"

Shankly didn't put any blame on Moran after the game, saying: "Unbelievable, unbelievable. I have never seen the boys play better. We could have scored 14 goals and yet here we are out of the cup."

On the evening of the Swansea game, an obviously disgruntled Liverpool 'fan' threw a lump of coal through Ronnie's front room window, but luckily for him he had vanished before Ronnie got hold of him. Ronnie brushed this off and used to jokingly remark when telling this story, that after scoring the winner against Burnley in a cup tie the previous season, no-one had come and posted pound notes through the front door!

All Liverpool's hopes for silverware were now lying on the League Championship. Having put six past Wolves and Stoke, the Reds were soon putting another six past Sheffield United as February dawned.

As the 1963/64 season entered into March, Liverpool were joint second, just three points behind leaders Tottenham Hotspur with two games in hand. Thirteen games were left to be played and Bill Shankly's Liverpool were in a very strong position to claim the First Division title for the first time in 17 years.

On March 9, 1964 inside forward Jimmy Melia was sold to Wolves for a fee in the region of £50,000. Melia, who played 286 games for Liverpool, had lost his place in Shankly's starting XI to Alf Arrowsmith after an injury he sustained the previous December. Melia told the press after his move: "I've spent 10 years at Anfield and I think a change will do me good. I did very well at Liverpool, but I see no reason why I shouldn't do well with Wolves. My wife is perfectly happy with the move and I am leaving Liverpool the best of friends."

A 2-2 draw away to Sheffield Wednesday, a 6-0 victory against Ipswich Town and a 1-0 defeat at Craven Cottage against Fulham were the results of Liverpool's following three fixtures as inconsistency proved their downfall as Liverpool dropped down the league table to fourth with 10 games to go. Liverpool needed to be at their strongest if they were going to compete with the teams around them during the final assault to capture the league title. However, this wasn't going to be the case, as their inspirational captain Ron Yeats was handed a 14-day ban for fighting with Arsenal's Joe Baker during the recent FA Cup fifth round match, an incident which saw both players red-carded.

The *Liverpool Echo* reported: "Seven minutes before half-time Arsenal's Baker and Yeats went down together. Both got up exchanging punches before Yeats went back down with a cut eye, leading to Bill Shankly coming onto the pitch to check he was ok. The referee, who had been following play, came back and promptly dismissed both men from the field and told Shankly to leave too, but not before he had quickly given some tactical instructions to players."

Yeats wasn't too pleased about his only sending-off in his Liverpool career after the game: "I have never struck a player in eight years and I never will. If I hit anyone I would expect to be sent off. But I swear I never hit him. I asked the referee if I had hit myself to get my cut and bleeding eye, but he would not listen."

Both players were banned but it was the Liverpool party who left the angrier of the two sides when they left the FA Commission in Leicester.

A grim-faced Yeats told the press: "If I had got seven days, I would have been choked, but 14..." The suspension cost him about £150 in wages and bonus but he added: "It's not the cash that bothers me, what it means to the club is what matters." Bill Shankly had been confident Yeats would be let off lightly but now said: "If I said what I am thinking I could land in jail. Disappointed? That's putting it mildly." During the two-week ban, Liverpool would be without their colossal captain for three games; against Bolton Wanderers at Anfield and away trips to White Hart Lane and Filbert Street. Twenty-year-old Chris Lawler was promoted from the reserves to replace Yeats and the young Liverpudlian didn't disappoint.

Lawler started his Liverpool career working for the Anfield ground staff, he told *Lfchistory.net*: "It was like a job at the ground. When I first went I thought we would just train during the day, but I never did that. We were working all day, it was hard going. I worked all day and then two nights a week I went training with the amateurs. I was there for three months before Bill Shankly came to the club and I bumped into him in the corridor. I was taking a tea break in the morning and he stopped me as I was going past his office and asked where I was going. He knew who I was as well. He said, 'You're Chris Lawler' because he was thorough like that. He asked me about my routine and I said, 'I'm in at half past eight every morning and two nights a week we go training with the amateurs'. And he said, 'That's no good. You're here to learn a trade. Football's your trade. Tomorrow morning you're going training at ten o'clock with the first team'. So after that I did my work in the afternoon and went training in the morning. And it made a big difference. When you're with the professionals they're giving you tips and advice and it made a big difference to me that."

Although Lawler was happy at Liverpool at this time, the main problem for him was that his way into the first team was blocked by a giant Scotsman. Lawler recalls: "I was a centre-back then in the second team. And I only played if Ron Yeats, the club captain, was injured. I thought there was no future for me at Liverpool. So, I went to see Bill Shankly and said I wanted a transfer. Well, he was shocked. He didn't expect that."

Another local lad, a 19-year-old by the name of Tommy Smith, was also getting restless about the lack of first team football. Lawler explained: "Tommy had seen I had gone in to speak to Shanks, so then he went in. It was in the papers that Matt Busby would take the two of us to Manchester United. We both wanted to stay at Liverpool, but we were desperate to break into the first team." Shankly realised he had blood in his youngsters. He later calmed Lawler and Smith's nerves inside his office and convinced them to stay. Lawler remembers: "Shankly said, 'I've got an idea. Leave it with me'. So in the next few weeks Ronnie Moran was coming to the end of his career and Gerry Byrne was playing right-back. So he moved Gerry Byrne over to left-back and tried me at right-back. I played nearly every game after that. I didn't miss many games. Only about four in five years, something like that!"

Despite, losing Yeats at such a vital time of the season, Liverpool achieved three wins from three in his absence. On April 4, third-place Manchester United visited Anfield, in what was a must-win match for both title-challenging sides. Liverpool won the encounter 3-0 over a Manchester United side that included George Best, Denis Law and Bobby Charlton. The game was a triumph for Alf Arrow-smith in particular, who scored twice. It was a spell of the season when Arrowsmith just couldn't stop scoring goals, netting 15 goals in 19 games. As the game blasted out to its close, the Kop choir were in full voice chanting out "Liv-er-pool, won the League". After the match, boxing fan Shankly echoed Cassius Clay when praising his players: "They're lions that go out hungry. Nothing will stop them. They're the greatest."

Left-back Ronnie Moran recalled a hairy incident from this game: "George Best rolled the ball to Nobby Stiles but under-hit it and I got to the ball at the same time as Nobby and went straight through him. Stiles jumped up looking angry and I thought he was going to attack me but fortunately he just marched straight past me. I then remember shouting to George Best, 'Bloody hell, George, you'll get me killed here!'"

Liverpool carried on their victorious run, which meant that if they beat Arsenal in the last home game of the season, they would be champions. The *Liverpool Echo* reported: "Although some turnstiles were still open an hour before kick-off, there was scarcely a soul in the streets outside, this presumably being due to the fact that count-less thousands must have taken the view that unless you were at Anfield by half-past one, then you had no chance of finding a place on the terraces. Roger Hunt had difficulty in getting through the crowds soon after mid-day to have his fitness test, but all was well and appropriately he was able to take his place in this final home game on which so much depended. Liverpool went ahead amid a great scene of enthusiasm at six minutes. Hunt came through at inside right avoiding a scything tackle by Skirton and turned the ball into Arrowsmith, who edged it across to St John, coming in fast, and able to slide it beyond the outcoming Furnell for what in view of its importance was the goal of the season. At 29 minutes, Arsenal got a penalty when Eastham, threading his way through at inside right, flicked the ball up with his head, and Yeats, finding he was going to be beaten, handed palpably. Not a soul protested at the justice of the penalty decision. Eastham chose to take it, and after having a word or two with the referee, lashed in a left-foot shot aimed just inside Lawrence's right hand post. The Scot brought off an outstanding save at the post edging the ball for a corner and sending the Anfield crowd wild with joy. All the Liverpool players came downfield to give their goalkeeper congratulations. Liverpool went further ahead and put the championship virtually in their pockets at 53 minutes when Thompson got their third. He brought the ball in from the wing, transferred it to his right foot, and fairly hammered it beyond the reach of Furnell for a goal which received a standing ovation. Liverpool went on now almost strolling in their triumph, and getting a further goal to Thompson at 57 minutes. He came into the centre to score from long range after weaving his way to an opening and probably unsighting Furnell thoroughly in the process.

"Hats, scarves, newspapers and everything throwable went into the air when Hunt got Liverpool's fifth at 60 minutes. Milne and Thompson had the part in the lead up to this, and again Furnell was completely beaten by a right-foot shot from a fair distance out.

"The noise when the referee finally did sound the end was so great the whistle could scarcely be heard. Everybody obeyed the instructions to stay behind the terraces except a few boys, and there were handshakes all round between Liverpool teammates and their Arsenal vanquished. The Liverpool players went down the subway to accompaniment of the chant: 'We won the the league' and calls for Yeats and manager Shankly. Final score: Liverpool 5-0 Arsenal."

Desmond Hackett from *The Daily Express* asked Bill Shankly after the game had finished how he planned on celebrating being confirmed league champions: "Celebrations? Maybe, but no time to think about that now. We still have three league matches to play." Hackett then asked him what his secret to success was: "There is no secret. We train to play football. Some people train for the marathon, some for a mile. Our business is football so we train to play hard, fast and accurately and carry our practice plans to the field. Players and manager must be bound together in their love of the game, pride in their club and mutual respect for each other. We are a working-class team. We have no room for fancy footballers. Just workers who will respond to the demands I lay down."

Incidentally, more than 4,000 fans missed the chance of seeing Liverpool clinch the league title against Arsenal and Shankly took the blame for it. The crowd of 48,623, 4,000 below capacity, provided the biggest surprise of a great day on Merseyside. After thousands had been locked out from the two previous home matches, Liverpool expected they had to close the gates in record time. Many of the gates were closed early, but in the hour before the kick-off anybody could have walked up and got into the Kop without queuing. After the match, Shankly said: "It's a pity there wasn't a full house. I certainly thought at mid-day that we would have to lock a lot of people out and that's probably why some fans missed the match. I told the BBC when they phoned up asking for the latest news that there were enough people outside to fill the ground already.

"When fans who weren't already at the ground heard this, they probably kept away. Quite a few went over to Goodison to watch Everton reserves without even bothering to come and see what the position was here."

Curiously enough, Everton also tried to play their part in helping Liverpool celebrate their success that day.

Liverpool were not allowed to parade the First Division trophy that afternoon, even though it was sat just under half a mile away in Everton's trophy room. The 'Old Lady' as it was known due to the design, could not be taken across Stanley Park as Manchester United still had an outside chance of pipping the Reds before their victory over Arsenal.

Everton did actually ask the Football League if they could courier the trophy over to Anfield at 4.45pm should Liverpool win. Relations were more cordial between the clubs in the carefree Sixties, but the Football League immediately refused and demanded it had to remain at Goodison.

There were also protocols in place, namely that the Football League had to retake guardianship and then officially present the silverware. If it was not to be after the title-clinching game or another match that season, it had to take place behind the scenes.

The Anfield board was disappointed as they had no more home

games remaining and were reluctant to be presented with the trophy at their midweek game at Birmingham City. Although Liverpool only gained one point from their final three games of the season, it didn't matter, the First Division title was already back at Anfield for the sixth time in their history. The prophet was right, Shankly's Red Army and a wonderful team had laid the foundations for a long period of Liverpool domination in England and Europe.

Three years after leaving Scotland, Ron Yeats had become captain of the First Division champions. Liverpool gambled when they signed him, as clubs do when they spend big money. Yeats gambled when he came south. Both parties came out winning. Yeats told *Football Monthly*'s scribe Jerry Dawson after the season had finished: "This title has given me great personal satisfaction. I have always thought I could make it in the big time. Now I have proof that I can. When I decided to leave Dundee United, I released I was accepting a big challenge. I felt I had got as far as I could there. I was pretty confident I would be all right. But at a time like that, no matter how confident you are, there are always those little doubts. Now that we have won the title they have all gone. I feel now I am as good as anybody and can play with anybody. That is what this title means to me. Now we look forward to playing in Europe with a lot of confidence – with Mr. Shankly planning for us and the Kop rooting for us, we could win the County Cricket Championship too! At Liverpool, I'm happily settled here with my wife and three daughters. They are very happy and I'm playing for a great club with a great manager, what more can I ask? Therefore, as long as I'm treated fairly as I have been so far, I can see myself ending my days – at the best club in the world, LI-VER-POOL!"

1963/64: Facts and Statistics

Final league table

		P	W	D	L	F	A	W	D	L	F	A	PTS
1	Liverpool FC	42	16	0	5	60	18	10	5	6	32	27	57
2	Manchester United	42	15	3	3	54	19	8	4	9	36	43	53
3	Everton	42	14	4	3	53	26	7	6	8	31	38	52
4	Tottenham	42	13	3	5	54	31	9	4	8	43	50	51
5	Chelsea	42	12	3	6	36	24	8	7	6	36	32	50
6	Sheffield Wednesday	42	15	3	3	50	24	4	8	9	34	43	49
7	Blackburn Rovers	42	10	4	7	44	28	8	6	7	45	37	46
8	Arsenal	42	10	7	4	56	37	7	4	10	34	45	45
9	Burnley	42	14	3	4	46	23	3	7	11	25	41	44
10	WBA	42	9	6	6	43	35	7	5	9	27	26	43
11	Leicester City	42	9	4	8	33	27	7	7	7	28	31	43
12	Sheffield United	42	10	6	5	35	22	6	5	10	26	42	43
13	Nottingham Forest	42	9	5	7	34	24	7	4	10	30	44	41
14	West Ham United	42	8	7	6	45	38	6	5	10	24	36	40
15	Fulham	42	11	8	2	45	23	2	5	14	13	42	39
16	Wolves	42	6	9	6	36	34	6	6	9	34	46	39
17	Stoke City	42	9	6	6	49	33	5	4	12	28	45	38
18	Blackpool	42	8	6	7	26	29	5	3	13	26	44	35
19	Aston Villa	42	8	6	7	35	29	3	6	12	27	42	34
20	Birmingham City	42	7	7	7	33	32	4	0	17	21	60	29
21	Bolton Wanderers	42	6	5	10	30	35	4	3	14	18	45	28
22	Ipswich Town	42	9	3	9	38	45	0	4	17	18	76	25

Games for the 1963/1964 season

(The number after date is league position after the game)

1	24.08.1963	5	W	2-1	Blackburn Rovers, Ewood Park, 1st Division
2	28.08.1963	8	L	1-2	Nottingham Forest, Anfield, 1st Division
3	31.08.1963	14	L	1-2	Blackpool, Anfield, 1st Division
4	03.09.1963	12	D	0-0	Nottingham Forest, City Ground, 1st Division
5	07.09.1963	9	W	3-1	Chelsea, Stamford Bridge, 1st Division
6	09.09.1963	4	W	3-1	Wolves, Molineux, 1st Division
7	14.09.1963	11	L	1-2	West Ham United, Anfield, 1st Division
8	16.09.1963	6	W	6-0	Wolves, Anfield, 1st Division
9	21.09.1963	10	L	0-3	Sheffield United, Bramall Lane, 1st Division
10	28.09.1963	8	W	2-1	Everton, Anfield, 1st Division

11	05.10.1963	8	W	5-2	Aston Villa, Anfield, 1st Division
12	09.10.1963	8	W	3-1	Sheffield Wednesday, Anfield, 1st Division
13	19.10.1963	5	W	1-0	West Bromwich Albion, Anfield, 1st Division
14	26.10.1963	3	W	2-1	Ipswich Town, Portman Road, 1st Division
15	02.11.1963	6	L	0-1	Leicester City, Anfield, 1st Division
16	09.11.1963	4	W	2-1	Bolton Wanderers, Burnden Park, 1st Division
17	16.11.1963	2	W	2-0	Fulham, Anfield, 1st Division
18	23.11.1963	1	W	1-0	Manchester United, Old Trafford, 1st Division
19	30.11.1963	1	W	2-0	Burnley, Anfield, 1st Division
20	07.12.1963	1	D	1-1	Arsenal, Highbury, 1st Division
21	14.12.1963	4	L	1-2	Blackburn Rovers, Anfield, 1st Division
22	21.12.1963	3	W	1-0	Blackpool, Bloomfield Road, 1st Division
23	26.12.1963	3	W	6-1	Stoke City, Anfield, 1st Division
24	04.01.1964		W	5-0	Derby County, Anfield, FA Cup 3rd round
25	11.01.1964	2	W	2-1	Chelsea, Anfield, 1st Division
26	18.01.1964	3	L	0-1	West Ham United, Upton Park, 1st Division
27	25.01.1964		D	0-0	Port Vale, Anfield, FA Cup 4th round
28	27.01.1964		W	2-1	Port Vale, Vale Park, FA Cup 4th round replay
29	01.02.1964	2	W	6-1	Sheffield United, Anfield, 1st Division
30	08.02.1964	3	L	1-3	Everton, Goodison Park, 1st Division
31	15.02.1964		W	1-0	Arsenal, Highbury, FA Cup 5th round
32	19.02.1964	3	D	2-2	Aston Villa, Villa Park, 1st Division
33	22.02.1964	2	W	2-1	Birmingham City, Anfield, 1st Division
34	29.02.1964		L	1-2	Swansea Town, Anfield, FA Cup 6th round
35	04.03.1964	2	D	2-2	Sheffield Wednesday, Hillsborough, 1st Division
36	07.03.1964	2	W	6-0	Ipswich Town, Anfield, 1st Division
37	14.03.1964	4	L	0-1	Fulham, Craven Cottage, 1st Division
38	20.03.1964	1	W	2-0	Bolton Wanderers, Anfield, 1st Division
39	27.03.1964	2	W	3-1	Tottenham Hotspur, White Hart Lane, 1st Division
40	28.03.1964	2	W	2-0	Leicester City, Filbert Street, 1st Division
41	30.03.1964	1	W	3-1	Tottenham Hotspur, Anfield, 1st Division
42	04.04.1964	1	W	3-0	Manchester United, Anfield, 1st Division
43	14.04.1964	1	W	3-0	Burnley, Turf Moor, 1st Division
44	18.04.1964	1	W	5-0	Arsenal, Anfield, 1st Division
45	22.04.1964	1	L	1-3	Birmingham City, St. Andrew's, 1st Division
46	25.04.1964	1	D	2-2	West Bromwich Albion, The Hawthorns, 1st Division
47	29.04.1964	1	L	1-3	Stoke City, Victoria Ground, 1st Division

Friendlies

1	08.05.1964	W	8-1	Boston Metros, Everett Memorial Stadium
2	10.05.1964	W	7-1	New York All Stars, Downing Stadium
3	13.05.1964	D	1-1	St. Louis's Catholic Youth Council All Stars, Public Schools Stadium
4	17.05.1964	W	3-0	Club de Fútbol Monterrey, Soldier Field
5	24.05.1964	L	0-2	Hamburg SV, Downing Stadium
6	27.05.1964	W	4-1	Meidericher Spielverein, University of Detroit Stadium
7	29.05.1964	D	0-0	Meidericher Spielverein, Soldier Field
8	03.06.1964	W	14-0	San Franciscan Select, Kezar Stadium
9	06.06.1964	D	1-1	Meidericher Spielverein, Empire Stadium
10	10.06.1964	W	2-0	Vancouver All Stars, Empire Stadium

Appearances for the 1963/1964 season

Name	League	FA Cup	League Cup	Total
Ian Callaghan	42	5	0	47
Gordon Milne	42	5	0	47
Peter Thompson	42	5	0	47
Roger Hunt	41	5	0	46
Tommy Lawrence	40	5	0	45
Ian St John	40	5	0	45
Willie Stevenson	38	5	0	43
Ron Yeats	36	5	0	41
Ronnie Moran	35	4	0	39
Gerry Byrne	33	4	0	37
Jimmy Melia	24	1	0	25
Alf Arrowsmith	20	4	0	24
Phil Ferns	18	1	0	19
Chris Lawler	6	0	0	6
Bobby Thomson	2	1	0	3
Jim Furnell	2	0	0	2
Gordon Wallace	1	0	0	1

Goalscorers for the 1963/1964 season

Name	League	FA Cup	League Cup	Total
Roger Hunt	31	2	0	33
Ian St John	21	1	0	22
Alf Arrowsmith	15	4	0	19
Ian Callaghan	8	0	0	8
Peter Thompson	6	2	0	8
Jimmy Melia	4	0	0	4
Gordon Milne	2	0	0	2
Ronnie Moran	2	0	0	2
Willie Stevenson	1	0	0	1
Own goals	1	0	0	1
Ron Yeats	1	0	0	1

The squad during the 1963/1964 season

Jim Furnell, Goalkeeper
Tommy Lawrence, Goalkeeper
Gerry Byrne, Defender
Ron Yeats, Defender
Chris Lawler, Defender
Ronnie Moran, Defender
Tommy Smith, Defender
Phil Ferns, Defender
Bobby Thomson, Defender
Ian Callaghan, Midfielder
Gordon Wallace, Midfielder
Alan A'Court, Midfielder
Peter Thompson, Midfielder
Willie Stevenson, Midfielder
Jimmy Melia, Midfielder
Alf Arrowsmith, Midfielder
Gordon Milne, Midfielder
Roger Hunt, Striker
Ian St John, Striker

Transfers for the 1963/1964 season

In:
Peter Thompson, Preston North End, £37,000, 14 August 1963
Phil Chisnall, Manchester United, £25,000, 15 April 1964

Out:
Kevin Lewis, Huddersfield Town, £18,000, August 1963
Jim Furnell, Arsenal, £15,000, 22 November 1963
Jimmy Melia, Wolves, £48,000, 9 March 1964

A collection of statistics for the 1963/1964 season

The season in numbers:
Total games: 47
Games won: 29
Games drawn: 6
Games lost: 12
Clean sheets – League: 13
Clean sheets – Overall: 16
Total goals: 101
Average attendance at home – League: 45,031
Average attendance at home – Overall: 45,710
Average goals per game – League: 2.86
Average goals per game – Overall: 2.75
Average goal minute – League: 52
Average goal minute – Overall: 53

Goals split down to competitions:
League – 92
FA Cup – 9

Player debuts:
Peter Thompson against Blackburn Rovers on 24.08.1963

Statistics and information provided by LFChistory.net

7 · CREATING A LEGEND

1965/66

L IVERPOOL'S LEAGUE CHAMPIONSHIP TRIUMPH of the 1963/64 season left fans hungry for more success. Only two seasons before, their team had been slogging it out in the Second Division and now under the leadership of Bill Shankly, the Reds were champions of England and heading into Europe for the first time.

The 1964/65 season was about to put Liverpool Football Club well and truly on the big stage.

Supporters who had followed the great recovery from Second Division mediocrity to First Division supremacy would sometimes have had to pinch themselves. Each success achieved since the great 'Shanks' took over seemed to be the probable apex of their expectations. In fact each success was merely a springboard to the next one.

On June 24, 1964, it was the end of an era for Liverpool Football Club as Mr. Thomas Valentine Williams (T.V. Williams), chairman of the club for the past eight seasons, told the shareholders at the annual general meeting that he was resigning the chair. Mr. Williams remained as a director and devoted more time to the selection, discipline and youth committees. Mr. Williams, a Liverpudlian from birth, devoted a great deal of his time during his chairmanship to the club and left a record of service "which will be difficult to equal". His ambition was always to see his club at the top, and that he achieved.

Mr. Williams reminded the shareholders that he had frequently informed them at annual meetings that he would not be satisfied until Liverpool were able to participate in the European Cup competition: "Now that this has been achieved, I feel the time has arrived when I should stand down to enable one of our younger directors to have the honour and opportunity of assuming this important office."

At the same board meeting at Anfield, Mr. Sidney Cecil Reakes, the current vice-chairman, was named as Williams' successor and Mr. Harold Cartwright was chosen as the new vice-chairman.

Bill Shankly, the dynamo behind the league champions, spoke to the *Daily Mirror* prior to the 1964/65 season: "The European Cup? It's a war! These foreign clubs stop at nothing to win. It's all politics with them, and sometimes even 'secret service.' They don't care about the game. They'd play eleven full-backs if they thought they could win. We have a chance of three titles this year. The league, the FA Cup and the European Cup. Of all of them, I'd pick the European Cup as the one I'd like to win most of all. We'll fear nobody in the world."

Around this time Shankly spent a lot of time planning for Europe and even admitted that he hardly knew Liverpool as a city: "My life revolves between my home, Melwood and the ground. I spend nearly all my time in these three places. It's the only way I know and I do it for the supporters. They are the greatest. A player who needs inspiring is not a player but with them behind you, you are doubly inspired. They know the game, too. If there's a great player on the park, they roar with delight every time he touches the ball – no matter whose side he's on."

Shankly was now entering into his sixth full season as manager and his relationship with the supporters was one of mutual admiration and respect, especially with the Kop. Shankly said: "It is difficult for me to talk about the Kop without sounding biased, because I am their greatest fan. But then I think there's a soft spot for these people in the heart of anyone who knows anything at all about football. The Kop are unique. They are fair, humorous, well-behaved and very well-educated on the game. They love to see good football being played and, if a team comes to Anfield and uses any foul methods the Kop will be on them like a shot. But if a team comes and plays well, they will be applauded almost as if they were the home team. It is said in football that the Kop is worth a goal start to Liverpool, and it may well be true because they do help to raise a player's game. But the other side nearly always play above themselves when they come to Anfield – such is the respect they have for the Kop. New players at Liverpool usually feel more than a little nervous when they play in front of the Kop for the first time, but they have nothing to fear. For the Kop are warm and they greet new players as though they have been in the team for years. This warmth and behaviour has earned the Kop the title of the best supporters in the land and, believe me, they deserve it. Forget the Beatles and all the rest. This is the real Liverpool Sound. It's real singing, and it's what the Kop is all about."

First-team trainer Bob Paisley also acknowledged the close-knit relationship between manager and fans alike: "Shankly and the Kop were made for each other. I knew the Kop crowd from my playing days, and I knew what sort of player and a man they appreciated. The more I saw of the Boss, the more I realised that he and the Kop would be married to each other."

The 1964/65 season started with the most unlikely set of fixtures. The first game at Anfield was the Charity Shield against West Ham on Saturday, August 15. In those days the Charity Shield was played at the ground of the reigning champions, before the authorities changed it to the fixed venue of Wembley.

The second game, a preliminary round of the European Cup, was played two days later, on August 15, in Reykjavik in Iceland. Most Liverpool fans had never heard of Reykjavik and some wouldn't have known where Iceland was. But they were not really surprised when their team won 5-0.

Liverpool's defence of the league title got off to a stuttering start. Despite winning their first two home fixtures, the Reds lost their first two away games. In fact, Shankly's team lost five of their first six away encounters and Liverpool were performing so badly in the league they found themselves 19th in the table at the end of October, 13 points behind leaders Manchester United.

After beating Anderlecht home and away, Liverpool were paired with FC Cologne of West Germany in the next round of the European Cup. The tie was to take three games to decide and even then it took the toss of a coin to find the winner! Liverpool captain, Ron Yeats, won the coin toss and as he left the pitch Shankly walked over to him and said, "Well done big man, what d'ya pick?" Yeats replied, "Tails boss" and Shanks said, "Good lad, I'd have picked that meself". Yeats, waiting for some form of congratulations, was to be disappointed as Shankly just walked away telling everyone who would listen that he would have picked tails too!

The drama of the Cologne tie had the effect of deflecting attention from the league performances, which remained erratic to say the least. However, Liverpool did manage to improve on their poor start to achieve a modest seventh-placed finish in the 1964/65 season.

Nonetheless, the FA Cup was a different story, as the Reds lifted the trophy for the first time in their history by beating Don Revie's

Leeds United 2-1 at Wembley. After the celebrations, Shankly's team then had the small matter of a European Cup semi-final first leg against Inter Milan to contest the following evening.

Before the game, Shankly employed a masterstroke, sending out Gordon Milne, a hugely popular player who had missed the FA Cup final through injury, and Gerry Byrne, who played all but the first three minutes of the final with a broken collarbone, to parade the FA Cup itself. Kop euphoria took over and the noise was just unbelievable, which helped Liverpool to a deserved 3-1 win over the Italians.

Less than 24 hours after cheering his team's European Cup victory over Inter Milan, Jimmy McInnes, a former player and current club secretary was found hanged at Anfield. Apparently McInnes had been overwhelmed by the size of his task at Liverpool and had resorted to sleeping on a camp bed at the ground. McInnes had been seen pulling at some cord earlier in the day, seemingly in quite good humour, but was later found hanging from a beam at the rear of the Kop.

Shankly worked with McInnes for five-and-a-half years at Liverpool, got to know him quite well and spoke about him in his autobiography: "Jimmy was honest and he was also quick-tempered. Sometimes he could be rude to people – some of them needed it, and he was right – but he would be gentlemanly with people he respected. There were some of us at Anfield with whom he never had a harsh word. Others would find him difficult to deal with and hard to understand. I've heard him calling somebody on the telephone and suddenly, bang! The phone would go down. Jimmy loved a game of snooker, and he was a good player. It was a change from his chores as secretary. When the club began to be transformed, Jimmy got the lash of the success. There were only a few seats in the stand in those days and when we won the Second Division championship, reached the FA Cup semi-final, won the First Division championship and then won the Cup, Jimmy's work was doubled and everything began to pile up on top of him. He needed help."

The Liverpool supporters' club secretary Mr. Arthur Mercer said: "Jimmy was a great guy to us. He must have been working under a terrific pressure during these last few months."

The second leg in Milan, of course, was one of the most contentious games that the Reds have ever played. Liverpool lost the game 3-0. There were many controversial incidents, but in the long term the game served as a good investment because the club, who were European novices, took due notes of what it took to be successful on the continent. Shankly and, to a greater extent, Bob Paisley filed the lessons away to be used in later and greater European triumphs.

Prior to the 1965/66 season Shankly made just one addition to his squad, John Ogston, who was always known as 'Tubby'. He was signed as a back-up goalkeeper to Tommy Lawrence and was destined to play only one game for the first team.

Shanks had incredible faith in his ability to pick out a player who would improve his team and unless a player would improve what was already there he would stick with what he had. As well as Ogston, Tommy Smith had now been introduced to the first team and had played outstandingly well as Ron Yeats' partner in the FA Cup final.

At a post-season celebration at the Liverpool Supporters' Club after winning the FA Cup, Yeats told fans: "I promise you that next season we will win something else. I don't know what, but we will bring something back."

Prior to the 1965/66 season, Shankly told Clive Toye of the *Daily Express* about his philosophy of always aiming high: "I wasn't interested in education. Football was the thing I wanted to be educated in. So I left school at 14, not just to be a footballer, but to be a

Scottish international footballer. I know I was aiming high, but if you aim as high as you can, do the right things, and believe in what you are doing, you will get there. What I'm really looking forward to is another crack at Europe's competitions, because our team works like soldiers on the front line, one gets shot and another one steps into his place."

Many clubs were now embarking on pre-season tours abroad, a new fashion that had not altogether won over Bill Shankly, who believed that European clubs should be learning from British teams and not vice versa. He called these jaunts "Dunkirk in reverse" and, in his own inimitable way, declared to the *Liverpool Echo*: "My very first thought, for the new season, is that we are becoming dazzled to the point of submission by the reputation of Continental sides. Don't get me wrong, I am not one of those people who believes the world ends at the white cliffs of Dover. I am all for the soccer Common Market. My only concern is to halt a naive swing in the opposite direction, and the belief that the Latins rule the waves. In the European Cup you meet cunning, bluff and gimmicks. You also meet some fine footballers. But so much of the Continental game is based on the safety-first principle, to the detriment of entertainment."

A Charity Shield confrontation at Old Trafford on August 13, 1965, provided the Reds with the perfect opportunity to serve warning that it would not be long before the League Championship trophy was back at Anfield. A 50,000 crowd witnessed a 2-2 draw, but it was very much a moral victory for Bill Shankly's men. The *Liverpool Echo* headline declared: 'LIVERPOOL'S RHYTHMIC EFFORT DOES IT AGAIN'. The report reflected the mood of the Red Army as another exciting season loomed large: "Not so much a football team, more an incoming tide. That is the most apt description of Liverpool these days. Time was when they were unpredictable. Not anymore. The waves of their inflowing football may be broken at times, but in the end that slow, steady rhythm of effort nearly always swamps the opposition. This was the way of it at Old Trafford, on Saturday, when Manchester, twice holding the lead, were finally worn down and had to play the match Liverpool's way. Only the most rabid United fan would deny that, though the League Champions led 1-0 and then went 2-1 up to within five minutes from the end, the initiative for the greater part of the game was with Liverpool. It would have been a great injustice if that second goal from Ron Yeats, a spectacular header, had not arrived to send the visiting fans home content with the 2-2 scoreline. The occasion confirmed Liverpool as the most talented and experienced club in the division."

Liverpool got the 1965/66 First Division campaign underway with a 3-1 away win at Leicester City on August 21. Leicester became known as Liverpool's bogey team as their magnificent goalkeeper Gordon Banks used to reserve his very best performances for games against the Reds. Following Liverpool's victory, the *Liverpool Echo* posed the million dollar question: "What is the secret of the Anfield success story?" In the same breath they came up with the answer, "Blend and team spirit." The *Liverpool Echo* reporter at Leicester said: "Whether this has come by design or accident makes no matter. It is there. All great teams have it. All managers aim at achieving it, but few of them ever satisfy themselves or their fans. But weigh up the Liverpool side which started the season excellently, with a solid, well-deserved victory at Filbert Street. There are internationals among them, some considered greater than others, but the essence of their play is surely their ability to act as a team. They come in all shapes and sizes, from the giant Ron Yeats to the pocket Hercules,

Milne, but all of them are playing for their club and none for them-selves. They fit each other's style, they understand each other's needs and when one is in trouble, he does not need to look far to get help. They move into attack from defence like well drilled soldiers, with no open spaces and a sustained power, which such teams as Leices-ter cannot match."

The first home game of the new season, four days later, against Sheffield United resulted in a 1-0 defeat and many Liverpool fans thought that the previous season's achievements of winning the FA Cup and reaching the semi-final of the European Cup was maybe as much as they could realistically expect from their team. However, at the same time they had come to learn never to underestimate Shankly's insatiable desire for success.

Although Liverpool's visit to Bramall Lane the following Wednes-day ended goalless and the Reds slumped to 14th in the league, Shankly's team went on to pick up maximum points at Bloomfield Road and Upton Park in the space of two days. When Liverpool beat West Ham 5-1 on September 6, the *Liverpool Echo* declared: "No honour is beyond Liverpool on this showing. They were given a fantastic sporting salute when they left the field at Upton Park. They did not flash in one or two positions, but sparked on every cylinder throughout the side. How easy it was to go into raptures over the combination and accomplishments of Ian St John and Roger Hunt. They teamed up so perfectly, so much so that Hunt scored a hat-trick in the space of eight minutes (42, 43 and 50). St John, the ace furnisher of chances, was also desperately unlucky not to register his first goal of the season. He has always been a football artist, making the most of almost every ball and every opportunity, applying thought to his work, which is a tribute to his dedication. Gordon Milne showed the way to goal with a corking left-foot drive, to complete a dazzling movement. Ian Callaghan added a second to rock West Ham, and they never recovered. All manner of honours are possible for a side which plays as convincingly as Liverpool did, but whatever the season may hold in store, the club's followers will not lack thrills or enjoyment. Tommy Smith and Yeats showed wonderful understanding to smash the threat posed by Geoff Hurst and Johnny Byrne, who were threatening to cut loose."

At the end of the strenuous two-games-a-week start to the season Liverpool had won 10 points from 16, which left them three points behind joint leaders West Brom and Sheffield United with a game in hand.

The Reds celebrated the start of the fixture programme up to Christmas by thrashing Everton 5-0 on a murky but memorable day at Anfield on September 25. Inevitably, the Merseyside derby captured the imagination of the whole city and Liverpool's astonishing victory left the Evertonians speechless.

Liverpool returned from a midweek game against Juventus in Turin to beat Aston Villa 3-1 on the Saturday. Peter Thompson scored twice, before St John added a third from point-blank range in the final stages. Shankly's admiration for his supreme winger grew from season to season. In 1978, Shankly wrote some very nice words in Thompson's testimonial brochure: "If Peter Thompson would not have taken up football he could have competed in the Olympic Games. That's how good an athlete he was. He could run forever, but more importantly in football he could run with the ball – probably the hardest thing to do. He could run every minute of every game, every week and every year better than anybody else. His work rate was outstanding, his fitness unequalled, his balance like a ballet dancer. I have no hesitation in placing Peter up among the all-time greats – alongside such players as Tom Finney, Stanley

Matthews and George Best. They say he didn't score enough goals, they said his final pass wasn't telling enough. Well, if he had scored goals as well as everything else he did, he would have been in the same category as Jesus Christ!"

From the Aston Villa game Chris Lawler went on to make 316 consecutive appearances for Liverpool until April 1971. In 1965, Lawler spoke to *Football Monthly* about his time at Liverpool so far: "I'm a lucky guy! Though my career so far consists of just one full season of First Division football I can already look back on achievements that many outstanding players have not realised after a lifetime in the game – a FA Cup winners' medal and playing in the European Cup until the semi-finals. And in addition I am playing for the best club (and team) in the world thus achieving an ambition that I have cherished since I was a schoolboy. Like so many Merseysiders, as a kid I was soccer-daft. Liverpool were my club and my individual idol was the legendary Billy Liddell, a great player and an off-the-field example to anyone in any walk of life. And I can't remember the day when I didn't want to follow the famous Scot and play for Liverpool. I was born in Norris Green and attended St. Teresa's School where I played centre-half. And it was in this position that I played for Liverpool Boys and England Boys. I didn't know it at the time, but I was being carefully watched by Liverpool's local scout, the late Thomas 'Tosh' Moore, and when I left school at 15 I was asked if I would like to join the Anfield ground staff. Would I like? Wild horses wouldn't have stopped me, and so began the usual climb through the junior and 'A' teams still as a centre-half and playing the odd game at full-back if required."

At the age of 21, Chris Lawler played 48 of the 60 games of the 1964/65 season. Lawler continued: "I must have pleased the boss, as before the season ended I had played in seven European Cup ties, and had gone through the FA Cup series, ending with our victory at Wembley. That is a day stamped on my memory. It was a wonderful feeling; we all felt so very proud!"

After losing 2-0 to the First Division champions Manchester United at Old Trafford, Liverpool's next away game was at The Hawthorns against West Brom on October 23. The Reds underperformed and lost their third consecutive away game, this time by three goals to nil and slipped down to seventh in the league. The fans were starting to become anxious and the club worried.

A rather unpleasant incident occurred during the game at the Hawthorns. A hard-boiled egg was thrown on to the pitch from the terraces. Tommy Smith handed it over to referee T.W. Dawes, who temporarily stopped the game while he spoke to the police. A loud speaker announcement then followed, threatening to call off the game in the event of other incidents.

Liverpool dispelled their supporters' fears by beating Nottingham Forest 4-0 the following week at Anfield. Hunt was emerging as a force to be reckoned with in any company. He blasted a double in the 4-0 victory over Nottingham Forest at the end of October as he enjoyed his best game of the season to that point. It's worth reflecting on his goal sense by assessing his strikes against Forest. After 72 minutes St John collected a clearance from Gerry Byrne and split the opposing defence with a fine pass to Hunt. He held off a Henry Newton tackle and hit a great shot on the run, which Peter Grummitt got his fingers to, but couldn't stop. Shortly after, Thompson got the ball across from the left and Yeats, having moved well forward, headed down to Hunt, who pounced in clinical fashion from close range. It was during this spell that Roger Hunt found the scoring touch that shaped Liverpool's success. In eight games from the beginning of November to the middle of December he only failed to score in one.

Despite the 4-0 victory against Forest, the club directors weren't completely satisfied; therefore, Bill Shankly added a new item to the Anfield battleplan. He started keeping the players together the night before away games. The system was put on trial for the trip to Hillsborough, which resulted in a 2-0 victory for the Reds. This important triumph shifted the worries about the team's inability to do well away, as the Hillsborough victory began a run of six away games in which Liverpool didn't concede a single goal, an achievement which Liverpool's goalkeeper Tommy Lawrence undoubtedly had a hand in.

Lawrence was now in this fourth season as Shankly's first-choice stopper. Strong, brave and consistent, he was a fearless goalkeeper, even if he was affectionately dubbed 'The Flying Pig' by supporters who felt he was carrying a bit too much weight!

Lawrence quit working in the Rylands wire factory in Warrington and signed professional forms at Liverpool on October 30, 1957, a few months after his 17th birthday. Lawrence had been at Anfield for five years when he got his opportunity during Liverpool's first season in the top-flight for eight years. Jim Furnell got injured 13 games into the 1962/63 season and Lawrence grabbed his chance with both hands.

The stockily-built Scotsman was the first sweeper-keeper, as Lawrence explains: "Shankly said, 'Right Tommy, you're not playing on the six-yard line. When the ball's on the halfway line, you've got to be on the 18-yard line. If the ball shoots through, you've got to be out to kick it – a sort of stopper'. At first I was frightened to death. We did it at Melwood a few times and then we tried at Anfield.

"Well, I'm standing there and the Kop is giving me some stick. 'Get back on your line!' they're all yelling. No goalkeeper did that in those days. I thought, 'Oh my God'. But it worked. I'd come out and do like they do today. You didn't get sent off in those days either. So I used to bring them down. If they pushed it past me, I'd just hit them."

The Reds ended the year on a high. A lone Gordon Milne goal was enough to beat Leeds at Elland Road on December 28, just 24 hours after the Yorkshire outfit had plundered a holiday victory at Anfield, also beating the Reds by a single goal. Shankly's men took revenge on Leeds far more decisively than the scoreline suggests. It was a hard, uncompromising game, Milne settling it when he rammed home a low centre from Hunt after 48 minutes. After the two duels against Leeds, the *Liverpool Echo* reflected on the importance of iron man Tommy Smith's contribution to the team: "He is a frightening figure as he goes in for the ball, with the undoubted intention of obtaining it at any cost. This sturdy young man gives the impression he would cheerfully charge through a brick wall, head first, if he thought it was necessary, and when he has acquired a little more maturity, he will be a truly great half-back."

At the end of the 1965 calendar year, the league table showed Liverpool on top with 34 points from 24 games. Burnley were battling well with 32 points from 23 games and Manchester United, Tottenham, Leeds and Stoke City were leading the chasing group. The Merseysiders kicked off the New Year on an important winning note, by beating Manchester United 2-1 at Anfield, the game ending in dramatic fashion, with the match winner secured in the closing minutes. The *Liverpool Echo* reported: "United had claimed the lead after just two minutes, when Denis Law withstood a Yeats challenge, kept his feet when the falling Lawrence tackled him, and then screwed the ball into the empty net, with the aplomb and adroitness of the football artist. Smith equalised after 39 minutes with a right-foot drive. United, with Charlton, Law and Best, had class and great ability, but Liverpool's never-say-die attitude proved crucial in the closing moments. Suddenly there was a pandemonium of flying bodies, goalkeeper Harry Gregg going down at the feet of the home forwards, without gaining the ball. A half clearance went to Reds' full-back Gerry Byrne, and when he played it straight back in, Gordon Milne conjured up a brilliant header that was to floor United. The eruption of sound, which was to greet this winning goal, must have been heard for miles."

When Shankly bought Gordon Milne during his first full season as manager in 1960 he knew the boy pretty well having been his dad's teammate at Preston for a few years. Joe Fagan, reserve team trainer at the time, later spoke of his admiration for Milne to the *Anfield Review*: "My memories of Gordon prompt me to say that possibly he was one of the unsung heroes of that fine Liverpool side of the 1960s. He was certainly one of the mainstays and, in my opinion, a very skilled exponent of the modern day game. Gordon had real quality in his play; and he also had the ability to close down an opponent, by which I mean he made it extremely awkward for the man in front of him to provide an accurate pass to a teammate. Sometimes I felt that not even the players around him realised just what an important role Gordon Milne was playing in what is essentially a team game."

By the end of January, the *Liverpool Echo* was reporting that Liverpool were within measurable distance of winning the league. This was because several of their remaining fixtures were against clubs concerned primarily with relegation. Yet Shankly's team was not performing quite as convincingly as usual. Were goalkeepers – and one in particular – saving their best for Liverpool? Gordon Banks of Leicester and England was always a tremendous adversary. The Kop gave him quite a welcome on January 29, even singing, "He's the finest goalkeeper in the land". Banks was to prove them right and it took a strange goal from a full-back after 75 minutes to secure victory for the Reds. The *Liverpool Echo* wrote: "Defender Chris Lawler, who gets into unusual forward positions with the stealth and mysticism of the cleverest of attackers, moved well inside the penalty box, but with his back half towards goal. There seemed no danger, when he flicked the ball with the outside of his boot, but it looped over the line. That Banks was beaten by an almost casual goal after withstanding a barrage of shots was remarkable. All the more remarkable was that between then and the final whistle, he saved fantastically from Callaghan twice and Hunt. No wonder the Anfield crowd rose to him." Final Score: Liverpool 1-0 Leicester City.

In their next three games against Blackburn, Sunderland and Blackpool, the Reds scored 12 goals, four in each game. In the wake of the 4-0 home win over Sunderland on February 12, which included another sensational Roger Hunt hat-trick, the *Liverpool Echo* reported that one of Hunt's goals was hit so hard that the ball struck the net support and rebounded, almost to the edge of the penalty box.

Liverpool's fine form had put them in a fantastic position; nine points clear at the top of the table. However, their run of eight unbeaten games ended with shattering impact to bottom-of-the-table Fulham. The Reds were defeated 2-0 at Craven Cottage, which ended in Ian St John being sent off for fighting. Alan Hoby of the *Sunday Express* wrote: "Three minutes from the end of this lurid and combative cliff hanger of a match with Fulham, crouching at the foot of the First Division table, racing to a fantastic victory over Liverpool, the runaway leaders, violence, raw and ugly, erupted. Mark Pearson, Fulham's chunky inside-left who had been pulled back in the second half to reinforce Fulham's unyielding defenders, clashed with the idol of Anfield, Ian St John. In a blurred few seconds of angry action, with the crowd booing and bawling, Pearson appeared to grab Liverpool's Scottish international centre forward by the head. There was a brief tugging and pulling before I saw the provoked St John aim a left hook worthy of British heavyweight champion Henry Cooper. Down slumped Pearson. Out roared the fury of the 31,000-plus crowd. There was a desperate straining mix-up of white and red shirts as referee Ray Aldous was surrounded by gesticulating players. It was a disgraceful scene as the lanky Mr. Aldous ordered St John from the field, following him nearly halfway across the pitch to make quite sure that he went. As St John slowly trudged off, his face set and flushed, a lone Liverpool supporter rushed on to the field to commiserate with his fallen hero. But Fulham's centre-back Johnny Dempsey, with a scowl worthy of the great Jack himself, shouted at the Anfield fan to get off and off he went."

The Liverpool forward later in life admitted: "The supporters and the Kop, they mean everything to me, when I come out on to the field on a Saturday, I'm prepared to die for these people! I have to be honest and say I did have a quick temper which was a bad thing, but the fact I wasn't frightened of anybody was a good thing." St John also recalls when the Kop was used for training sessions: "The one thing I always remember about the Kop was that I had to run up and down it. On wet days, when we didn't go out to Melwood for any training, Reuben Bennett, our trainer, used to take us on to the Kop and make us run up and down it countless times. I don't know how many steps there are but I do know that they have been covered many times in my sweat."

Liverpool had two European games with Honved to get over the defeat at Craven Cottage. They did not concede a goal to the Hungarian team and got back into the habit. They did not concede one in the next five League games either, which included a 1-0 victory against Sheffield Wednesday at Anfield on April 6. The *Liverpool Echo* reported on Willie Stevenson's winning goal: "Geoff Strong began the movement with a pass to Callaghan out on the right and from the winger's cross into the goalmouth, Stevenson connected with the ball on the bounce and it fairly flew high into the net."

Willie Stevenson was a skilful midfielder with an eye for a sensational pass. He arrived on Merseyside from Rangers in October 1962 and took over the left-half spot from Tommy Leishman. He was the dressing room joker and a big favourite with the fans. When Kenny Dalglish went on trial at Liverpool at 15 years of age he became the victim of Stevenson's humour. Dalglish asked for Stevenson's autograph when the players were relaxing in the changing room. "I went to Billy Stevenson and said, 'Would you please sign this, Billy?' He said, 'No'. As I walked away all the players burst out laughing. Billy was only kidding."

Long before Chris Lawler had developed his goalscoring habit, an extraordinary incident occurred involving Stevenson. Ron Yeats recalls: "Whilst changing for a game at Turf Moor getting ready to face Burnley, Willie Stevenson said to Chris Lawler: 'I dreamed last night that you scored one today.' Sure enough late in the game when we were already 4-1 up, Willie spotted Chris moving into a favourable spot and slipped the ball to him for him to score his first goal for the club. Chris turned dream into fact, which is why, for a time 'Steve' was known as 'Willie the Dreamer'. From that day he received many lucrative offers to dream up the winners at the races."

Liverpool were yet to recapture the rhythm of their great spell just before and after Christmas, but they were picking up points, which is a sign of a really good team. Any side can pick up points when they are playing well. Liverpool were not playing well, but they went into the vital Easter programme top of the league, seven points ahead of Burnley, in second place.

Liverpool's two away draws against Northampton and Sunderland must have given their title challengers a glimpse of hope. However, after the round of games played on Easter Monday, Burnley were still seven points behind. Nevertheless, the Clarets still had five games to play and could still overhaul the Reds, as one of their remaining fixtures was a visit from the Anfielders to Turf Moor. Against Northampton, being without leading scorer Roger Hunt through injury was bad enough, but to have St John hurt in the opening minutes and be absent for nearly 20, thanks to a kick to the side of the face, added considerably to Liverpool's problems. A cut on the jawbone required three stitches and St John's reply to an injury which shook him up and left him dazed was one of great courage, as Shankly's wounded solider returned to the battlefield to complete the game.

In April 1966, Bill Shankly spoke to *Football Monthly*: "My team have won one League title and are well on the way to a second. They have won the FA Cup and they have become one of Europe's most powerful and most feared teams. There's only one way to do anything in football – that's flat-out. I want a man who will go through a brick wall with a broken leg... and still come out the other side shooting for goal. If he can do that, then he is good enough to play for Liverpool! If there is anything I can demand in a footballer, it is courage and roughness. Nobody can assure them of lacking either quality."

After beating Celtic over two legs to qualify for the European Cup Winners' Cup final, it was widely predicted that the game against Burnley on April 23 would be the Championship decider and, indeed, by the time Liverpool went to Turf Moor, they needed just one point to settle matters. It proved to be an anti-climax, as the Reds lost 2-0.

Defeat at Turf Moor did at least set up a glory day on home soil, with the visit of Chelsea to Anfield on April 30. The *Liverpool Echo* reported: "All the gates except for ticket holders were closed half-an-hour before the kick-off, and just before the teams came out a Liverpool fan emerged from the packed Kop and went to the centre of the field, where he planted a replica of the Championship trophy on the centre spot. There was no doubt who Chelsea thought were going to be champions because they came out first and lined up in two rows and applauded the Liverpool players as they ran between them on to the pitch. Liverpool, defending the Kop, got a quick free-kick when St John was impeded by Hinton, but from this Yeats could not reach Stevenson's lob. Chelsea were moving the ball quickly. A brilliant piece of work by Osgood took him beyond two players and Houseman's shot from the pass was not very wide. St John got up to reach a Thompson corner, but his header went straight at Dunn who made a fine save. Chelsea were always willing to open out the game and were particularly dangerous on the left. They got another free-kick near the edge of the penalty area, but this time the shot was only half hit and did not even reach Lawrence. A dangerous cross from Robson was cut off by Yeats, and when Liverpool got a free-kick on the left St John headed the ball across the Chelsea goal-mouth, with no other Liverpool player there to take what would have been a gift. Osgood was lying deep, and many of the good-looking moves began with him, but there was little finishing power from the Londoners. Osgood slipped a through pass in front of Tambling and the inside right, from near the edge of the penalty area, lashed the ball first time just over the angle. This was a good move, and the Liverpool defence was not too confident dealing with these fine passes from Osgood. Liverpool were striving hard enough, but they were against a defence which was playing coolly and competently, and all St John's efforts could not create an opening. We were not getting much action, but Chelsea were in luck when Hunt made his own opening and then cracked a right-footer which hit the inside of the post and rebounded into Dunn's arms. Liverpool had done most of the pressing, but although this Chelsea defence had been hard put to on occasions to hold them it had also played well. Half-time: Liverpool 0-0 Chelsea.

"Liverpool went ahead in 48 minutes and it looked like an own goal from Dunn. Byrne got possession in midfield and slid the ball through for Hunt. The Liverpool man took it almost to the line before pulling it back and the next thing we knew was the ball in the net. One must assume that it struck Dunn and rebounded in, although, the Liverpool players gave their congratulations to Hunt. Naturally the Kop was in an uproar, and they nearly had cause for more celebration when St John bore down the left and saw his shot hit a defender and glance outside for a corner. And from this Liverpool almost scored, because Yeats' header was sneaking in at the angle when Dunn went up to make a good catch. The atmosphere was here now in full measure and how Stephenson missed connecting from six yards was amazing. Dunn made a fine leap to stop Callaghan's cross reaching St John, then, while Robson was lying injured Smith went on from a pass by the winger only to stub his shot and give Dunn an easy pick up. Offside twice, and then the long leg of Yeats stopped Chelsea in their tracks. But it was Liverpool who were doing the attacking, and a shot from Stevenson slewed well wide, while St John's effort to get his head to Callaghan's chip was foiled by Hinton.

"Yeats came up to make a header which passed over and then Chelsea grabbed a surprise equaliser in the 62nd minute. Tambling switched the ball down the right and Murray outpaced Yeats and then guided it into the net as Lawrence came out. Chelsea became more menacing after their goal and a mistake by Yeats very nearly let in Robson, who retrieved the situation for Liverpool by trying to take the ball forward instead of shooting first time when Lawrence was off his line. But Liverpool went into the lead again on 69 minutes and this was a fine goal. Hunt beat one man and then came right and then went left again, leaving him with the chance to make a left-foot shot. He hit this hard and low and although Dunn partly made a stop, the power was too much and the ball rolled on over the line. This set the Kop off again and they gave us pretty well their whole repertoire. They groaned when a St John header slipped outside instead of inside the post because if anyone deserved to score it was St John, who had played so well. It had now become a case really of waiting for the end because Chelsea were not getting within range and Liverpool, too, were happy to coast along. One can hardly blame them in the view of the tough job at Hampden Park on Thursday night. With minutes left the Kop began their 'Ee-aye-addio, we've won the League' chant. Final Score: Liverpool 2-1 Chelsea.

"When the final whistle went and Liverpool's seventh First Division title was confirmed, several Liverpool supporters raced on to the pitch, and as Yeats was congratulated by the Chelsea players one boy gave him the replica of the trophy. An elated Bill Shankly then strode onto the pitch to congratulate each and every player individually. The lap of honour followed, with the Kop a kaleidoscope of red and white. A shout then went up for the injured Geoff Strong and when he appeared the place erupted. Sentiment, adulation, sheer ecstasy... it was a day to savour. Tommy Docherty, the

Chelsea manager, described the Liverpool crowd as the best in the world. The best of British would have been good enough for Shankly. The rest of the world, in his eyes, were not good enough to lace the boots of his boys. Incredibly, Liverpool used just 14 players throughout the campaign and, almost every week, Shanks would nod his head and say, 'Same Again.' Five players, Tommy Lawrence, Gerry Byrne, Ron Yeats, Ian Callaghan and Tommy Smith, were ever-present. Willie Stevenson and Ian St John missed just a game apiece, Chris Lawler and Peter Thompson two apiece. It was a side that will never be forgotten, the names of men like Roger Hunt, Gordon Milne and Geoff Strong, all earning a place in the Anfield Hall of Fame. Alf Arrowsmith and Bobby Graham made just four appearances between them, but they were still part of Shankly's famous football family."

Bill Shankly told the press after the game: "We've been living in a pressure cooker. Everybody expected us to take the title because we have been at the top for so long. But it hasn't been easy. Everybody has been trying extra hard to beat us because we were the leaders. It was different the last time we won it in 1964, when we came with a late burst to overtake all our rivals."

When Liverpool won the League Championship in 1964 and 1966 the trophy wasn't present at Anfield in either instance, but due to the foresight of the Curlett brothers, who had made one at home, the players still had a trophy to parade.

This famous trophy, now known as the Curlett Cup, is today on permanent display at the Liverpool museum and the homemade cup has become the focal point of these watershed moments in Liverpool's history. The mother of the Curlett brothers had a dressing table with a set of vases on top.

One of them broke, so their mother was going to throw them both away. "My youngest brother Terry had other plans," Peter Curlett told the *LFC Magazine*. "He took the intact vase up to his room and started decorating it. Being a Liverpool fan, he naturally painted it red and white. He also cut out pictures of the players from newspapers and football magazines and stuck them on it. It was the day of the Arsenal game and we didn't know whether the Championship trophy was going to be there. We brought the trophy with us on to the Kop and as Ron Yeats had no trophy to lift, we handed it to him and he took off on a lap of honour. When the same scenario developed two years later, we also came to the players' rescue. As the team were standing in the middle of the pitch applauding the supporters our Terry ran on and gave our cup to Ron Yeats. My brother immediately disappeared back into the crowd while the players did a lap of honour with it and then got their medals. When Yeats went up to get his medal on the podium, he banged it down on the table and broke the base of the trophy. After the celebrations were over, we were invited into the dressing room with the team and each player signed under their own photo of the cup".

Liverpool lost to Borussia Dortmund at Hampden Park in the European Cup Winners' Cup final, but there were some great victories along the way over Juventus, Standard Liege, Honved and Celtic. That summer three Anfield players – Hunt, Byrne and Callaghan – were all included in Alf Ramsey's squad that won the World Cup. Roger Hunt, who for the fifth consecutive season finished Liverpool's top scorer, was preferred to famous rival Jimmy Greaves in the final as England won the Jules Rimet trophy for the first and only time.

Liverpudlian Gerry Byrne added a second League Championship medal to his collection. Byrne signed professional forms with Liverpool aged 17 after coming through the junior ranks at Anfield. He was spotted by chain-smoking Liverpool scout Tosh Moore at 15 when featuring for the Liverpool Catholic Schoolboys in Dublin. He made his league debut at Charlton Athletic on September 28, 1957 but that was his only outing that season, the reason being perhaps that Liverpool lost 5-1 but certainly because he scored an own goal! The experienced full-back pairing of John Molyneux and Ronnie Moran prevented Byrne from making more than a handful of appearances during the next two years, but Bill Shankly's arrival in 1959 changed his prospects completely as the new manager seemed to take a liking to the tough-tackling left-back, who got a break when Moran got seriously injured in the autumn of 1960. Byrne played in the remaining 33 league games of the 1960/61 season and remainded a regular after that.

Byrne was an uncompromising character on the field and might not have been as well-known as some of his colleagues but his courage was never in question, and that was never shown more clearly than on the day Liverpool finally won the FA Cup in 1965 for the first time. He was injured very early on in the final against Leeds United at a time before substitutes were allowed. Bob Paisley was Liverpool's physio at the time and ran on to the field. "Gerry had clattered into the chunky Bobby Collins. As soon as I reached him I knew that my initial touchline diagnosis had been painfully accurate. He had broken his collar bone." Byrne asked Paisley not to tell anyone and kept on playing. The extent of his injury was not revealed until the final was over, by which time Byrne had a winner's medal in his pocket and important involvement in the first, vital breakthrough goal scored by Roger Hunt early in extra-time. Shankly was in awe of Byrne's performance: "It was a performance of raw courage from the boy."

Shankly also added: "Gerry wasn't flashy and he wouldn't score you goals. But he was hard and skilful and gave you everything he had. More than that, he was totally honest, which is the greatest quality of all. He was a true Liverpudlian who couldn't look his fellow Scousers in the face after a game unless he'd given everything he had for 90 minutes."

Byrne later talked to *LFChistory.net* about the type of player he regarded himself as: "I was nicknamed 'the Crunch'. I was a clean, hard but fair player. I used to wait for the ball to come and then I was on my way. You hit someone when the ball was there and that was it. That's how I got 'the Crunch.' I didn't go after players intentionally and I was never sent off in my life."

Captain Ron Yeats became the first player since Alex Raisbeck to captain Liverpool to two First Division championships and thanked the fans for their contribution to the team's success on the pitch: "On behalf of the boys, the thanks of us all for the wonderful support which we have received. This encouragement, particularly when things are not going our way, means more than we can say, and we want supporters to know that it is truly appreciated."

The League Championship-winning side of 1966 were not a great team of great players but a great team of good players with tremendous strength, fight and confidence. They had confidence in themselves and each other. It is an odds-on formula for success and knowing all this, perhaps Ron Yeats was not taking such a chance when he made his promise to the fans at the start of the season!

Yeats later said: "The Sixties teams laid the foundations, the Seventies teams built the walls and the Eighties teams added the roof to the soccer fortress that is now Anfield. But for sheer entertainment value, that 65/66 Championship side takes some beating."

After winning two First Division league titles and the FA Cup in three seasons Shankly predicted more success to come. He said: "Not for a minute do I believe that we are at the end of our achievements. We are at the beginning. Ours is not an old team. Some of our players are matured. Others are maturing fast and I do not fear to look into the future. Since we took the lead in Division One this season, we have led all the way and in recent weeks have had points to spare. But don't let anybody try to kid you that winning the English League Championship is easy. It is anything but that and it is getting harder."

In the same speech to the press, Shankly also dedicated some words to his players: "To our players I would say don't let our successes impair your ambition. There is no room for complacency. Other goals remain to be conquered. The challenge is to maintain and, if possible, improve the standard set. We have had five years of achievement. Let us look on that only as a start. Everybody needs to get it into their heads that forward movement is still possible and is the way we must keep on going – FORWARD. The players are still young enough to become even better. The cunning and craft that comes with experience should carry them on and on. We have nobody in the veteran stage. I am not guilty of wishful thinking when I say I honestly believe we can be even better next season. The older you are, up to a point, the more experienced you are. The more you know, the better you play. You get to the stage when you don't just hope to play, but when you know you are going to play well. Players become tradesmen. If you are a plumber and you go to repair a burst pipe you know exactly what you have to do. Similarly with football, if you know what to do, and how to do it, you must be better for it.

"In conclusion, I would say, ambition rides higher at Anfield today than it has ever done before. The sky's the limit as far as we are concerned. Thanks from all of us to all of you who helped us to put LIFE IN LIVERPOOL!"

1965/66: Facts and Statistics

Final league table

		P	W	D	L	F	A	W	D	L	F	A	PTS
1	Liverpool FC	42	17	2	2	52	15	9	7	5	27	19	61
2	Leeds United	42	14	4	3	49	15	9	5	7	30	23	55
3	Burnley	42	15	3	3	45	20	9	4	8	34	27	55
4	Manchester United	42	12	8	1	50	20	6	7	8	34	39	51
5	Chelsea	42	11	4	6	30	21	11	3	7	35	32	51
6	WBA	42	11	6	4	58	34	8	6	7	33	35	50
7	Leicester City	42	12	4	5	40	28	9	3	9	40	37	49
8	Tottenham	42	11	6	4	55	37	5	6	10	20	29	44
9	Sheffield United	42	11	6	4	37	25	5	5	11	19	34	43
10	Stoke City	42	12	6	3	42	22	3	6	12	23	42	42
11	Everton	42	12	6	3	39	19	3	5	13	17	43	41
12	West Ham United	42	12	5	4	46	33	3	4	14	24	50	39
13	Blackpool	42	9	5	7	36	29	5	4	12	19	36	37
14	Arsenal	42	8	8	5	36	31	4	5	12	26	44	37
15	Newcastle United	42	10	5	6	26	20	4	4	13	24	43	37
16	Aston Villa	42	10	3	8	39	34	5	3	13	30	46	36
17	Sheffield Wednesday	42	11	6	4	35	18	3	2	16	21	48	36
18	Nottingham Forest	42	11	3	7	31	26	3	5	13	25	46	36
19	Sunderland	42	13	2	6	36	28	1	6	14	15	44	36
20	Fulham	42	9	4	8	34	37	5	3	13	33	48	35
21	Northampton Town	42	8	6	7	31	32	2	7	12	24	60	33
22	Blackburn Rovers	42	6	1	14	30	36	2	3	16	27	52	20

Games for the 1965/1966 season

(The number after date is league position after the game)

1	14.08.1965		D	2-2	Manchester United, Old Trafford, Charity Shield
2	21.08.1965	5	W	3-1	Leicester City, Filbert Street, 1st Division
3	25.08.1965	9	L	0-1	Sheffield United, Anfield, 1st Division
4	01.09.1965	14	D	0-0	Sheffield United, Bramall Lane, 1st Division
5	04.09.1965	9	W	3-2	Blackpool, Bloomfield Road, 1st Division
6	06.09.1965	3	W	5-1	West Ham United, Upton Park, 1st Division
7	11.09.1965	4	W	2-1	Fulham, Anfield, 1st Division
8	15.09.1965	6	D	1-1	West Ham United, Anfield, 1st Division

9	18.09.1965	8	L	1-2	Tottenham Hotspur, White Hart Lane, 1st Division
10	25.09.1965	6	W	5-0	Everton, Anfield, 1st Division
11	29.09.1965		L	0-1	Juventus, Stadio Communale, ECW Cup 1st round 1L
12	02.10.1965	2	W	3-1	Aston Villa, Anfield, 1st Division
13	09.10.1965	6	L	0-2	Manchester United, Old Trafford, 1st Division
14	13.10.1965		W	2-0	Juventus, Anfield, ECW Cup 1st round 2L
15	16.10.1965	3	W	2-0	Newcastle United, Anfield, 1st Division
16	23.10.1965	7	L	0-3	West Bromwich Albion, The Hawthorns, 1st Division
17	30.10.1965	5	W	4-0	Nottingham Forest, Anfield, 1st Division
18	06.11.1965	2	W	2-0	Sheffield Wednesday, Hillsborough, 1st Division
19	13.11.1965	2	W	5-0	Northampton Town, Anfield, 1st Division
20	17.11.1965	1	W	5-2	Blackburn Rovers, Anfield, 1st Division
21	20.11.1965	1	D	0-0	Stoke City, Victoria Ground, 1st Division
22	27.11.1965	1	W	2-1	Burnley, Anfield, 1st Division
23	01.12.1965		W	3-1	Standard Liege, Anfield, ECW Cup 2nd round 1L
24	04.12.1965	1	W	1-0	Chelsea, Stamford Bridge, 1st Division
25	11.12.1965	1	W	4-2	Arsenal, Anfield, 1st Division
26	15.12.1965		W	2-1	Standard Liege, Stade de Sclessin, ECW Cup 2nd round 2L
27	18.12.1965	1	D	0-0	Newcastle United, St. James' Park, 1st Division
28	27.12.1965	1	L	0-1	Leeds United, Anfield, 1st Division
29	28.12.1965	1	W	1-0	Leeds United, Elland Road, 1st Division
30	01.01.1966	1	W	2-1	Manchester United, Anfield, 1st Division
31	08.01.1966	1	W	1-0	Arsenal, Highbury, 1st Division
32	15.01.1966	1	D	2-2	West Bromwich Albion, Anfield, 1st Division
33	22.01.1966		L	1-2	Chelsea, Anfield, FA Cup 3rd round
34	29.01.1966	1	W	1-0	Leicester City, Anfield, 1st Division
35	05.02.1966	1	W	4-1	Blackburn Rovers, Ewood Park, 1st Division
36	12.02.1966	1	W	4-0	Sunderland, Anfield, 1st Division
37	19.02.1966	1	W	4-1	Blackpool, Anfield, 1st Division
38	26.02.1966	1	L	0-2	Fulham, Craven Cottage, 1st Division
39	01.03.1966		D	0-0	Honved, Nep Stadium, ECW Cup 3rd round 1st leg
40	08.03.1966		W	2-0	Honved, Anfield, ECW Cup 3rd round 2L
41	12.03.1966	1	W	1-0	Tottenham Hotspur, Anfield, 1st Division
42	19.03.1966	1	D	0-0	Everton, Goodison Park, 1st Division
43	26.03.1966	1	W	3-0	Aston Villa, Villa Park, 1st Division
44	06.04.1966	1	W	1-0	Sheffield Wednesday, Anfield, 1st Division
45	09.04.1966	1	D	0-0	Northampton Town, County Ground, 1st Division

46	11.04.1966	1	D	2-2	Sunderland, Roker Park, 1st Division
47	14.04.1966		L	0-1	Celtic, Celtic Park, ECW Cup Semi-Final 1L
48	16.04.1966	1	W	2-0	Stoke City, Anfield, 1st Division
49	19.04.1966		W	2-0	Celtic, Anfield, ECW Cup Semi-Final 2L
50	23.04.1966	1	L	0-2	Burnley, Turf Moor, 1st Division
51	30.04.1966	1	W	2-1	Chelsea, Anfield, 1st Division
52	05.05.1966		L	1-2	Borussia Dortmund, Hampden Park, ECW Cup Final
53	10.05.1966	1	D	1-1	Nottingham Forest, City Ground, 1st Division

Appearances for the 1965/1966 season

Name	League	FA Cup	ECWC	CS	Total
Gerry Byrne	42	1	9	1	53
Ian Callaghan	42	1	9	1	53
Tommy Lawrence	42	1	9	1	53
Tommy Smith	42	1	9	1	53
Ron Yeats	42	1	9	1	53
Ian St John	41	1	9	1	52
Willie Stevenson	41	1	9	1	52
Chris Lawler	40	1	8	1	50
Peter Thompson	40	1	9	0	50
Roger Hunt	37	1	7	1	46
Gordon Milne	28	1	6	1	36
Geoff Strong	22	0	4	1	27
Alf Arrowsmith	5	0	1	0	6
Phil Chisnall	0	0	1	0	1
Bobby Graham	1	0	0	0	1

Goalscorers for the 1965/1966 season

Name	League	FA Cup	ECWC	CS	Total
Roger Hunt	29	1	2	0	32
Ian St John	10	0	2	0	12
Chris Lawler	5	0	4	0	9
Gordon Milne	7	0	0	0	7
Geoff Strong	5	0	2	0	7
Peter Thompson	5	0	1	0	6
Willie Stevenson	5	0	0	1	6
Ian Callaghan	5	0	0	0	5
Tommy Smith	3	0	1	0	4
Ron Yeats	2	0	0	1	3
Own goals	1	0	0	0	1
Alf Arrowsmith	1	0	0	0	1
Gerry Byrne	1	0	0	0	1

The squad during the 1965/1966 season

Tommy Lawrence, Goalkeeper
Ron Yeats, Defender
Gerry Byrne, Defender
Tommy Smith, Defender
Chris Lawler, Defender
Alf Arrowsmith, Midfielder
Ian Callaghan, Midfielder
Gordon Wallace, Midfielder
Peter Thompson, Midfielder
Geoff Strong, Midfielder
Willie Stevenson, Midfielder
Ian St John, Midfielder
Gordon Milne, Midfielder
Bobby Graham, Striker
Roger Hunt, Striker
Phil Chisnall, Striker

Transfers for the 1965/1966 season

In:
John Ogston, Aberdeen, £10,000, September 1965

Out:
George Scott, Aberdeen £12,000, 1965
Phil Ferns, Bournemouth & Boscombe Athletic, £5,000, August 1965
Bobby Thomson, Luton Town, £3,000, 1 August 1965

A collection of statistics for the 1965/1966 season

The season in numbers:
Total games: 53
Games won: 31
Games drawn: 11
Games lost: 11
Clean sheets – League: 19
Clean sheets – Overall: 23
Total goals: 94
Average attendance at home – League: 46,334
Average attendance at home – Overall: 47,428
Average goals per game – League: 2.48
Average goals per game – Overall: 2.38
Average goal minute – League: 52
Average goal minute – Overall: 51

Goals split down to competitions:
League – 79
European Cup Winners Cup – 12
Charity Shield – 2
FA Cup – 1

Player debuts:
N/A

Statistics and information provided by LFChistory.net

8 : REBUILDING THE FORTRESS

1972/73

THE GREAT LIVERPOOL SIDE OF THE SIXTIES HAD gained promotion from the Second Division, won the First Division twice, the FA Cup once, and progressed in Europe. However, after their second First Division title triumph in 1966, Bill Shankly's Liverpool went through a six-year period without any tangible success. Shankly's mistake was to let his side rumble on for too long without any major rebuilding. "We were all at the same age when we started so around 1967 we were all around 30," Ron Yeats explained to *LFChistory.net*. "He then started to change the side, changing tactics, changing players; it took maybe three years to come together." By the middle of 1972 that rebuilding process was almost complete and it would bear fruit in a quite remarkable way.

Although Liverpool went trophy-less for six seasons, they never finished lower than fifth in the league and came incredibly close to winning honours in both the league and the FA Cup. Arsenal beat Liverpool 2-1 in the 1971 FA Cup final and the Reds drew 0-0 at Highbury in the final league game of the 1971/72 season when Shankly's team needed a win to snatch the title away from Derby.

John Toshack scored a goal against the Gunners to give Liverpool a crucial lead but it was cruelly ruled offside by referee Roger Kirk-patrick.

During the late Sixties, not all of Bill Shankly's signings turned out to be as successful as he would have liked. Players like Alun Evans and Tony Hateley had short Anfield careers but Emlyn Hughes was one player who certainly did thrive at the club.

Emlyn Walter Hughes was born in Barrow-in-Furness in 1947. Although his father Fred was a Welsh rugby union and professional rugby league player during the Forties, football had always been Emlyn's passion. Shankly saw Hughes play in one of his first games for Blackpool and offered £25,000 for him immediately. Blackpool were not keen on selling him but manager Ron Suart promised Liverpool first refusal if Hughes ever became available.

Shankly phoned Hughes every Sunday morning to tell him he'd be a Liverpool player soon. "I'd be just about to make short work of a plate of eggs, bacon and black pudding when the phone would ring. It would be Shanks," Hughes said. "'Hey, Emlyn, son, don't eat that stuff you've got on your plate there. I'll be signing you shortly. I want you lean and hungry, son. Lean and hungry!' Today, thirty years later, I still associate the smell of bacon frying with the telephone ringing at 8.30 sharp on a Sunday morning."

When Suart was sacked in February 1967, Liverpool knew they had to react quickly. Suart wasted no time in serving as an intermediary between Shankly and Hughes, contacting his former player the day after his sacking to advise him to join Liverpool. Shankly finally got his man but for a considerably higher fee of £65,000.

Hughes recalls the most important day of his career in an interview with *Shankly.com* in 1999: "We had to get to Lytham St. Annes to complete the signing so I could play straight away in Liverpool's next match and Shanks drove us both down there. It's only about ten minutes from Bloomfield Road but he was the worst driver in the world. He had this old brown Corsair and just as we left the ground he half went through a set of lights and a woman shunted into the back of us and smashed all the lights in. Next thing, a police car flags us down and the young officer comes up to the car and Shanks winds down the window. 'What is it, officer?' he asked. 'I'm sorry sir you can't continue the journey in that car as you've got no lights', said the policeman. 'Do you know who's in this car?' said Shanks, and I thought he was doing the old, 'Do you know who I am routine'. 'No', said the officer. 'I don't recognise you'. 'No, not me you fool', he said. 'I've got the future captain of England alongside me.'"

Shanks threw Hughes straight into the side and he played 10 First Division games before the end of that 1966/67 season, mostly at left-back. The Kop took him quickly to their hearts and he got the nickname "Crazy Horse" after he rugby-tackled Newcastle's forward Albert Bennett, who was slipping through his grasp, in his fifth game for Liverpool.

Hughes revealed in his autobiography that Shanks had inspired him to do something special in this game: "Shanks took me to one side and said, 'The crowd are looking for a new name to take to. They need a new hero after the Sixties side. They want someone to take over as their own. Go out and give them something to remember you by'." Hughes duly obliged. He took over Willie Stevenson's left-half position in the following season and was not only a hit with the Anfield crowd but also with the girls as he was voted the most attractive Football League player at the end of the 1968/69 season, polling 5,000 more votes than second place, receiving 36,000 votes in total.

Hughes' strong runs from midfield made numerous openings for his colleagues, although he possessed a venomous shot which brought him nearly 50 goals as a Liverpool player. His goal celebrations were usually a sight to behold as he ran the length of the field like a wild man, displaying his great love for the game.

Hughes' Liverpool career started alongside most of the names that had brought the club so much success in the mid-Sixties like Ian St John, Ron Yeats and Roger Hunt but he was never going to be one of the casualties in Shankly's clear-out. Shankly knew what a gem he had found and his was one of the first names on the teamsheet.

One cold afternoon in February 1970, Liverpool were dumped out of the FA Cup at Second Division Watford. "After Watford I knew I had to do my job and change the team," recalled Shankly. "It had to be done and if I didn't do it I was shirking my obligations." Most of the old guard were phased out and in their place came the likes of Ray Clemence, Larry Lloyd, John Toshack, Steve Heighway and Brian Hall, not to mention the inspirational signing of Kevin Keegan from Scunthorpe United.

These newcomers, plus the younger players from the 1960s like Tommy Smith, Chris Lawler, Ian Callaghan and Emlyn Hughes who had survived the post-Watford cull, would be the nucleus for Shankly's next team. Shankly's marquee signing of 1972 was Peter Cormack from Nottingham Forest for a fee of £110,000. Cormack had already attracted Shankly's attention as a 20-year-old Scottish international with Hibernian, possibly under the recommendation of Bill's brother Bob, who managed Cormack while he was on loan at Toronto City in 1967.

He entertained fans with his brilliant tricks on the ball. His experience and creativity added something extra to the Liverpool squad that had narrowly missed out on the League Championship in 1971/72. Cormack's transfer from Nottingham to Liverpool was described by the *Daily Mail* as a lightning deal. Forest secretary

Ken Smales told the newspaper: "Liverpool moved fast. I didn't know anything about the transfer until a few hours before it went through." Cormack had a few weeks of pre-season training behind him at Forest when he arrived at Melwood, mainly consisting of running through the woods. When he told Shankly how he had been preparing for the season, Shankly looked incredulously at him and said: "Snooker champions don't go swimming every day."

During the summer of 1972, Shankly also signed defender Trevor Storton from Tranmere Rovers for £25,000. Storton featured in over 100 games for Rovers from 1968, but only managed to make 12 first team outings for the Reds, before returning to the lower divisions with Chester in July 1974, for whom he made 468 appearances in all competitions until 1984.

On July 20, 1972, Bill Shankly told more than 100 shareholders at Liverpool's annual meeting at Anfield: "We've got the youngest and, incidentally, the smallest playing staff we've ever had with most of them either still in their teens or in their early twenties. We can only get better. Two years ago a lot of men came here, and ripped it to pieces. During that time, the season before last we nearly won the cup and last season we nearly won the league. We didn't lose it at the beginning of the season and we didn't lose it at the end. We lost it in the middle. It is difficult to put your finger on any particular occasion but we suffered injuries to Tommy Smith, Larry Lloyd and Kevin Keegan and were without them for long periods. Any one of those three players, great players, could have won us that extra point."

Before the new season got underway, Shankly also spoke to the *Daily Mirror*'s Colin Dunne: "We have done well, but even now I still think we can do better for the fans. I have lived amongst them. I know what they are like. They worship the team and I want to give them a team they can be proud of. They talk about these young lads breaking a few windows and so on, and say it's football that causes it. But it isn't. Football is a safety valve for these people. There would be far more violence without football, I'm sure of that. I set high standards. We've got a lot of history behind us here. We are a great team by Christ. We've got to have high standards. I want to be able to look around like John L. Sullivan and say I can lick anyone in the world, that's what I want for Liverpool, to conquer everybody! Losing? I hate losing, I don't even like to lose to the wife at cards!"

Twenty-year-old Kevin Keegan exploded into First Division football with Liverpool during the 1971/72 season and promised to become one of the game's superstars. He was a prime example of Bill Shankly's genius, snapped up from unfashionable Scunthorpe United for £35,000, the club where Ray Clemence was also spotted.

The nippy front man had the craft, cheek and strength to become Europe's top player and England captain. Impossible to shackle, 'Mighty Mouse' became a Kop idol due to his almost telepathic partnership with John Toshack. Keegan's vital goals, many of which were headers, despite his lack of height, were paramount to Liverpool's future successes at home and abroad.

Kevin Keegan trained like a man possessed, he played like a man possessed and everyone around him was to become infected by his desire for success. Everybody hated being paired with Kevin in training because his efforts at Melwood were as vivid as they were on match days. Kevin was a pocket dynamo, perhaps not a natural footballer, but he trained hard and deserved all the plaudits he gained.

Winger Steve Heighway assessed his team's strength and depth ahead of the forthcoming season with the *Liverpool Daily Post*: "Like every other player at Anfield, I'm well aware of the competition for first-team places and I've got to play well enough to hold down a spot. But I would like to be credited now as a player who has been a regular, for two seasons and my tally of close on 100 games proves it beyond doubt. It's surprising how swiftly matches come and go. It seems only a short time since I made my debut in a League Cup tie against Mansfield, and that was followed by my league bow against Tottenham at White Hart Lane. Liverpool's team now has a mixture of experience and comparative newcomers, when you consider that Tommy Smith and Chris Lawler have each played in 46 European ties, that Chris is nudging the 450-game mark and that Ian Callaghan has chalked up more than 525 appearances, including 43 in Europe. I referred to comparative newcomers because players such as myself, Brian Hall, Alec Lindsay, Larry Lloyd, Ray Clemence and Kevin Keegan are cracking on with first-team appearances. Perhaps now, the most important thing is that we should steer clear of injuries so that we can keep a settled team. Given that break the rest is up to us and I feel we can be called upon to do something this year."

The squad that kicked off the 1972/73 campaign was one of the strongest the club had had for years. A valuable member of the team was the hardworking and intelligent midfielder Brian Hall, who joined the club as an amateur in 1966. All Hall wanted to do in his teens was to go to Liverpool, but not to play football. He wanted to study at the university and chose Liverpool because he was a Beatles nut! He studied mathematics and graduated three years later with a Bachelor of Science degree. In 1966, aged 19, a friend of his arranged a trial for him at Liverpool and he went along not knowing what to expect. The training staff at Melwood liked what they saw and Hall trained and played as an amateur for three years while he carried out his university course. He eventually made his first-team debut in April 1969 at Stoke City, replacing Roger Hunt, who had picked up a shoulder injury, as a second-half substitute. Hall was an industrious player who always gave his all for Liverpool. He was small in stature but clever and a very efficient footballer.

Hall recalls his 1972/73 pre-season memories: "Although there was great optimism in the camp at the start of the 1972/73 season, it was no different to any other season. That was very much the nature of Bill Shankly. He inspired confidence into the lads with ease. If he told us once, he told us a thousand times, that we were the greatest. It gave us a tremendous self-belief and I don't remember one time when we ran out with doubts that we wouldn't win."

On August 12, the opening round of fixtures got underway and the Reds were trying to preserve a nine-year record of not having lost their first game of the season. In that time they had recorded eight wins and a draw. Blackpool were the last team to inflict an opening-match defeat upon them, back in 1962 at Anfield, and when Championship dark horses Manchester City made the short journey, they hoped to follow suit.

Before kick-off, Kevin Keegan was given a tremendous welcome as he received last season's Young Player of the Year Award from the Liverpool chairman, Mr. Eric Roberts, and Football League secretary, Mr. Alan Hardaker. In an eventful first half, Brian Hall gave the Reds a third-minute lead when his strike beat Manchester City's goalkeeper Joe Corrigan from the edge of the area and just before the interval, Larry Lloyd and Wyn Davies received their marching orders for fighting. Six minutes from the end, the consistent Ian Callaghan added a second.

Shankly wasn't happy with his defender's sending off as it was clearly Davies who was the culprit by simply head-butting Lloyd. Consequently, Liverpool became the first team to fight a three-match ban of a player before the newly-formed independent disciplinary tribunal and won. Lloyd told the *Liverpool Echo*: "I was pushed in the back and went down. The whistle went for a free-kick to us and as I got up and went to turn away. I was only a foot from Davies and he butted me on the nose."

The incident was recorded by the Match of the Day cameras and after Lloyd's initial appeal was dismissed by an FA Disciplinary Commission a month later, Shankly used the footage to help clear the defender's name and said: "I would not have allowed the appeal to go this far if I had not been convinced Larry was innocent."

Three days later, the Reds played host to Manchester United but they too suffered the same fate as City. Frank O'Farrell's team were beaten 2-0 in front of 54,779 fans thanks to an impressive performance from Welsh striker John Toshack. Six-footer 'Tosh' had joined Liverpool from Cardiff City for a club record of £110,000 and became the perfect foil for Kevin Keegan. "Welcome to Liverpool son, you have come from Sunday school into church," were Bill Shankly's words to Toshack when he greeted him at Lime Street Station on November 11, 1970.

His tremendous heading ability not only provided an abundance of ammunition for strike partner, Keegan, to fire, it also earned him his own respect as a lethal goalscorer. 'TOSHACK RECLAIMS ANFIELD CROWN' was how the *Liverpool Echo* headline described his display. In the 12th minute, the tall striker strode on to Callaghan's pass to beat Alex Stepney comprehensively, and seven minutes later, after slipping Martin Buchan superbly down the right, he laid on the second goal for Steve Heighway. The *Liverpool Echo* wrote: "This was a Toshack the Kop had never seen before. He was hungry for the ball and anxious to come back and win it in midfield, careful to distribute it in the most constructive manner possible, and always there in the penalty area looking to add the finishing touch."

Kevin Keegan later paid tribute to 'Tosh' and the partnership that brought Liverpool an abundance of success in front of goal for much of the 1970s: "John Toshack was a wonderful player to play alongside. His aerial ability was fantastic and I always knew that he was going to win the high balls. From then on it was just a question of me reading which way the ball was going to go and from those situations we created many chances. I always admired Tosh's honesty as a player. He was a nice approachable lad and he did a really great job for the club during his time here."

Liverpool's victory against Manchester United was a joyful occasion in more ways than one. Ian Callaghan, now aged 30, broke Billy Liddell's appearance record, playing his 535th game for the club. Liverpool-born 'Cally' joined the Reds for a £10 fee and became Anfield's greatest servant. He was applauded off the field by his teammates when he made his debut in the 1959/60 campaign.

Steve Heighway paid tribute to Callaghan: "He's never played better since I joined the club and I'm convinced he'll go on for at least three or four seasons yet. Cally is small, but he's well built. He's very fit, and has tremendous energy. And he's by no means at the veteran stage even though he's packed so much experience into his career. Take it from me, he's one of those players whose presence in the team is invaluable – he's like Chris Lawler and Tommy Smith. These lads have been more or less permanent fixtures at Anfield and they have developed a tremendous relationship with everyone."

Liverpool played six league fixtures in August 1972, losing only the last one, 3-2 at Leicester City. On September 2, the Reds travelled to the Baseball Ground for a crunch match against reigning champions Derby. Goalkeeper Ray Clemence was forced to miss the clash with a thigh injury so Frank Lane, a £20,000 purchase from Tranmere Rovers 12 months previously, stepped in for what was to be his only First Division outing for the Reds. The game at Derby also marked the league debut of summer signing Peter Cormack, who replaced Brian Hall in midfield and it was also Bill Shankly's 59th birthday. Toshack opened the scoring for Liverpool in the 16th minute, after Keegan had again done the spadework, but Lane, who otherwise had a good debut, carried Alan Hinton's cross over his own goalline and the Rams were level. A John O'Hare strike later helped Derby to the win.

On September 16, one of the most bizarre incidents of the 1972/73 season occurred. An injury to linesman Dennis Drewitt during Liverpool's clash at Highbury resulted in former footballer-turned-TV pundit Jimmy Hill taking over with the flag in a sky blue tracksuit. A PA announcement had been put out for any qualified referees in the crowd, which Hill was, and stepped forward so the game could continue. Shankly and Arsenal manager, Bertie Mee, seemed to find the whole thing rather amusing. The match finished 0-0 and Shankly commented: "He was the best linesman I have ever seen."

By the time Sheffield United came to Anfield on September 23, Liverpool, along with Wolverhampton Wanderers, were the only First Division sides with a 100 per cent home league record. However, Toshack was missing, the legacy of a knee injury sustained four days earlier against Carlisle United in a League Cup replay. Curly-haired Phil Boersma had replaced him in that match and scored twice in a 5-1 victory, and the Kirkby youngster was given the chance to shine from the start against the Blades. Again he showed his scoring prowess by setting the Reds on their way to a 5-0 romp with a superb 28th-minute goal. Others followed from Lindsay, Heighway, Cormack and Keegan (penalty). It was a result which put the Anfield club top of the table from Tottenham Hotspur on goal average and prompted the Saturday *Liverpool Echo* headline: '(SHEF)

FIELD DAY FOR LIVERPOOL'. Monday's *Liverpool Echo* report elaborated slightly: "Liverpool didn't just beat Sheffield United 5-0, they annihilated them."

The following week Elland Road was the venue for another crucial league confrontation. Leeds United had lost 3-2 at Newcastle seven days earlier, and so were one point adrift of the Reds before the start of play. Liverpool drew a 46,000 crowd but had to make do without the services of injured skipper Tommy Smith. An uncompromising, powerful defender, the Anfield hard-man was never short of fight or determination, ever since he signed professional forms on his 17th birthday. He epitomised all that manager Bill Shankly stood for, and his efforts had been rewarded the previous year with his first and only full cap for England. The absence of Smith at Leeds gave Trevor Storton his debut in a defence which started nervously and lacked composure. Mick Jones' spectacular overhead kick put United ahead on the half-hour but Larry Lloyd and Phil Boersma replied to claim two valuable points. Final score: Leeds United 1-2 Liverpool.

Liverpool's next match was the first of two thrilling Merseyside derbies. Shankly kept an unchanged side for the Anfield occasion against an Everton team which had made a good start to the season, even topping the table early on. Almost 56,000 people packed the ground to see Peter Cormack score the only goal on his derby debut with a flying header in the 77th minute from Steve Heighway's cross. It was a match played at a frantic pace which the Blues could count themselves unlucky to lose. The result, however, did the Reds a power of good, increasing their unbeaten run to 10 games in all competitions. Liverpool received Stoke City on October 21, which turned out to be Gordon Banks' last appearance in competitive football and his 11th domestic game at Anfield. The following day, Banks was returning home from the Victoria Ground having received treatment as a consequence of the Liverpool game when he was involved in a traffic accident that resulted in him losing the sight in his right eye.

Although Liverpool picked up maximum points beating the Potters 2-1 and remained league leaders, captain Tommy Smith apologised to the fans at Anfield for the team's performance. Smith told the press: "I'm sorry if all of you who turned up at Anfield on Saturday were a bit let down. When you get a side like us steaming away at the top and a team of Stoke's skills banging them in away from home, you expect action all the way. Well, we tried our hardest, but what can you do when the opposition pull all their players back in defence at the slightest hint of pressure?"

On October 28, Liverpool drew 1-1 against Ron Saunders' Norwich City. Although the likes of Derby, Arsenal and Spurs were all beaten at Carrow Road, the point Liverpool got was not much satisfaction to them. For the result was more a point thrown away than a point held. After featuring as a substitute on two occasions, Phil Thompson made his first start for his boyhood team that Saturday afternoon in Norwich, replacing the injured Emlyn Hughes in Liverpool's midfield.

This debut was described in the *Liverpool Echo*: "Phil Thompson thoroughly justified Mr. Shankly's confidence in him, contributing considerably to Liverpool's midfield dominance with a lot of intelligent work. He did the simple things well without trying to be spectacular and over-reach the limits of his experience."

Thompson was born in Ling Street, Kensington (L7), but when he was a toddler, he moved out of inner-city Liverpool to Kirkby with his family. After making his full first-team debut, 'Thommo', spoke to the *Liverpool Echo*: "Whatever the future holds for me I don't think

I'll ever be as thrilled as I was at ten past two on Saturday. We were in the dressing room at Carrow Road when Mr. Shankly came over to me and took me outside into the corridor. He said to me: 'Do you want to play for Liverpool, son?' I took a breath and said: 'Oh, yes please. I love this club and it would make me feel really proud.' The boss replied: 'All right, Phil, you go out there and play.' I could hardly believe it was true. I'd made two appearances as a substitute before against Manchester United at Old Trafford last season and against AEK Athens at Anfield last week but this was something quite different.

"To play in a red shirt for a full game is a great feeling and it's not really registered with me yet. I've been a Liverpool fan all my life. When I was a kid I used to write all the names of the Liverpool players in coal on the walls of the coal shed at my mum's house in Kirkby. My mother, my two brothers and my four sisters are all Liverpudlians as well. My father's the only exception. He's an Evertonian but that's not made any difference at all. He feels as proud as I do. The whole family is over the moon. My elder brother Owen, who's 20, two years older than me, wanted to be a footballer as well but he had to give it up because of a chest complaint. Ever since then he's been right behind me in my career. When he found out I'd played at Norwich he was overjoyed. Liverpool are a great club. There's never been any other for me. When I was in the reserves I used to stand in the Kop and watch the first team. All these thoughts were running through my mind as we waited for kick-off plus the fact that I had the task of stepping in for Emlyn. But then the great team spirit of Liverpool shone through. My teammate, John McLaughlin, obviously disappointed that he hadn't been chosen, came to me and said: 'Congratulations Phil, and the best of luck, go out there and show them!' As the game wore on I almost forgot it was in my full senior game and I grew more confident all the time. But something that did stick in my mind were some words of advice our trainer Joe Fagan once gave me. It was when Joe was in charge of the reserve team and I made my debut in a Central League game against Sheffield Wednesday at Hillsborough. That game remains a nightmare. Nothing seemed to go right for me and although we got a draw, I came off the field feeling very dejected. It was then that Joe had a little talk with me. He told me to remember to go forward whenever possible and not to put too many balls back. I've never forgotten that and I think it came very useful at Norwich. I tried to give forward passes whenever possible and I also managed to get in a couple of shots at the Norwich goal. I realise that if Emlyn is fit he'll play against Leeds in the League Cup tomorrow night, but what I've got to do now is put Saturday's game behind me and concentrate on the future because to be quite honest I'm still walking on air."

High-flying Chelsea travelled to Anfield on November 4 and became Liverpool's first double victims of the season, having gone down 2-1 at Stamford Bridge in August.

That result moved the Reds three points ahead of second-placed Arsenal with a game in hand, as the Gunners crashed 2-0 at home to Coventry City.

John Toshack and Kevin Keegan took most of the credit for Liverpool's 3-1 win, the Welshman in his first match back from injury scoring the opener from Keegan's pass in the 34th minute. On the hour, Toshack's flighted centre returned the compliment, and five minutes later, the striker got his second from Steve Heighway's cross.

Seven days later, Liverpool suffered their first league defeat since September 2 at the Baseball Ground, when they lost 2-0 to bottom-of-the-table Manchester United at Old Trafford. It was their first reversal in 18 fixtures, covering all competitions, and made even more surprising by coming straight after a morale-boosting 3-1 UEFA Cup success away to AEK Athens.

The Reds claimed they were denied a first-half penalty when Steve Heighway appeared to be fouled by Alex Stepney, and that the linesman had flagged an instant before Wyn Davies opened the scoring on the stroke of half-time. Ted MacDougal put the result beyond doubt after the interval.

There then followed three successive league victories with Newcastle, Tottenham and Birmingham being the victims. The Reds fought back from being 3-1 down to beat Birmingham 4-3 at Anfield and increased their lead at the top to three points.

Alec Lindsay was the scorer of two of the four Liverpool goals at Anfield that afternoon. Lindsay was signed by Liverpool from his hometown club Bury in March 1969 when he was 21. Bill Shankly gave him his first-team debut in a 10-0 Fairs Cup thrashing of Dundalk in September that year but he didn't taste any First Division action until the middle of October when he came off the bench to strike an equaliser against Ipswich Town at Portman Road. That would be one of just six league matches he figured in that debut season as he was tried all over the forward line.

Shankly was left questioning whether he had bought the right player and told him: "Listen son. I want you to take men on, go past them and lash in those shots that brought you the goals when you were playing at Gigg Lane." "But that wasn't me boss, that was Jim Kerr," protested Lindsay. "Jesus Christ, Bob," said Shankly to Paisley. "We've signed the wrong bloody player."

Lindsay was frustrated with life at Liverpool and handed in a transfer request which was accepted, but his Liverpool career then changed unexpectedly for the better. Lindsay had been a half-back before arriving at Liverpool and Shankly moved the naturally right-footed player to left-back against Newcastle on September 12, 1970, after previously experimenting with Ian Ross and Roy Evans in that position.

Despite lacking pace, this decision launched his Liverpool career. Shankly was happy: "The lad looked as if he had been playing at left-back all his life. He places passes up the touchline with tremendous accuracy." Liverpool had moved Lindsay further back but he still put his attacking skills to good use. He was clever at overlapping the defence on the left flank. He always chipped in with a couple of goals himself, possessing a powerful left foot.

On December 6, Spurs got their revenge on the Reds for their previous defeat by beating Liverpool 3-1 at White Hart Lane in a League Cup quarter-final replay. Shankly said after the match: "Frankly I wouldn't have minded if we'd lost for the sake of the players. The more games they play, the more likely they are to get injured."

Shankly's side hit a rich vein of form, ending the year unbeaten in the league since the Old Trafford setback on November 11. On December 30, Liverpool's last game of 1972 and 39th game of the season, Liverpool beat Bert Head's Crystal Palace 1-0 at Anfield. Shankly's team set a new record in top-flight football of 21 consecutive home league wins.

Local scribe Alan Pinch wrote in the *Liverpool Daily Post*: "Peter Cormack's 66th-minute winner was a long time coming, but when it finally arrived it immediately gained a nomination for the BBC TV's Goal of the Month competition and rightly, too. Liverpool marched confidently into the New Year with an impressive three-point lead at the top of the First Division table, and in view of their astonishing home record the rest of League must begin to ask: who can stop their drive to the championship?"

On Boxing Day, Liverpool visited Bramall Lane, and returned from Sheffield with two points, after beating the Blades 3-0 in what would turn out to be their biggest away win of the season.

During the final weeks of 1972 Liverpool were without their commanding captain Tommy Smith as he was hospitalised with broken ribs due to a car crash. He made his return to action during the first game of 1973, against West Ham at Upton Park, which the Reds won 1-0. During Smith's 10-game absence Emlyn Hughes took over as team captain.

Despite Smith's return to action, 1973 started with hiccups for Liverpool as they took just two points from four outings between January 20 and February 17. On January 20, Liverpool failed to extend their consecutive home league record to 22 victories as the Reds drew 1-1 against Brian Clough's Derby.

The following Saturday, Liverpool were hoping to bounce back at Molineux, but were defeated 2-1 by Wolves, a defeat which was followed by elimination from the FA Cup in a fourth round replay against Manchester City at Maine Road. Shankly's team had just won one game in their last five outings and results weren't to improve.

Three days later on February 10, Liverpool received Bertie Mee's Arsenal, who were just one point behind the Reds in second place. An Alan Ball penalty and a well-taken John Radford goal gave the visitors a 2-0 victory and the Gunners took over from Liverpool as league leaders. It was the Reds' first home defeat in all competitions since January 1 of the previous year against Leeds, a run of 32 games. After the game, Shankly said: "From now on, the first team won't be reporting to training until Wednesdays, the players who have led the First Division since September have not suddenly lost their skills, they have just run themselves out. They have played 47 competitive games and not surprisingly they lost their competitive edge."

Tommy Smith, who played up front alongside Billy Liddell when he first started out with the reserves and played his first five games of the 1964/65 season as a forward, scoring two goals, was now in his ninth season as a first-team regular. In February 1973, Smith, who had now fully recovered from his car crash caught up with *Football Monthly*: "They say I'm the hardest man in football but there's no truth in the rumour that my studs are screwed straight into my feet. They couldn't penetrate my skin anyway! But seriously, I'm proud of my reputation as a tough guy. That's the way I like to play the game, hard but always fair, 50-50 tackling and no other nonsense. Since I was a youngster I've had to live with this rough and tough image! Let me say right now that I have never deliberately set out to injure a player, that's not me at all. I'd pack up the game altogether if that ever happened. It's a man's game but I want no part of anything vicious. My reputation seems to worry a lot of players and when they are more conscious of you than the actual game itself, they cannot be doing their jobs properly. Perhaps I'm being a little conceited when I say that some strikers don't want to know when I'm around. That's their fault, I never shy away from a tackle and when I go in I give it everything I've got. My job is to win the ball and I reckon I'm fairly useful at doing just that.

"Bill Shankly has done a marvellous job in re-fashioning the team so quickly after the club's brilliant success of the Sixties. He is such a fabulous character, when you live and work with someone like Shanks you tend to accept his humour as part of the normal way of life at Anfield! He is famous for standing by our dressing-room door when the opposition turn up and as they walk in he'll turn around and state in all seriousness: 'Na trouble lads, they all look as if they've had a few pints on the way here. And that centre-back! He looks as if he's been up all night.' However, what does get his back up is when we are trailing at Anfield. He'll walk into the dressing room at half-time with a grim face and pound the floor for a while. Then he starts: 'There are 50,000 fans out there and 49,500 are for you. You've let them all down. We can't let it happen to these people.' That's Shanks, despite his Scottish ancestry he is a Scouser through and through. The lads on the terraces are his people. They're the only ones he really wants to know. All this does not disguise his real abilities as a manager. You don't need me to remind you just what he has achieved in his years at Anfield. What the lads respect most is his tremendous enthusiasm which continuously inspires us. He is as fit and raring to go as ever and still puts a few of us in our place during training. Above all, he has the knack of being able to turn little-known players into world-beaters; hence his shrewdness in the transfer market, which is reflected in the likes of Kevin Keegan, Steve Heighway, Ray Clemence and Larry Lloyd who were all picked up at bargain prices.

"I was born in the famous Scotland Road district of Liverpool so it was only natural that I should be a devoted Reds fan as a youngster. But it was only the unfortunate death of my father when I was 15 that prompted me into becoming a professional footballer. Would you believe that I wanted to become an architect? I was attending college and receiving a grant of £52 a year to help in my studies when my father caught pneumonia and died. It meant that I had to become the bread-winner for the family and Liverpool's £8-a-week offer to join the ground staff was an opportunity that couldn't be turned down. Even now I can remember the day my mother took me along to Anfield and asked Mr. Shankly to take care of me. I have never regretted the decision for soccer has enabled me to see the world and provided some outstanding experiences."

By February 24, 1973, the day Ipswich Town travelled to Anfield, the title race was really hotting up. Arsenal's 1-0 beating of Leicester City shot them to first place, two points ahead of Liverpool, who had a game in hand. Leeds were four points behind the leaders, having played two matches fewer and Ipswich, who also had two games in hand, were six points adrift. February 24 was also the day Arsenal were involved in FA Cup action, giving Liverpool a great chance to go above them on goal average. Steve Heighway opened the scoring in the 67th minute only for former Everton and future Reds striker David Johnson to equalise soon afterwards. But 10 minutes from time, a pinpoint centre from Phil Boersma was controlled by Kevin Keegan on his chest and as the ball dropped, he hammered it into the bottom corner of the net for the winner. It was a most important result for Liverpool even if they had failed to impress.

Their next match, despite the now dangerously low position of their opponents, was sure to be another stiff test. It was the Goodison derby in front of 54,269 spectators on March 3, and it was a cracker.

With action at both ends, the deadlock was finally broken in the 80th minute when Emlyn Hughes scored a brilliant goal. Bringing the ball out of defence, he slipped it to Ian Callaghan, while continuing his run forward. The winger's through pass was glorious, and Hughes rounded goalkeeper David Lawson before firing a low right-foot shot into the net.

Hughes, labelled "the best all-round player in English football today" by The *Liverpool Echo's* Michael Charters, had a storming game and his day was not over. Eight minutes later, after Lawson had punched out Alec Lindsay's cross, he caught the ball beautifully on the volley to increase the lead and secure a 2-0 victory. 'EMLYN RAPS OUT A TITLE WARNING... BUT WHAT LIES AHEAD FOR THE BLUES?' was how the *Liverpool Echo* headline spelled out the significance of the derby.

The Reds, having played a match less than Arsenal, joined the Gunners at the top of the table, but battling Everton had slipped to only three points off a relegation place.

Liverpool went on to win their next three league fixtures against Southampton, Stoke City and Norwich City but on April 7, while Arsenal were losing to Second Division Sunderland in the FA Cup semi-final, the Reds crashed 2-1 at lowly Birmingham City, where Hughes was sent off. Local scribe Roger Kelly wrote: "On December 11, 1954, Liverpool suffered their record 9-1 defeat at St. Andrew's, so perhaps Saturday's events didn't come as a surprise. Emlyn Hughes sent off, a disputed goal, arguments, a vehement penalty appeal, brawls and the bitter pill of defeat to swallow – all make Birmingham a very unwelcome name around Anfield, anyone might be forgiven for thinking.

"Fred Goodwin had hired his own voodoo man to put a hex on Liverpool. Sir Alf Ramsey was in the stands to watch his English international Hughes ordered off in injury time after a conflagration with Trevor Francis. Hughes and Francis were chasing upfield when the Liverpool player caught the Birmingham forward with an elbow in the face. Was it accidental? Tommy Smith clearly thought so and told the referee all the way down the players' tunnel when the final whistle blew. In my opinion it was the antics of Francis, a brilliant player who can electrify a crowd without the need for gamesmanship, which hastened Hughes' departure. He collapsed in a seemingly unnecessary heap clutching his face which was later seen to be unmarked."

Hughes appealed the sending off and was later cleared of punishment by the Disciplinary Committee.

The league was looking like a two-horse race, with Liverpool lying one point ahead of Arsenal after 37 games. The following week, a

Kevin Keegan penalty at home to West Bromwich Albion increased the Anfield club's lead over Arsenal as the Gunners could only draw with local rivals Tottenham, at Highbury.

A Howard Kendall penalty against Chelsea ensured Everton's First Division survival on April 17, and on the same night Phil Boersma struck twice at Highfield Road to earn Liverpool, playing their 60th match of the season, a 2-1 win against Coventry City.

It took his season tally to 13 from 27 outings in all competitions, hence the *Liverpool Echo* headline: 'BOERSMA IS TOAST OF MERSEYSIDE'. The newspaper reported: "Last night's display was Liverpool at their mean, disciplined and powerful best away from home." What it meant was that if Everton beat Arsenal four days later, and the Reds won at Newcastle, the title race was virtually over. But Alan Ball, making his first appearance at Goodison since his record breaking £220,000 transfer in 1971, helped his team to a goalless draw.

To make matters worse for Liverpool, a brace from John Tudor cancelled out Kevin Keegan's opener at St. James' Park, as the Geordies claimed both points. By thumping Crystal Palace 4-0 at Elland Road, Leeds had re-entered the Championship battle, with the top three positions thus: Liverpool 57 points from 40 games; Arsenal 54 points from 39 and Leeds 51 points from 38.

Don Revie's men, who were a team the Reds respected, came to Anfield for a title showdown just 48 hours after their Palace victory and gates were locked more than an hour before kick-off. The clash received worldwide press coverage, even as far away as Japan, and it was broadcast live on West German radio. More than 55,000 fans turned up, too, and most went home happy after watching Liverpool almost claim the First Division crown with a 2-0 triumph.

In the 47th minute, following a corner on the right, teenager Phil

Thompson played the ball forward for Larry Lloyd to knock on. Chris Lawler brought it down on his thigh and kicked it over his head for Kevin Keegan, rising above taller men, to head on and Peter Cormack's left foot did the rest.

Keegan got on the scoresheet himself five minutes from time, and the *Liverpool Echo* was already acclaiming the title. 'SUPER REDS TOP THE LOT!' read the headline and their scribe Chris James wrote: "Only freak results, which are best left to the mathematicians and computers, can stop Liverpool winning the Championship now. And in the eyes of the entire football world both at home and abroad they are the new Champions." Keegan was the hero, making one goal, scoring another, and he paid tribute to the fans: "They're the people we do it for. They're the people who make it all worthwhile."

It was Bill Shankly's third top-flight League Championship success. Although the Reds could still mathematically be caught by Arsenal and the champagne remained on ice, the legendary Scot still allowed himself words of reflective praise: "The players have done an incredible job considering the number of matches they've had to play, I think we can call ourselves champions now. I'm delighted for the players, for the club, and especially for the fans, who have again proved themselves the greatest in the world."

For Shankly, though, football wasn't just about players, it was about supporters too and he had a special relationship with Liverpudlians. "They excelled themselves, they really did," Shankly added. "They really gave the lads all the encouragement they needed. It was only Liverpool that mattered to them, the club and the colour of the jersey. Who was wearing the jerseys didn't matter. It was Liverpool they were cheering. There were fantastic scenes at the end. I've never seen such a sea of colour."

Two days after the Leeds game, the Reds went down 2-1 at Tottenham in the UEFA Cup semi-final, second leg, but qualified for the final on away goals. Shankly said: "For both teams to give that sort of display after each playing more than 60 games this season was unbelievable. It was a fantastic game and so close, but we are obviously glad to be in the final and will now go for the double."

There was even more joy for Shankly and his side on Saturday, April 28, when they wound up their league programme with a goalless draw against Leicester City at Anfield, taking the necessary point to secure the title. Liverpool finished on 60 points with nearest challengers Arsenal lying on 57, but with only one match remaining. 'TITLE TANGO AS THE FANS PAY HOMAGE' was how the *Liverpool Echo* headline described the scenes at Anfield, as the iced champagne was finally cracked open.

"Champions, Champions", "Ee-aye-addio, we've won the league", and "You'll Never Walk Alone" chanted most of the 56,000 crowd when Tommy Smith collected the trophy and went on a lap of honour with his teammates. Banners and flags were waved and Shankly answered the calls of the fans to join the jubilant squad on the pitch.

Because of their success, Liverpool could not afford too many celebrations. After all, they had a UEFA Cup final looming with the opposition none other than West German side Borussia Moenchengladbach. During the first leg at Anfield torrential rain turned the pitch into a pond and Austrian referee Erich Linemayr had no alternative but to lead the players off after a goalless 27 minutes. He suspended the action for 20 minutes pending a pitch inspection and then finally abandoned the game as the rain continued to lash down. Liverpool and Borussia officials immediately agreed on a return match for the following night, rain gods permitting. The game went ahead and two goals from Kevin Keegan, and one from Larry Lloyd, gave the Reds a 3-0 lead to take to Germany. Thirteen days later, Liverpool suffered in the return, conceding two goals by half-time. However, showing true grit they held on for a 2-0 defeat, a result which brought them an aggregate victory and their first European trophy in an unforgettable season.

But their conquest of the Continent had only just begun.

Tommy Smith recalls Liverpool's first European honour: "We'd gone close before in 1965 when a dodgy referee cost us a place in the final of the European Cup and then the following year we got beat in the Cup Winners' Cup final. Shanks was delighted to get his hands on a European trophy and there's no doubt we deserved it. The UEFA Cup was always regarded as the lesser of the three European competitions but it was the hardest of them all to win. There was an extra round for starters, and the two-legged final didn't make it any easier. You'd also come up against emerging clubs who were on the verge of great things, like Monchengladbach for example. In the first leg at Anfield, the ground was so hard the water wouldn't drain away. It was like trying to play football in a pool. The ref called the game off but Shanks had seen enough in that time to change his tactics for the following night. I think someone was looking down on us that night. We were struggling without the big man Toshack up front and the rain proved to be a blessing in disguise. In the second leg the boss told us to contain them and hit them on the break. It was an aerial battle and it was up to me as captain to organise us so we conceded no further goals. Joe Fagan said afterwards that it was the best game I'd ever played for Liverpool as skipper. I never realised how big the cup was. It had a big stone base and weighed a ton. I remember on the lap of honour some big fat guy jumped on my back and I nearly collapsed. After such a gruelling match I was absolutely knackered. I eventually made it to the dressing room and

I said to Shanks, 'Here you are boss, the cup's yours'. I handed it to him, but I don't think he realised how heavy it was either. He nearly dropped it."

On May 25, 1973 over a quarter of a million people lined the streets to celebrate the most momentous season in the history of Liverpool Football Club.

Shankly and his players were joined by Toxteth-born and reigning British light-heavyweight boxing champion John Conteh, on an open-top bus victory parade of the city. Three trophies were paraded to the fans: the League Championship, which was won for a record-equalling eighth time, the UEFA Cup and the Central League title, won by Ronnie Moran's reserve side for the fourth time in five years. But it was the big one in the middle, the UEFA Cup that attracted the most attention. It meant that Liverpool had finally arrived in Europe. To Bill Shankly, UEFA Cup success meant so much. The title win may have been the bread and butter, but glory in Europe was the realisation of a long-held ambition and the culmination of eight consecutive seasons of continental action, a feat no other English club could boast.

Liverpool's energetic powerhouse Emlyn Hughes reflected on the Reds' monumental season with *Football Monthly*: "We came through in the end because everyone was prepared to run until they dropped. That's how much it meant to us. It was the culmination of two years' bloody hard slog. The boss has drummed into us the need to do things collectively, as one compact unit, and that's why Liverpool will never have to rely on one individual to do the work for us.

"Then there's Shanks who never lets you forget what a privilege it is to be at Anfield! You get the feeling that he'll gladly swap positions for the chance to score in front of the Kop. When we practically clinched the league by beating Leeds 2-0 at Anfield on Easter

Monday he was near to tears. It's typical of the man that. When he walked on to the field to salute the Kop, he took off his jacket to reveal a red shirt. They lapped it up. He's really a Scouser through and through. He played an important part in that victory. Before the game we were sitting down in the dressing room and hardly a word was spoken because we were so nervous. It was a match we had to win. Then Shanks arrived with half-an-hour to go. 'Nothing to worry about today,' he said casually. 'I've just seen the Leeds boys. They look white with fright'. Incredible isn't he?"

After the misfortunes of the 1970/71 and 1971/72 seasons, many fans often look back and question; had Liverpool not achieved what they did during the 1972/73 season, would the many successes of later years have happened?

Only 17 players were involved in the 66 games of this historic season with one of them only appearing once for a 15-minute substitute appearance (Jack Whitham) and another (reserve goalkeeper Frank Lane) only playing twice when first-choice Ray Clemence was injured. A gruelling schedule for which manager Bill Shankly had to shuffle the pack without having the advantage of selecting his team from the massive squads of today's game.

Shankly was immensely proud of the "young men who played like veterans". He also had to cope with the intransigence of the football authorities as his team closed in on its double target. Both the Football League and the Football Association had been decidedly lukewarm about English clubs participating in European competitions, despite the reflected glory they could bask in should an English club be successful in winning one of the three cups.

1972/73: Facts and Statistics

Final league table

		P	W	D	L	F	A	W	D	L	F	A	PTS
1	Liverpool FC	42	17	3	1	45	19	8	7	6	27	23	60
2	Arsenal	42	14	5	2	31	14	9	6	6	26	29	57
3	Leeds United	42	15	4	2	45	13	6	7	8	26	32	53
4	Ipswich Town	42	10	7	4	34	20	7	7	7	21	25	48
5	Wolves	42	13	3	5	43	23	5	8	8	23	31	47
6	West Ham United	42	12	5	4	45	25	5	7	9	22	28	46
7	Derby	42	15	3	3	43	18	4	5	12	13	36	46
8	Tottenham	42	10	5	6	33	23	6	8	7	25	25	45
9	Newcastle United	42	12	6	3	35	19	4	7	10	25	32	45
10	Birmingham City	42	11	7	3	39	22	4	5	12	14	32	42
11	Manchester City	42	12	4	5	36	20	3	7	11	21	40	41
12	Chelsea	42	9	6	6	30	22	4	8	9	19	29	40
13	Southampton	42	8	11	2	26	17	3	7	11	21	35	40
14	Sheffield United	42	11	4	6	28	18	4	6	11	23	41	40
15	Stoke City	42	11	8	2	38	17	3	2	16	23	39	38
16	Leicester City	42	7	9	5	23	18	3	8	10	17	28	37
17	Everton	42	9	5	7	27	21	4	6	11	14	28	37
18	Manchester United	42	9	7	5	24	19	3	6	12	20	41	37
19	Coventry City	42	9	5	7	27	24	4	4	13	13	31	35
20	Norwich City	42	7	9	5	22	19	4	1	16	14	44	32
21	Crystal Palace	42	7	7	7	25	21	2	5	14	16	37	30
22	WBA	42	8	7	6	25	24	1	3	17	13	38	28

Games for the 1972/1973 season

(The number after date is league position after the game)

1	12.08.1972	1	W	2-0	Manchester City, Anfield, 1st Division
2	15.08.1972	1	W	2-0	Manchester United, Anfield, 1st Division
3	19.08.1972	2	D	1-1	Crystal Palace, Selhurst Park, 1st Division
4	23.08.1972	1	W	2-1	Chelsea, Stamford Bridge, 1st Division
5	26.08.1972	1	W	3-2	West Ham United, Anfield, 1st Division
6	30.08.1972	4	L	2-3	Leicester City, Filbert Street, 1st Division
7	02.09.1972	6	L	1-2	Derby County, Baseball Ground, 1st Division
8	05.09.1972		D	1-1	Carlisle United, Brunton Park, League Cup 2nd round
9	09.09.1972	4	W	4-2	Wolves, Anfield, 1st Division

10	12.09.1972		W	2-0	Eintracht Frankfurt, Anfield,
					UEFA Cup 1st round 1L
11	16.09.1972	5	D	0-0	Arsenal, Highbury, 1st Division
12	19.09.1972		W	5-1	Carlisle United, Anfield,
					League Cup 2nd round replay
13	23.09.1972	1	W	5-0	Sheffield United, Anfield, 1st Division
14	26.09.1972		D	0-0	Eintracht Frankfurt, Waldstadion,
					UEFA Cup 1st round 2L
15	30.09.1972	1	W	2-1	Leeds United, Elland Road, 1st Division
16	03.10.1972		D	1-1	West Bromwich Albion, The Hawthorns,
					League Cup 3rd round
17	07.10.1972	1	W	1-0	Everton, Anfield, 1st Division
18	10.10.1972		W	2-1	West Bromwich Albion, Anfield,
					League Cup 3rd round replay
19	14.10.1972	1	D	1-1	Southampton, The Dell, 1st Division
20	21.10.1972	1	W	2-1	Stoke City, Anfield, 1st Division
21	24.10.1972		W	3-0	AEK Athens, Anfield, UEFA Cup 2nd round 1L
22	28.10.1972	1	D	1-1	Norwich City, Carrow Road, 1st Division
23	31.10.1972		D	2-2	Leeds United, Anfield, League Cup 4th round
24	04.11.1972	1	W	3-1	Chelsea, Anfield, 1st Division
25	07.11.1972		W	3-1	AEK Athens, Nikos Goumas Stadium,
					UEFA Cup 2nd round 2L
26	11.11.1972	1	L	0-2	Manchester United, Old Trafford, 1st Division
27	18.11.1972	1	W	3-2	Newcastle United, Anfield, 1st Division
28	22.11.1972		W	1-0	Leeds United, Elland Road,
					League Cup 4th round R
29	25.11.1972	1	W	2-1	Tottenham Hotspur, White Hart Lane,
					1st Division
30	29.11.1972		D	0-0	Dynamo Berlin, Sportforum,
					UEFA Cup 3rd round 1L
31	02.12.1972	1	W	4-3	Birmingham City, Anfield, 1st Division
32	04.12.1972		D	1-1	Tottenham Hotspur, Anfield,
					League Cup 5th round
33	06.12.1972		L	1-3	Tottenham Hotspur, White Hart Lane,
					League Cup 5th round R
34	09.12.1972	1	D	1-1	West Bromwich Albion, The Hawthorns,
					1st Division
35	13.12.1972		W	3-1	Dynamo Berlin, Anfield,
					UEFA Cup 3rd round 2L
36	16.12.1972	1	D	1-1	Ipswich Town, Portman Road, 1st Division
37	23.12.1972	1	W	2-0	Coventry City, Anfield, 1st Division
38	26.12.1972	1	W	3-0	Sheffield United, Bramall Lane, 1st Division
39	30.12.1972	1	W	1-0	Crystal Palace, Anfield, 1st Division
40	06.01.1973	1	W	1-0	West Ham United, Upton Park, 1st Division

41	13.01.1973		D	0-0	Burnley, Turf Moor, FA Cup 3rd round
42	16.01.1973		W	3-0	Burnley, Anfield, FA Cup 3rd round replay
43	20.01.1973	1	D	1-1	Derby County, Anfield, 1st Division
44	27.01.1973	1	L	1-2	Wolves, Molineux, 1st Division
45	03.02.1973		D	0-0	Manchester City, Anfield, FA Cup 4th round
46	07.02.1973		L	0-2	Manchester City, Maine Road, FA Cup 4th round replay
47	10.02.1973	2	L	0-2	Arsenal, Anfield, 1st Division
48	17.02.1973	2	D	1-1	Manchester City, Maine Road, 1st Division
49	24.02.1973	1	W	2-1	Ipswich Town, Anfield, 1st Division
50	03.03.1973	1	W	2-0	Everton, Goodison Park, 1st Division
51	07.03.1973		W	2-0	Dynamo Dresden, Anfield, UEFA Cup 4th round 1L
52	10.03.1973	1	W	3-2	Southampton, Anfield, 1st Division
53	17.03.1973	1	W	1-0	Stoke City, Victoria Ground, 1st Division
54	21.03.1973		W	1-0	Dynamo Dresden, Rudolf Harbig Stadion, UEFA Cup 4th round 2L
55	24.03.1973	1	W	3-1	Norwich City, Anfield, 1st Division
56	31.03.1973	1	D	1-1	Tottenham Hotspur, Anfield, 1st Division
57	07.04.1973	1	L	1-2	Birmingham City, St. Andrew's, 1st Division
58	10.04.1973		W	1-0	Tottenham Hotspur, Anfield, UEFA Cup Semi-final 1st leg
59	14.04.1973	1	W	1-0	West Bromwich Albion, Anfield, 1st Division
60	17.04.1973	1	W	2-1	Coventry City, Highfield Road, 1st Division
61	21.04.1973	1	L	1-2	Newcastle United, St. James' Park, 1st Division
62	23.04.1973	1	W	2-0	Leeds United, Anfield, 1st Division
63	25.04.1973		L	1-2	Tottenham Hotspur, White Hart Lane, UEFA Cup Semi-final 2L
64	28.04.1973	1	D	0-0	Leicester City, Anfield, 1st Division
65	10.05.1973		W	3-0	Borussia Moenchengladbach, Anfield, UEFA Cup Final 1st leg
66	23.05.1973		L	0-2	Borussia Moenchengladbach, Bökelberg, UEFA Cup Final 2nd leg

Friendlies

1	25.07.1972	W	2-0	Chester, Sealand Road, Friendly
2	02.08.1972	W	2-0	Bochum, Bochum, Friendly
3	05.08.1972	W	1-0	Utrecht, Stadion Galgenwaard, Friendly
4	13.03.1973	L	1-2	Everton, Goodison Park, Testimonial*
5	30.04.1973	W	4-2	Chelsea, Anfield, Testimonial**

* Testimonial for former Everton player Brian Labone.
** Testimonial for Ian St John.

Appearances for the 1972/1973 season

Name	League	FA Cup	LC	UEFA	Total
Ian Callaghan	42	4	8	12	66
Chris Lawler	42	4	8	12	66
Larry Lloyd	42	4	8	12	66
Emlyn Hughes	41	4	8	12	65
Kevin Keegan	41	4	8	11	64
Ray Clemence	41	4	7	12	64
Steve Heighway	38	4	8	12	62
Alec Lindsay	37	4	7	11	59
Peter Cormack	30	4	8	10	52
Tommy Smith	33	2	4	10	49
John Toshack	22	4	6	8	40
Brian Hall	21	0	2	8	31
Phil Boersma	19	1	3	8	31
Phil Thompson	14	2	1	3	20
Trevor Storton	4	0	4	2	10
Frank Lane	1	0	1	0	2
Jack Whitham	0	0	0	1	1

Goalscorers for the 1972/1973 season

Name	League	FA Cup	LC	UEFA	Total
Kevin Keegan	13	0	5	4	22
John Toshack	13	2	1	1	17
Phil Boersma	7	0	2	4	13
Emlyn Hughes	7	0	2	3	12
Steve Heighway	6	0	2	2	10
Peter Cormack	8	1	0	1	10
Alec Lindsay	4	0	0	1	5
Ian Callaghan	3	0	1	0	4
Chris Lawler	3	0	1	0	4
Brian Hall	2	0	0	1	3
Larry Lloyd	2	0	0	1	3
Tommy Smith	2	0	0	1	3
Own goals	2	0	0	0	2

The squad during the 1972/1973 season

Ray Clemence, Goalkeeper
Frank Lane, Goalkeeper
Grahame Lloyd, Goalkeeper
Roy Evans, Defender
Chris Lawler, Defender
Alec Lindsay, Defender
John McLaughlin, Defender
Tommy Smith, Defender
Larry Lloyd, Defender
Trevor Storton, Defender
John Webb, Defender
Peter Cormack, Midfielder
Emlyn Hughes, Midfielder
Steve Heighway, Midfielder
Phil Thompson, Midfielder
Peter Thompson, Midfielder
Ian Callaghan, Midfielder
Brian Hall, Midfielder
Steve Arnold, Midfielder
Hughie McAuley, Midfielder
Peter Spiring, Midfielder
Phil Boersma, Striker
Jack Whitham, Striker
Kevin Keegan, Striker
John Toshack, Striker
Kevin Kewley, Striker
Derek Brownbill, Striker

Transfers for the 1972/1973 season

In:
Peter Cormack, Nottingham Forest, £110,000, 14 July 1972
Trevor Storton, Tranmere Rovers, £25,000, 29 July 1972
Jimmy Case, South Liverpool, £500, 1 May 1973

Out:
Alun Evans, Aston Villa, £72,000, 9 June 1972

A collection of statistics for the 1972/1973 season

The season in numbers:
Total games: 66
Games won: 37
Games drawn: 18
Games lost: 11
Clean sheets – League: 14
Clean sheets – Overall: 26
Total goals: 108
Average attendance at home – League: 48,103
Average attendance at home – Overall: 44,863
Average goals per game – League: 2.14
Average goals per game – Overall: 2.18
Average goal minute – League: 47
Average goal minute – Overall: 49

Goals split down to competitions:
League – 72
UEFA Cup – 19
League Cup – 14
FA Cup – 3

Player debuts:
Peter Cormack against Derby on 02.09.1972
Frank Lane against Derby on 02.09.1972
Trevor Storton against Frankfurt on 26.09.1972

Statistics and information provided by LFChistory.net

9 A CHANGING OF THE GUARD

1975/76

ON JULY 26, 1974, AT THE AGE OF 55, BOB PAISLEY became the successor to Bill Shankly.

Some thought that Shankly had made a hasty decision he would later regret. New chairman John Smith offered him a contract on an increased salary but it wasn't about money. Shankly had been at Liverpool for nearly 15 years and it was a terrible wrench to leave.

He recalls in his autobiography that he suggested to the directors that "the only way to make the changeover was to promote the rest of the staff". He even added that he had "elevated them earlier with a view to what I was going to do later on".

Having signed professional forms in May 1939, Paisley had already been at Anfield twice as long as Shankly and despite his reluctance to take the job, if the position was going to remain in-house, he was the only logical candidate. Paisley knew the club and the game inside out and was a fine judge of a player. He had an almost uncanny ability of being able to correctly diagnose an injury and treat it accordingly.

But where personality was concerned, Bob was the complete opposite to Bill. He had been in the background for so long that the responsibility of dealing with the press was frightening. Paisley knew the enormity of the task and said the job was "like being given the Queen Elizabeth to steer in a force 10 gale". Chief executive Peter Robinson confirms Paisley had to be virtually manhandled into accepting the responsibility: "When we approached Bob he said 'no'. In the end the chairman, directors and I had to gang up on him."

Ray Clemence recalls the moment Paisley told the players that he had agreed to take over the reins from Shankly: "I think when Bob first succeeded Shanks he was a bit overawed. I'll never forget him standing in the dressing room in the summer of 1974 on the first day of pre-season training and telling us, 'Shanks has gone and they have given me the job even though I don't really want it. But we must try to carry on from what Bill has started here'. I think in the end, he realised it was his duty to take the job."

While Paisley prepared for his first league game against Luton Town on August 17, 1974, Shankly spent his first Saturday afternoon in retirement watching his local home match: Everton versus Derby County. Even though Paisley wasn't the darling of the media like Shankly he showed early on that he was also capable of a one-liner.

When the press asked Bob what Shankly was doing this particular afternoon, he replied: "He's trying to get right away from football. I believe he went to Everton." Paisley's first season in charge was not a success, not by the high standards set by his predecessor anyway. The team fought hard to reclaim the league title but defeat at Middlesbrough on the penultimate weekend of the season meant their challenge was over. There was disappointment in the cups too with a late Ipswich goal at Portman Road putting the holders out of the FA Cup and Middlesbrough beating them in the League Cup at Anfield in November. Liverpool enjoyed their biggest-ever competitive victory with an 11-0 thrashing of the Norwegian part-timers, Strømsgodset, in the opening round of the Cup Winners' Cup but conceding a last-minute equaliser at home to Ferencvaros in the next round was a blow the team was unable to recover from. They eventually went out of the competition on the away goals rule a fortnight later. As things turned out, that 1974/75 season would be the only one during Paisley's reign that no silverware was won.

With one full season now under his belt, Paisley gave a fascinating insight into his relationship with the man he had replaced. Paisley sat down with the *Liverpool Echo* and said: "Everybody calls Bill Shankly a great manager. But I'm the only one who knows how great, because I worked more closely with him than anyone else for 15 years. In all that time at Liverpool we never missed a headline league game together. So that makes 630 consecutive league matches we worked together and tried together. In fact, in those 15 years, we were only "separated" for a total of two games, both cup ties. When we played Stockport in the FA Cup, Bill was on his way back from Germany after watching our European opponents. In another FA Cup tie against Chelsea the year after we had won at Wembley, I was missing through tonsillitis. In nearly a thousand Liverpool matches we missed only two together.

"Basically, Bill managed by example. He lived a simple life, his whole life was on a simple level and he approached football in exactly the same way. He never tried to complicate things: he was down to earth. He was completely dedicated to fitness. He didn't drink or smoke; he lived like an athlete. So when he demanded these qualities from his players, they could see in front of them the living example of what he was preaching – a fitness fanatic who could play a game of five-a-side football at 60 as well as he could when he was a younger man.

"In fact, he is so fit that I think he believes that when he goes up there (pointing to the skies) he will step right into a five-a-side team –

on merit. Fitness was everything in his football creed. He looked on the game as simple, based on movement and possession, with players fit enough to move around fluently. He would not have complicated ideas in training or playing. He scorned fancy phrases. Tactics have not changed, but new names have been put to them. His personality was overwhelming. Even now, as I walk around Anfield and Melwood, I can feel his presence in the air. It is everywhere. You open a drawer, sit in a chair, work at a desk, walk down a corridor...and he's there around us still. It was this terrific personality, his passion for the game, which enabled him to lift players. He did it by personality, not by tactical talks. He didn't have tactical talks at Anfield as most people understand them. We had a tactical board which we used – in the oddest way. It was my job to lay out 22 counters which represented the two teams. I used to do this before we had a team talk. Notice, not a tactical talk. The players would be sitting around the board when he walked in. The first thing he did, every time before a match, was sweep up the five opposing forwards and put them in his pocket. 'They can't play,' he said – always. So our 11 men were faced with just six opponents and that was before he really started. And some of the forwards he swept into his pocket included people like Johan Cruyff, Charlton and company, some of the best in the world! But that was his method – your opponents couldn't play.

"His favourite word was 'rubbish'. He would tell the Liverpool players that their opponents were rubbish and they were the greatest. It may seem silly but it worked with Bill Shankly because of his personality. He made his players believe. After Liverpool had won, their beaten opponents would become a fine team – even though he had said they were rubbish 90 minutes earlier. After Liverpool had lost, their successful opponents still remained rubbish.

"If Liverpool lost, it was never because our opponents had been a better team. Bill would blame the pitch, the weather, the referee, the players' boots, even the strip they were wearing – never that they had lost to a better team on the day. That was his reaction immediately after the game was over. But about Tuesday of the following week, he would be telling his men what they had done wrong and how bad they had been the previous Saturday. It was his psychology never to criticise his players immediately after they had lost. He reserved that for days later. He knew that our opponents had deserved to win but he'd never say so. Not for days, anyway. That was his psychology. It was remarkable that grown men, intelligent men, would take it week after week. He would tell them one thing and, 90 minutes later, tell them the exact opposite. Yet they accepted it without question because of his personality. That was what made him a great manager; it was the secret of his success.

"He was the best motivator I ever knew: he could lift a player better than anyone else. But he could also knock them down if he thought they were getting a bit too big for their boots. He usually did it by telling them that Tom Finney could play better than them – with his overcoat on! When he came to Liverpool from Huddersfield, a friend at Huddersfield told me I'd never be able to work with Bill for more than two years. I wouldn't be able to stand the strain, he said. Well, I stuck it for 15 years and I think, probably, that I became the best foil for him. Together, we struck a balance off the field which we liked to achieve on the field with the team. Playing in the five-a-side games was his great outlet, the one activity he had to release the tensions and the pressures. His tracksuit was like his second skin; he loved kicking the ball. After a particularly tough Saturday game, perhaps we had lost a vital match, the atmosphere would be electric at Anfield all over the weekend. The pressure and the tensions were there so much you could feel them. You kept away from Bill at those times, if you could. But on Monday morning, he would bounce out at Melwood in his tracksuit, the pressure over, his eyes shining like a schoolboy because he was going to have a five-a-side game.

"He always wanted to be totally involved in all things Liverpool. His passion and honesty for the game were there for all to see. He gave this club the finest successes of its history. It has not been easy for me to follow him. People have told me I should have copied him, do as he did. How can you copy a man who is unique? The players wouldn't accept from me the sort of man-management he used. No, I must go about things my way, be my own man. It is up to me to follow him as the Liverpool manager. But what a job that is – to follow the greatest manager Liverpool have ever had, one of the greatest in the long history of the game."

Continuity on the pitch was vital to the club's success. The sort of wholesale buying and selling that would be commonplace long after his retirement was not part of Paisley's agenda. Changes were made gradually and the newcomers integrated carefully into an already successful side. Phil Neal arrived in 1974, soon replacing Alec Lindsay, the only change to the regular 11 from Shankly's last campaign in Paisley's debut season. Terry McDermott, who had arrived from Newcastle, was having trouble adjusting as well as the final signing of the Shankly era, Ray Kennedy.

In 1975/76 the most vital changes to Paisley's side took place in midfield. Peter Cormack's days were numbered following Paisley's successful transformation of Ray Kennedy into a left-sided midfielder and Jimmy Case was promoted from the reserves to replace the industrious Brian Hall.

In July 1975 there was increased speculation that Paisley was about to swoop for star talent north of the border. His tongue-in-cheek sense of humour came through when he told the *Liverpool Echo*:

"From some of the reports I have read, it seems that I am going to sign everybody in Scotland, and even some from Scotland Road as well! There will be no signings from Scotland before the UEFA Cup deadline."

Paisley kept his word, as his only signing in the summer was Joey Jones from Third Division side Wrexham, costing the club £110,000. Jones was an enthusiastic and tough-tackling left-back whose uncompromising style quickly endeared him to the Liverpool crowd. The charismatic Welshman, whose mother was from Dingle in Liverpool, became a cult figure on the Kop even though he only actually played for the club during three different seasons. Wrexham manager John Neal was furious when Jones was sold to Liverpool: "The directors went over my head. Now I'll have to consider if I have any future with the club."

The former self-confessed youth delinquent was 20 when Paisley brought him to Liverpool and was still a bit raw. Even though Jones started the season as first-choice left-back, he only appeared in 13 First Division matches in total during the 1975/76 campaign as the gulf in class between the Third Division he left behind and the First Division became too apparent in his performance.

As the Reds entered into the 1975/76 season, Chris Lawler, Ian Callaghan and Tommy Smith were the only survivors from Shankly's 1965 FA Cup-winning side. However, after only featuring in 17 matches in a season-and-a-half following Bob Paisley's appointment, two days after his 32nd birthday, in October 1975, Lawler moved to Portsmouth, who were managed at the time by his former teammate, Ian St John.

Callaghan was still a first-team regular and only missed two of the 53 games played in Paisley's debut season, as was his good friend Smith who played 45 games during the 1974/75 season.

On July 24, 1975, Paisley addressed the board of directors and shareholders at the club's annual meeting. He first spoke about his disappointment of failing to win a trophy during the previous season: "In trying to analyse why we did not win a trophy, I believe the main factor was the injury to Phil Thompson early in the season. We were playing so well at the time and if he had not been injured I think we could have won the championship. The players, backroom staff and myself are bitterly disappointed that we did not win something. We thought we could have done so. It was a funny old season, a topsy turvy start and it carried right on in that fashion up to April. I've never known such an uneven season in my career. At the start, I thought we were playing as well as, if not better than, at any time in my years at the club. Hence the increased disappointment at not winning an honour. Excuses don't rate much but it must be remembered that we had the Kevin Keegan incident in the Charity Shield even before the season began, and then Thompson's injury which put him out of the game because he needed a cartilage operation. Another factor was the exceptionally wet winter. The 1965 team, being heavier than the present team, would have walked off with the title. That is not to decry the present side, because the pitches prevented them showing consistent fluency in their game. The weather became the great leveller."

Paisley followed by paying a handsome tribute to the newest member of his backroom staff – Roy Evans. Just 26, Evans, who began the season in the Central League team but then gave up his playing career to become the reserve team coach, had guided them to their sixth championship success in the past seven years.

After thanking his colleagues who had, he said, "leant over backwards to help me in my first season as manager", Paisley added: "We go into the new season confident and optimistic. We have a very experienced squad and a very good staff so that, given the run of the ball and with all things equal, we'll be there with a shout in all the major competitions. We set about our task with the utmost confidence. Of course, we know the squad can be improved and I'm conscious that our supporters, the best in the country, deserve the best from us. We realise the high standards the club has enjoyed in the past and we'll do our utmost to maintain them."

With skipper Emlyn Hughes and full-back Phil Neal fit again after injury and along with the signing of Joey Jones, Tommy Smith suddenly found his place under threat. Smith realised that he might be relegated to the substitutes' bench for the opening game of the season at Queens Park Rangers. His fears were confirmed as he had to make do with being Liverpool's 12th man at Loftus Road. After naming his team for the QPR clash, Paisley said: "Tommy is such a professional that he will not lie down and this is the kind of spirit I want at Liverpool."

Paisley's team went on to lose 2-0 in their first test of the season in Shepherd's Bush. Gerry Francis blunted Liverpool's hopes of a decent start to the season with a fine goal a minute before half-time. The Reds fell further behind to a headed goal by Michael Leach after 72 minutes as Rangers clinched their first ever victory over Liverpool. Three days after their defeat in the capital, Liverpool kicked off their season at Anfield.

Admission prices for the forthcoming season were set at 65p – £1.30. Supporters were charged slightly more for home European games to help the club manage the high travel costs involved in the European away ties.

In that opening Anfield match, 40,564 supporters witnessed their team draw 2-2 against John Lyall's West Ham United. The *Liverpool Echo* reported: "Liverpool have made an uncharacteristically shaky start, with just one point from the opening two games, but they proved one thing at Anfield last night. That old battling spirit is beating as strongly as ever. The Hammers looked to be heading for a surprise win when John Toshack pounced, nine minutes from time, after Kevin Keegan had cleverly allowed Peter Cormack's pass to run through his legs."

Ian Callaghan missed the subsequent game against Tottenham with a thigh injury, a highly unusual occurrence because he had been virtually ever-present for four years. Up-and-coming local player Jimmy Case replaced him for only his second senior appearance. Incredibly, Liverpool slumped to a 2-0 half-time deficit but staged one of their famous fightbacks. Keegan rammed home a penalty, Case scored his first goal in senior football for the equaliser, and Steve Heighway raced in at the right hand post to beat Pat Jennings for a sensational winner. Final score: Liverpool 3-2 Tottenham Hotspur. The First Division after three games read: Manchester United top with maximum points, chased by Newcastle, QPR, Coventry, West Ham and Leeds United. Liverpool were just below halfway.

Local lad Jimmy Case experienced the hero's acclaim on his first appearance at Anfield by scoring the equaliser. The tough-tackling midfielder who took no prisoners was also renowned for his ferocious shooting ability and went on to score more than a fair amount of goals for Liverpool.

Case learnt to survive on the football field while playing for dockers' club Blue Union in Garston aged just 16, regularly facing 30-somethings who showed the teenager no mercy.

A year later he started playing for a non-league side South Liverpool where he was noticed by Liverpool scouts Tom Saunders and John Bennison.

When Case was first taken from the amateur league in 1973, Liverpool gave South Liverpool a donation of £500, but in 1975, in appreciation of Case's rapid advance to the first team, a cheque for £1,500 was posted as a goodwill present. Liverpool had no need to give South Liverpool any additional payment for Case. Chairman John Smith said: "We decided to send South Liverpool the money on the instigation of our president, Mr. Thomas Valentine Williams (T.V. Williams), and manager Bob Paisley, who put it to the Board. "We have had a fine relationship with South for many years and we hope we can develop that even further to the benefit of both clubs. We believe that boys coming through from junior and non-league clubs like South Liverpool form the basis for First Division clubs' recruitment of players. Local boys like to play for their local teams and it is with clubs like South that they get the right start."

Manager Paisley also paid his tribute to non-league clubs with this comment: "They make a very valuable contribution to the game. Without their work, professional football could not exist."

Steve Heighway was injured and replaced by Phil Boersma for the Reds' next game at Leeds on August 26. Paisley also rested Toshack and brought in Ray Kennedy. It was Keegan and Ian Callaghan who inspired a marvellous 3-0 victory, a performance which warned the rest of the First Division not to underestimate the Anfield challenge.

Inconsistency then crept into Liverpool's play. They drew at Leicester, beat Sheffield United 1-0, but lost 2-0 at Ipswich. A 3-0 Anfield victory over Aston Villa livened things up with Keegan once again in sparkling form.

One player who was unhappy with his lot was Terry McDermott, signed from Newcastle United for £150,000 the previous November. He was left out against Villa and only made two more appearances the whole season, both as a substitute. His future greatest moments, including Footballer of the Year and PFA Players Player of the Year accolades, were nothing but dreams at that moment.

The 113th derby game, played at Goodison Park on September 27, produced the fourth successive goalless draw between the two neighbours. Ray Clemence was superb for Liverpool, producing one miracle save. He raced almost to the edge of the box to try to prevent Gary Jones from centering, but the winger took the ball away from him. Jones crossed to the far post where Bob Latchford aimed a firm header towards the roof of the apparently unguarded net. Clemence suddenly arrived from nowhere, leaping to turn the ball over the bar, after sprinting back into position. The *Liverpool Echo* scribe Michael Charters described it as: "One of the greatest saves I have ever seen."

Clemence was a fresh-faced 18-year-old at Scunthorpe United when Shankly brought him to Anfield in June 1967. Despite his young age he had still made 46 appearances for the Third Division club. Shankly even told him Lawrence was over the hill and he would be in the team inside six months to convince him to join.

Clemence had to serve a two-and-a-half-year frustrating apprenticeship in the reserves apart from being selected for a League Cup tie against Swansea in September 1968. Clemence's second and third game came one year after his debut but he could hardly showcase his talent as Liverpool conquered Dundalk 10-0 and 4-0 in the European Fairs Cup.

As the 1960s moved into the 1970s and Shankly started to break up the team which had brought him so much success, Clemence was given his full league debut at Nottingham Forest on the last day of January 1970. Tommy Lawrence's last appearance for the club was in an awful FA Cup quarter-final defeat at Watford the next month and seven days later Clemence was one of a number of changes made for the visit of Derby County and he had established himself firmly as first-choice goalkeeper by the end of that season. Clemence's teammate Ian Callaghan held his keeper in high regard: "Ray was one of the best goalkeepers I have ever seen. He is in England's top three alongside Gordon Banks and Peter Shilton. No one dominated the box as well as Clem. He made things look easy which is the sign of a top keeper. Ray was one of those people who was really enthusiastic in training. He always wanted people to take shots at him. He defied you to try and put the ball in the net. That's the sign of someone who was always on top of the job and confident in his own ability."

Birmingham City's visit to Anfield on October 11 saw an old Everton favourite, Howard Kendall, dropped by the visitors for the first time. 'NO STOPPING TOSH' roared the *Liverpool Echo* headline after a 3-1 victory, in which the big striker claimed a hat-trick, his second in 11 days following his UEFA Cup achievement against Hibernian. His first goal was a freak, a headed clearance by Gallagher, striking Toshack on the back of the head and rebounding at pace into the top corner. His other two goals came from perfectly-struck shots.

On November 1, Liverpool travelled to Ayresome Park to face Jack Charlton's Middlesbrough. The game ended in a 1-0 victory for the Reds as substitute Terry McDermott's second-half strike was enough to secure his team the two points. Full-back Joey Jones received a red card for fighting with Boro's John Hickton in Liverpool's goalmouth six minutes from time. Hickton fell to the floor, so it was Joey who was sent off. It was reported in the press that Hickton, lost five, albeit synthetic, teeth in the incident. Joey's antics carried an automatic one-match suspension.

Eighteen-year-old David Fairclough made his first-team debut that afternoon on Teesside and caused his opponents an abundance of problems with his speedy forward runs. Alex Goodman from the *Liv-*

erpool Echo reported on the teenager's start to his Liverpool career: "David Fairclough, still only 18, is going to become a First Division star of some considerable stature with Liverpool. Probably not this season but certainly in the not too distant future. Young Fairclough with 10 Central League goals to his credit this season was plunged into his First Division debut at Middlesbrough on Saturday. And manager Bob Paisley could scarcely conceal his delight at Fairclough's performance, which helped in no small way towards Liverpool's record-breaking 1-0 win. It was record breaking because Terry McDermott's second-half effort which clinched the points was the first goal Middlesbrough had conceded at home that season in league and cup games. In fact it was the first goal scored against them in a competitive match at Ayresome Park since last April. But it was the showing of Fairclough as much as Liverpool's win that pleased Mr. Paisley. He said: 'I knew the lad would not let us down and that's why I put him in. If he had scored I would not have been surprised and although he tired in the second half, Middlesbrough could not leave him alone and Willie Maddren, one of their best defenders, had to stay with him.' Mr. Paisley added: 'He is exciting to watch and is the kind of player every manager in the country would like to have. Fairclough, who twice came close to scoring, was equally pleased: 'I was apprehensive and excited more than frightened before the start but I was looking forward to the game and I enjoyed it. I thought it was not bad for a debut but of course the game was a lot faster than in the Central League'."

At the time Fairclough was in dreamland and he told *LFChistory.net*: "I grew up about half a mile from the ground and I went to school just 500-600 yards away from the stadium. Anfield was very much my patch. I played football in the streets. Comic book stuff really. I remember standing in the street where we lived listening to the crowd in the Inter Milan game in '65. I was only eight and my dad didn't allow me to go to that game. We knew obviously the game was going Liverpool's way and you could hear them singing. We lived literally in the shadows of Anfield."

A fascinating clash now loomed on November 8. Manchester United arrived at Anfield as leaders with 21 points from 15 games. Liverpool had moved up to fifth with 19 points from 14 games. The Reds won 3-1 and the *Liverpool Echo* headline said it all: 'ALL THE BEST AT ANFIELD... SKILLS, THRILLS, ENTERTAINMENT. WHAT AN ADVERT FOR ENGLISH SOCCER!' Although Manchester United took the game to Liverpool, the home side met the challenge head on. Heighway, Toshack and Keegan scored vital goals to send the Liverpool fans wild with delight.

West Ham and Derby moved joint top, Liverpool claimed third with United relegated to fourth place but just a single point separated the top five. Paisley's side then took second spot behind Derby after a 2-1 win at Newcastle on November 15. Ray Kennedy's late goal at St. James' Park opened up golden vistas of further league glory. Unbeaten in the First Division for two months, Liverpool now had three home games in succession to help them consolidate their challenge. Incredibly, they failed to win a single one, drawing against Coventry and Arsenal, and losing in between to Norwich. Yet there was much to report, not least a visit by former manager Bill Shankly to his beloved Kop terraces for the first time.

It happened when the Sky Blues arrived at Anfield on November 22, the crowd greeting him with the chant: "Shankly is our king." The following Monday, he told the *Liverpool Echo*: "When I was a boy I used to watch Celtic and Rangers play with 100,000 people there, and that was nothing to us. I was in it again on Saturday. The wheel had turned full circle. This time it was with a red and white scarf. I got it from a boy and brought it home. I promised to go on the Kop long ago and to see games from all parts of Anfield. It has taken a long time to get round to going. You get a view of the game, but the pitch looks different. It looked wider and bigger, and it was difficult to judge what was going on at the other end.

"At first, the people were surprised to see me, but, in fact, when I went in, the Coventry team were coming out at eight minutes to three. People were concentrating on that. Then, all of a sudden, it struck them I was walking and talking to the people there. I am a citizen of Liverpool and I wanted to go there to see the fans who have done so much for me. The handshakes are real, they aren't false. It was an enjoyable experience, and not as tiring as you might think. The jostling was not too bad, but there were a lot of kids in the ten-year-old bracket, and some of them couldn't see at all. That surprised me."

Local boy Phil Boersma had lost his place in Paisley's starting eleven. Boersma was mostly on the bench in the first months of the 1975/76 season and on December 2, he moved to First Division Middlesbrough.

Failing to capitalise on home fixtures meant that on December 2, after the 2-2 draw with Arsenal, the league table showed Derby on top by one point, followed by QPR, West Ham, Manchester United, Leeds and then Liverpool. Fortunately the other clubs had also struggled and just two points separated the top six. Liverpool's gate against the Gunners of 27,447 was their fourth lowest since being promoted in 1962 and there was little to cheer following a visit to Burnley which produced a goalless draw.

The halfway stage to the season came with a trip to Tottenham, where it finally all came right. With Tommy Smith now back in the side, a 4-0 victory catapulted Paisley's men joint top. Toshack was the Tottenham tormenter, laying on three of the four goals which were claimed by Keegan, Case, Neal and Heighway. The Reds then put the skids under title rivals QPR with a 2-0 win at Anfield. The Londoners, leading the pack on goal average, had been conducting a war of words in the build-up. Skipper Gerry Francis boldly predicted the Merseysiders' downfall. Paisley simply named a side to produce the goods: Clemence, Smith, Neal, Thompson, Cormack, Hughes, Keegan, Case, Heighway, Toshack, Callaghan. Toshack's ninth goal of the season gave Liverpool the edge and a Neal penalty clinched matters and helped move Liverpool to the top of the league for the first time this season.

Manchester United and Derby also won to match the Reds' points total of 30. Things were clearly hotting up but Liverpool were just edging it on goal average.

First place disappeared on January 10 when United beat QPR at Old Trafford while Liverpool were drawing 3-3 at Anfield against Ipswich. News that Peter Cormack would need a cartilage operation further disappointed the camp.

Two days later, even sadder news was reported as the man entitled to be called Liverpool's greatest fan had died – Mr. Thomas Valentine Williams, life-president of the club.

A former postman and cotton broker, he was a proud Liverpudlian who had been a long-time shareholder before joining the board of directors in 1948. He went on to serve the club for 28 years and was an inspirational figure in the shaping of its future. In the early 1950s he instigated the move to purchase an unkempt school field in West Derby that now homes the club's famous Melwood training base.

Williams then played a key role in bringing together Bob Paisley, Reuben Bennett and Joe Fagan – the three wise men who would play key roles in the legendary Boot Room dynasty. His greatest legacy of all, though, was without doubt the appointment of Bill Shankly as manager in 1959; together they worked in tandem to drag Liverpool Football Club back to the top.

Michael Charters at the *Liverpool Echo* wrote: "Born in 1890, he would have been 86 in a month's time… on St. Valentine's Day. He was known throughout football as T.V. rather than by his Christian name. And wherever he went, the cause of Liverpool was his first concern. He remembered going to Anfield with his father as a boy of five and his devotion to the club grew from that day before the start of the 20th century. Although he had been failing in health for some time, he still managed to go to his beloved Anfield on match days. The club was his whole life, particularly after the death of his wife. He and the late John McKenna (Honest John), one time president of the Football League, and the original father figure of Liverpool, will be remembered as Liverpool's greatest directors and administrators."

On the pitch, a goalless draw at Sheffield United could have been costly but United and Leeds failed to cash in so the status quo was retained at the top. Three draws in four games was clearly frustrating but the situation was not desperate. A 4-0 away success at West Ham, including another Toshack hat-trick, had the Kopites smiling again. He steered a shot past Mervyn Day after 63 minutes, latched on to a Ray Kennedy free-kick to volley home his second and then soared to head the third in typical fashion, after Heighway had left two defenders for dead with a devastating run. Keegan volleyed the fourth but United still held on to top spot. Two crucial games now loomed against rivals Leeds and Manchester United. Leeds were to bow to the genius of Keegan, who inspired a majestic performance and a 2-0 home win.

The League Championship now seemed to rest between Liverpool and Manchester United and it seemed fitting that a draw was the end product of a battling game between the teams on February 18. Three days later, Keegan and Case scored the goals that beat Newcastle, an absolutely crucial win on the day United crashed to defeat at Villa. The Reds were now two points clear but they stumbled at Arsenal, whose winner came 28 seconds into injury time. It was all looking very tense at the top, particularly when Derby held the Reds 1-1 at the Baseball Ground.

After 32 games played, Liverpool, Queens Park Rangers and Manchester United sat at the summit of the First Division, all on 43 points apiece. However, in their next game on March 6 disaster struck the Merseysiders in the shape of a 2-0 home defeat at the hands of Middlesbrough. The *Liverpool Echo* remained optimistic, reporting: "This is a major upset to the club's Championship hopes, but with nine games to play there is still time to recover."

Recover they did, in spectacular style.

Liverpool now gathered all their resilience and experience together to leave their rivals gasping. They picked themselves up from the Boro defeat to secure a sensational eight wins from nine remaining fixtures, also drawing with Villa. It was like a heavyweight champion rising to the roar of the crowd in the last round, unleashing a flurry of blows to take the crown. Local lad Fairclough was to steal much of the limelight. He scored a crucial match-winner at Norwich and came off the bench to strike twice at home to Burnley. He repeated his super sub act with a lone effort against Everton, also getting on the scoresheet against Stoke and Manchester City. He only made five full appearances but plundered nine absolutely vital goals and looked deadly when thrust into the action from the bench. Against Everton he came on for Toshack, sprinting from his own half to unleash a powerful right-foot drive that flew past Dai Davies. During this period of splendid form, Paisley's team also progressed to the UEFA Cup final after beating Johannes Weisweiler's Barcelona over two legs. On March 30, the magnificent setting of the Camp Nou in Cataluña was the scene for one of the club's best-ever European performances. Playing in an all-white strip, the team's defensive performance was immense and they snuffed out the threat of the brilliant Johan Cruyff and the creativity of Johan Neeskens. John Toshack drove home the only goal of the game after just 13 minutes to keep the home supporters quiet. A noisy Anfield awaited the Catalans but this tie was still in the balance and the first half was very even. Five minutes after the interval, Phil Thompson scored from close range and it looked to be over but within a minute Carlos Rexach had equalised. Just as against Dynamo Dresden in the previous round, this led to a very tense finish but Liverpool held out. The Reds heard that their final opponents would be FC Bruges, who had beaten Hamburg 1-0 at home after a 1-1 draw in Germany.

One of the most exciting seasons on record went to the bitter end and on May 4, the final match day of the 1975/76 season, Liverpool had 58 points with QPR a point behind on 57. The Reds went into their final league game knowing that due to their superior goal average a point against Wolves would be enough to clinch a ninth league title. Despite being a goal down until 15 minutes from the end, goals from Keegan, Toshack and Ray Kennedy brought a truly amazing campaign to a thrilling climax. 'HAIL THE NEW KING OF THE KOP' said the *Liverpool Echo*'s back page headline, that man being an ecstatic Bob Paisley. The paper went on to report: "On a night of a thousand and one memories, an occasion when Liverpool made football history by winning the League Championship for a record-breaking ninth time, one outstanding fact emerged. This was the night when the Liverpool fans finally took Bob Paisley to their hearts, recognising him as a great manager. They will always have a special affection for Bill Shankly, but now, at the end of Bob's second season at the helm, they have their own recognition for him as well. Perhaps it will never be as flamboyant as Shanks' links with the Kop, but it is a deep, sincere acknowledgement of this man's special qualities. It overflowed last night as Liverpool, players and fans, took over Wolverhampton completely, before, during and after the 3-1 win." Paisley said: "This is the greatest night of my football life. It is my fifth Championship medal, one as a player in 1947, three as coach in 64, 66 and 73 and now this as a manager." Bob had arrived in a big way. His glorious reign was now underway in earnest.

Ian Callaghan, who made his first-team debut more than 16 years earlier, had just played his 767th Liverpool game, which won him his fourth First Division title. After the game he told the press: "I can't remember too much about the other three championships, only tonight matters now. I started to despair when the goal didn't come, but once it did, it was all over, because the tension had gone."

Fifteen days later, the Reds completed a hard-fought 4-3 aggregate victory over FC Bruges which gave Liverpool their second UEFA Cup title. A repeat of the double Bill Shankly's team had managed three years earlier was now achieved by his successor, Bob Paisley. The Reds came back from two down at half-time in the first leg to win the match 3-2, and then fought back to claim a 1-1 draw courtesy of a Kevin Keegan goal in the second leg.

From way down in the Fourth Division to the top of the First, from being next to unknown to winning an England cap – all this happened to full-back Phil Neal inside 18 months. He told *Football Monthly*: "I arrived at Anfield in October 1974 and was told by Bob Paisley I had been bought as cover for the back four. I was delighted even at that. But going straight into the team? You can imagine how I felt. The first season was a tremendous experience as we finished runners-up in the championship to Derby County. I was delighted, but the other lads were downhearted because they hadn't finished on top. That's the sort of drive which fires the club. Then came this season, the England call-up, the championship and success in Europe. Being capped by Don Revie was just as big a shock as was my signing for Liverpool. So completely unexpected, I felt out of this world.

"I have so many people to thank for the help I've been given at Liverpool. People who have made this last couple of years so memorable for me. There's the coaching staff who point out improvements that can be made. Bob Paisley and Reuben Bennett, with their tips on strengths and weaknesses of opponents. The players themselves, like Tommy Smith and Emlyn Hughes, who have taught me never to panic. Ray Clemence, in goal behind me, has been a particular help with his intelligent calling and calming influence. Without them I couldn't have achieved what I have in such a short time."

Paisley's team, as distinct from Shanks' which he had inherited, was gradually taking shape. The players he was bringing in along with the now established nucleus of Clemence, Neal, Thompson, Hughes, Keegan, Heighway, Toshack and Callaghan were starting to look more than the part. In other words he was combining the great players left from the Shankly era with his own men to form one master team. The League Championship and UEFA Cup were won in what, after all, was only Bob's second season. As a physio he made a bloody good manager. As a "trainer" he made a great tactician. Maybe even he didn't realise he was a coaching genius. Never frightened to discipline a player who had stepped out of line. Never frightened to drop a player who wasn't doing the business, no matter who they were. A banner at Molineux when Liverpool won the First Division for a record ninth time summed it up: 'QPR: QUALITY FROM PAISLEY'S REDS.'

1975/76: Facts and Statistics

Final league table

		P	W	D	L	F	A	W	D	L	F	A	PTS
1	Liverpool FC	42	14	5	2	41	21	9	9	3	25	10	60
2	QPR	42	17	4	0	42	13	7	7	7	25	20	59
3	Manchester United	42	16	4	1	40	13	7	6	8	28	29	56
4	Derby	42	15	3	3	45	30	6	8	7	30	28	53
5	Leeds United	42	13	3	5	37	19	8	6	7	28	27	51
6	Ipswich Town	42	11	6	4	36	23	5	8	8	18	25	46
7	Leicester City	42	9	9	3	29	24	4	10	7	19	27	45
8	Manchester City	42	14	5	2	46	18	2	6	13	18	28	43
9	Tottenham	42	6	10	5	33	32	8	5	8	30	31	43
10	Norwich City	42	10	5	6	33	26	6	5	10	25	32	42
11	Everton	42	10	7	4	37	24	5	5	11	23	42	42
12	Stoke City	42	8	5	8	25	24	7	6	8	23	26	41
13	Middlesbrough	42	9	7	5	23	11	6	3	12	23	34	40
14	Coventry City	42	6	9	6	22	22	7	5	9	25	35	40
15	Newcastle United	42	11	4	6	51	26	4	5	12	20	36	39
16	Aston Villa	42	11	8	2	32	17	0	9	12	19	42	39
17	Arsenal	42	11	4	6	33	19	2	6	13	14	34	36
18	West Ham United	42	10	5	6	26	23	3	5	13	22	48	36
19	Birmingham City	42	11	5	5	36	26	2	2	17	21	49	33
20	Wolves	42	7	6	8	27	25	3	4	14	24	43	30
21	Burnley	42	6	6	9	23	26	3	4	14	20	40	28
22	Sheffield United	42	4	7	10	19	32	2	3	16	14	50	22

Games for the 1975/1976 season

(The number after date is league position after the game)

1	16.08.1975	18	L	0-2	Queens Park Rangers, Loftus Road, 1st Division
2	19.08.1975	15	D	2-2	West Ham United, Anfield, 1st Division
3	23.08.1975	13	W	3-2	Tottenham Hotspur, Anfield, 1st Division
4	26.08.1975	8	W	3-0	Leeds United, Elland Road, 1st Division
5	30.08.1975	8	D	1-1	Leicester City, Filbert Street, 1st Division
6	06.09.1975	5	W	1-0	Sheffield United, Anfield, 1st Division
7	10.09.1975		W	1-0	York City, Bootham Crescent, League Cup 2nd round
8	13.09.1975	7	L	0-2	Ipswich Town, Portman Road, 1st Division

9	17.09.1975		L	0-1	Hibernian, Easter Road,
					UEFA Cup 1st round 1L
10	20.09.1975	4	W	3-0	Aston Villa, Anfield, 1st Division
11	27.09.1975	8	D	0-0	Everton, Goodison Park, 1st Division
12	30.09.1975		W	3-1	Hibernian, Anfield, UEFA Cup 1st round 2L
13	04.10.1975	6	W	2-0	Wolves, Anfield, 1st Division
14	07.10.1975		D	1-1	Burnley, Anfield, League Cup 3rd round
15	11.10.1975	4	W	3-1	Birmingham City, Anfield, 1st Division
16	14.10.1975		L	0-1	Burnley, Turf Moor,
					League Cup 3rd round replay
17	18.10.1975	5	D	0-0	Coventry City, Highfield Road, 1st Division
18	22.10.1975		W	3-1	Real Sociedad, Atocha,
					UEFA Cup 2nd round 1L
19	25.10.1975	5	D	1-1	Derby County, Anfield, 1st Division
20	01.11.1975	5	W	1-0	Middlesbrough, Ayresome Park, 1st Division
21	04.11.1975		W	6-0	Real Sociedad, Anfield,
					UEFA Cup 2nd round 2L
22	08.11.1975	4	W	3-1	Manchester United, Anfield, 1st Division
23	15.11.1975	2	W	2-1	Newcastle United, St. James' Park, 1st Division
24	22.11.1975	3	D	1-1	Coventry City, Anfield, 1st Division
25	26.11.1975		W	2-1	Slask Wroclaw, Olimpijski Stadium,
					UEFA Cup 3rd round 1L
26	29.11.1975	6	L	1-3	Norwich City, Anfield, 1st Division
27	02.12.1975	5	D	2-2	Arsenal, Anfield, 1st Division
28	06.12.1975	5	D	0- 0	Burnley, Turf Moor, 1st Division
29	10.12.1975		W	3-0	Slask Wroclaw, Anfield, UEFA Cup 3rd round 2L
30	13.12.1975	2	W	4-0	Tottenham Hotspur, White Hart Lane,
					1st Division
31	20.12.1975	1	W	2-0	Queens Park Rangers, Anfield, 1st Division
32	26.12.1975	1	D	1-1	Stoke City, Victoria Ground, 1st Division
33	27.12.1975	1	W	1-0	Manchester City, Anfield, 1st Division
34	03.01.1976		W	2-0	West Ham United, Upton Park,
					FA Cup 3rd round
35	10.01.1976	3	D	3-3	Ipswich Town, Anfield, 1st Division
36	17.01.1976	3	D	0-0	Sheffield United, Bramall Lane, 1st Division
37	24.01.1976		L	0-1	Derby County, Baseball Ground,
					FA Cup 4th round
38	31.01.1976	2	W	4-0	West Ham United, Upton Park, 1st Division
39	07.02.1976	1	W	2-0	Leeds United, Anfield, 1st Division
40	18.02.1976	1	D	0-0	Manchester United, Old Trafford, 1st Division
41	21.02.1976	1	W	2-0	Newcastle United, Anfield, 1st Division
42	24.02.1976	1	L	0-1	Arsenal, Highbury, 1st Division
43	28.02.1976	1	D	1-1	Derby County, Baseball Ground, 1st Division
44	03.03.1976		D	0-0	Dynamo Dresden, Rudolf Harbig Stadion,

					UEFA Cup 4th round 1L
45	06.03.1976	2	L	0-2	Middlesbrough, Anfield, 1st Division
46	13.03.1976	2	W	1-0	Birmingham City, St. Andrew's, 1st Division
47	17.03.1976		W	2-1	Dynamo Dresden, Anfield,
					UEFA Cup 4th round 2L
48	20.03.1976	3	W	1-0	Norwich City, Carrow Road, 1st Division
49	27.03.1976	4	W	2-0	Burnley, Anfield, 1st Division
50	30.03.1976		W	1-0	Barcelona, Nou Camp,
					UEFA Cup Semi-final 1st leg
51	03.04.1976	2	W	1-0	Everton, Anfield, 1st Division
52	06.04.1976	2	W	1-0	Leicester City, Anfield, 1st Division
53	10.04.1976	2	D	0-0	Aston Villa, Villa Park, 1st Division
54	14.04.1976		D	1-1	Barcelona, Anfield, UEFA Cup Semi-final 2L
55	17.04.1976	1	W	5-3	Stoke City, Anfield, 1st Division
56	19.04.1976	1	W	3-0	Manchester City, Maine Road, 1st Division
57	28.04.1976		W	3-2	Club Brugge, Anfield, UEFA Cup Final 1st leg
58	04.05.1976	1	W	3-1	Wolves, Molineux, 1st Division
59	19.05.1976		D	1-1	Club Brugge, Olympic Stadium,
					UEFA Cup Final 2nd leg

Friendlies

1	02.08.1975	W	2-0	Utrecht, Utrecht, Friendly
2	05.08.1975	W	2-0	Borussia Dortmund, Westfalen Stadion, Friendly
3	08.08.1975	D	1-1	Roda, Sportpark Kaalheide, Friendly
4	21.04.1976	L	5-6	Tranmere Rovers, Prenton Park, Testimonial*
5	27.05.1976	L	1-3	Hercules, Estadio Jose Rico Perez, Friendly

* Testimonial for Tranmere Rovers player Ray Mathias

Appearances for the 1975/1976 season

Name	League	FA Cup	LC	UEFA	Total
Ray Clemence	42	2	3	12	59
Phil Neal	42	2	3	12	59
Kevin Keegan	41	2	3	11	57
Ian Callaghan	40	2	3	12	57
Emlyn Hughes	41	2	3	11	57
Phil Thompson	41	2	3	11	57
Steve Heighway	39	2	2	11	54
John Toshack	35	2	2	11	50
Ray Kennedy	30	2	1	10	43
Jimmy Case	27	2	1	9	39
Tommy Smith	24	2	0	9	35
Brian Hall	13	1	2	9	25
Peter Cormack	17	0	3	4	24
David Fairclough	14	0	0	5	19
Joey Jones	13	0	0	1	14
Alec Lindsay	6	0	3	2	11
Terry McDermott	9	0	1	0	10
Phil Boersma	3	0	1	1	5
Brian Kettle	1	0	0	1	2
Chris Lawler	0	0	0	1	1
Max Thompson	0	0	0	1	1

Goalscorers for the 1975/1976 season

Name	League	FA Cup	LC	UEFA	Total
John Toshack	16	1	0	6	23
Kevin Keegan	12	1	0	3	16
Jimmy Case	6	0	1	5	12
Ray Kennedy	6	0	0	4	10
David Fairclough	7	0	0	1	8
Phil Neal	6	0	0	1	7
Steve Heighway	4	0	0	2	6
Ian Callaghan	3	0	0	1	4
Emlyn Hughes	2	0	0	0	2
Phil Thompson	0	0	0	2	2
Brian Hall	2	0	0	0	2
Peter Cormack	1	0	0	0	1
Alec Lindsay	0	0	1	0	1
Terry McDermott	1	0	0	0	1

The squad during the 1975/1976 season

Ray Clemence, Goalkeeper
Peter McDonnell, Goalkeeper
Emlyn Hughes, Defender
Joey Jones, Defender
Brian Kettle, Defender
Phil Thompson, Defender
Alec Lindsay, Defender
John McLaughlin, Defender
Phil Neal, Defender
Tommy Smith, Defender
Chris Lawler, Defender
Max Thompson, Defender
Ian Callaghan, Midfielder
Jimmy Case, Midfielder
Peter Cormack, Midfielder
Steve Heighway, Midfielder
Ray Kennedy, Midfielder
Terry McDermott, Midfielder
Brian Hall, Midfielder
Phil Boersma, Striker
Alan Waddle, Striker
Kevin Keegan, Striker
David Fairclough, Striker
John Toshack, Striker
Kevin Kewley, Striker

Transfers for the 1975/1976 season

In:
Joey Jones, Wrexham, £110,000, 14 July 1975

Out:
Frank Lane, Notts County, Free, July 1975
Chris Lawler, Portsmouth, Free, 22 October 1975
Phil Boersma, Middlesbrough, £72,000, December 1975

A collection of statistics for the 1975/1976 season

The season in numbers:
Total games: 59
Games won: 33
Games drawn: 18
Games lost: 8
Clean sheets – League: 23
Clean sheets – Overall: 29
Total goals: 95
Average attendance at home – League: 41,670
Average attendance at home – Overall: 39,847
Average goals per game – League: 1.95
Average goals per game – Overall: 2.14
Average goal minute – League: 60
Average goal minute – Overall: 58

Goals split down to competitions:
League – 66
UEFA Cup – 25
FA Cup – 2
League Cup – 2

Player debuts:
Joey Jones against QPR on 16.08.1975
David Fairclough against Middlesbrough on 01.11.1975
Brian Kettle against Real Sociedad on 04.11.1975

Statistics and information provided by LFChistory.net

10 : REDS REMAIN RESPLENDENT

1976/77

LIVERPOOL REPORTED FOR PRE-SEASON IN THE summer of 1976 with the shadow of the Kevin Keegan bombshell hanging over them.

The England star had caused a sensation by revealing that he was embarking on his last season with the Reds as he wanted a new challenge abroad, with all the financial awards that such a move would entail. Spanish giants Real Madrid wasted no time in declaring an interest. The *Daily Express* reported on June 28: "England football star Kevin Keegan lay in hospital last night unaware that his club Liverpool had turned down a Real Madrid offer of around £700,000, that would make him the highest priced player in British football history. Keegan is in hospital with stomach trouble and knew nothing of yesterday's drama. Agustín Dominguez, Real's general secretary, rang John Smith with an open ended offer worth up to £700,000, but was told politely, 'Nothing done.' Last night Smith said: 'It was a most friendly discussion, but Señor Dominguez was told we were just not interested in doing business.' Dominguez also spoke with Liverpool's secretary Peter Robinson, who said: 'Keegan is under contract; we are in the European Cup and we are all looking forward immensely to the new season.' Miljan Miljanic, the Real manager, made his fourth and final check in two months on Keegan, in an exhibition match in Paris last week. He said: 'I have watched several players extensively in Europe and South America, and Keegan is unquestionably the type of player who we want to replace Günter Netzer with. There is no other player I know of in world football today who has the same kind of professionalism and energy as Keegan.' Liverpool's refusal was predictable in spite of the price. The Reds were expecting the offer, and knew that money was no object to Real. But as manager Bob Paisley said: 'Money is of no use to us.'"

Despite Keegan's intentions to leave Merseyside, spirits were high during the club's annual meeting on July 23. The *Liverpool Echo* reported: "Liverpool are ready for next season's challenge in the European Cup and they are prepared to plunge into the transfer market for the right man. That was the message to shareholders from manager Bob Paisley at last night's annual meeting at the Holiday Inn. Mr. Paisley said: 'We are in good heart and we are optimistic about the European Cup. I do not see anyone who we should be afraid of and if we get the breaks at the right time I am quite convinced that we can do well. And if there is a player out there who I think will help us to a European Cup win we will go for him.'"

Recalling the season in which Liverpool won the First Division title, the UEFA Cup, and the Central League, Paisley paid tribute to the backroom men at the club, including Joe Fagan, Ronnie Moran, Roy Evans, Tom Saunders and Ken Addison and said: "Without the team spirit we have, Liverpool would not be the club it is. It runs from top to bottom and if I have achieved anything it is entirely due to the co-operation I have received."

On August 12, Paisley found the player he was looking for in the form of Liverpudian, David Johnson from Ipswich Town. The following day the *Daily Mirror* reported: "England striker David Johnson signs for Liverpool for a club record fee of £200,000 and said: 'It's great to be home.' Merseyside-born Johnson dashed to Anfield yesterday after Liverpool moved in with a late bid to pip Spurs at the post for the Ipswich centre-forward. Johnson, who moved to East Anglia from Everton four years ago in a cash plus Rod Belfitt exchange deal, has been unsettled at Portman Road for several months. And last week Ipswich manager Bobby Robson made him officially available for transfer. After completing all the formalities last night a delighted Johnson said: 'I feel tremendous. It's a relief that I've finally put pen to paper and that it's all over, I never really wanted to sign for any other club. Spurs showed a lot of interest and offered a lot of money and I saw them out of courtesy. But I told them honestly that I'd prefer to go back North. I didn't fancy a London club'."

The boyhood Red started his career at Everton which Johnson says came as a "great shock" to his family who were all Reds. He certainly got Liverpool's attention when he scored the winning goal as a 20-year-old against Liverpool at Goodison on November 13, 1971, a feat he would repeat for the Reds at Goodison in 1978. Bill Shankly made two enquiries for Johnson while at Everton but Harry Catterick wouldn't let him go across the park. Shankly also asked for him on a couple more occasions while Johnson's career flourished at Ipswich, who at the time were usually a top-three team.

Johnson was soon to become known as 'The Doc' as he used to suffer from a sore throat so he always kept cough sweets in his bag along with headache tablets. "Everyone used to go to my bag to use my gear," Johnson explained. "Terry Mac went in there one time and took out all these pills and stuff and said, 'It's like a flippin' doctor's bag' and after that, it just stuck."

Although Johnson was Paisley's only new recruit ahead of the upcoming 1976/77 season, Brian Hall, who only featured in 13 league games the previous season, moved on to pastures new at Second Division Plymouth Argyle for a fee of £50,000.

On August 14, Liverpool took on Southampton at Wembley in the Charity Shield. John Toshack scored early in the second half to give his side an important pre-season boost while serving notice that he would not be stepping aside for new signing David Johnson. After his team claimed their first piece silverware of the season, manager Bob Paisley spoke to the *Liverpool Echo*: "A week today we start what I believe will be the most demanding season I have ever known for Liverpool. It is always hard to defend the Championship and we do accept that. Opponents always try that little bit harder to beat the Champs. But a new feature will make it that much more difficult, the new demands of international fixtures and co-operation with England manager Don Revie in his preparation for World Cup qualifying games. We have a duty to our public to maintain our standards at the highest level and to do that we need new faces. That is why I paid a club record fee for Johnson this week. I hope there will be more incomings to give us fresh strength in other departments."

Paisley was refusing to allow the Keegan affair to rock the boat as Liverpool's first league game against Norwich loomed, but the player's declaration of intent clearly stunned Liverpudlians. Under the headline: 'KEEGAN, IT'S THE LAST GOODBYE' the *Liverpool Echo* reported: "Liverpool supporters must start accepting, as a fact of football life, that Keegan will be leaving in a year's time to play for a Continental club. This is what he stated publicly, and nothing short of a drastic loss of form or injury will make him change his mind. Keegan said: 'I know my worth. The rewards of playing for a big club abroad are so staggering that, by going out of the country, I could be a millionaire in five years. I am not pleading poverty now, but with income tax at 83p in the pound for me, what's the point of sticking around indefinitely?' Paisley reacted calmly, saying: 'I'll cross the Keegan bridge when I come to it. There's nothing I can do about it now. People should try and put themselves in his position and ask what they would do if they had the chance to earn money like that'." He then revealed that David Johnson, if fit, would make his league debut at home to Norwich, in the opening league game of the season, but told the fans that Toshack would not necessarily be the man to make way. He was ready to experiment early on.

Jimmy Case turned out to be the odd man out and in. The *Liverpool Echo*'s Michael Charters wrote: "Liverpool open the season tomorrow with a 12-man team. And if that breaks the laws of football, manager Bob Paisley has explained that all 12 will play at some time. Johnson will wear the number eight shirt, Case will be substitute, but he will be used." The reserve team, selected for a game at West Brom that weekend, included Alec Lindsay, Peter Cormack, Terry McDermott, David Fairclough and Brian Kettle.

Clearly, the battle for places was going to be as strong as ever.

At a lunch in Glasgow in May 1976, shortly after winning his first league title as manager, Bob Paisley, accompanied by Bill Shankly, was named Football Manager of the Year and was presented with a cheque for £1,000. Prior to kick-off at Anfield that afternoon against Norwich, Paisley received his award, presented to him by Mr. R. C. Miquel, chairman and managing director of Bell's Scotch Whisky.

A second-half Steve Heighway strike from close range was enough for the champions to claim an important first-day victory over the Canaries and new signing David Johnson made a satisfying start to his Liverpool career, linking up well with Toshack and Keegan.

News then broke that Liverpool's five-man England contingent had been cut to three for the game against the Republic of Ireland at

Wembley, with the omission of Phil Neal and Ray Kennedy, but that was certainly not going to worry Paisley.

The Reds followed up their opening-day win against Norwich by taking maximum points at The Hawthorns, thanks to a John Toshack goal. Johnson then got his first goal for the club in a game at Birmingham, but Liverpool lost 2-1. The Keegan-Toshack-Johnson combination put things right by inspiring a 3-1 home success over Coventry. Slowly, but surely, Liverpool were settling into the pattern of play Paisley wanted, but there was still some work to be done before Johnson would fit smoothly into the jigsaw. After four games played, Aston Villa, Bristol City and Middlesbrough were the three teams who joined Liverpool at the summit of the First Division with six points apiece.

After being eliminated from the League Cup by West Bromwich Albion, Liverpool visited the Baseball Ground to face Dave Mackay's Derby County in what turned out to be a superb encounter.

The Derby matchday programme reported: "Liverpool took the lead in the third minute as Archie Gemmill fouled David Johnson eight yards outside the penalty area, and from Keegan's free-kick Ray Kennedy moved in to lob Graham Moseley on the volley. The Rams drew level after 16 minutes, Leighton James collecting a throw curled over a centre, which Charlie George side-footed past Ray Clemence. Nine minutes later the Rams took the lead. George lobbed a pass through to Kevin Hector, Tommy Smith falling as he went in to challenge, and when Hector fired in a cross-shot Phil Neal turned it into his own net. So the Rams had a 2-1 interval lead but were pegged back in the 50th minute. Neal received a long pass by Steve Heighway, sent in a cross, and as the Rams' defence hesitated, Liverpool striker John Toshack scored. He nearly put Liverpool ahead, when Kennedy slipped the ball through, but Moseley managed to divert the Welshman's shot. As Liverpool mounted their customary second-half pressure the Rams defence had looked wobbly at times. Liverpool took the lead with seven minutes left; Neal's cross was headed on by Toshack for Keegan to slam the ball home." Final score: Derby County 2-3 Liverpool.

After coming back from 2-1 down to take maximum points at Derby, another victory over Tottenham at Anfield the following Saturday encouraged the defending champions even more. However, a 1-0 defeat at Newcastle, and a goalless home draw against Middlesbrough forced the side to keep their feet on the ground.

Liverpool now faced a fortnight without a game because of the international situation. One man who refused to remain inactive was the evergreen Ian Callaghan, who asked to play for the reserves. Callaghan, Mr Perpetual Motion, had totted up a fantastic 771 senior games, but he was still keen to turn out in the Central League against Sunderland. Paisley said: "He is a wonderful example to some of the youngsters in football. He doesn't want to break the rhythm of a game a week. That is the true professional speaking."

On October 14, Liverpool's new souvenir shop was opened by Ray Clemence and club director Mr. Corkish, which was a part of the new development complex, costing £300,000, situated at the back of the Kop and run by development officer Ken Addison. The *Liverpool Echo* reported: "Reds fans will find Ken Addison and his staff housed in palatial new surroundings on Saturday. The brand new development office and souvenir shop was officially opened today. It's a far cry from the car park, which was where Ken's first office was when he was first appointed in 1962.

"Addison was working for a charity at the time, when he answered an advertisement in a national newspaper for 'an organiser for a First Division club.' As a self-confessed 'dyed-in-the-wool Liverpudlian,' he was keeping his fingers crossed that it was Liverpool. He started organising draws, introduced the Golden Goal tickets the following year. Liverpool were one of the first top division clubs to set up such initiatives and other money raising events. At first these raised around £16,000 a year – now that figure has grown to £50,000 a year, and Ken now has a staff of six to keep things ticking over."

After the international break, on October 16, neighbours Everton visited Anfield and were only a point behind the Reds in the standings. Everton boss Billy Bingham was confined to a hospital bed after a minor operation and Liverpool threatened to give him a relapse by storming to a 3-1 victory.

New signing David Johnson was injured and bitterly disappointed to be missing a clash against his old club but Toshack returned to boost the Reds. Four goals ended the derby scoring drought but the game would be remembered for much more than that. Liverpool's first-half display was so brilliant, so masterly in design and execution,that they obliterated their great rivals and by half-time it was all over as a contest. A Toshack header from a McDermott corner led to Heighway opening the scoring from close range. Then Neal hammered home a penalty after Keegan was brought down by Ken McNaught. Liverpool's play was magnificent at this point and when Everton were denied a penalty of their own, after Neal clearly appeared to handle, the Blues despaired. On the stroke of the interval, Joey Jones set off on a 40-yard run, crossing for Toshack to glance home a header. Dobson was to reduce the deficit but there was no way back.

Four days later, Liverpool played Trabzonspor in Turkey where Ian Callaghan set a new record of European appearances with 79 games, previously held by Norman Hunter at Leeds United. Ray Clemence doesn't have the fondest memories from that game: "Trabzonspor, in

1976, was the worst European trip ever. The pitch had rocks all over it. The hotel was awful, we were woken by the noise of farm animals at 5am, the food was terrible and we lost 1-0."

The following Saturday the Reds could only manage a 1-1 draw against Jimmy Armfield's Leeds at Elland Road. Phil Neal set a Liverpool record from this game on by making 417 consecutive appearances until September 24, 1983.

The point Liverpool gained at Leeds was followed by triumphs over Midlands outfits Leicester City and Aston Vllla, which saw the Reds secure a three-point advantage at the top. Aston Villa proved to be the best team Liverpool had met up to that point, despite the 3-0 scoreline. Villa were to exact their revenge over Liverpool and hammer home their potential in sensational fashion in the not too distant future but for the time being Paisley's lads were on top of the pile.

The Reds pushed on with a lone goal victory at Sunderland and an emphatic 5-1 win over Leicester at Anfield on November 9. England boss Don Revie watched the game, keeping an eye on Emlyn Hughes who was dramatically recalled for the crucial World Cup qualifier against Italy after 18 months in the international shadows.

Hughes later revealed to the BBC the phone call conversation he had with Revie at that time: "I remember I was at home one day and the phone went and he said, 'It's the boss here' and I said, 'Who, Bob Paisley?' and he said, 'No it's Don Revie', so I asked him sarcastically, 'Ah, are you my boss now then?' He answered, 'I'm going to recall you for the England squad'. I said, 'What? You're recalling me after 18 months, after I've been playing the best football of my career, while you've been playing all of the garbage that you've been picking for the England side. Anyway, I gave him so much stick on the phone for about twenty minutes my wife thought I had blown it."

After that storming performance against Leicester, the *Liverpool*

Echo reported: "Who, on this form, can stop Liverpool?" Paisley was glowing, his side holding a commanding five-point lead after just 14 games, with Ipswich, Villa, Manchester City, Newcastle, Leicester and Middlesbrough all trailing in their wake. Paisley said: "This is as great a team as Liverpool have ever had in its history. It's the equal of the marvellous mid-Sixties side which won the League-Cup-League in successive years and they are getting better! Our performances in the last few weeks since we beat Everton have been, collectively, the best displays in such a short time that I can recall from any Liverpool team in my 37 years with the club.' But Paisley, ever the realist, added: 'Now we must cash in on our lead, not sit back and admire it. You have to work harder when you are on top. You have to keep your heads down and keep going.'"

Midfielder Peter Cormack had been unable to regain his place in Liverpool's starting XI after sustaining a knee injury in December 1975 and on November 10, he was transferred to First Division Bristol City for a fee of £50,000.

His move came as no real surprise as the Scot had been turning out for the reserves since the season began. Liverpool remained unbeaten throughout the remainder of November, drawing with Arsenal and beating Bristol City. The Robins' manager Alan Dicks made Cormack the captain for the day to face his former teammates and the former Red received a tremendous reception from the Kop when he led out the City team.

Despite looking in such good form, the team Paisley had saluted so warmly were to soon feel the heat in what can only be described as a disastrous December.

It began with a 1-0 defeat at Ipswich, continued with a shock 5-1 reversal at Villa and became almost a mini-crisis after a 2-0 setback at West Ham. The Villa game, in the middle of the month, was the talk of the whole country. The home side exacted sweet revenge for that result at Anfield a month and a half earlier, the Reds suffering their heaviest defeat for 10 years. Villa had shown great promise in defeat at Anfield. Now, it bubbled to the surface, Andy Gray opening the scoring with a deadly header, John Deehan adding a double, and Brian Little floating a superb fourth over Ray Clemence. Ray Kennedy got one back but Gray rubbed it in by claiming his second and Villa's fifth before the referee blew for half-time. Paisley held a no-holds-barred inquest, declaring: "Some of them, because they have gone top after winning the league last season, think it's all going to be easy. This will convince them that nothing is easy in this game. You don't win championships by what you do at home. You have to produce the goods away. I couldn't believe we could play so badly."

After the West Ham reversal at Upton Park three days later, Paisley handed out a warning: "If players do not fight for Liverpool, they will not be in the team." A 4-0 home win over Stoke finally reversed the trend after three defeats in four games.

Liverpool ended the month with a visit to Maine Road on December 29. An own goal by Dave Watson three minutes from time dramatically denied City a place alongside the Reds at the top of the First Division. The game finished 1-1 and after a dire end to 1976, incredibly Liverpool finished the calendar year top of the First Division, albeit having played two more games than their nearest rivals, Ipswich Town and Manchester City.

Liverpool marked the turn of the year with a 2-0 home win over Sunderland but were disappointed by a 1-1 draw with West Brom at Anfield on January 15. The only other league game played in January produced a defeat at Norwich and this lack of consistency was worrying.

Liverpool also made hard work of their third round FA Cup tie against Third Division opponents Crystal Palace. The Reds needed a replay to beat the Eagles 3-2 at Selhurst Park after a stalemate encounter at Anfield. Steve Heighway scored twice to take his goal-scoring tally to eight for the season.

Not only did Steve Heighway so often take the "highway" up the left wing, riding tackles, showing perfect ball control at breathtaking speeds, delivering great passes and assists, he also chipped in with his fair share of goals.

The Dubliner possessed an unorthodox style and pace which caused many a problem for defenders and he was now in his sixth season as a regular first-team starter after being spotted playing for non-league Skelmersdale United by Bob Paisley's sons, Graham and Robert. Bob Sr. himself decided to have a look and was very impressed: "When I first saw him, he was playing for Skelmersdale against South Liverpool and he almost took my breath away because he had 'star' written all over him. I even told one of our coaches that he was the best amateur footballer I'd ever seen."

Heighway signed for Shankly's Liverpool in May 1970 when he was 22. Like his teammate Brian Hall, Heighway was a university graduate, a very different background to most professional sports-men. He achieved his degree in economics and politics at the University of Warwick in Coventry. He explained to the *Daily Mail* how he became a First Division footballer fresh from the lecture halls: "When I went to university it was not at the expense of a football career. I wasn't good enough at that stage. I became an amateur with Manchester City after they saw me playing for the England grammar schools team. It was never a very serious relationship. It wasn't until Roy Rees, who was manager of the English universities team, took me to Skelmersdale that I joined Liverpool. I was never what you might call an academic, an intellectual. I had no difficulty in deciding to be a footballer when I finished at university. There was no risk involved in going into football. I had these qualifications behind me. I knew that I could still do what I intended doing when I went to university – and that was to become a teacher. At university it's a do-as-you-please life. If you don't feel like doing your own work one day there's always tomorrow. Whatever discipline there is, is self-imposed. As a footballer you have to get used to more regular working hours and doing what you are told. Now you take orders, but I'm loving it and I love Liverpool. I would rather pack in the game than move. The thought of being a transfer market footballer depresses me. As long as Liverpool are happy with me I'm delighted."

It was due to Heighway's academic achievements that he got his nickname 'Big Bamber'. Teammate and fellow academic Brian Hall was dubbed 'Little Bamber' after the television programme University Challenge host Bamber Gascoigne.

Heighway told the *Liverpool Echo* of the dressing room camaraderie he received owing to his previous academic studies: "I think the other lads expected me to walk into the ground in a cap and gown. It's funny really. Anyone without a degree is the odd man out among my friends. Now I'm the odd man out because I've got one. Not that it makes any difference to me. I am not an academic or an intellectual. Sport has always meant more to me. I would probably have got a better degree if I hadn't spent so much time at university playing football. But the lads do take the mickey and a lot! It's difficult to know how much they mean it because professional footballers are the world's biggest mickey-takers. I think it's all just good humoured. I hope so, anyway. I'm perhaps too self-conscious."

Tommy Smith recalls one incident that showed Heighway could, in fact, stand up for himself, even when facing the frightening Bill Shankly: "Shortly after Steve Heighway first joined we were at a meeting with Shanks. Now Steve in those days was still an amateur player in his mind as well as having a university degree, and he would take offence pretty quickly. He's a great lad, terrific fella, but I remember a time when Shanks called him out for not helping a teammate in a situation where he could have helped. Shanks said, 'Tell me, son, if your neighbour's house was on fire what would you do?' Would you get a bucket of water and help him put it out, or would you watch it burn down?' I don't know how everybody kept a straight face, because Steve in his wisdom gets up and says, 'Well, all I can say is till you ask me a serious question, I can't answer. If you ask me silly questions, all you're going to get is silly answers'. That knocked Shanks back on his heels and set the place rocking, I can tell you."

Bob Paisley couldn't praise his winger enough: "I've never seen a footballer move more gracefully than Steve Heighway. He should have been an Olympic athlete because he was so beautifully balanced."

February was much brighter on the league front for Paisley's men, with three wins in four outings. When they completely outplayed Birmingham City on February 5, the *Liverpool Echo* reported: "Liverpool are building up a formidable head of steam as they enter the home stretch in the defence of their title.

After the Reds' 3-1 home victory over Derby County on February 19, the league table showed Liverpool top with 38 points from 28 games, Ipswich second with 36 from 25 and Manchester City, Middlesbrough and Manchester United all in the chasing pack.

March was to be unforgettable for Liverpool fans. Mention David Fairclough and St Etienne to any Liverpudlian from that era and their face will light up. Two European Cup games against the French giants were to be remarkable to say the least as the Reds sought a place in the semi-finals. Kevin Keegan was ruled out of the first game right at the start of the month, with an injured right knee. Terry McDermott took over in midfield and the St Etienne stadium was a cauldron, as Liverpool came to within an ace of conjuring up a tremendous first-leg result. Ten minutes from time, Dominique Bathenay volleyed home to give the home side a crucial advantage for the return.

Liverpool then had to put the European Cup out of their minds and concentrate on the domestic competitions they were still fighting for. A brilliant Steve Heighway header was enough to beat Newcastle after fine work by Fairclough. Keegan was back for the game at Tottenham, but the Reds lost 1-0. It was a doubly disappointing day as the news broke that influential defender Phil Thompson had undergone a cartilage operation. At Middlesbrough, a dress rehearsal for an impending FA Cup quarter-final, a 30-yard rocket from Emlyn Hughes proved crucial. The Reds were top, with 42 points from 31 games, but Ipswich and Manchester City, with matches in hand, were still threatening. A tension-packed week loomed in which Liverpool would aim for two semi-finals.

On March 16, Liverpool welcomed St Etienne to Anfield, when a capacity crowd packed the ground, willing the Merseysiders to wipe out the French side's one-goal first leg advantage. It was to be the night of the super sub. The *Liverpool Echo* reported: "With their European Cup hopes vanishing in an atmosphere of almost unbearable tension and drama, Bob Paisley found the man for the moment. Fairclough, brought on for Toshack 18 minutes from the end, showed the skill, the cool nerve and the calmness of a veteran to stroke in the winning goal, which made Anfield almost take off with excitement into the night air. Super sub indeed! Fairclough has scored some vital goals in his 12 months as Liverpool's secret weapon. He is the man who lopes on from the bench to win matches for the Reds, but this was the most vital. Keegan scored after just 1 minute 45 seconds to level matters on aggregate. St Etienne stormed back to regain the lead, when Bathenay struck with a swerving shot from 30 yards. Ray Kennedy equalised on the 58-minute mark, and then Fairclough stepped into the heat of battle to bring the house down."

Liverpool now had to entertain Middlesbrough in the FA Cup, giving Ipswich the chance to make their mark in the league, but the men from Portman Road lost 1-0 at Sunderland. Paisley's men secured a smooth 2-0 win over Boro, Fairclough producing another moment of individual brilliance to swing the game their way. During the second half there was a flare-up between Jimmy Case and Boro's Graeme Souness near the halfway line. The two midfielders tangled and after throwing a couple of missed punch at Case, the Scot shaped up to punch his future teammate again whilst he held the Scouser down by the neck. Both players were booked and Souness was lucky to stay on.

The bookies were now quoting Liverpool at 12-1 to win the treble of league, FA Cup and European Cup, odds Paisley described as ridiculous, bearing in mind the magnitude of the challenge.

April 9 was the day for an absolutely crucial top-of-the-table match with third-placed Manchester City. Lifted by the sheer quality of another fine European display, a 3-1 win in Zurich, Liverpool produced the goods to edge out the men from Maine Road. Brian Kidd wiped out a Keegan opener in the second half but Heighway responded a minute later when he pounced for the winner after a Jimmy Case shot had rattled the bar.

Two days later Liverpool visited Stoke hoping to regain the top spot from Ipswich, who since their defeat at Sunderland went on to win four of their five following league games. In what would be Liverpool's 50th game of the season, Paisley fielded the exact same eleven that beat Manchester City just 48 hours prior. *The Times* reported: "A precious point was swept away from Liverpool in their pursuit of the championship at Stoke yesterday, though it would be more accurate to suggest that they preserved a point for it was Stoke City who looked more likely winners as the match evolved."

Despite the setback at Stoke, the Reds bounced back five days later beating Terry Neill's Arsenal 2-0 at Anfield. The *Liverpool Echo* reported that it was: "A massacre in all but the scoreline. Terry McDermott had an outstanding game, his use of the ball being meticulous and his variety in the attacking play had the fans enthralled."

McDermott, after needing two seasons to settle into the Liverpool side, had now blossomed and during the 1976/77 season he became paramount to Liverpool's midfield. Kirkby-born McDermott supported Liverpool as a boy and used to play in the Sacred Heart school team at Kirkby with future boxer John Conteh. He later played for Kirkby Boys, where his teammates included Aston Villa's Dennis Mortimer and John McLaughlin, a former Liverpool player.

He signed for Bury as a 16-year-old midfielder and was immediately placed on a malt and milk diet to build him up. Four years later he moved to Newcastle – only to find Liverpool had been interested in him, and might have made a bid. When first selected for England's Under-23 team, he was asked if his next ambition was to play for the full England side, but he replied: "No, it's to play for Liverpool." He played in 56 league matches for the Magpies and just like future Kop hero, Alan Kennedy, played against Liverpool in the 1974 FA Cup final before moving to Anfield.

McDermott returned to his native Merseyside in November 1974 when he was a few weeks short of his 23rd birthday as one of Bob Paisley's earliest signings.

Three days after his arrival, McDermott played in six successive league games in place of Brian Hall, but it was a frustrating time for him as he was in and out of the team as he settled in at his new club. In 1975/76 he was selected in the starting XI for the opening eight games but was then replaced by Hall whose place was taken by Jimmy Case later in the season. McDermott was stuck in the reserves as Liverpool captured the league title and the UEFA Cup and looked like a change of club would be the only way to resurrect his career.

Terry recalls the frustration he felt during his early days at Anfield: "There were many times when I went to see Bob Paisley and slammed the door so hard it almost came off its hinges. On numerous occasions I told him to stick his club where he wanted it. I just felt aggrieved at times because there were days I thought I'd played well and the pop-up toaster would come up showing 8 or 11, or I never played the next game. Maybe that was just a learning curve for me, for them to say to me, 'Hey, you think you've made it. You bloody haven't!'"

Phil Thompson, John Toshack and Ian Callaghan, three players who started the season against Norwich in Paisley's team of '12' were now sidelined due to injury. Emlyn Hughes told the *Liverpool Echo* how the team was coping without the influential trio: "Success breeds success and we've had loads of that in my time. This is the best team I've played in at Liverpool. Twelve months ago I was saying the same thing and I would say we could be just a little bit better now. The spirit is tremendous, the confidence sky-high and although we've been hit by a lot of injuries recently, the team pattern seems to have gone on just the same. Tommy Smith has come in for Phil Thompson and done better than at any time I can recall in my ten years playing alongside him. He's been simply fantastic. Terry McDermott has come in for Ian Callaghan, David Fairclough for John Toshack. Phil, Ian and Tosh have been out for a long time but we've kept rolling along."

At the end of April title rivals Ipswich, who were just one point behind the Reds, came to Merseyside for a real crunch clash, which turned out to be one of the most controversial games of the season. Liverpool won 2-1, thanks to goals from Kennedy and Keegan, but five players were booked, four Reds and one visitor. Referee Peter Willis infuriated the home supporters. He failed to clamp down on a running battle between Tommy Smith and Paul Mariner. Smith was consequently knocked out in a head-on collision with Mariner. "Tommy's gonna getcha," the crowd chanted when Smith finally wobbled erect, glaring in Mariner's direction.

Tough Tommy did "get him" twice in the next 10 minutes. Smith remained unpunished and went on to play an eventually outstanding part in Liverpool's victory. Brian Talbot and Jimmy Case then clashed as tempers flared. Heighway was stretchered off with blood pouring from a wound over his eye after Mick Mills had clattered into him. And a fan ran onto the pitch to hand the referee a pair of spectacles! Mr. Willis then called both captains together to try and calm things down. The only thing that really mattered was that Paisley's lads had the points in the bag and Ipswich boss Bobby Robson conceded that his team were now out of the title race.

Bob Paisley told the *Daily Mirror* after the game: "That was the closest there has ever been to a riot here. Certainly it was the worst I've seen on this ground. The sheer pressure of the game affected both teams and the crowd – this made me nervous."

Liverpool had beaten Everton in a Maine Road replay to reach the FA Cup final, and a league game now loomed against the side they would face at Wembley, Manchester United. It was to be no contest, simply because the Old Trafford outfit refused to break sweat. The *Liverpool Echo* report read: "They didn't compete, rarely challenged or made an effort to tackle. The oddity is that while Liverpool had 95 per cent of the play, they only scored once through a first-half Kevin

Keegan header." This victory gave the Reds a four-point lead over second-place Manchester City and one hand on retaining the First Division trophy.

On May 5, Liverpool suddenly swooped into the transfer market, a move Bob Paisley described as "insurance for next season". The player in question was a 21-year-old Scot by the name of Alan Hansen, who joined the Reds from Partick Thistle for £100,000. Curiously, Hansen was turned down by Liverpool when he attended trials at Melwood as a teenager. Chief scout Geoff Twentyman sent Alan a letter which simply read: "Dear Alan, It was decided after trails that you did not reach the standard required. Thank you for attending."

It was thought at the time that the £100,000 fee for Hansen would look like peanuts when the Scot reached his full potential. Bolton made a desperate bid of £80,000 just before the transfer deadline in March, but Partick Thistle manager Bertie Auld had no hesitation in turning it down flat. Southampton and Newcastle were also said to be interested, but there was no way Hansen was going to be allowed to leave Firhill for anything under £100,000. Liverpool had watched him on several occasions and eventually agreed to pay Auld's asking price.

The talented Hansen had the ability to surge into attack and set up moves and finish them off. At the time of putting pen to paper the young Scot was aware that he wouldn't walk straight into the first team. He told the press: "As far as I am concerned this could not have been a better move. Liverpool are the best team in the business and they have proved that conclusively over the years. However, I realise I am about to start my soccer education. I'm going to be put through the mill. Liverpool will want to groom me before I even get close to the first team. I'm really looking forward to life as a Liverpool player and I'm determined not to let them down."

At the time no one realised how important Paisley's recruit would be in seasons to come but Liverpool's priority was simply to get at least one trophy in the bag, in what had developed into a truly remarkable campaign.

In the end Liverpool were to edge to the title, rather than storm to it. They drew 1-1 at QPR and 0-0 at Coventry which meant that just one point was needed to settle it and end Manchester City's mathematical miracle of catching them. They got the point that was needed in a successive goalless draw, this time in front of their home fans against West Ham United on May 14.

Michael Charters reported for the *Liverpool Echo*: "The capacity crowd at Anfield on Saturday did their best, the players did their best, but somehow it fell a bit flat. The expected spectacular did not come up to other Anfield special occasions. The goalless draw against West Ham gave Liverpool the point they needed to end the title issue under any mathematical doubt. At the same time, the lack of attacking thrills put the game into the forgettable class."

Bob Paisley told the press after his team secured Liverpool's 10th First Division Championship: "The team would have liked to have clinched it in style but we have proved our right to the Championship over the whole season. The players deserve to be champions." Paisley was absolutely right. Only outstanding teams win this marathon race twice in succession. Liverpool deserved the salutes and the acclaim of the football public in general.

Liverpool finished the 1976/77 season with a visit to Ashton Gate to face relegation-fighting Bristol City. Although they lost 2-1 at Bristol, the Reds were still smiling as not only were they league champions, they had also sustained no injuries ahead of the FA and European Cup finals.

Two days before the FA Cup final against Manchester United,

Paisley told the *Daily Mirror*: "If you had told me we would be in the running for three trophies after losing three key players this season – Phil Thompson, Ian Callaghan and John Toshack – I'd have laughed at you. I would have settled for halfway. But when one door closes another opens – even if it sometimes smacks you in the face first. Other players have come through tremendously."

On May 21 at Wembley, Tommy Docherty's Manchester United put an end to Liverpool fans' dreams of achieving a historic treble. *The Times* reported: "After a distinguished season in which they had come to expect victory even on their poorer days, Liverpool suffered the rare irony of playing well and losing in Saturday's excellent FA Cup final at Wembley. With their 2-1 defeat by Manchester United went the hopes of an illustrious treble, also embracing the championship and European Cup. Too much was expected of them and when the moment came to draw on the strength that had previously been so reliably summoned, there was not enough left. Yet this was not a day when sympathy ranked high among the emotions. Liverpool had already enjoyed one prize-giving when retaining the championship title and on Wednesday in Rome they may revive their spirits in time to lift the European Cup in another final against Borussia Moenchengladbach. Such is their proven resilience that the tears of disappointment can quickly turn to those of pleasure. The treble would have been the fully ripened fruit of a decade but perhaps it was too perfect, too tidy for the ever unpredictable game of football."

Prior to Liverpool's European Cup final showdown in Rome, Bill Shankly, who longed for this one prize during his many years as manager, caught up with the *Sunday Express* writer Richard Bott: "I wanted to win the European Cup and I will be the happiest man in the world if Liverpool win in Rome. When the boys come out I will feel proud, tremendously proud. This is the moment they have been building for, the trophy we all wanted when I took the club into Europe 11 times in succession. I will feel proud, too, for the wonderful Liverpool public: that I have had something to do with them and the team. I started this side off, gave them their first lessons... Cally... Emlyn... Smithy... Kevin. But I will also feel sad and distant as I am no longer part of the Anfield scene. I'm not jealous of Bob Paisley. I will have my own satisfaction that all the years of trial and error; building up a system, attention to detail would have paid off."

Only four days after their defeat at Wembley, the Reds were to bounce back stronger with one of their most famous victories, on a never-to-be-forgotten night in Rome that was to be Kevin Keegan's swansong.

Thirty years earlier, Bob Paisley had rode into Rome on board a tank as a member of the liberating army. This time Paisley led a red army into the Italian capital to fight the final battle of Europe's league champions. In a way it was a similar rumbling, unstoppable, menacing vehicle which carried him there again.

Liverpool defeated the German champions 3-1 and achieved their long-term goal of winning the European Cup. *The Guardian* reported: "Liverpool gained their ultimate reward for 13 years of dogged perseverance in Continental competitions when they became the second English and third British club to win the European Cup, beating Borussia Moenchengladbach 3-1 in the final in Rome. After taking the lead and dominating the first half, they conceded a goal early in the second and for a time were in danger of being overwhelmed by the Germans' formidable attacking skill. But Tommy Smith put them back in front with his first goal of the season, probably the last and certainly the most important of his long career at Anfield, and Neal completed a famous British victory with a penalty seven minutes from the end.

"As the game finished, the 24,000 Liverpool supporters who had regaled the Olympic Stadium throughout with songs from home, silencing the German followers and reducing the Italian section of the audience almost to the role of intruders, reacted not with relief but with the jubilation of those who had known all along that the result would be right. Indeed, for the major part of the game there was little doubt that Liverpool would win."

After referee Robert Wurtz blew the final whistle, Emlyn Hughes later told the *BBC* what his and Bob Paisley's first word was to each other: "I remember walking over to Bob straight after the game, giving him a hug and we both looked at each other and at the same time said, 'Shanks'. We just both knew that it was 'Shanks' who had given us the players, and Bob, a chance to win that trophy."

Earlier in the season Tommy Smith, who had fallen out of favour as an automatic starter in Paisley's XI, announced that the 1976/77 season would be his last. Phil Neal and Joey Jones were regulars at full-back and Phil Thompson was proving to be reliable in other positions that Smith could cover with equal competence. Smith had only featured three times in the league when he won a regular spot back following Phil Thompson's injury in March. Consequently, 'The Anfield Iron' went on to play in the last 13 league fixtures, made his fourth FA Cup final appearance and in Rome, what was thought to be his 604th and final game for the club, scored the Reds' second goal.

On May 27, Smith's testimonial fixture was held at Anfield, against a Bobby Charlton Select XI, just two days after the European Cup was won. Smith and Hughes proudly paraded the giant trophy to an ecstatic reception from the home crowd. Although 35,694 fans turned up to say farewell to one of their most loyal servants, Anfield was far from its full capacity. This was mainly due to the fact that many Liverpool fans were still making their way back from Rome via rail and road.

What a season it had been for Liverpool Football Club and the awards kept on coming! Emlyn Hughes was honoured by the Football Writers' Association as their 1977 Footballer of the Year. Hughes described the award as an honour for all the Liverpool team. In addition to his captain's personal feat, Bob Paisley retained the Manager of the Year award and at the end of the 1977 calendar year, he was also presented with the BBC Sports Team of the Year Award by Scotland manager Ally MacLeod.

During the 1976/77 campaign, the Reds didn't lose a single top-flight league game at Anfield for only the third time in their history, the other two times coming during the 1893/94 and 1970/71 seasons. Kevin Keegan got his wish to play abroad and joined Hamburg for a fee of £500,000.

Yet, the Reds were not weakened as another Kop hero was soon to arrive from north of the border. Liverpool would simply go from strength to strength and the bombshell 'Mighty Mouse' dropped at the start of the season would soon become a distant memory in the minds of Liverpool fans.

1976/77: Facts and Statistics

Final league table

		P	W	D	L	F	A	W	D	L	F	A	PTS
1	Liverpool FC	42	18	3	0	47	11	5	8	8	15	22	57
2	Manchester City	42	15	5	1	38	13	6	9	6	22	21	56
3	Ipswich Town	42	15	4	2	41	11	7	4	10	25	28	52
4	Aston Villa	42	17	3	1	55	17	5	4	12	21	33	51
5	Newcastle United	42	14	6	1	40	15	4	7	10	24	34	49
6	Manchester United	42	12	6	3	41	22	6	5	10	30	40	47
7	WBA	42	10	6	5	38	22	6	7	8	24	34	45
8	Arsenal	42	11	6	4	37	20	5	5	11	27	39	43
9	Everton	42	9	7	5	35	24	5	7	9	27	40	42
10	Leeds United	42	8	8	5	28	26	7	4	10	20	25	42
11	Leicester City	42	8	9	4	30	28	4	9	8	17	32	42
12	Middlesbrough	42	11	6	4	25	14	3	7	11	15	31	41
13	Birmingham City	42	10	6	5	38	25	3	6	12	25	36	38
14	QPR	42	10	7	4	31	21	3	5	13	16	31	38
15	Derby	42	9	9	3	36	18	0	10	11	14	37	37
16	Norwich City	42	12	4	5	30	23	2	5	14	17	41	37
17	West Ham United	42	9	6	6	28	23	2	8	11	18	42	36
18	Bristol City	42	8	7	6	25	19	3	6	12	13	29	35
19	Coventry City	42	7	9	5	34	26	3	6	12	14	33	35
20	Sunderland	42	9	5	7	29	16	2	7	12	17	38	34
21	Stoke City	42	9	8	4	21	16	1	6	14	7	35	34
22	Tottenham	42	9	7	5	26	20	3	2	16	22	52	33

Games for the 1976/1977 season

(The number after date is league position after the game)

1	14.08.1976		W	1-0	Southampton, Wembley, Charity Shield
2	21.08.1976	4	W	1-0	Norwich City, Anfield, 1st Division
3	25.08.1976	1	W	1-0	West Bromwich Albion, The Hawthorns, 1st Division
4	28.08.1976	7	L	1-2	Birmingham City, St. Andrew's, 1st Division
5	31.08.1976		D	1-1	West Bromwich Albion, Anfield, League Cup 2nd round
6	04.09.1976	3	W	3-1	Coventry City, Anfield, 1st Division
7	06.09.1976		L	0-1	West Bromwich Albion, The Hawthorns, League Cup 2nd round replay
8	11.09.1976	1	W	3-2	Derby County, Baseball Ground, 1st Division
9	14.09.1976		W	2-0	Crusaders, Anfield, European Cup 1st R 1st L

10	18.09.1976	1	W	2-0	Tottenham Hotspur, Anfield, 1st Division
11	25.09.1976	1	L	0-1	Newcastle United, St. James' Park, 1st Division
12	28.09.1976		W	5-0	Crusaders, Seaview, European Cup 1st R 2nd L
13	02.10.1976	3	D	0-0	Middlesbrough, Anfield, 1st Division
14	16.10.1976	1	W	3-1	Everton, Anfield, 1st Division
15	20.10.1976		L	0-1	Trabzonspor, Trabzon Sehir Stadt, European Cup 2nd R 1st L
16	23.10.1976	3	D	1-1	Leeds United, Elland Road, 1st Division
17	27.10.1976	1	W	1-0	Leicester City, Filbert Street, 1st Division
18	30.10.1976	1	W	3-0	Aston Villa, Anfield, 1st Division
19	03.11.1976		W	3-0	Trabzonspor, Anfield, European Cup 2nd R 2L
20	06.11.1976	1	W	1-0	Sunderland, Roker Park, 1st Division
21	09.11.1976	1	W	5-1	Leicester City, Anfield, 1st Division
22	20.11.1976	1	D	1-1	Arsenal, Highbury, 1st Division
23	27.11.1976	1	W	2-1	Bristol City, Anfield, 1st Division
24	04.12.1976	1	L	0-1	Ipswich Town, Portman Road, 1st Division
25	11.12.1976	1	W	3-1	Queens Park Rangers, Anfield, 1st Division
26	15.12.1976	1	L	1-5	Aston Villa, Villa Park, 1st Division
27	18.12.1976	2	L	0-2	West Ham United, Upton Park, 1st Division
28	27.12.1976	1	W	4-0	Stoke City, Anfield, 1st Division
29	29.12.1976	1	D	1-1	Manchester City, Maine Road, 1st Division
30	01.01.1977	1	W	2-0	Sunderland, Anfield, 1st Division
31	08.01.1977		D	0-0	Crystal Palace, Anfield, FA Cup 3rd round
32	11.01.1977		W	3-2	Crystal Palace, Selhurst Park, FA Cup 3rd round replay
33	15.01.1977	1	D	1-1	West Bromwich Albion, Anfield, 1st Division
34	22.01.1977	1	L	1-2	Norwich City, Carrow Road, 1st Division
35	29.01.1977		W	3-0	Carlisle United, Anfield, FA Cup 4th round
36	05.02.1977	1	W	4-1	Birmingham City, Anfield, 1st Division
37	16.02.1977	2	D	0-0	Manchester United, Old Trafford, 1st Division
38	19.02.1977	1	W	3-1	Derby County, Anfield, 1st Division
39	26.02.1977		W	3-1	Oldham Athletic, Anfield, FA Cup 5th round
40	02.03.1977		L	0-1	Saint-Étienne, Stade Geoffroy-Guichard, European Cup 3rd R 1st L
41	05.03.1977	1	W	1-0	Newcastle United, Anfield, 1st Division
42	09.03.1977	1	L	0-1	Tottenham Hotspur, White Hart Lane, 1st Division
43	12.03.1977	1	W	1-0	Middlesbrough, Ayresome Park, 1st Division
44	16.03.1977		W	3-1	Saint-Étienne, Anfield, European Cup 3rd R 2nd L
45	19.03.1977		W	2-0	Middlesbrough, Anfield, FA Cup 6th round
46	22.03.1977	2	D	0-0	Everton, Goodison Park, 1st Division
47	02.04.1977	1	W	3-1	Leeds United, Anfield, 1st Division
48	06.04.1977		W	3-1	FC Zürich, Letzigrund Stadium,

					Eur. Cup Semi Final 1st L
49	09.04.1977	2	W	2-1	Manchester City, Anfield, 1st Division
50	11.04.1977	2	D	0-0	Stoke City, Victoria Ground, 1st Division
51	16.04.1977	1	W	2-0	Arsenal, Anfield, 1st Division
52	20.04.1977		W	3-0	FC Zürich, Anfield, Eur. Cup Semi Final 2nd L
53	23.04.1977		D	2-2	Everton, Maine Road, FA Cup Semi-final
54	27.04.1977		W	3-0	Everton, Maine Road, FA Cup Semi-final replay
55	30.04.1977	1	W	2-1	Ipswich Town, Anfield, 1st Division
56	03.05.1977	1	W	1-0	Manchester United, Anfield, 1st Division
57	07.05.1977	1	D	1-1	Queens Park Rangers, Loftus Road, 1st Division
58	10.05.1977	1	D	0-0	Coventry City, Highfield Road, 1st Division
59	14.05.1977	1	D	0-0	West Ham United, Anfield, 1st Division
60	16.05.1977	1	L	1-2	Bristol City, Ashton Gate, 1st Division
61	21.05.1977		L	1-2	Manchester United, Wembley, FA Cup Final
62	25.05.1977		W	3-1	Borussia Moenchengladbach, Stadio Olimpico, European Cup Final

Friendlies

1	04.08.1976		L	0 - 2	Feyenoord, Stadion Feyenoord, Friendly
2	07.08.1976		D	1 - 1	Roda, Sportpark Kaalheide, Friendly
3	10.08.1976		L	0 - 2	Twente, Sportpark Diekman, Friendly
4	22.11.1976		D	2 - 2	Northampton Town, County Ground, Testimonial
5	27.05.1977		D	9 - 9	Bobby Charlton Select XI, Anfield, Testimonial

Appearances for the 1976/1977 season

Name	League	FA Cup	LC	UEFA	Other	Total
Ray Clemence	42	8	2	9	1	62
Emlyn Hughes	42	8	2	9	1	62
Ray Kennedy	41	8	2	9	1	61
Phil Neal	42	8	2	8	1	61
Joey Jones	39	8	2	9	1	59
Steve Heighway	39	7	2	9	1	58
Kevin Keegan	38	8	2	8	1	57
Ian Callaghan	33	5	2	7	1	48
Jimmy Case	27	7	1	6	1	42
David Johnson	26	4	2	6	0	38
Terry McDermott	26	5	0	7	0	38
Phil Thompson	26	4	2	3	1	36
John Toshack	22	2	1	4	1	30
David Fairclough	20	5	2	3	0	30
Tommy Smith	16	4	0	7	0	27
Brian Kettle	2	0	0	0	0	2
Alec Lindsay	1	0	0	0	0	1

Alan Waddle	0	0	0	1	0	1
Peter McDonnell	0	0	0	0	0	0
Sammy Lee	0	0	0	0	0	0
Peter Cormack	0	0	0	0	0	0

Goalscorers for the 1976/1977 season

Name	League	FA Cup	LC	UEFA	Other	Total
Kevin Keegan	12	4	0	4	0	20
Steve Heighway	8	3	0	3	0	14
Phil Neal	7	2	0	4	0	13
John Toshack	10	1	0	1	1	13
Ray Kennedy	7	1	0	1	0	9
David Johnson	5	0	0	3	0	8
Jimmy Case	1	4	0	2	0	7
David Fairclough	3	1	0	1	0	5
Terry McDermott	1	1	0	2	0	4
Joey Jones	3	0	0	0	0	3
Ian Callaghan	1	0	1	0	0	2
Phil Thompson	2	0	0	0	0	2
Tommy Smith	0	0	0	1	0	1
Emlyn Hughes	1	0	0	0	0	1
Own goals	1	0	0	0	0	1

The squad during the 1976/1977 season

Ray Clemence, Goalkeeper
Peter McDonnell, Goalkeeper
Joey Jones, Defender
Brian Kettle, Defender
Phil Thompson, Defender
Tommy Smith, Defender
Emlyn Hughes, Defender
Alec Lindsay, Defender
Phil Neal, Defender
Ian Callaghan, Midfielder
Jimmy Case, Midfielder
Steve Heighway, Midfielder
Sammy Lee, Midfielder
Ray Kennedy, Midfielder
Terry McDermott, Midfielder
Peter Cormack, Midfielder
David Fairclough, Striker
Alan Waddle, Striker

David Johnson, Striker
Kevin Keegan, Striker
John Toshack, Striker
Kevin Kewley, Striker

Transfers for the 1976/1977 season

In:
David Johnson, Ipswich Town, £200,000, 12 August 1976
Alan Hansen, Partick Thistle, £100,000, 5 May 1977

Out:
Brian Hall, Plymouth Argyle, £50,000 July 1976
Peter Cormack, Bristol City, £50,000, 10 November 1976
Kevin Keegan, Hamburg SV, £500,000, 3 June 1977

A collection of statistics for the 1976/1977 season

The season in numbers:
Total games: 62
Games won: 36
Games drawn: 14
Games lost: 12
Clean sheets – League: 18
Clean sheets – Overall: 27
Total goals: 103
Average attendance at home – League: 47,284
Average attendance at home – Overall: 46,171
Average goals per game – League: 2.24
Average goals per game – Overall: 2.23
Average goal minute – League: 54
Average goal minute – Overall: 52

Goals split down to competitions:
League – 62
European Cup – 22
FA Cup – 17
League Cup – 1
Charity Shield – 1

Player debuts:
David Johnson against Norwich City on 21.08.1976

Statistics and information provided by LFChistory.net

11 : A KING IS BORN

1978/79

SIMILAR TO ALAN HANSEN, ANOTHER TEENAGE Scot by the name of Kenneth Mathieson Dalglish also attended a trial at Liverpool as a 15-year-old boy in August 1966, and even wore the Liverpool shirt for the 'B' team in a friendly against Southport Reserves, which Liverpool won 1-0. Dalglish's association with the Reds ended there – for then, at least.

Dalglish also attended a trial at Ron Greenwood's West Ham United and randomly crossed paths with Liverpool manager, Bill Shankly. Dalglish recalls: "Liverpool's first team were due to play West Ham the same weekend as my trial. As I walked through to the players' area at Upton Park, Shanks came along in the other direction. I was overwhelmed with embarrassment. I couldn't speak to him. I just kept my head down and hurried past. I heard his voice shouting, 'Kenny, Kenny', but I said to myself, 'Just keep walking'. I regret not talking to Shanks but I was only 15 and very shy. If anybody spoke to me back then, I'd blush."

After his trials in England, Kenny returned to Scotland where he signed a professional contract with Celtic in May 1967. "There were a lot of good youngsters about at that time, and I think Kenny got overlooked. After all he was only 15 or so at the time," Shankly later stated.

Almost 11 years later, on August 9, 1977, Liverpool manager Bob Paisley's bid to sign Kenny Dalglish reached a dramatic climax. For the previous two weeks Celtic had been saying no to all Liverpool's attempts to sign their Scottish international. Then late that afternoon, Celtic manager Jock Stein finally agreed to listen to Liverpool's proposals.

Immediately, Paisley and chairman John Smith made an M6 car dash north and booked into a hotel at Moffat, some 30 miles outside Glasgow. False names were used so that outsiders would not be alerted to their presence in Scotland. Celtic wanted everything done secretly because if the deal fell through they did not want other clubs to know that they were even willing to talk about Dalglish.

That night, Celtic played at Dunfermline, Dalglish's swansong, and Paisley and Jock Stein finally got together for talks at 10.30pm. Both parties entered Celtic Park by the back door and the negotiations began. The fee was agreed between the clubs and the deal to shatter the existing British transfer record was on.

The following morning, Paisley brought Dalglish to Anfield by car and before he left Glasgow, the 26-year-old Scottish international said: "This really was the offer I could not refuse. There was no way I could turn down such a fabulous offer although I am very sad to be leaving Celtic. But I am happy to be going to such a great club as Liverpool." Celtic manager Jock Stein added: "If Kenny had wanted to stay at Celtic Park I would have turned down any amount of money offered for him. Now where do I find another player like Dalglish?"

Dalglish arrived in Liverpool that afternoon ready to become the costliest player in British history. After agreeing a fee of £440,000 the previous night, the transfer was completed late that afternoon after Dalglish had a medical check and agreed his personal terms.

As Dalglish had not asked for a transfer from Celtic, he was entitled to five percent of a fee over £400,000 and immediately became £20,000 richer. If he had asked for a move he would not have been entitled to any money. What's more, Dalglish was almost certain to become one of the highest paid players in the First Division. Liverpool paid a generous salary to their first team and they also paid out big bonuses for success. So, he expected to receive over £20,000 in his first year at Liverpool and that fee was to be increased by off-the-field activities such as personal appearances.

'WHERE WILL THE NEW BOY FIT IN?' was the headline in the *Liverpool Echo*, which Michael Charters tackled, answering: "Kenny Dalglish is possibly the only player in Britain with the basic style to fill the gap left by the departure of Kevin Keegan – that's why Liverpool were prepared to pay a record transfer fee to sign him. The big question is what role manager Bob Paisley has in mind for him. He can play in midfield and attack – as did Keegan. He can score goals and make them – as did Keegan. A big pointer to this crucial question could come with the line-up for Saturday's Charity Shield against Manchester United at Wembley. I expect Dalglish to fit into Liverpool's playing pattern very quickly in the same sort of role as Keegan had.

"Like Keegan, Dalglish had been a target for European clubs. Informed Scottish circles believed the Celtic star was bound to sign for a leading club in West Germany. But Liverpool have beaten them to it. Paisley had recently asked Stein to keep him informed of any Dalglish developments. I understand the feeling was fairly general that Dalglish was bound for Europe, but suddenly, Celtic were ready to let him go – to Anfield. The arrival of Dalglish will bring repercussions at Anfield. It seems certain that if unsettled striker David Johnson goes through with his intention of asking for a move, he will be allowed to go."

The following day, August 11, Kenny was introduced to his teammates at Melwood and was put through his paces by first-team trainer Ronnie Moran, who later said: "Kenny took to the place immediately. It didn't take him six months to settle in like it took some of the other players; it was more like six minutes with Kenny. He was the near perfect professional. He was a winner."

Bob Paisley, obviously pleased with his latest recruit, told the press when he was asked how vital it was that Liverpool should buy a star like Kenny Dalglish to replace the star of Kevin Keegan: "Well, it was vital in as much that the tax from the money would have gone to the government and I'm like any other professional manager – players is what it's all about and the money was there available from Kevin. The board instructed me to try and get the best and I'm hoping with Kenny I have gone and got the best. They talk about this, he can do that, he can go both ways and all the jargon that goes with him, but he's a good all-round player, an all-purpose player. He's skilful, he can finish, he can read the game and this all adds up to good players and I like good players in my side and I think the more good players you get the better chance you have of winning something."

At the request of Bob Paisley, Tommy Smith decided to play on for one more season and during the Reds' 1977/78 defence of the League Championship and the European Cup, 'The Anfield Iron' went on to make another 34 first-team appearances. Paisley told the *Liverpool Echo* in July 1977: "I asked for a new contract for Tommy Smith following his testimonial because I wanted cover for the first team, cover he gave us so splendidly when it was needed last season.

I feel he still has something to offer and it was to our mutual benefit that he should be available."

However, an unfortunate accident in his garage at his Crosby home in April 1978, when he dropped a pickaxe on his foot, cut short Smith's Liverpool career a month too soon and ended his hopes of making Paisley's team for their second successive European Cup final. After turning down an offer to become Walsall's player-manager later in the year, Smith moved to Swansea City to join his former teammate John Toshack who had been appointed the Swans' player-manager at the Vetch Field.

The 1977/78 season was also Ian Callaghan's last for Liverpool, in which the marathon man played another 41 times for the Reds, taking his tally to an incredible 857 appearances, which remains a record to this day.

Unlike his friend Tommy Smith, Callaghan was included by Paisley in Liverpool's squad to face Club Brugge at Wembley, albeit as an unused substitute. That was to be the last time his name appeared on Liverpool's teamsheet. Cally had gone through the whole of his Liverpool career without being sent off or even booked until the referee took his name down in Callaghan's penultimate game for Liverpool in March 1978 against Nottingham Forest in the League Cup.

In September 1978, after 19 seasons with Liverpool, Callaghan called it a day at the club having enjoyed the summer in the States on loan at Fort Lauderdale. On his return, Callaghan also signed for John Toshack's Swansea City where he was reunited on the field with Tommy Smith.

As Liverpool entered 1978, the Reds were sitting in third place, six points behind league leaders Nottingham Forest. Therefore, Paisley was quick to bring reinforcements into his squad. On January 10, 1979, he paid £352,000, a record transfer fee between English clubs and £2,000 more than Manchester United paid for Leeds' Joe Jordan a week earlier, for Middlesbrough midfielder Graeme Souness.

The *Daily Mail* reported: "Liverpool smashed another transfer record yesterday when they bought Graeme Souness from Middlesbrough for £352,000. Their outlay on the talented Scottish midfield man they have pursued for six weeks represents a new record cash deal between English clubs. Liverpool already hold the records for incoming and outgoing British transfers with their £500,000 sale of Kevin Keegan to Hamburg and the £440,000 purchase of Kenny Dalglish. And their latest bid for 24-year-old Souness finally landed their man."

After putting pen to paper, Bob Paisley showed his new signing around Anfield, introduced him to the club's prize possession – the European Cup – and told the Scot that it was a taste of things to come.

Souness then sat down with the *Anfield Review* and took a realistic view on the situation regarding competition for places: "I'm not anticipating anything. Just because Liverpool have signed me for a big fee doesn't mean that I see myself as an established player in the first team here. I know, without being told, that I've got to do my stuff out there on the park, and so far as I'm concerned, this move means that I'm starting afresh. I'm hoping that I'll be able to settle in quickly and that things go well for me. And I'm certain about one thing, the competition for first-team places will keep me on my toes!"

During pre-season for 1978/79, Liverpool played five friendly games. Such change from Liverpool's routine showed Paisley's determination to have his players reach peak fitness earlier than usual. In the past decade, the Reds played three or no more than four games in their build-up to a season. But now, they had five matches in 12 days, which was a heavy programme, even if the games were only designed as warm-up sessions.

Paisley told the *Liverpool Echo* on August 2: "It is unusual for us to cover five countries in our pre-season schedule. But I look on tonight's game at Lansdowne Road as a replacement for the match we usually play at Chester behind closed doors. The three games next week against Basel, Bayern Munich and FC Austria involve more travelling than normal but should provide the type of training matches I am looking for. And our fifth game, a week on Monday, against Celtic for the Jock Stein testimonial is to help an old friend, and is a match between two of the only three British clubs to have won the European Cup. It is a harder pre-season programme than usual, but it's all part of the increased tempo of training we have adopted this time because we have to be right for our cup final in September against Nottingham Forest in the European Cup."

The left-back position had been a bit of a problem area for Liverpool in 1977/78 with Joey Jones, Tommy Smith and Alan Hansen all wearing the No. 3 shirt at some stage of the season. Therefore, on August 13, Paisley signed 23-year-old England 'B' full-back Alan Kennedy from Newcastle for £330,000, which at the time was a British record amount for a full-back.

Although joining the European champions was a dream move for Kennedy, the day he signed didn't go as smoothly as he would have liked. Kennedy later told *LFChistory.net*: "I had what's called a nightmare travelling down. My car broke down, the weather was so bad and it was wet and windy. My windscreen wipers broke on the car so I couldn't see. This car was a brand new one and it was absolutely hopeless. I thought because it had a gold stripe along the side it was a good, reliable car. The car broke down in Leeds and I had to wait for a while. There were no mobile phones in those days and I couldn't get in touch with anyone at the club so I had to get on with it. I was late meeting Bob Paisley and Peter Robinson, the secretary. In the end it all worked out well and I made it to the hotel in Liverpool. I had my medical, signed the forms and had some pictures taken. To be honest, even at the time I couldn't believe how quick my medical was. The doctor just put me on the bed, took my temperature, took my pulse, took a couple of other things and said to Bob Paisley that I was as fit as a fiddle and that I could run forever! I was with my girl-friend at the time. It was dead funny. Bob Paisley made a sweeping statement. He said, 'If this lad doesn't play for England I'll throw myself in the Mersey' and then he said to a couple of the reporters, 'when the tide is out'. It was a nice way of putting things. Bob felt as though I would play for England for a long time. Unfortunately a lad called Kenny Sansom had beaten me to the England left-back spot. He never got injured and I didn't get that many caps."

Paisley was quite pleased with his new signing who he captured two days before the European deadline of August 15 and told the press: "He will be a first-class capture. He is fast, likes to move up into attack and should fit into our side very quickly. Now I have seven men challenging for the back four positions – Hughes, Thompson, Hansen, Neal, Jones, Kennedy and Irwin. I wanted Kennedy because I wanted more competition for places."

The following day, Kennedy's first match for his new club was a 3-2 win against Glasgow Celtic in Jock Stein's testimonial, where he managed to get on the scoresheet. The wily Scot was convinced that once again Liverpool had made a more than useful purchase. "They've bought a good one," said the Celtic boss. "He will add more width to their attack and he'll also make more room for the forwards as he comes through."

Ahead of the 1978/79 season there was an important change to the Kop grandstand at Anfield. After many decades, the infamous Boys' Pen – which started off in the lower Kemlyn Road stand – was removed, increasing the Kop's capacity by 1,000. Former Anfield tour guide Ray Hughes explains: "There was no announcement or explanation given by the club. I suspect that it was for a couple of reasons. Firstly, people had a bit more money, so kids were paying the extra to go into the Kop and the Anfield Road end, so the Boys' Pen was half empty for most anyway. Therefore, I think the club simply decided they could take the railings down and allow more adults in the ground and also save on stewarding. Secondly, the pen was said to be somewhat feral and caused the club concerns in that respect. Peter Robinson, the club secretary, would regularly receive complaints from parents about their children being bullied and robbed."

However, some youngsters were bitterly disappointed to hear the news of the removal of the Boys' Pen. David Findlay from Maghull told the *Liverpool Echo* of his anguish: "The decision to close the pen is rather stupid; I don't agree that the pen wasn't fully used. A lot of youngsters are only able to watch matches because of the cut-price admission available, and this is even more apparent this season now that the minimum admission charge is £1." In addition, while some young Kopites expressed the view that there would be more chance of getting hurt and injured in the congestion of the Kop and that in fact their safety was virtually guaranteed in the Boys' Pen by the presence of two police officers, others were more concerned that they would now be deprived of a view of the pitch in a packed Kop full of adults.

It was also brought forward by some senior Kopites that the closing of the pen would have consequences for the thousands of fans who filled the Kop at each of Liverpool's home games. Some Kopites declared that the only blight of watching a match from the Kop was the droves of small children constantly wriggling between the spectators, searching for a barrier on which they could perch without being forcibly removed by irate Kopites.

Liverpool kicked off the 1978/79 campaign without a domestic honour to their name. Winning the title, of course, has always been the club's priority and as Bill Shankly said: "The league is our bread and butter." On August 19, Paisley's men began their championship assault with a predictable result against visitors Queens Park Rangers, who made the dreaded trip up north.

Before his official debut, of all the men new signing Alan Kennedy could have bumped into, he bumped into the great Shankly.

Kennedy told *LFChistory.net*: "Before my first game Bill Shankly was rushing around the corridors of Anfield. He stopped and looked at me, 'Hi ya, son. How are you doing?' I was like, 'That is the great Bill Shankly. I am alright, Mr. Shankly, I am a little bit nervous'. He went into his pocket and pulled out... and I don't know what he had given me, but he gave me a couple of tablets. I thought, 'What has he given me here?', but it's Mr. Shankly and whatever he says is right. All of a sudden my mind was going back to the 1978 World Cup where there was a Scottish player who had taken some kind of drug, Willie Johnston, and so in the end... he might have given me drugs. I better have a little look. When I brought them out there were two sweets, that's all they were, just two sweets. I thought to myself, if Mr. Shankly has given me them they must do me good, so I ate them. I felt great, I didn't really! It's like somebody telling you to eat a steak before a game, it makes you feel good. It doesn't actually make you feel good. It makes you feel terrible. It just made me feel a bit more relaxed, I think!"

The gates were closed half an hour before kick-off. It was like carnival time at Anfield with the ground looking in superb order. A pre-match presentation of a gallon of Scotch was made to Bob Paisley along with an inscribed silver salver for retaining the European Cup. 'IT'S HEIGHWAY TO THE RESCUE' read the *Liverpool Football Echo* headline as the Republic of Ireland winger popped up in the 76th minute with the winner. Kenny Dalglish, who was to have a quite marvellous season, had put the home side ahead following 26 minutes of all-out attack. But a freak equaliser from Paul McGhee soon afterwards meant that the Reds had to work just that little bit harder for their victory.

However, after his first official appearance, new signing Kennedy came down to earth. He explained: "Early on in the game I mis-kicked with my right foot – the one I use for standing on – and knocked a policeman's helmet off! I just wanted half-time to come to get some reassurance from the manager but when I got back to the dressing room, Bob said to me, 'I think they shot the wrong Kennedy!'"

Following their 2-1 opening-day victory over QPR, three days later Liverpool travelled to Portman Road for a Tuesday night fixture against Ipswich Town. The *Liverpool Echo* reported: "Liverpool gave a display of rich authority and class in winning 3-0 at Ipswich last night. They combined elegance with power, discipline with a gift for the unexpected and teamwork with individual brilliance. A poor Ipswich, short of some of their top players through injury, were out-played and might have suffered a defeat of staggering proportions had Liverpool not eased up in the second half and missed three or four clear-cut chances. There were outstanding displays from Graeme Souness and Steve Heighway. Souness was at the heart of everything, spreading the ball around with effortless precision as Liverpool took a grip in midfield which they never relaxed." Once into their stride, Liverpool were looking rather impressive. After their 4-1 slaughtering of Manchester City at Maine Road on August 26, the Reds showed their true class, producing one of their finest performances ever as Tottenham Hotspur were drubbed 7-0 at Anfield.

Tottenham, who were seeking their first Anfield win in over 60 years, came to Merseyside with midfielders Osvaldo Ardiles and Ricardo Villa in their ranks, fresh from a World Cup triumph with Argentina. Gifted ball-players, the South American pair were, however, powerless against a well-oiled red machine and Paisley described his team's seventh strike as: "The best goal Anfield has ever seen scored."

Liverpool continued their impeccable start in the league with victories over Birmingham City at St. Andrew's and Coventry City at Anfield but although the Reds had won their first six league matches, they lost their grip on the European Cup at the first hurdle, going down 2-0 on aggregate to Brian Clough's talented Nottingham Forest outfit in September.

Graeme Souness later recalled a vital moment that occurred in the home leg to *The Sunday Times*: "I was taught a harsh lesson in my early days at Liverpool that stood me in good stead for the rest of my playing career. We were 1-0 down with three minutes to go against Nottingham Forest in the European Cup and I went chasing the game from central midfield and ended up in their left-back area. The ball was played into where I should have been, then back out to the left wing, squared and they scored to make it 2-0. Joe Fagan tore a strip off me afterwards. We would have taken 1-0 but 2-0 made it twice as difficult. Forest got a 0-0 draw back at Anfield and we were out. That was my lesson."

One of the great strengths of every Liverpool team is the ability to put setbacks behind them and immediately rejoin the winning trail. Three days later, the Forest elimination was forgotten and Liverpool were able to beat Bolton Wanderers 3-0, thanks to a Jimmy Case hat-trick at Anfield, which was followed up by thrashing Norwich City 4-1 and Derby County 5-0 in successive weeks.

Well balanced and supremely confident, the Reds looked almost unbeatable. At the back, Alan Hansen was filling Emlyn Hughes' role perfectly as an ideal central partner for Phil Thompson; in midfield, powerhouse Graeme Souness was spraying passes with ease and style in his first full season at the club while up front the evergreen Heighway was linking superbly with Dalglish and Johnson to form a lethal attacking force.

Dalglish now wore the captain's armband as Emlyn Hughes was no longer a regular and if he already wasn't, Dalglish was becoming a world-class player. He used his strength to hold up the ball with ease against any man twice his size; he could bring teammates into play or take it on himself. He wasn't the fastest, but that didn't matter.

His pace was in his head. He was the attacking equivalent of Bobby Moore, in that he read the play better than anybody. Off the field, the stocky Scot was a man of few words, a reporter's nightmare. He shunned the limelight and shrugged his shoulders whenever anyone tried to hang a laurel wreath around his neck. "Glamour and publicity don't bother me," he said. "If I score goals, so what? Isn't that what Liverpool pay me for? I am no more important than the people who make and save goals. And my strengths as a player are the players around me."

Liverpool did not suffer their first league defeat until October 28, when they met second-place Everton at Goodison Park in a top-of-the-table battle. An Andy King drive was enough to give the Toffees their first derby victory since 1971 and ended the Reds' impressive start to the season of 10 wins and one draw in their first 11 games, scoring 35 goals and conceding only four.

Following a 1-1 draw at home to Leeds the following Saturday, the Reds soon got back to winning ways with a 3-1 victory over Queens Park Rangers at Loftus Road on November 11, *The Guardian* reported: "Any thoughts that Liverpool's sniffle, a loss at Everton and then a draw with Leeds at Anfield, was going to turn into a full scale cold were dispelled by Saturday's full scale victory at Loftus Road. It is quite usual for Liverpool to catch some sort of cold in the two months before Christmas; this time last year they had just lost their third game in a row, at Queens Park Rangers and two years ago they lost three games in December. Rangers were to have no such luck this time for Liverpool were back to their best, oozing class, professionalism, necessary toughness and luck.

"Pity poor QPR, half of whose players took to the field with one ailment or another and were then faced with a barrage of accurate passing in a non-stop attack that was a joy to watch. Souness led the charge with some crisp ground through passes to Dalglish, who has that tremendous ability to receive the ball with his back to goal and turn around his marker, in this case the hardworking John Hollins. It is coupled with the knack of laying the ball into the paths of his colleagues. Two men are needed to mark him effectively. Souness and Dalglish, both expensive signings, are part of an upward spiral. Liverpool are a successful football club, they draw the crowds to draw the money to buy the players to make them more successful to draw more money etc. However, at the same time they drop and discard those you fall with an accepted ruthlessness which belies their family image."

Following their first goalless draw of the season at White Hart Lane, the Anfielders beat Middlesbrough 2-0 to finish November top of the pack, two points clear of Everton. As was the case two seasons earlier when the Reds won their 10th First Division title, again the month of December proved to be the most disappointing of the season.

Not only did they lose the European Super Cup over two legs to Anderlecht, they were beaten in the league at Arsenal and Bristol by a single goal on both occasions. Although Liverpool were only able to pick up two points from six, not once were they overtaken by Everton at the top of the table as the Toffees themselves dropped points to Leeds and Coventry.

On Boxing Day, Liverpool travelled to Old Trafford and returned with a 3-0 victory thanks to Ray Kennedy, Jimmy Case and a brilliant goal from David Fairclough, who was making his first league appearance of the season. *The Guardian* reported: "Liverpool are boring chanted a somewhat desperate Stretford End, but the only criticism that could seriously have been made of the First Division leaders after their comprehensive and sometimes brilliant victory at Old Trafford yesterday was that it should have been more decisive. After taking a lead of two goals through Kennedy and Case in the first half while Manchester United plumbed uncharted depths of inadequacy, they simply toyed with the home side and seemed a little put out when a succession of late attacks failed to add to a glorious third goal from Fairclough."

At the end of 1978, Liverpool led Everton on goal difference at the top of the First Division. West Bromwich Albion were sat in third, just two points behind and remained in close contention. The Reds were excelling both in attack and defence, having netted 47 goals in 21 games and letting in only nine at the other end. Paisley's side was striking the perfect balance of a champions-elect team.

In one of the worst winters in Football League history, a great amount of matches were postponed due to the weather. Britain froze and ice-age weather conditions buried the country beneath a blanket of snow, hail and frost, freezing playing fields and submerging terraces up and down the country.

Although Liverpool were able to compete in FA Cup games, passing through the third and fourth rounds against Southend United and Blackburn Rovers, their next league game following the emphatic victory at Old Trafford came no fewer than 39 days later when West Bromwich Albion visited Anfield.

By the time Ron Atkinson's side arrived at Anfield on February 3, they had leapfrogged Liverpool and Everton into top spot with the intention of having a say in the title race. Bob Paisley in his programme notes said: "This is a stern test. We are in our own stronghold and the match is a four-pointer. Over the years, people have become accustomed to seeing Liverpool score victories on this ground, but the interest today will centre on West Brom's performance. The simple fact is that this season West Brom have emerged as one of the most entertaining teams in English Football. Make no mistake, West Brom ARE real challengers."

Phil Thompson, who was fit again after recovering from a knee injury, was not recalled to the side and opted to play for the reserves that day in order to obtain valuable match practice before joining up with the England squad for a midweek international. Despite his absence, Liverpool again impressed.

A 2-1 home win restored order with Liverpool taking pole position again, but only after a couple of late scares from the Baggies in what was an enthralling top-of-the-table clash. 'DALGLISH SPELLS IT OUT FOR ALBION' was the *Liverpool Echo*'s headline after the Scot produced a masterclass to oust West Brom from the top spot.

Michael Charters wrote: "Liverpool were inspired by a matchless

display from Dalglish, who revealed for our delight all the fascinat-
ing facets of his multi-coloured talents to torment and destroy the
Albion defence. It was his finest performance for Liverpool. The
Reds totally dominated proceedings for the first hour and it was
Dalglish who opened the scoring on twenty-one minutes, rounding
off a slick move involving Graeme Souness and Terry McDermott.
King Kenny was central to the second goal too; his run finding
McDermott, who rolled David Fairclough in on 53 minutes. The
result should have been out of sight by this point, Liverpool missing
a host of chances to see the visitors off. As it was, the Baggies gave
themselves a lifeline when Alistair Brown headed in a corner in the
67th minute. This breathed life into West Brom, who then went
close through Cyrille Regis but to no avail. Albion's recovery kept
interest at fever pitch until the end. Yet there could be no argument
about the result. Liverpool had proved once again that, when the
pressure and tensions are at their greatest, they have the experience,
maturity and talent to rise to the special occasion."

On February 13, a pitch inspection early in the day gave Liverpool's already rearranged home fixture against Birmingham City
the green light. Local referee Joe Worrall quickly gave the game
the go-ahead and the Anfield ground staff got to work, clearing the
slight covering of snow to get the surface playable. This handed Liverpool the chance to send out another message of intent in the title
race, this time to neighbours Everton who had now overtaken both
the Reds and the Baggies into first place due to Liverpool's run of
postponed games.

Despite being embroiled in a relegation battle with only eight
points from 23 games, Birmingham came to Anfield hoping history
would repeat itself. They were the last side to beat the Reds there
just over 12 months before in a 3-2 thriller in which all goals came

in the second half. It was a very different story this time, though. Graeme Souness' solitary first-half strike, Liverpool's 50th goal of the season, proved decisive at the final whistle as the Reds laboured to a 1-0 win.

However, the game was marred by inflammatory comments made by Birmingham boss Jim Smith afterwards, who left Anfield claiming Souness' matchwinner was fisted into the net by Steve Heighway. "We made more chances than they did," barked Smith. "We deserved to get a result. The ball was going straight to our goalkeeper when Heighway pushed out a fist and deflected it onto the post and into the net."

In reply, Heighway acknowledged making contact with the ball, but not with his fist and certainly not intentionally. The winger said: "I tried to get out of the way of the shot, but the ball brushed the top of my arm and went into the net." Either way, this wasn't Liverpool at their best. It seemed they dropped to Birmingham's level and the performance was a far cry from the stylish display that saw off West Brom 10 days earlier.

Paisley blamed the weather conditions for Anfield's "dead as doornails pitch" claiming it was impossible to play flowing, fluent football on it.

Liverpool were soon back in form though as they produced a fine show on February 21 in a re-arranged clash with Norwich City.

Striker David Johnson, who had not started a senior outing for over two months, was recalled to the side in place of the injured David Fairclough. He knew a win would put his team three points clear with two games in hand over nearest rivals Everton and Arsenal, who after a good run of form had joined the title race, and Johnson didn't let his manager down as he bagged a brace in a 6-0 romp.

The *Liverpool Echo* ran the headline: 'RED DESTROYERS IN

SIX-STAR SHOW' with Michael Charters beginning his report: "It was a privilege to watch Liverpool at Anfield last night. With a classic exhibition of all the arts of football, they dismissed Norwich City from their presence by six goals and a performance of such all-round brilliance that it is difficult to find adequate superlatives to describe it. Dalglish, with two goals and a thousand touches of breathtaking artistry, almost destroyed Norwich on his own. He dazzled them with his genius and was involved in everything."

However, if the Reds were banging in the goals at one end, they were miserly when it came to conceding them. The various defensive combinations comprising Phil Neal, Alan Kennedy, Alan Hansen, Phil Thompson and Emlyn Hughes had looked more than solid, but in goal Ray Clemence was masterly.

Once that four-man red rearguard was pierced, how demoralising it must have been for opposing forwards to realise they still had the great Clemence to beat. The former Skegness deckchair attendant was now rated by many observers as the best keeper in the world.

Ian Hargraves wrote in the *Liverpool Echo* praising Paisley's majestic stopper: "One of only two players to have turned out regularly for Liverpool throughout the Seventies (Emlyn Hughes being the other), Ray Clemence has possibly had a greater influence on events at Anfield than any other single individual. It's not for nothing that the club chose the word "goalkeeper" as their telegraphic address, for they have long recognised the supreme importance of having the right person between the sticks, and Clemence is merely the latest in a long line of famous men. However, what makes him so important to Liverpool's plan of campaign is that he is much more than just a goalkeeper. It is generally conceded amongst many of the Anfield faithful, that had he been playing for Bill Shankly's team of the Sixties, then they would have won as many trophies as their successors, instead of being narrowly pipped in several competitions."

After hitting Norwich for six, the Reds travelled to the Baseball Ground and beat Tommy Docherty's Derby County 2-0 to increase their lead at the top of the table to five points.

However, Liverpool's three following league fixtures at the start of March all ended in draws. This included Everton's point at Anfield on March 13, with the gap between the two Merseyside clubs now just two points, albeit Gordon Lee's side had played three games more than their neighbours.

On March 24, the Reds received visitors Ipswich Town to Anfield. Kenny Dalglish's 50th goal for Liverpool in 101 appearances was enough to secure the two points and re-establish Liverpool's five-point cushion at the top. Kenny Dalglish now averaged a goal every two games for Liverpool.

Michael Charters summed up perfectly Dalglish's worth to his team, writing in the *Liverpool Echo*: "To find and groom a player to world class stardom must be about the ultimate for any club. To lose that player and manage to replace him instantly with another of equal world class quality is stretching football experience to its limits.

"Yet, that is what Liverpool have achieved in the amazing outgoing of Kevin Keegan to Hamburg and Continental pastures new and the incoming of Kenny Dalglish from Glasgow Celtic. When Keegan was transferred, his departure left a massive gap. That is an understatement really because, from the evidence of one match alone when he destroyed Moenchengladbach's Berti Vogts in Rome to play the major part in Liverpool's supreme European victory, he could not be replaced. But he was.

"Dalglish has proved himself a fascinating mixture of the individualist and at the same time, the ideal team man. Very few stars are blessed with both attributes. Dalglish and Keegan are alike in their world class status but are totally different types on and off the field. Keegan is more an individual than Dalglish, more of a one-man force than Dalglish, whose ability to play with others, to distribute the ball and lead the attack unselfishly is on the highest level of that difficult art."

How would they play as partners – if it could ever be arranged? Bill Shankly has no doubts. He told Charters: "They would have to form a society for the prevention of cruelty to opponents, if the two of them were in the same team."

Charters added: "Bob Paisley, who knows better than anybody what a gem he has in Dalglish, describes him quite simply as 'the best player in the country: 'Even when he had that lean scoring spell earlier this season, his contribution to the team never let up for a moment. When his teammates are in trouble, they'll always find Kenny available to take the ball off them. I've never known a player with such a quick football brain. In fact, he thinks too quickly at times for some of them but now they're getting to know him, it must help the general team performance. He has a matchless eye for the scoring chance, can turn players on a sixpence, works hard and never quits. He is tremendously strong although he is not a big man and shrugs off injuries. Just about perfect isn't he?'"

Hopes of a Liverpool 'double' were dashed on April 4 when Manchester United beat the Reds in an FA Cup semi-final replay at Goodison, which turned out to be Emlyn Hughes' 665th and final appearance in a Liverpool shirt.

The Reds soon bounced back and within a week defeated Arsenal 3-0 at home and Wolves 1-0 at Molineux, taking their unbeaten league run to 12 games and putting the Reds six points clear of second-place West Brom who had taken over from Everton as leaders of the chasing pack.

With 10 games to go, Liverpool were in pole position to clinch their 11th First Division championship.

The game against Arsenal at Anfield marked the first time Phil Thompson captained Liverpool. Kenny Dalglish, who during the season had skippered the Reds in Emlyn Hughes' absence, no longer felt comfortable as captain. It just wasn't his thing and he had no special interest in captaining the side. Therefore, Bob Paisley appointed boyhood Liverpool fan Thompson as the club's new permanent skipper.

On Saturday, April 14, Liverpool faced Manchester United for the third time in 14 days, giving a majestic exhibition of quality football. This time round the Reds outplayed their FA Cup conquerors at Anfield, beating them 2-0. United manager David Sexton, who has seen more than enough of Liverpool recently, told the press: "It would take something catastrophic to keep them from the title."

On April 21, Liverpool mourned the death of one of their most loyal and trusted off-the-pitch servants, Mr Eric Sawyer. The *Liverpool Echo* reported: "A mastermind of finance – Liverpool director Eric Sawyer, who died over the weekend, was the man whose financial expertise played a vital part in the club's emergence from its Second Division days in the early Sixties to its pre-eminence today as one of the greatest clubs in the world."

During the latter half of April, the Reds only managed one win in four games and suffered their biggest league defeat of the season at Villa Park. This was the Reds' first league defeat since the loss at Bristol City on December 16.

The *Liverpool Echo* reported: "The best defence in football, heading for an all-time record, had an attack of the jitters at Aston Villa yesterday. Runaway leaders, Liverpool tumbled to a 3-1 defeat which sent a shock wave through the game as challengers West Bromwich and Forest must have taken fresh heart from this unexpected result. They made more mistakes in one match than they had made all season. Villa accepted the gifts for a victory which their elated fans greeted as though they had won the European Cup and the championship all in one dizzy afternoon."

Despite only adding two points from eight to their tally, Liverpool entered into the final month of the season with a seven-point lead over the chasing pack. Liverpool only had four fixtures left to play and it was becoming increasing safe for many a Kopite to say that their team had one hand firmly gripped on to the First Division title and the second hand was only a matter of days away.

On April 24, 20-year-old Liverpudlian Sammy Lee made his full first-team debut against Southampton at The Dell. Sammy Lee was a true Scouser, having been brought up in St. Andrew's Gardens, better known locally as the Bull Ring, but it was only when he failed seven O-Levels that he decided he wanted to become a footballer.

Until then Sammy had dreams of being a surveyor or a physicist but he was denied the chance of going to university when he only passed English Language and English Literature exams while at St Francis Xavier College in Woolton.

Sammy recalled: "I was so ashamed that I did not go back to the school to pick up my certificate. I wanted to stay on at school and had even taken up physics at night school. I felt if I was good enough at football to be offered a chance at 16 then I would still be good enough at 18 when clubs have to decide if they will offer you an apprenticeship or let you go."

As a schoolboy, Sammy was training at Melwood one night a week under Tom Saunders who offered him an apprenticeship but with the warning he used to give to any youngster about how hard and exacting it would be if he hoped to make the grade.

Bob Paisley soon became a big fan of little Sammy Lee, who graduated from Roy Evans' Central League winning reserve team into the first team with distinction. Paisley later said: "If they had put that heart of his into Big Ben they would never have to carry out any maintenance. He could run, run and run. And he was another of the hard workers who seemed to thrive the tougher it got. For most of his time at the club he was the smallest player on the staff – he was certainly the smallest I can remember making it as a first-team regular – at a fraction under five foot five but he made up for any lack of height with his bulk and effort. I had no hesitation in naming him as substitute only a couple of weeks after his 18th birthday and I wouldn't have over worried if I had been forced to pitch him into the game in front of the Kop. He had to wait another year before his first experience of playing in the First Division but people at the club had already earmarked him as the new Ian Callaghan. With the character and attitude he shows they'd make him Mayor of Liverpool if he was a few inches taller."

On Tuesday, May 8, 1979, Aston Villa, plus a crowd of 50,576 were present at Anfield knowing that a win would give Liverpool their 11th League Championship. The Reds won the game 3-0; Alan Kennedy gave the Reds the ideal start with a goal after just 47 seconds. Dalglish, with his last league strike of the season, and Terry McDermott completed the proceedings.

Fittingly, this was also the day Bob Paisley celebrated his 40th anniversary of joining the club as a player. The Liverpool boss had now led his team to three First Division triumphs and the jubilant Paisley allowed himself a moment's reflection: 'We have won three championships and been runners-up twice in my five years as manager and I wouldn't like to drop down as low as third position. This season we have played better and more consistent football than at any other time since I became manager.' Paisley joined his players in a triumphant march across the pitch to their delighted fans. Only the trophy was not present. It will be brought to Anfield in due course."

An incredibly proud skipper Phil Thompson led the team on a lap of honour and then expressed his feelings to the *Liverpool Echo*: "The greatest thing that ever happened to me was playing for Liverpool. The next greatest thing is skippering the side. For me, a boy from the Kop, to lead out Liverpool on the night they won the title, at Anfield, is the most fabulous feeling. I always hoped to make skipper one day. Captains tend to be defenders and l have always been a bit of a talker on the pitch. This season has been exceptional even by our own standards. Our consistency has been remarkable, and of our four defeats, three were by 1-0. But, overall, it has been tremendous and that's all down to the manager and his backroom staff."

Anfield legend Billy Liddell saluted his former teammate and friend after Paisley clinched his third league title as manager. Both men signed professional for Liverpool together, on the same day, although Billy had been on the books as an amateur for 10 months before. Liddell told the *Liverpool Echo*'s Michael Charters: "I have always been very pleased to know Bob; he has always been a very special friend of mine. We used to live opposite to each other when we were players and the day we moved in, Bob was the first person across our doorstep to welcome us. I played in front of him for years at Liverpool. It was a great comfort to have him there, pushing the ball through for me. He was a left-half in the old style – tremendously strong and rugged, never quitting, a wonderful tackler, and off the field, a tremendous joker among the players. He kept us laughing with his practical jokes and comments. He was born in Durham but he's been a Liverpudlian by adaption for many years. I regard him as the greatest servant Liverpool have ever had. A matchless record of 40 years' service as player, coach and manager. No one could have done more to help to make Liverpool the great club they are today and I'm proud to be his friend."

While the title race was over, the Reds' quest for glory was not. They knew that if they beat Leeds United in their final game of the season on May 17, they would overtake by one point Leeds' record points haul of 67 set 10 years earlier by Don Revie's great side. More than 41,000 fans saw David Johnson score twice and Jimmy Case once in a 3-0 Elland Road win. This latest victory took Liverpool's league goals total to 85, an average of over two per game.

Their tally of only 16 goals conceded, two of which were own goals, is five fewer than the previous record over 42 matches in all divisions, shared by Southampton and Port Vale, and eight fewer than the previous First Division record Liverpool had shared with Nottingham Forest.

To put the latter achievement in even sharper perspective: Preston's 'Invincibles' of 1888/89 conceded 15 goals in 22 matches when winning the championship without losing a match. Liverpool lost only four. Apart from the number of league goals conceded, the four that flew in at Anfield was the lowest number ever and the Reds' 30 victories also signalled a club record. In typical Liverpool style, those achievements would be put aside by the start of the following season.

Roy Evans recalls how his former Boot Room colleague Ronnie Moran would never allow the players to get carried away with the success they had on the pitch: "When Ron used to hand out medals to the players on the first day back at pre-season, there were never any presentations or anything. He just made them think it was their job to be doing this and nothing special was ever made of it. Ronnie would just say something along the lines of, 'These things don't mean anything now, but come and pick one up if you think you deserve one and same again this season, lads'."

Although David Fairclough made four league appearances and Sammy Lee two, Bob Paisley only needed to use another 13 players to complete a 42-game season and win the First Division title by eight points. Four players featured in all 42 games; Ray Clemence, Phil Neal who hadn't missed a game since October 1976, the phenomenal Kenny Dalglish and the brilliant Ray Kennedy.

Before joining Liverpool, Kennedy had already tasted success in his first full season as a professional. He was a vital part of the triumphant Arsenal side that had achieved the First Division and FA Cup 'double' in 1970/71. Kennedy's arrival at Anfield on July 12, 1974 was completely overshadowed by the shock news on the same day that Bill Shankly, the man who had signed him from Arsenal, had decided to step down from the manager's chair with immediate effect.

Shankly was happy with his last task as manager: "There is no doubt Kennedy will do a good job for Liverpool. He is big, brave and strong. His signing means that we now have the greatest strength in depth that we have ever had. Kennedy will cause plenty of trouble to defences. He fights all the way and he was at the top of my list of wanted men. Maybe it will be said that one of the last things I did at this club was to sign a great new player." Kennedy was physically very strong and that impressed Shankly who was still around Melwood: "I've seen him in training and he looks good. He reminds me of Rocky Marciano."

Jimmy Case and Ray Kennedy were inseparable off the pitch and Case held his best friend in the highest regard as a footballer. "Tactically Ray was in a different league," recalls Case. "He had a delicate touch, a sweet left foot and his movement was phenomenal.

I used to cover much more ground and tackle more and he'd cover less ground but use his head more. We worked well together. His best point has to be his timing. I'd have the ball, I'd look up and he was gone. A perfectly timed run, ghosting in from the left, losing his marker, I'd put in the simplest of balls and bang! One-nil."

Bob Paisley was named Manager of the Year for the third time in four years. He had led his team to three League Championships, two European Cup triumphs, a UEFA Cup, an FA Cup Final and a League Cup Final. No-one else in the game could match that sequence.

Paisley told the *Liverpool Echo*: "You're always learning in this game! There are always surprises. But, at Liverpool it's team work first that brings success and creates a good team. We encourage individuals to show their own skills but those skills must fit into the team pattern. We have harmony and stability throughout the club, from the chairman down. We are a family; if any member of a family is in trouble, the rest of them should help. This is what we do at Liverpool."

Continuity was the theme at Anfield and the coaching staff were the perfect example of it. Including the manager, there was more than 150 years of service at the club. In this collection of behind-the-scenes talent, Bob Paisley himself led the long-serving list with 40 years, followed by Ronnie Moran with 27 years' experience since signing professional forms in 1952, Joe Fagan 20, Reuben Bennett 20, Geoff Twentyman 19, Roy Evans 15, Tom Saunders 9 and John Bennison 8. That stability was the secret of the Anfield success story.

Kenny Dalglish scored 56 goals in 116 games in his first two seasons at Liverpool and his contribution had won over the media that voted him Player of the Year in 1979.

Dalglish linked up well with David Johnson, a striking partnership which produced 37 league goals. Paisley sounded more than happy with his new established front pairing when he spoke to the *Liverpool Echo* shortly after the season had ended: "You ask me if I've seen a better finisher, I haven't seen many better players than Kenny Dalglish! A dream of a player for any manager to have, he is so consistent, strong, dedicated to the betterment of the team and with such outstanding individual ability. David Johnson has had his best spell since he joined us and has the hardest job of the front two, doing all the leg work, the running and the chasing. He is a fine foil for Kenny and fits into the blend because of his pace and work rate. A player like Dave is ideal alongside a player like Kenny."

From the diligent Boot Room to the deafening roar of Kop and from the ingenious manager to the gifted players on the pitch, Liverpool Football Club had emphatically become a force to be reckoned with at home and abroad.

It was a family-orientated organisation, ran on pure simplicity with no real special formulas or secrets to justify their success. That said, an immense collective effort was responsible for the multi-record breaking 1978/79 season – a team who went unbeaten at home in the league and a team who had won the First Division by their greatest ever points margin.

On previous occasions, Liverpool teams had won it by six points, but this season Paisley's red machine went two points further and won it by eight. Coupled with the records broken and the quality of the football on show, the 1978/79 season is regarded by many Liverpool fans as the greatest of all time.

1978/79: Facts and Statistics

Final league table

		P	W	D	L	F	A	W	D	L	F	A	PTS
1	Liverpool FC	42	19	2	0	51	4	11	6	4	34	12	68
2	Nottingham Forest	42	11	10	0	34	10	10	8	3	27	16	60
3	WBA	42	13	5	3	38	15	11	6	4	34	20	59
4	Everton	42	12	7	2	32	17	5	10	6	20	23	51
5	Leeds United	42	11	4	6	41	25	7	10	4	29	27	50
6	Ipswich Town	42	11	4	6	34	21	9	5	7	29	28	49
7	Arsenal	42	11	8	2	37	18	6	6	9	24	30	48
8	Aston Villa	42	8	9	4	37	26	7	7	7	22	23	46
9	Manchester United	42	9	7	5	29	25	6	8	7	31	38	45
10	Coventry City	42	11	7	3	41	29	3	9	9	17	39	44
11	Tottenham	42	7	8	6	19	25	6	7	8	29	36	41
12	Middlesbrough	42	10	5	6	33	21	5	5	11	24	29	40
13	Bristol City	42	11	6	4	34	19	4	4	13	13	32	40
14	Southampton	42	9	10	2	35	20	3	6	12	12	33	40
15	Manchester City	42	9	5	7	34	28	4	8	9	24	28	39
16	Norwich City	42	7	10	4	29	19	0	13	8	22	38	37
17	Bolton Wanderers	42	10	5	6	36	28	2	6	13	18	47	35
18	Wolves	42	10	4	7	26	26	3	4	14	18	42	34
19	Derby	42	8	5	8	25	25	2	6	13	19	46	31
20	QPR	42	4	9	8	24	33	2	4	15	21	40	25
21	Birmingham City	42	5	9	7	24	25	1	1	19	13	39	22
22	Chelsea	42	3	5	13	23	42	2	5	14	21	50	20

Games for the 1978/1979 season

(The number after date is league position after the game)

1	19.08.1978	2	W	2-1	Queens Park Rangers, Anfield, 1st Division
2	22.08.1978	1	W	3-0	Ipswich Town, Portman Road, 1st Division
3	26.08.1978	1	W	4-1	Manchester City, Maine Road, 1st Division
4	28.08.1978		L	0-1	Sheffield United, Bramall Lane, League Cup 2nd round
5	02.09.1978	1	W	7-0	Tottenham Hotspur, Anfield, 1st Division
6	09.09.1978	1	W	3-0	Birmingham City, St Andrew's, 1st Division
7	13.09.1978		L	0-2	Nottingham Forest, City Ground, European Cup 1st R 1st L
8	16.09.1978	1	W	1-0	Coventry City, Anfield, 1st Division
9	23.09.1978	1	D	1-1	West Bromwich Albion, The Hawthorns, 1st Division

10	27.09.1978		D	0-0	Nottingham Forest, Anfield, European Cup 1st R 2nd L
11	30.09.1978	1	W	3-0	Bolton Wanderers, Anfield, 1st Division
12	07.10.1978	1	W	4-1	Norwich City, Carrow Road, 1st Division
13	14.10.1978	1	W	5-0	Derby County, Anfield, 1st Division
14	21.10.1978	1	W	2-0	Chelsea, Anfield, 1st Division
15	28.10.1978	1	L	0-1	Everton, Goodison Park, 1st Division
16	04.11.1978	1	D	1-1	Leeds United, Anfield, 1st Division
17	11.11.1978	1	W	3-1	Queens Park Rangers, Loftus Road, 1st Division
18	18.11.1978	1	W	1-0	Manchester City, Anfield, 1st Division
19	22.11.1978	1	D	0-0	Tottenham Hotspur, White Hart Lane, 1st Division
20	25.11.1978	1	W	2-0	Middlesbrough, Anfield, 1st Division
21	02.12.1978	1	L	0-1	Arsenal, Highbury, 1st Division
22	04.12.1978		L	1-3	Anderlecht, Stade Émile Versé, European Super Cup 1st leg
23	09.12.1978	1	W	2-0	Nottingham Forest, Anfield, 1st Division
24	16.12.1978	1	L	0-1	Bristol City, Ashton Gate, 1st Division
25	19.12.1978		W	2-1	Anderlecht, Anfield, European Super Cup 2nd leg
26	26.12.1978	1	W	3-0	Manchester United, Old Trafford, 1st Division
27	10.01.1979		D	0-0	Southend United, Roots Hall, FA Cup 3rd round
28	17.01.1979		W	3-0	Southend United, Anfield, FA Cup 3rd round replay
29	30.01.1979		W	1-0	Blackburn Rovers, Anfield, FA Cup 4th round
30	03.02.1979	1	W	2-1	West Bromwich Albion, Anfield, 1st Division
31	13.02.1979	1	W	1-0	Birmingham City, Anfield, 1st Division
32	21.02.1979	1	W	6-0	Norwich City, Anfield, 1st Division
33	24.02.1979	1	W	2-0	Derby County, Baseball Ground, 1st Division
34	28.02.1979		W	3-0	Burnley, Anfield, FA Cup 5th round
35	03.03.1979	1	D	0-0	Chelsea, Stamford Bridge, 1st Division
36	06.03.1979	1	D	0-0	Coventry City, Highfield Road, 1st Division
37	10.03.1979		W	1-0	Ipswich Town, Portman Road, FA Cup 6th round
38	13.03.1979	1	D	1-1	Everton, Anfield, 1st Division
39	20.03.1979	1	W	2-0	Wolves, Anfield, 1st Division
40	24.03.1979	1	W	2-0	Ipswich Town, Anfield, 1st Division
41	31.03.1979		D	2-2	Manchester United, Maine Road, FA Cup Semi-final
42	04.04.1979		L	0-1	Manchester United, Goodison Park, FA Cup Semi-final replay
43	07.04.1979	1	W	3-0	Arsenal, Anfield, 1st Division
44	10.04.1979	1	W	1-0	Wolves, Molineux, 1st Division
45	14.04.1979	1	W	2-0	Manchester United, Anfield, 1st Division
46	16.04.1979	1	L	1-3	Aston Villa, Villa Park, 1st Division

47	21.04.1979	1	W	1-0	Bristol City, Anfield, 1st Division
48	24.04.1979	1	D	1-1	Southampton, The Dell, 1st Division
49	28.04.1979	1	D	0-0	Nottingham Forest, City Ground, 1st Division
50	01.05.1979	1	W	4-1	Bolton Wanderers, Burnden Park, 1st Division
51	05.05.1979	1	W	2-0	Southampton, Anfield, 1st Division
52	08.05.1979	1	W	3-0	Aston Villa, Anfield, 1st Division
53	11.05.1979	1	W	1-0	Middlesbrough, Ayresome Park, 1st Division
54	17.05.1979	1	W	3-0	Leeds United, Elland Road, 1st Division

Friendlies

1	02.08.1978	W	3-1	Bass League Select, Lansdowne Road, Friendly
2	06.08.1978	W	6-0	Basel, Saint Jakob Stadium, Friendly
3	08.08.1978	D	1-1	Bayern Munich, Olympic Stadium, Friendly
4	11.08.1978	W	1-0	Austria Vienna, Wienerstadion, Friendly
5	14.08.1978	W	3-2	Celtic, Celtic Park, Testimonial*
6	02.10.1978	D	1-1	Saudi Arabia, Jeddah, Friendly
7	11.10.1978	W	3-2	Swansea City, Anfield, Testimonial**
8	12.12.1978	D	1-1	Werder Bremen, Weserstadion, Friendly
9	27.01.1979	W	4-1	Bangor City, Farrar Road, Friendly
10	27.03.1979	L	0-1	Borussia Moenchengladbach, Anfield, Testimonial***
11	28.05.1979	D	3-3	Israel, Ramat-Gan Stadium, Friendly

* Testimonial for Celtic manager Jock Stein.
** Testimonial for Chris Lawler
*** Testimonial for Emlyn Hughes

Appearances for the 1978/1979 season

Name	League	FA Cup	LC	UEFA	Total
Kenny Dalglish	42	7	1	4	54
Ray Kennedy	42	7	1	4	54
Phil Neal	42	7	1	4	54
Graeme Souness	41	7	1	4	53
Ray Clemence	42	7	1	3	53
Phil Thompson	39	6	1	3	49
Terry McDermott	37	7	1	4	49
Jimmy Case	37	6	1	4	48
Alan Kennedy	37	2	1	3	43
Alan Hansen	34	6	0	2	42
Steve Heighway	28	5	1	3	37
David Johnson	30	4	0	3	37
Emlyn Hughes	16	7	1	4	28
David Fairclough	4	3	1	2	10
Sammy Lee	2	0	0	0	2

Steve Ogrizovic	0	0	0	1	1
Brian Kettle	0	0	0	0	0
Joey Jones	0	0	0	0	0

Goalscorers for the 1978/1979 season

Name	League	FA Cup	LC	UEFA	Total
Kenny Dalglish	21	4	0	0	25
David Johnson	16	2	0	0	18
Ray Kennedy	10	1	0	0	11
Graeme Souness	8	1	0	0	9
Jimmy Case	7	1	0	1	9
Terry McDermott	8	0	0	0	8
Phil Neal	5	0	0	0	5
Steve Heighway	4	0	0	0	4
Alan Kennedy	3	0	0	0	3
David Fairclough	2	0	0	1	3
Alan Hansen	1	1	0	0	2
Emlyn Hughes	0	0	0	1	1

The squad during the 1978/1979 season

Ray Clemence, Goalkeeper
Steve Ogrizovic, Goalkeeper
Alan Kennedy, Defender
Phil Thompson, Defender
Phil Neal, Defender
Joey Jones, Defender
Brian Kettle, Defender
Emlyn Hughes, Defender
Alan Hansen, Defender
Colin Irwin, Defender
Ian Callaghan, Midfielder
Jimmy Case, Midfielder
Steve Heighway, Midfielder
Ray Kennedy, Midfielder
Sammy Lee, Midfielder
Terry McDermott, Midfielder
Kevin Sheedy, Midfielder
Graeme Souness, Midfielder
David Johnson, Striker
Kenny Dalglish, Striker
David Fairclough, Striker

Transfers for the 1978/1979 season

In:
Kevin Sheedy, Hereford United, £80,000, 13 July 1978
Alan Kennedy, Newcastle United, £330,000, 13 August 1978
Frank McGarvey, St. Mirren, £300,000, May 1979

Out:
Peter McDonnell, Oldham Athletic, Free, August 1978
Tommy Smith, Swansea City, Free, 17 August 1978
Ian Callaghan, Swansea City, Free, 14 September 1978
Joey Jones, Wrexham, £200,000, 18 October 1978
Trevor Birch, Shrewsbury Town, £45,000, March 1979

A collection of statistics for the 1978/1979 season

The season in numbers:
Total games: 62
Games won: 36
Games drawn: 14
Games lost: 12
Clean sheets – League: 18
Clean sheets – Overall: 27
Total goals: 98
Average attendance at home – League: 47,284
Average attendance at home – Overall: 46,171
Average goals per game – League: 2.24
Average goals per game – Overall: 2.23
Average goal minute – League: 54
Average goal minute – Overall: 52

Goals split down to competitions:
League – 85
FA Cup – 10
European Super Cup – 3
League Cup – 0
European Cup – 0

Player debuts:
Alan Kennedy against QPR on 19.08.1978

Statistics and information provided by LFChistory.net

12 : DOING IT HIS WAY

1979/80

DURING THE 1978/1979 POST-SEASON, BOB Paisley, who had just won his third League Championship as manager during his 40th year at the club, explained to the *Liverpool Echo* that not all his years at Liverpool had been glorious ones: "My years at Liverpool have been hard years but I've enjoyed every one of them. There have been many more ups than downs and I don't think that can be said very often in football, being the game it is. Probably it was only the last half of my forty years at Anfield that you can call glorious, since Bill Shankly started it all. In the mid-Sixties, Bill created a great team, but from 1966 to 1972 we didn't win anything. Yet, by that time, Liverpool had become a great club again, becoming recognised in Europe and the world.

"We don't have any secrets about our success, we regard football as a simple game but perhaps what gives us something extra is the spirit in the club. We are dedicated to two things – family and winning. We are a family club, everyone helping everybody else in every department. That is the spirit that runs right through all club policy. We never want to lose; we make a custom of winning.

"For myself, as manager, I have two things – my own family,

without which nothing could be achieved. Without that as the basis no man can succeed. And I have the staff at Anfield, helping me along the line. Without them, I couldn't achieve anything at Anfield. As a manager, the pressures are greater now than I've ever known as a player or a coach. When you're at the top the pressure is on you to stay there. Nevertheless, I would never want to work without pressure and I also know if you become complacent, you are dead! It is possible to look at a team of 22-year-old players and think they will go on forever but they won't – you must keep building.

"In my first year as manager, I made a habit of counting to 10 before I made a decision. I was being deliberately cautious. I took my bends wide instead of hugging the rails, probably because I was so keen not to trip up. Now I'm learning, I only count to two before I make a decision. That's what man-management teaches you. We go about our business at Liverpool on a day-to-day basis, we have our patterns and our way of life. We set our targets and ambitions at the very top, and it's not easy to stay there. But I wouldn't want it any other way, I wouldn't change a day of it. I'm happy, in good health and I'm surrounded by good friends and helpers. I've no thoughts of retiring. I'm 60 but I believe I've got a few more years left in the job. I hope so anyway as I enjoy my work."

Despite his success and fame within the game, during the little time off he has away from Anfield, Paisley had no interest in luxury cruises and Caribbean holidays. Instead, he would go to work as a stable lad and spend a fortnight getting up at dawn and "doing out" the thoroughbreds for a trainer friend, simply because he enjoyed doing it. The summer holidays best epitomised Bob Paisley. He did the things he liked to do; not those which others might think a man in his position ought to have done.

In July 1979, Abraham 'Avi' Cohen was the first foreign player to sign for Liverpool and go on to represent the first team since South African Doug Rudham, who had arrived 24 years earlier. His transfer successfully concluded six months of Liverpool interest in the player. The club had received glowing reports about the defender and in February 1979 he spent a week training with the first team at Melwood under the watchful eye of Paisley.

The club also completed another deal during the summer of 1979, but it wasn't for a player. Liverpool decided to wear shirt advertising and the sponsor was Japanese TV and electronics giant Hitachi, which was also the name Anfield old boy Kevin Keegan wore on his Hamburg shirt in Germany.

The shock behind the pioneering move by Liverpool, the most successful club in the league, is that they claimed they were doing it to stay alive. "We are fighting for our existence," chairman John Smith told the *Liverpool Echo* as he announced a one-year £50,000 deal with Hitachi. The money may not have seemed a lot at this stage but Liverpool were hoping it would be a trailblazer. The aim was to challenge regulations which banned shirt advertising in televised matches, FA Cup ties and European games.

Quoting figures that emphasised the grim financial position in football, Smith revealed: "From a turnover of £2.4 million last year, Liverpool's profit at the end of the day was a meagre £71,000... this for one of the leading clubs in Europe. It shows the paucity of money in British football. Our neighbours, Everton, for instance, made a profit of £2,000 last year and the year before their figure was just £184. And only a handful of clubs make a profit at all. The days are gone when a club like ours could control their destiny on the money coming through the turnstiles. It is absolutely essential to generate income from other sources. We have agreed to this deal to help safeguard the long-term financial interest of the club."

On August 2, long-serving skipper Emlyn Hughes was sold to Wolverhampton Wanderers for £90,000. Hughes told the press shortly after joining John Barnwell's side: "I have been impressed with everything and everyone at Wolves. Whether it's this year, next year or three years' time, this club is going places – and I'm looking forward to being part of it. Of course, it was a hard decision to leave Liverpool. They have treated me fantastically and made it clear that I could have stayed there. I spent a lot of time thinking about whether I should leave – and exploring the alternatives like the eight offers I received to become a player manager in the Second, Third or Fourth Division. I sought advice from those I respected most in the game – people like Bill Shankly, Ron Greenwood and Joe Mercer – and they all told me: 'Carry on playing, you have plenty of time later to be a manager'. More importantly, I felt I could continue to play First Division football and I chose Wolves from the four clubs who offered me that opportunity."

Despite selling Hughes, Paisley knew that in captain Phil Thompson and Alan Hansen he had no central defensive worries. Therefore, apart from Hughes, Paisley had the rest of his title-winning squad at his disposal plus the arrival of Cohen, and striker Frank McGarvey, a £300,000 buy from St Mirren.

Liverpool's pre-season work had gone well and when they beat FA Cup winners Arsenal 3-1 at Wembley in the Charity Shield, with goals by Terry McDermott (2) and Kenny Dalglish, it appeared they were about to begin their championship defence in ruthless fashion.

But strangely, in contrast to their previous campaign, Liverpool took time to move into top gear. They were scheduled to open their league fixtures against Hughes' Wolves team, but that match was postponed because a new stand at Molineux had not yet been completed. Instead, while the rest of the First Division went into league action, the Reds defeated a League of Ireland XI 2-0 in a friendly across the water.

Liverpool's season proper got underway three days later when they faced Bolton Wanderers on August 21. The Trotters, who had told the world they would come to Anfield to attack, failed to keep their promise and spent the whole evening trying to keep the Reds at bay. They succeeded, too, as the match finished disappointingly goalless and Liverpool failed to score for the first time in a league game at home for 15 months. 'ANFIELD'S NIGHT OF FRUSTRATION' read the *Liverpool Echo* headline, with Bob Paisley quoted as saying: "It will bring us down to earth."

However, four days later Liverpool scored three times when Ron Atkinson's West Brom visited Anfield. A double from David Johnson and a Terry McDermott goal gave Liverpool their first league victory of the season. Colin Irwin made his Liverpool debut that after-noon, coming in for the injured Alan Hansen. The Liverpudlian came through the junior ranks at Anfield and carried out an electri-cal apprenticeship before signing professional forms for the Reds shortly after his 17th birthday. Irwin's only other previous call-up to the first-team squad came, remarkably, in the 1978 European Cup final. Although the young Scouser did not get on the pitch, he did collect a winner's medal.

On September 19, Bob Paisley brought teenager Ronnie Whelan to Merseyside from his native Ireland. Whelan's background always made it likely that he would be successful in the sport as it had become something of a tradition in the family. His father was an Irish international and his younger brother Paul also played in the League of Ireland for many years. Ronnie impressed as a young-ster with Home Farm in the city of his birth, Dublin. A number of English clubs showed interest including Manchester United where he was a trainee but it was Liverpool who made a definite move shortly before his 18th birthday for £35,000. Like many young players brought to the club by Paisley, Whelan had to be patient for his chance to show that he was worth a place in the team.

Besides West Bromwich Albion, Coventry City were the only other team to taste league defeat at the hands of Liverpool by the time the champions faced Nottingham Forest at the City Ground on September 29. The Reds had taken only seven points from their opening seven games and were lying 10th in the table. Surprisingly, Crystal Palace were level at the top with Manchester United and Forest with 12 points from eight outings. The South London outfit was already being dubbed the team of the Eighties but it turned out to be a premature label to attach, especially as they were to leave the top-flight in 1981. Against Forest, Liverpool crashed to a Garry Birtles effort and the *Liverpool Echo* headline read: 'LOOK BACK IN ANGER' highlighting the amount of possession and chances, not only in that match but so far through the season, that the Reds had failed to convert.

Goalkeeper Ray Clemence missed the trip to Nottingham with flu, so Steve 'Oggy' Ogrizovic, took over in goal for only the fourth time since he joined in 1977. Ogrizovic served as a police officer at Mansfield Police Station in Nottinghamshire prior to signing as a professional footballer and was also an accomplished cricketer, reaching the Minor Counties as a medium-fast bowler during a spell with Shropshire. Oggy arrived at Anfield from Chesterfield as cover for Clemence after playing only 18 games in Chesterfield's first team. Ogrizovic conceded four goals on his Liverpool debut at Derby County's Baseball Ground on March 8, 1978, the first game Clemence had missed since September 9, 1972, after having made 336 appearances in a row. The turning point, albeit a painful one, of the season came three days later when Liverpool again went out of the European Cup in the first round. This time their conquerors were the useful Russians, Dinamo Tbilisi, who turned a 2-1 first leg reversal into a 4-2 aggregate win.

From that moment, Liverpool were stung into action, embarking on a run of 16 league matches without defeat. This started the following Saturday at Anfield when the Reds put four past Bristol City in the club's 3000th league game.

On October 20, neighbours Everton crossed Stanley Park for the first derby clash of the campaign. The game ended 2-2, but controversy reigned in the 70th minute when a hard tackle by Garry Stanley on David Johnson caused a mass brawl resulting in Terry McDermott and Everton's Stanley becoming the first players to be sent off in a Merseyside derby in the 20th century.

McDermott couldn't help but laugh at the situation: "I made contact with Garry's teeth – or vice versa. I've still got the scar on my hand today and the referee sent us both off. The irony was that Garry and I are good friends and we'd often be out for a drink together. That plus the fact we were both just about the two softest players on the park. I remember sitting in the bath and laughing when I thought of all those hard men still running about out there while us two softies had been sent off. I think it was for dropping our handbags." This colourful game also featured a female streaker running the length of the field.

A week later the Reds thumped Manchester City 4-0 at Maine Road which moved them to within three points of league leaders Manchester United, having played a game less. Before the game, manager Paisley explained his side's disappointing form: "The whole crux to this season has been the way Kenny (Dalglish) has been playing. He has not hit form. He could have had a few more goals. If Kenny starts attacking the way he can then I cannot see anything wrong with us."

The Scottish striker answered that call and Liverpool's form that day against City was devastating, as Malcolm Allison's young Mancunians were ripped apart. Dalglish sparkled and laid on the opening goal for David Johnson after 16 minutes and just after the half hour mark, he was on the scoresheet himself, beating Joe Corrigan with a low shot from 10 yards. Dalglish struck again in the 65th minute, hooking the ball home after Ray Kennedy, scorer of the fourth goal, had headed down Phil Neal's cross. The *Liverpool Echo* headline: 'DAZZLING DALGLISH' summed up the afternoon, with the match report elaborating: "Dalglish, back to his superb best, played the major part in a magnificent display by the champions, which was far too good for the immature, though promising, young men Malcolm Allison has assembled."

On November 3, Emlyn Hughes returned to Anfield with his new club Wolves and was given a rapturous ovation by the Kop. Kenny Dalglish's inspiring leadership of the Liverpool attack was paramount in a 3-0 victory. The talented Scot scored the first two and was involved in the attack that led to Ray Kennedy's fourth goal of the season. Dalglish's second goal was a flawless team creation, a perfect example of scoring quickly on the break and Liverpool made it look so easy.

Six players were involved in the move which began with a short goalkick from Ray Clemence to captain Phil Thompson. Thompson pushed the ball upfield to Phil Neal who turned, looked up and spotted David Johnson unmarked 15 yards inside the Wolves half. Neal's long right-foot pass was right to the feet of Johnson who instinctively flicked on a superb first-time ball to Terry McDermott, running hard on the blind side of Emlyn Hughes. McDermott cut into the box and as goalkeeper Paul Bradshaw advanced to narrow the angle he unselfishly slipped a delightful square ball to Dalglish on the penalty spot, leaving Dalglish with the sort of chance he doesn't miss and he side-footed the ball home past the wrong-footed keeper.

The following weekend Dalglish continued his exceptional form, adding two more goals at the Goldstone Ground against Brighton, bringing his tally to six in his last three league outings. It was now safe to say that Dalglish's dip in form at the start of the campaign was well and truly over.

On November 20, Tommy Smith re-signed for Liverpool as a junior coach, joining the most professional backroom staff in English Football. Smith had had to cut short his contact with John Toshack's Swansea the previous month after being told by a specialist that his playing days were over at the age of 34 due to a knee injury.

Liverpool, always the realists in such situations, didn't make room for Smith to join the coaching staff and no-one had been disturbed to create a position for him as Bob Paisley explained to the *Liverpool Echo*: "Tommy asked us if he could come on the staff, and as there was a position available as a junior coach, he was offered the job. He now has to learn a totally different side of football that he was used to. There is much to learn and he will find a very big change."

Liverpool ended November on 22 points from 16 games in second place and were now just a point behind leaders Manchester United who had notched up 23 points from 17 games. Liverpool were going from strength to strength and the following month achieved a feat which was previously achieved by a Liverpool team in 1962.

During the month of December, Liverpool played seven league games and won all seven, matching the achievement of Bill Shankly's team's debut season in the First Division.

Liverpool's match against Middlesbrough at Anfield on December 1 coincided with the 20th anniversary of Shankly's arrival on Merseyside. The Reds demonstrated once more that their former manager's basic principles; fitness, simplicity and unselfish teamwork were the main strengths of their game as the Teessiders were well beaten, 4-0.

Liverpool entered into the festive period as league leaders, albeit on goal difference ahead of rivals Manchester United. On December 22, the Reds travelled to the Baseball Ground to take on Colin Addison's Derby County and left with a 3-1 victory.

Four days later, Liverpool faced Manchester United at home on Boxing Day in a top-of-the-table clash. Dave Sexton's United had plenty of big names on view such as Joe Jordan, Lou Macari, Mickey Thomas, Steve Coppell, Sammy McIlroy and Ray Wilkins, but against a Reds team unchanged for the ninth successive League fixture, they were powerless, and went down 2-0 before a 51,000 crowd. 'ANFIELD KINGS RULE ON' was the *Liverpool Echo* headline, with the sub-heading reading: "Pretenders punished by the crown bearers..." Alan Hansen opened the scoring in the 15th minute with a superb effort, rounding off a seven-pass move to finish with a one-two with Ray Kennedy before beating Gary Bailey. The young United keeper was having a fine match but five minutes from time he allowed David Johnson's fierce volley to slip through his arms and legs. The *Liverpool Echo*'s Michael Charters was again liberal with his praise for Liverpool, writing: "The point they hammered home in beating Manchester United 2-0 was that they are outstandingly the best team in the land."

At the end of 1979, midfielder Ray Kennedy, now in this sixth season at Liverpool, gave an insight into the club's approach in bringing success. Kennedy told the *Daily Express*: "It's no big deal really, the answer is simplicity. We don't have any magic formula. The whole basis of our game is doing the simple things well. We are told to play the simple ball early, not to run with the ball and not to try and complicate the game. It's as easy as that. When you join the club, they condition you to become a Liverpool player. It really is a special feeling."

Kennedy was right, the efficiency and simplicity of how the club was run applied at all levels of its administration. From chairman John Smith, via the best club secretary in the business, Peter Robinson, through manager Bob Paisley and his coaching staff and, not least, the players themselves.

Everything started in pre-season when, in an era of physical fitness, Liverpool got their players fitter than almost any other club. As a consequence, they had fewer injuries, and, in turn, needed to make fewer team changes. There was fanatical loyalty, an increasingly rare commodity during those days. Within the club, no player was bigger than the club itself. With unerring regularity one or two players were integrated each season, and one or two older players, no matter how famous, were moved on before they became a liability. Yet the players are financially rewarded to the extent that there were few, if any, pay rows or cases of players refusing to re-sign.

Football is a game of chance, yet Liverpool went as far as it is possible to eliminate it and that occasionally exposed them to the accusation – which is also a compliment – of being boring. During this period they were so efficient it could have seemed that way.

In the previous seven seasons Liverpool hadn't finished outside the top two and didn't stop adding silverware to their trophy room and Terry McDermott later confessed he thought even Liverpool's own fans could have got bored at times. He claimed: "I mean nobody in the right mind would admit they would ever get bored of winning!

"However, I think our fans did every now and again, I honestly do. I think it was expected that we would go and pummel teams but you had to entertain them as well as win trophies and if you didn't do that, then you were the first to know about it!"

Liverpool's first game of the new decade was on January 5, when Grimsby Town came to Anfield in the third round of the FA Cup. The Reds were expected to win handsomely and did so by five clear goals, but David Johnson, who scored his only hat-trick for Liverpool that afternoon, remembers the sufferings on the way: "Grimsby were the far better team for about half an hour. There was no doubt about that. They brought tremendous support and had us on the run for a long, uncomfortable period. Some lesser teams had the ability to lift their game on a rare visit to Anfield.

"I also remember the great rivalry between the two sets of supporters that day and how Grimsby sparked off the Kop by chanting, 'You only sing when you're winning'. The Kop responded, 'You only sing when you're fishing' and then our fans went through some of our team shouting, 'Jimmy Plaice', 'Stingray Kennedy', 'Kenny Dogfish', 'Phil Eel' and so on. They were hilarious and so quick with their humour. So what could have been a disaster day turned out well in the end but the fun from the supporters has lasted long in my memory."

In spite of starting 1980 in stylish fashion in the FA Cup, the same wasn't to be said about their league form. In January, the Reds could only manage a 1-1 draw when third-place Southampton visited Anfield and their visit to Highfield Road the following weekend ended in a 1-0 defeat, Liverpool's first league reversal since September 29. Defensively, the Reds were not at their best when visiting Carrow Road on February 9, but their lively attack compensated for their deficiencies at the back and ensured the team of the points in an eight-goal thriller against Norwich City.

Bob Paisley was forced to make changes after 17 successive matches. Johnson was absent with a head wound and Graeme Souness was suspended, thus allowing midfield dynamo Sammy Lee his first outing of the season and David Fairclough his first appearance since the Nottingham Forest defeat in September.

The flame-haired striker, fed up with the 'Super Sub' tag he had been given because he always felt he could produce the goods throughout 90 minutes, underlined his point with a well-taken hat-trick. His first goal came after four minutes, to cancel out Martin Peters' opener, and he gave the Reds the lead 14 minutes later. Kevin Reeves pulled one back for the Canaries but Fairclough completed his first treble in senior football in the second half, following a magnificent run by Kenny Dalglish.

With nine minutes remaining, Justin Fashanu scored that now famous long-range volley but Dalglish and Jimmy Case put the game beyond Norwich's reach. The *Liverpool Echo* headline read: 'BREATH-TAKING SHOW' with the match report making the point that this remarkable Liverpool team relied on guts, as well as skill, to see them through. It read: "It was the character of the Liverpool players, even more than their ability, which won them two priceless points on a day when rivals Manchester United lost 1-0 at home to Wolves. Liverpool are the original misers in refusing to concede opponents anything and it was their determination to battle to the end which brought them victory at the last gasp."

Hat-trick hero Fairclough, was again relegated to the bench the following Tuesday when Nottingham Forest visited Anfield for the League Cup semi-final second leg. Fairclough was upset by Paisley's decision: "Despite just scoring my first hat-trick for Liverpool away at Norwich, I was named as a substitute for the following midweek League Cup game against Forest. It was a massive personal blow but was something I was becoming used to, so I shouldn't have felt totally surprised about being omitted by Bob Paisley. I'm sure it wouldn't have happened at any other club."

Looking back Fairclough wasn't very pleased with Paisley's treatment of him at Liverpool. He told *LFChistory.net*: "Down the years I've had lots of time to think about why I didn't fulfil my potential. Obviously, Paisley had to keep 14-16 people happy, but he made life difficult for me. I broke into the England squad and I was very much on Ron Greenwood's list of players who were perhaps going to break in. I came back to Anfield and Bob Paisley decided to play me as sub or leave me out. I thought I had a lot more to offer."

Nottingham Forest were still thought of as a bogey team, even if Liverpool had knocked them out of the FA Cup in January, and there was some justification for that tag as Brian Clough's side gained revenge with an aggregate win over the Reds in the League Cup semi-final. However, in a sense, Liverpool still had the last word in that competition for Emlyn Hughes went on to captain Wolves to victory in the final.

On February 19, Nottingham Forest were back at Anfield, a week after the League Cup semi-final, for their fifth meeting of the season. Still with a game in hand, Liverpool established a three-point lead over second-placed Manchester United with a 2-0 victory, thanks to a thunderous shot from Terry McDermott and a Ray Kennedy drive, both goals coming in the final 10 minutes.

Liverpool ended February exactly the same way they started their league proceedings in January; a home draw followed by an away defeat. The Reds were denied maximum points at Anfield against Ipswich Town on February 22, when Frans Thisssen threw mud in Terry McDermott's way as he was about to take a late penalty.

The referee refused to have it retaken. *The Guardian* reported: "Terry McDermott's failure to convert a penalty three minutes from the end of Saturday's match at Anfield cost Liverpool, the league leaders, a championship point, enabled Ipswich to establish a club record of 15 matches without defeat and provided a controversy that proved more interesting than the match as a whole.

"The central subject of the debate was the refereeing of Bert Newsome of Broseley, Shropshire, who awarded the penalty on seeing Butcher, the Ipswich central defender, pull Dalglish's jersey as the Liverpool striker attempted to shield the ball with his back to goal. Ipswich contended that Dalglish had obstructed the defender with his buttocks and having scored an unexpected equaliser only four minutes earlier, they allowed their anger and frustration to well into vehement protest. Mr Newsome refrained from booking several Ipswich players, including their frantic captain, Mills.

"The referee also took no action when he saw Ipswich's midfield player Frans Thijssen throw a handful of mud between McDermott and the ball as the Liverpool player was about to take the penalty kick and disregarded Liverpool's claim that Cooper had moved before the ball was kicked when making a fine save at the foot of his right hand post. While one did not question Mr Newsome's right, as the arbiter, to decide that Butcher, and not Dalglish, had committed an offence and accepted in the understanding way in which he overlooked the Ipswich protests, his handling of the 'mud-slinging incident' was a source of concern."

McDermott described Thijssen's action as "the type of gamesmanship practised in five-a-side training matches". However, he also admitted that the mud missile had not affected his kick: "I didn't hit it hard enough." Meanwhile Thijssen agreed that he was lucky to escape a booking for ungentlemanly conduct.

The following Tuesday, Liverpool travelled to Molineux to play their long-awaited game in hand, which was originally scheduled to take place on the first day of the season but was postponed due to building work at Molineux. A well-taken goal by John Richards after

71 minutes proved to be the winner for Wolves after being outplayed by Liverpool for most of the game.

Despite their fourth loss of the season, Liverpool remained two points ahead of Manchester United at the top of the First Division, with both teams now having played the same amount of games (28).

Goodison Park provided the venue for Liverpool's first game in March. Although the Reds won 2-1, the result was of minimal importance as Everton's greatest ever player, 73-year-old Dixie Dean, died of a heart attack while attending the game, a few minutes from the final whistle.

There was a special lunch before the derby at Liverpool's Moat House Hotel on Paradise Street to launch the Liverpool and Everton annuals. Dixie, Bill Shankly, Billy Liddell and many other greats were all in attendance. Shankly and Dixie got up and spoke fondly about each other. Shankly delivered the following words as a tribute to Dixie: "Dixie was the greatest centre forward there was and will ever be. His record of goalscoring is the most amazing thing under the sun. He belongs in the company of the supremely great, like Beethoven, Shakespeare and Rembrandt."

On March 11, after only a year at Liverpool, Frank McGarvey left the club, as he had not been able to break into the starting XI. McGarvey returned to Scotland to join Celtic for a fee of £275,000 without having played a single game for Liverpool's first team.

By the time the Reds visited White Hart Lane on March 29, Liverpool had won their previous four league games, conceding just one and had extended their lead at the top to six points. However, against Keith Burkinshaw's Tottenham Hotspur, the Reds simply weren't on their game and slumped to their fifth league defeat of the season, losing 2-0.

Liverpool's next away trip was to Old Trafford, where the Reds were defeated 2-1 – their second consecutive away defeat in seven days. Dropping four points in such a short space of time allowed Dave Sexton's team to narrow the gap at the top to four points with six games still to be played by both teams. However, the reality is that Manchester United would need to gain five points on Liverpool due to the champions being a long way ahead on goal difference; plus 44 against plus 23.

Paisley's side bounced back three days later, beating relegation-stricken Derby County 3-0 at Anfield. The headline that the *Daily Mirror* went with summed up the game in three words, 'DERBY KOP IT!' And the following write up read: "Liverpool moved a big step nearer to their fourth league championship in five seasons last night. And they destroyed Derby's faint hopes of First Division survival at the same time. Goals from stand-in Colin Irwin, David Johnson and an own goal from Keith Osgood rubbed in Liverpool's superiority."

For the sixth successive season, the Reds were going to have no success in the domestic knock-out competitions, going out of the FA Cup on May 1 to eventual runners-up Arsenal at Highfield Road in a semi-final third replay.

On the very same day as Liverpool's FA Cup exit, Paisley added a relatively unknown striker to his ranks, a Welsh teenager by the name of Ian Rush. Rush was born and raised with four sisters and five brothers in a town called Flint in North Wales. When he was 13 playing for Deeside Primary Schools his scoring prowess alerted scouts at Liverpool and Manchester United. He eventually went on trials to Burnley, Wrexham and Chester. Cliff Sear, the youth team manager at Chester, put him at ease and Rush felt at home at Chester. Liverpool scout Geoff Twentyman was a regular visitor at Chester's games and by 1980, Bob Paisley was convinced enough about his talent to persuade the club to splash out £300,000 on the 19-year-old, which was the highest fee ever paid for a youngster at the time in the world.

What clinched the deal for Rush was that Chester manager, Allan Oakes, told him: "If you don't make it, you can always go back to Chester." Rush left Chester after scoring 17 goals in 39 matches.

He later recalled his first moments at Liverpool with *LFChistory. net*: "Allan Oakes, the manager at Chester, told me that Liverpool wanted to sign me. This was in February or March 1980. I refused to go to Liverpool at first because I didn't feel I was good enough to play for them. They were such a big club and I didn't think I was ready to go. They came again back in April. Paisley invited me to Anfield and Melwood and I realised it was such a great club and it would be too good of a chance to turn it down. I thought to myself, if I wasn't good enough, I could always go back to Chester, and that I had nothing to lose to go and see what it was like. After three or four months I realised I was good enough to play for them. Even though there were some good players there, I wasn't out of place. I started out in the reserves and most of the players in the reserves were good enough for the first team. I knew I was as good as them so that's when I knew I could make it at the top given the chance."

Initially, first teamer Alan Hansen wasn't that convinced by Rush's abilities: "I watched Rushie in training and I thought to myself, 'He's got no pace, he can't head it, he can't score, we'll get rid of him at the end of the season'. It just goes to show how good a judge of a player I was."

A few weeks later Paisley also added 24-year-old former England Under-21 international Richard Money to his squad, who arrived from Fulham for £50,000. Born in Lowestoft, Money played for Suffolk Boys in his time and was signed by Ipswich Town on associated schoolboy forms. He had ideas of being a PE teacher after achieving five O-Levels at grammar school and realised being a professional footballer was not the be all and end all of his young life.

He decided to turn professional when Ron Ashman, the Scunthorpe manager, gave him the chance. Money told the *Liverpool Echo*: "Of course, the names of Kevin Keegan and Ray Clemence, Scunthorpe players before they joined Liverpool, were hammered at the young players. We were always being told by Scunthorpe people what they had done so the ambition of playing for Liverpool was planted in me then. You can imagine my delight when I was told to go to Anfield and see Mr. Paisley. I knew Liverpool were watching me and Bobby had told me he would do his best to recommend me and he kept his word."

Bob Paisley always spoke of the constant need to add new recruits to an already perfect team. He told the *Liverpool Echo* after signing his two latest incomings: "We must never sit still and enjoy the good times; we must constantly be looking ahead to maintain the success and build further on it. Rush and Money are players whom we believe will strengthen the squad. They have been bought to maintain challenge and competition for first-team places. Regulars must never be allowed to believe that their positions are secure. We will always make sure that there is competition for places at Anfield."

On May 3, 1980, history had the chance of repeating itself when Liverpool faced Aston Villa in their last home game of the season. Ron Saunders' Villa were the Reds' opponents almost a year earlier when they clinched League Championship number 11 at Anfield. Therefore, once again Paisley and his men had the opportunity of taking the title in front of their magnificent home fans. Ultimately, occasions like this belonged to the Kop.

The terraces were packed two hours before the kick-off with thousands still outside. The Reds beat Aston Villa comprehensively and once more, ended the season unbeaten at home. The 51,541 spectators saw Liverpool round off their Anfield fixtures in style. Avi Cohen made amends for a first-half own goal, one of only eight conceded in Anfield league matches, with a goal in the right net as they won 4-1. A double from David Johnson took his championship total to 21 goals, 27 in all competitions with Kenny Dalglish weighing in with 16. David Johnson's second goal which secured the championship was a tremendous strike. Johnson recalls: "Ronnie Moran used to have go at me for not scoring enough goals with my left foot. I remember Graeme Souness laying the ball off to me and from just outside the box I lashed one with my left, it hit the post and flew into the net at the Kop end."

After the final whistle, the two injured first-team players, David Fairclough and Alan Kennedy, strolled out to hand English football's hardest-won trophy to captain, Phil Thompson.

The plinth was momentarily lost and careered around the centre circle. After the Kop and the players had exchanged mutual salutations, Bob Paisley appeared to salute the Kop with his traditional waves of gratitude.

His record since succeeding Shankly as manager in the summer of 1974 is, to use his own words: "Something you would never even dream about." In the ensuing six seasons, Liverpool won the league four times, the European Cup twice, the UEFA Cup once and the European Super Cup once.

Of equal importance, in many respects, was the reserve team's habit of winning the Central League, which including the 1979/80 season. They had won the league an incredible 10 times in the past 12 seasons. This demonstrated the underlying strength of the club, namely its strong sense of continuity and Liverpool's ability to fill positions weakened by injury or loss of form with players who had been trained to play the Liverpool way.

Statistically, Liverpool's record suffered by comparison with their record-breaking success of 1978/79. Then they accumulated 68 points, compared to this season's total of 60; and while they scored a similar number of goals, 81 compared to 85, they conceded nearly twice as many, 30 against 16.

All these figures prove is that Liverpool's season flowed less evenly than its predecessor and it was hard for any supporter to disagree with Paisley's assertion that: "During our unbeaten run of 16 league games up to and just into the New Year, Liverpool produced some of the best football that has ever been seen at the club. And in spite of not achieving silverware in the three cup competitions, I don't think the season has been too bad at all."

Terry McDermott had scored some truly memorable goals during his Liverpool career, but none so great as his sublime strike against Tottenham in the sixth round of the FA Cup at White Hart Lane in March.

The *Anfield Review* perfectly depicted McDermott's masterpiece: "It was seven minutes before half-time and Spurs' Argentinian international Ossie Ardiles was deep in his own half and in charge of the ball. He was seeking perfection, as always, and attempted to find a teammate with a delicately weighted pass. That was his style. But Jimmy Case was promptly moving in to make an interception and the ball ran kindly for McDermott, positioned just outside the right corner of the Spurs penalty area. Seconds later, it was nestling in the top corner of the net after a McDermott strike, angled from 22 yards, that was simply unstoppable."

As well as this mesmerising strike and his constant wizardry in midfield, McDermott deservedly became the first player to win the

Football Writers' and Professional Footballers' Association's Player of the Year awards in the same season.

Despite achieving such a feat, his introverted personality held him back from going to collect the awards. Terry explains: "I'm not one of these people who likes the adulation. I'd sooner be in the background. Even when I won the Player of the Year in 1980, I never turned up. I never went down to London to get it from the sports writers. I think I am the only one who has ever done that. I'm not proud of having done that but now I feel so proud when I see it and think to myself that I actually won that award.

"At that time though, it just wasn't me. I'd sooner have gone to the pub for a pint and a pie rather than go to a big function like that. That's no disrespect to anybody, that's just the way I was and to a certain extent I'm still like that now. I don't go to hardly any functions with the former players because I don't like the limelight. People might think that's strange, because he's an outgoing fellow, but that's just the way I am!"

As Liverpool entered into a new decade, they remained at their invincible best. Who could topple Liverpool's dynasty? That was the question everyone in football was asking. They had just won the League Championship for the 12th time, Paisley's fourth triumph in six seasons and when he was asked by a reporter if he had any ambitions left in the game, Liverpool's manager simply replied: "Yeah, to win it next year."

Paisley had already assured fans that he had no plans to retire, which only meant one thing, many more league titles and honours would be on the horizon.

Bob Paisley was a man who had to follow a legend, and consequently had become one himself.

1979/80: Facts and Statistics

Final league table

		P	W	D	L	F	A	W	D	L	F	A	PTS
1	Liverpool FC	42	15	6	0	46	8	10	4	7	35	22	60
2	Manchester United	42	17	3	1	43	8	7	7	7	22	27	58
3	Ipswich Town	42	14	4	3	43	13	8	5	8	25	26	53
4	Arsenal	42	8	10	3	24	12	10	6	5	28	24	52
5	Nottingham Forest	42	16	4	1	44	11	4	4	13	19	32	48
6	Wolves	42	9	6	6	29	20	10	3	8	29	27	47
7	Aston Villa	42	11	5	5	29	22	5	9	7	22	28	46
8	Southampton	42	14	2	5	53	24	4	7	10	12	29	45
9	Middlesbrough	42	11	7	3	31	14	5	5	11	19	30	44
10	WBA	42	9	8	4	37	23	2	11	8	17	27	41
11	Leeds United	42	10	7	4	30	17	3	7	11	16	33	40
12	Norwich City	42	10	8	3	38	30	3	6	12	20	36	40
13	Crystal Palace	42	9	9	3	26	13	3	7	11	15	37	40
14	Tottenham	42	11	5	5	30	22	4	5	12	22	40	40
15	Coventry City	42	12	2	7	34	24	4	5	12	22	42	39
16	Brighton & H A	42	8	8	5	25	20	3	7	11	22	37	37
17	Manchester City	42	8	8	5	28	25	4	5	12	15	41	37
18	Stoke City	42	9	4	8	27	26	4	6	11	17	32	36
19	Everton	42	7	7	7	28	25	2	10	9	15	26	35
20	Bristol City	42	6	6	9	22	30	3	7	11	15	36	31
21	Derby	42	9	4	8	36	29	2	4	15	11	38	30
22	Bolton Wanderers	42	5	11	5	19	21	0	4	17	19	52	25

Games for the 1979/1980 season

(The number after date is league position after the game)

1	11.08.1979		W	3-1	Arsenal, Wembley, Charity Shield
2	21.08.1979	14	D	0-0	Bolton Wanderers, Anfield, 1st Division
3	25.08.1979	9	W	3-1	West Bromwich Albion, Anfield, 1st Division
4	29.08.1979		D	0-0	Tranmere Rovers, Prenton Park, League Cup 2nd round 1L
5	01.09.1979	16	L	2-3	Southampton, The Dell, 1st Division
6	04.09.1979		W	4-0	Tranmere Rovers, Anfield, League Cup 2nd round 2L
7	08.09.1979	8	W	4-0	Coventry City, Anfield, 1st Division
8	15.09.1979	8	D	1-1	Leeds United, Elland Road, 1st Division

9	19.09.1979		W	2-1	Dinamo Tbilisi, Anfield, European Cup 1st R 1st L
10	22.09.1979	7	D	0-0	Norwich City, Anfield, 1st Division
11	25.09.1979		W	3-1	Chesterfield, Anfield, League Cup 3rd round
12	29.09.1979	9	L	0-1	Nottingham Forest, City Ground, 1st Division
13	03.10.1979		L	0-3	Dinamo Tbilisi, Dinamo Stadium, European Cup 1st R 2nd L
14	06.10.1979	8	W	4-0	Bristol City, Anfield, 1st Division
15	09.10.1979	7	D	1-1	Bolton Wanderers, Burnden Park, 1st Division
16	13.10.1979	6	W	2-1	Ipswich Town, Portman Road, 1st Division
17	20.10.1979	5	D	2-2	Everton, Anfield, 1st Division
18	27.10.1979	3	W	4-0	Manchester City, Maine Road, 1st Division
19	30.10.1979		W	2-0	Exeter City, Anfield, League Cup 4th round
20	03.11.1979	3	W	3-0	Wolves, Anfield, 1st Division
21	10.11.1979	2	W	4-1	Brighton & H A, Goldstone Ground, 1st Division
22	17.11.1979	1	W	2-1	Tottenham Hotspur, Anfield, 1st Division
23	24.11.1979	2	D	0-0	Arsenal, Highbury, 1st Division
24	01.12.1979	2	W	4-0	Middlesbrough, Anfield, 1st Division
25	05.12.1979		W	3-1	Norwich City, Carrow Road, League Cup 5th round
26	08.12.1979	1	W	3-1	Aston Villa, Villa Park, 1st Division
27	15.12.1979	1	W	3-0	Crystal Palace, Anfield, 1st Division
28	22.12.1979	1	W	3-1	Derby County, Baseball Ground, 1st Division
29	26.12.1979	1	W	2-0	Manchester United, Anfield, 1st Division
30	29.12.1979	1	W	2-0	West Bromwich Albion, The Hawthorns, 1st Division
31	05.01.1980		W	5-0	Grimsby Town, Anfield, FA Cup 3rd round
32	12.01.1980	1	D	1-1	Southampton, Anfield, 1st Division
33	19.01.1980	1	L	0-1	Coventry City, Highfield Road, 1st Division
34	22.01.1980		L	0-1	Nottingham Forest, City Ground, League Cup Semi-final 1L
35	26.01.1980		W	2-0	Nottingham Forest, City Ground, FA Cup 4th round
36	09.02.1980	1	W	5-3	Norwich City, Carrow Road, 1st Division
37	12.02.1980		D	1-1	Nottingham Forest, Anfield, League Cup Semi-final 2L
38	16.02.1980		W	2-0	Bury, Anfield, FA Cup 5th round
39	19.02.1980	1	W	2-0	Nottingham Forest, Anfield, 1st Division
40	23.02.1980	1	D	1-1	Ipswich Town, Anfield, 1st Division
41	26.02.1980	1	L	0-1	Wolves, Molineux, 1st Division
42	01.03.1980	1	W	2-1	Everton, Goodison Park, 1st Division
43	08.03.1980		W	1-0	Tottenham Hotspur, White Hart Lane, FA Cup 6th round

44	11.03.1980	1	W	2-0	Manchester City, Anfield, 1st Division
45	15.03.1980	1	W	3-1	Bristol City, Ashton Gate, 1st Division
46	19.03.1980	1	W	3-0	Leeds United, Anfield, 1st Division
47	22.03.1980	1	W	1-0	Brighton & H A, Anfield, 1st Division
48	29.03.1980	1	L	0-2	Tottenham Hotspur, White Hart Lane, 1st Division
49	01.04.1980	1	W	1-0	Stoke City, Anfield, 1st Division
50	05.04.1980	1	L	1-2	Manchester United, Old Trafford, 1st Division
51	08.04.1980	1	W	3-0	Derby County, Anfield, 1st Division
52	12.04.1980		D	0-0	Arsenal, Hillsborough, FA Cup Semi-final
53	16.04.1980		D	1-1	Arsenal, Villa Park, FA Cup Semi-final replay
54	19.04.1980	1	D	1-1	Arsenal, Anfield, 1st Division
55	23.04.1980	1	W	2-0	Stoke City, Victoria Ground, 1st Division
56	26.04.1980	1	D	0-0	Crystal Palace, Selhurst Park, 1st Division
57	28.04.1980		D	1-1	Arsenal, Villa Park, FA Cup Semi-final 2R
58	01.05.1980		L	0-1	Arsenal, Highfield Road, FA Cup Semi-final 3R
59	03.05.1980	1	W	4-1	Aston Villa, Anfield, 1st Division
60	06.05.1980	1	L	0-1	Middlesbrough, Ayresome Park, 1st Division

Friendlies

1	01.08.1979		W	4-2	Borussia Moenchengladbach, Bökelberg, Friendly
2	03.08.1979		D	2-2	Feyenoord, Parkstadion, Friendly
3	05.08.1979		D	1-1	Benfica, Parkstadion, Friendly
4	07.08.1979		W	5-2	FBU Select, Odense Idraetspark, Friendly
5	18.08.1979		W	2-0	League Of Ireland, Dalymount Park, Friendly
6	06.11.1979		L	1-3	Lille, Stade Grimonprez Jooris, Friendly
7	14.05.1980		L	6-8	Anderlecht, Anfield, Testimonial*
8	26.05.1980		W	2-1	Bahrain XI, Unknown, Friendly
9	29.05.1980		W	8-0	Al Nasr, Al Wasl, Friendly

*Testimonial for Ray Clemence.

Appearances for the 1979/1980 season

Name	League	FA Cup	LC	UEFA	CS	Total
Kenny Dalglish	42	8	7	2	1	60
Phil Neal	42	8	7	2	1	60
Phil Thompson	42	8	7	2	1	60
Graeme Souness	41	8	7	2	1	59
Ray Clemence	41	8	7	2	1	59
Ray Kennedy	40	8	6	1	1	56
David Johnson	37	8	6	2	1	54
Terry McDermott	37	6	7	2	1	53
Alan Hansen	38	8	5	1	1	53
Jimmy Case	37	5	7	2	1	52
Alan Kennedy	37	5	7	1	1	51
David Fairclough	14	5	5	2	0	26
Colin Irwin	8	2	2	2	0	14
Steve Heighway	9	0	1	1	0	11
Sammy Lee	7	4	0	0	0	11
Avi Cohen	4	1	0	0	0	5
Steve Ogrizovic	1	0	0	0	0	1
Brian Kettle	0	0	0	0	0	0
Howard Gayle	0	0	0	0	0	0
Frank McGarvey	0	0	0	0	0	0

Goalscorers for the 1979/1980 season

Name	League	FA Cup	LC	UEFA	CS	Total
David Johnson	21	3	2	1	0	27
Kenny Dalglish	16	2	4	0	1	23
Terry McDermott	11	2	1	0	2	16
David Fairclough	5	3	5	0	0	13
Ray Kennedy	9	0	0	0	0	9
Own goals	6	0	0	0	0	6
Jimmy Case	3	1	0	1	0	5
Alan Hansen	4	0	0	0	0	4
Colin Irwin	2	0	0	0	0	2
Graeme Souness	1	1	0	0	0	2
Phil Thompson	0	0	1	0	0	1
Phil Neal	1	0	0	0	0	1
Avi Cohen	1	0	0	0	0	1
Alan Kennedy	1	0	0	0	0	1

The squad during the 1979/1980 season

Ray Clemence, Goalkeeper
Steve Ogrizovic, Goalkeeper
Avi Cohen, Defender
Colin Irwin, Defender
Alan Kennedy, Defender
Phil Thompson, Defender
Phil Neal, Defender
Brian Kettle, Defender
Alan Hansen, Defender
Steve Heighway, Midfielder
Sammy Lee, Midfielder
Terry McDermott, Midfielder
Ray Kennedy, Midfielder
Kevin Sheedy, Midfielder
Graeme Souness, Midfielder
Jimmy Case, Midfielder
Howard Gayle, Striker
David Johnson, Striker
David Fairclough, Striker
Kenny Dalglish, Striker
Frank McGarvey, Striker

Transfers for the 1979/1980 season

In:
Avi Cohen, Maccabi Tel Aviv, £200,000, 18 July 1979
Ronnie Whelan, Home Farm, £35,000, 19 September 1979
Richard Money, Fulham, £50,000, May 1980
Ian Rush, Chester, £300,000, 1 May 1980

Out:
Emlyn Hughes, Wolves, £90,000, 2 August 1979
Frank McGarvey, Celtic, £275,000, 11 March 1980
Brian Kettle, Wigan Athletic, £35,000, August 1980

A collection of statistics for the 1979/1980 season

The season in numbers:
Total games: 60
Games won: 35
Games drawn: 15
Games lost: 10
Clean sheets – League: 19
Clean sheets – Overall: 27
Total goals: 111
Average attendance at home – League: 44,578
Average attendance at home – Overall: 42,233
Average goals per game – League: 2.19
Average goals per game – Overall: 2.32
Average goal minute – League: 48
Average goal minute – Overall: 50

Goals split down to competitions:
League – 81
League Cup – 13
FA Cup – 12
Charity Shield – 3
European Cup – 2

Player debuts:
Colin Irwin against WBA on 25.08.1979
Avi Cohen against Leeds United on 15.09.1979

Statistics and information provided by LFChistory.net

13 : STATE OF TRANSITION

1981/82

ANY OTHER CLUB BUT LIVERPOOL WOULD STILL
have been celebrating their previous successes at the start of
the 1981/82 season.

Bob Paisley's men had not only won their first League Cup by
defeating West Ham in a dramatic replay, they had also carried off
the greatest prize of all, the European Cup, for the third time.

Full-back Alan Kennedy's lone goal had given them victory
over Real Madrid in Paris, hence the fact that few fans bothered
to remember that Liverpool had finished fifth in the league, their
lowest position in 10 seasons.

At management level, there was much greater realism. Paisley
knew that several of his stars had passed their peak and was well
aware of the need for rapid reinforcement.

During the previous spring he had made two signings which were
to prove of great significance buying the effervescent Kevin Keegan
look-alike Craig Johnston from Middlesbrough for £650,000 and
then acquiring animated goalkeeper Bruce Grobbelaar from the
Canadian club Vancouver Whitecaps on the recommendation of
their manager, former England keeper and Liverpool coach, Tony

Waiters. Paisley recalls: "I will never forget going to see Bruce Grobbelaar play for the first time. I had an idea that he would become the next Liverpool goalkeeper even before the match had kicked off. He was playing in the Fourth Division for Crewe Alexandra at Doncaster in April 1980. Before the game, he had three of his teammates lined up on the edge of the penalty area firing in shots at him. Bruce was dancing about like a cartoon character stopping every attempt. I turned to Tom Saunders, who was sitting next to me, and said, 'We can go, 'I've seen enough'."

Paisley and Saunders were in for a slight shock when they approached the Railwaymen showing their interest in who they thought was a Crewe player. Grobbelaar explained to *LFChistory.net*: "A couple of weeks after they watched me briefly at Doncaster, they came to Crewe... 'You know the goalkeeper who played...' They said, 'Oh yeah, but he was never our player, we had him on loan from Vancouver and he's gone back now'. They looked on the map: 'Oh shit, we have to fly all the way there?' Bob didn't like flying and wasn't too pleased that he had to come all the way over to Vancouver. However, he did, just to ask me one question and wanted to hear my answer in person. 'Would you like to play for...' 'Yes, I'd love to play for Liverpool, Mr. Paisley!' And that was that, he went back to the airport and that very same day caught the 23.30 flight back to Heathrow. If he would have stayed any longer, he would have had to stay overnight and he wouldn't have liked that."

Paisley had hoped to introduce his new recruits into the first team gradually, in Liverpool's time-honoured style, but events defeated him. Shortly before the big kick-off, England goalkeeper Ray Clemence suddenly announced that he wished to embrace a new challenge and after all attempts failed to change his mind, he left to start a new career with Tottenham.

Clemence spoke to *LFChistory.net* regarding his departure from Merseyside: "My last game for Liverpool was the European Cup final in Paris. We won it 1-0 and you don't get a more spectacular game than that. It was my third European Cup final. I came off the field afterwards and went into the dressing room. There was champagne everywhere and TV cameras. All of the sorts of things you expect when you've won the European Cup final. I sat in the corner of the dressing room and just sat there in silence. It was just another day at the office for me. It was that exact moment when I made the decision to leave. I said to myself, that in order to perform at the level I had always pushed myself to, I just needed a new challenge.

"I had won everything there was to win at Liverpool. I was 32 years of age and for me to play longer at the level I wanted to play, it needed to be at a new club. I didn't go obviously to speak to Bob Paisley straight after the cup final. I went in a couple of weeks later and said this is what I want to do. Bob and Peter Robinson, said: 'Well, are you sure it's nothing else, can we do anything?' I'm sure they would have probably given me a bigger contract if I had pushed for it. But I said 'it's not that, it's just literally I need to change. I loved every minute of being here and I didn't want it to turn sour.' I had seen other great players stay a little bit too long at Liverpool and when they moved on to a smaller club, they had difficulties in motivating themselves. I didn't want anything like that to happen to me. It was important if I was going to move, I had to move at a time when a big club wanted me. It was a difficult decision for me because I loved Liverpool and I had another two years left of my contract. It has certainly nothing to do with the fairy stories people came up with. I was literally in a situation in which I felt I needed a new challenge."

Grobbelaar, a man with remarkably fast reflexes and a taste for adventure rare in a goalkeeper, had never lacked confidence but he was undoubtedly short on experience, and his instant promotion into the senior side caused many a flutter among the fans. "When I signed him, I thought I had a good competitor for Ray, a rival to make him compete and perhaps put a couple of years on his career," Paisley told the *Liverpool Echo*. "Now Ray has left, Bruce is going in at the deep end. I hope he will be judged on what he is and not against what Ray is now. I feel he is as good as Ray was at his age."

Craig Johnston was a different proposition. Quick, hard working and highly unorthodox, he was not the sort of goalscorer needed to partner Kenny Dalglish, but a possible candidate for several positions. "Johnston is an individualist, and it might take a bit of time to run him in," Paisley warned.

At the age of 14, Johnston wrote to various English clubs asking for trials and received some encouragement from Middlesbrough. Weeks later he arrived at Ayresome Park after his parents paid his expenses for the 12,000-mile journey, only for Jack Charlton to tell him he couldn't play. Liverpool had seen him in action at Boro while they were tracking Graeme Souness, and Tom Saunders had listed him as a possible for the future.

At the same time Johnston became available, Paisley wanted to strengthen his squad and a deal was agreed. Ronnie Moran held the Australian in high regard. "Craig was certainly different," Moran later told the *Anfield Review*. "But he gave his all and deserved all the prizes. Craig faced his Anfield challenge with courage after leaving the North East, although he wasn't always an automatic choice because of the wealth of talent available."

A third newcomer arrived just as the team were setting out on their usual pre-season Continental excursion. Mark Lawrenson, a defender who had started his career with Preston before moving to unfashionable Brighton, had already been capped by the Republic of Ireland and was sought by Arsenal when Liverpool decided he was just the man for them.

The fee of £900,000 was a Liverpool record and there were many who wondered where he would play, with internationals Alan Hansen and Phil Thompson also available, but as Paisley said: "Mark has all the hallmarks of a Liverpool player. He wants to win, has quite a bit of style and can play in several positions."

Lawrenson recalls the night he signed for Liverpool: "I was nervous as a kitten. I had on my best suit, shirt and tie, my best bib and tucker. I went down to reception at the Atlantic Tower hotel in Liverpool and the doorman spotted me and said, 'Mr Paisley is waiting for you in his car outside'. When I got in the car, I saw that Bob was wearing his slippers and an old-looking cardigan. I couldn't believe it! That was my first meeting with Bob Paisley and I knew I'd come to the right place. They'd just won the European Cup and there was this fellow, who everyone in football thought was an absolute god, driving me to Anfield in his slippers and cardigan! I thought, 'You'll do for me!' By the time we went through the contract formalities, it was around midnight on a perfect summer's night and I decided to go on to the pitch just to soak up the surroundings. It was incredible, every player's dream come true. That exact moment changed my career, a turning point in my life and one that I will never forget."

Lawrenson's arrival from Brighton was followed almost immediately by the departure of hard-tackling, hard-shooting local boy Jimmy Case in the opposite direction, as Paisley had now introduced Sammy Lee on the right side of midfield.

Lee was less effective as an attacking player than Case had been, but his virtues of solid hard graft and remarkable consistency were to prove invaluable assets to a team in a state of transition. Despite Grobbelaar's inexperience, there seemed little wrong with the

defence, but queries remained over the attack, which were intensi-
fied once the team got down to serious business. And despite the
passing ability of Graeme Souness, a player capable of finding his
man from 40 yards distance or more, there were obvious queries
over midfield. That moustachioed buccaneer Terry McDermott was
running as hard as ever but was starting to drift out of the game
from time to time, while Ray Kennedy, whose trusty left foot had
dominated Liverpool's opponents for several years, had clearly lost
a yard of pace.

Ahead of the 1981/82 campaign, a change had also been made in
the points system. In an effort to encourage more positive play, the
Football League had increased the points for a victory from two to
three, so making the scoring of goals even more important.

Liverpool's opening league match was at Molineux against Wolves
on August 29 and manager Paisley gave an early indication of just
how ruthless he was prepared to be by omitting Alan Kennedy, the
hero of Paris, in favour of Lawrenson. Kennedy admitted later that
he was completely stunned as he had not even thought of Lawrenson as a contender for his position, but the shock was to prove beneficial in the long run, for both player and club.

Souness, who had missed most of the pre-season preparations
through injury, was able to resume alongside McDermott, David
Johnson continued at centre forward and Craig Johnston was made
substitute, but came on in the second half to deputise for his new
club. Grobbelaar also played his first game and subsequently went
on to make 317 consecutive appearances for Liverpool.

The season could hardly have got off to a worse start. A single
goal by Mike Matthews cost them a 1-0 defeat, which inspired the
Liverpool Echo headline: 'REDS LACK THE KILLER TOUCH'
and a comment that the team had been guilty of missing numerous

chances in a game they dominated territorially for long periods. The next match brought little improvement, a penalty from Phil Neal being needed to cancel out an early score from David Shearer in an uninspired draw with Middlesbrough.

A 2-0 victory over Arsenal at Anfield was mildly encouraging but the following week the Reds were defeated at Portman Road and slumped to 16th in the league. Liverpool had only managed to take four points from their first four games and Paisley was fed up. He told the press: "They have got to be professional not playboys or fly-by-nights. I am talking about the attitude. The players seem to be saying sorry and think it's over and done with. They will have to change their attitude."

Although Paisley was considered a man of few words and would never be seen walking through Anfield shouting the odds, his players would immediately know when their boss wasn't happy. Graeme Souness recalls: "He may have been regarded as a fatherly figure by the supporters but, let me tell you, he ruled at Anfield with a rod of iron. You could tell when he was about by the changed atmosphere in the dressing rooms and training ground. He was a commanding man and there were few who dared mess around with him. If we looked as though we were becoming a little complacent or if we were not performing up to the standard Bob would say, 'If you have all had enough of winning, come and see me and I will sell the lot of you and buy 11 new players'. I also soon learnt that praise from Bob Paisley was rather like a snowstorm in the Sahara. It took a while before he trusted you, he had great respect in the dressing room. But it would be wrong to give the impression that we all walked around in fear and trepidation. His knowledge was fantastic and his judgement of players was exceptional and when he was talking about football you were hearing the right things from the right man. At times, maybe outsiders who met him for the first time found that he didn't communicate easily with strangers and I think that people found that a bit strange, as obviously a big part of management is communication. The players would take the mick sometimes, like they did out of everyone, as he had his own particular sayings with some North East terminology that some of the other lads didn't understand."

Phil Neal recalls a classic example of one of Paisley's Geordie sayings being the cause of a dressing room joke: "Terry McDermott once got us hysterical in the dressing room, laughing at Bob Paisley's expense. The boss had a habit of saying the word 'doings' all the time. He'd refer to opposition players as 'doings' instead of naming them, mainly because he couldn't remember their names. So, one time, Bob came into the dressing room and started a talk. Terry stood behind him with a big grin on his face and every time Bob said 'doings' he held a finger up. By the time he got to six, Terry was starting to titter and we were all trying not to laugh. Ray Kennedy was kicking me and when he got to 10, Ray just turned and legged it into the toilet, he was in absolute fits. We were like a bunch of school kids."

Paisley explained to the *Anfield Review* the approach he tried to take on at Liverpool, regarding discipline: "My biggest job is to stop anybody getting out of line at any level, manager, director, player, coach. It only needs one person to get a bit carried away with our success and the whole lot could be blown sky high. You look at clubs where there has been trouble and it is usually the result of somebody having too much of an ego, feeling too important for the club. I know groundsmen who run some clubs. At others it is the chairman, manager, secretary or someone else. It would be so easy for me to start shouting my mouth off. I've had enough success but that would be fatal. And that's why I try to keep a low profile. It's not easy to get a family atmosphere but that is what we have at Anfield and what we must keep."

The famous Boot Room was an informal place where Bob and the coaching staff discussed matches past and present, players, tactics and anything to do with the club really. The Boot Room was a place where all men were equal and everybody's input was appreciated, whether the discussion revolved around the senior team, the reserves or the youth teams. Shankly was never part of the Boot Room boys as he had his own office. He stayed well away from the Boot Room after games, he finished off his press duties and hurried home to his wife and kids, leaving his coaching staff to their own devices.

Paisley, who had been a part of the original Boot Room, would no longer hang up his coat there after he took over as boss, but was in there far more frequently than Shankly had ever been during his reign. Paisley felt more at home in the Boot Room than he did in his carpeted office. On match days, visiting trainers were invited inside for a drink. When they have yelled their lungs out for 90 minutes, some-times at each other in the heat of battle, they shook hands and opened a bottle. Apart from Brian Clough and his assistant Peter Taylor, who were always a bit sceptical about going in, opposition managers and staff would look forward to their invite into the Boot Room. Not only would they go over the game with the Boot Room boys but would also be interested in how things were done at Liverpool. You could enter by invitation only. Any other approach was frowned on, no matter who it was. Mark Lawrenson tells the story of knocking on the Boot Room door one day, putting his head inside and being greeted by the words "what do you want? You're a first teamer ....you're one of the big 'eds. Go away!"

"Myself, Joe and Roy would always be in there, even during the week after training," Ronnie Moran explained in the *Anfield Review*. "You'd have your lunch and do a bit of work, sorting the kits or whatever. Then we'd sit down and have a natter. The club is a big happy family. Don't ask me the secret. I don't know what it is. We all have our say, but there's no bickering. There's so much enjoyment in the job that I don't feel I've been here all that time. The players make it easy for us. One or two float in the clouds, but we knock them on the head. At training sessions, we say, 'Big head from Saturday over here'. They always know who we are referring to and would walk over with a smile on their face. It's the same with the training staff. Joe Fagan and me have a weekly joke. If we win, we say, 'OK for another week'. If we lose it's, 'We could be out of a job now'. There's no way you can afford to sit back. There's no magic about Liverpool. When it boils down to it, you've got to have the players – and the results."

Even though Liverpool had the players, during the first few months of the 1981/82 season they weren't getting the results. Liverpool's first eight games brought only eight points out of a possible 24, with four of their eight goals coming from penalties. That eighth match, on October 3, was a 2-2 draw with Swansea City but Liverpool's sluggish form in that encounter was entirely overshadowed by a far more important, and tragic, event.

Swansea City were managed by Anfield old boy John Toshack, who had looked forward to the visit as one of the highlights of his career.

Instead, he found himself sharing in the widespread mourning of an Anfield icon.

For the great Bill Shankly was dead.

Shankly had died in Broadgreen Hospital on September 29, to the stunned disbelief of his adopted city.

Toshack had owed much of his success, both as player and manager, to Shankly's influence and as a special mark of respect, joined his players on the pitch during the minute's silence, wearing a Liverpool shirt with his old number 10 on it.

After the final whistle Toshack waited until the last man had left the field, and then, with tears streaming down his face, walked alone across the pitch, received Shankly's ashes and carried on until he reached the Kop.

Bill Shankly seemed indestructible; however, he was unable to recover from a heart attack he suffered from in his West Derby home and passed away shortly after in hospital with his wife Nessie at his side. Ian St John expressed the feelings of all the players, past and present, when he addressed the assembled congregation at his funeral held at St. Mary's Church, West Derby. St John said: "The legend will live on but I wish the man had been around a bit longer. We were honoured as players to have a man like Bill Shankly to take us to his club and mould us from boys into men. He gave us all the attributes you need in life – play the game hard, play it fair, think of your fellow players and people around you, and always try to be honest in whatever you do. Words can't express what we feel that Bill is not still with us. For those still in the game their loss is even greater. I would like to thank Mrs. Shankly for allowing the Boss to spend the time he devoted to the game. We know how much he loved his home life, he got terribly homesick after a day away with the team."

Bill Shankly's legacy can be seen at Anfield today, but not just in the gates that bear his name or the statue at the back of the Kop. Shankly was the catalyst that Liverpool Football Club needed. Other men carried on the job that he started but he was the father of the modern-day Liverpool and did as much as anyone and more than most to turn them into one of the great powers of first English and then European football.

The debt the club owes him can never be repaid.

The Swansea match featured two young Irishmen, rivals for the position in left midfield filled so brilliantly in the past by Ray Kennedy. Ronnie Whelan came in from the start while the substitute was Kevin Sheedy, who was transferred across the park to Everton the following May after making only five first-team appearances for the Reds.

Whelan made a good impression and kept his place in mid-week for the League Cup tie with Exeter City at Anfield. David Johnson was suffering from a cut over his eye so manager Paisley suddenly promoted a young man who was to become one of Anfield's favourite sons – Ian Rush, a lean, coltish youngster with a rare eye for goals.

Rush had joined Liverpool in May 1980 but had been confined mainly to the reserves with the exception of nine first-team outings, including playing in the replayed final of the League Cup at Villa Park in April 1981. Rush also had trouble adapting socially to his new surroundings. He was shy and didn't like how Dalglish and the senior players used to wind him and the other new recruits up. Not happy with the game time he was given, Rush knocked on Paisley's door and declared he wanted more chances with the first team or else he would leave. Paisley said he would make him available for transfer and Rush left his office determined to show him he could score an abundance of goals with the reserves that would alert other clubs. Rush scored five goals in his first four reserve games of the season. Paisley's trick had worked as he never intended to sell him. However, Paisley did tell Rush to become more selfish and start shooting more often.

How he took that excellent advice is now football history.

At the end of September, Rush broke his duck at Anfield against Oulu Palloseura from Finland in the European Cup after coming on as a second-half substitute for David Johnson. On October 7, two more goals from Rush against Exeter and one from Whelan helped Liverpool win a relatively unimportant match 5-0 and inspired the *Liverpool Echo* headline: 'YOUNG REDS HEAD FOR THE HEIGHTS'.

Impressed, Paisley kept Rush in the side for the home league game with Leeds on October 10 but relegated Whelan to substitute on Ray Kennedy's return. A solid 3-0 victory, featuring two more goals from Rush, his first league goals, caused the *Liverpool Echo*'s Ken Rogers to comment: "Rush has the vital gift of doing the unexpected, and his first goal certainly took Lukic by surprise! He squeezed the ball just inside an upright, instead of blasting a shot as the goalkeeper expected." Precision rather than sheer power was already proving to be the Welshman's trademark.

Rush took a knock in the next match, a frustrating 3-3 draw at Brighton after the Reds had been two goals in front, and missed the 2-1 defeat by Manchester United caused by Arthur Albiston's last-minute winner, but thereafter became an automatic selection. Whelan, too, was now established in place of the slowing Kennedy, but the player winning most of the plaudits was Sammy Lee, showing immense strength and consistency down the opposite flank. Lawrenson, a tower of strength whether at left-back, in central defence or even in midfield, had also become a regular and despite a few scares due to his impetuosity and enthusiasm for trying to catch every cross wherever it went, Grobbelaar was doing the club proud in goal.

Bob Paisley bought 19-year-old Scottish Under-21 full-back, Steve Nicol on October 26, 1981, as an eventual replacement for right-back Phil Neal. He was another promising young player following Liverpool traditions in signing young talent from north of the border, where he had been playing for Ayr United as a part-time player and an out-of-work building labourer. Various clubs were queuing up to sign Nicol but Liverpool jumped to the front with a £300,000 offer.

Nicol told the press shortly after arriving on Merseyside: "If I'd been given the choice of club to join, I would have picked Liverpool. They are the best side in the country, the side that any young player wants to go to. I didn't say to Ayr that Liverpool was the only place I'd go to, but when the boss there, Willie McLean, told me Liverpool were in then it was just perfect for me. I'd play anywhere the club wants me to, but either of the full-back positions is where I prefer. I don't really care; I'm looking forward to going full-time and I hope that I can do well enough to get a chance in the first team soon."

During this period Kenny Dalglish, subtle, skilful and surprisingly unobtrusive, had been soldiering on bravely, without scoring many goals. For much of the time, he was playing a lot deeper, but with the emergence of Rush, his attacking brilliance began to shine again. After the 3-1 victory over Everton on November 7, in which he scored twice with Rush getting the third, the *Liverpool Echo* said: "Dalglish has become a victim of his own high standards. People expect perfection from him and are sometimes disappointed."

Results were still very much in and out with nobody at Anfield seriously thinking in terms of First Division title number 13. On December 5, a victory at Nottingham Forest, Liverpool's third away league win of the season, restored some confidence within the ranks.

At the City Ground, Mark Lawrenson scored the first of his 11 league goals for Liverpool and two minutes later Ray Kennedy scored the last of his 51 league goals for Liverpool. *The Guardian* reported: "With a victory stolen in their old piratical style Liverpool hoisted a warning to the clubs milling around at the top of the First Division that they are very much back in contention. They gave Forest almost a free hand in the first half at the City Ground, but two headed goals of remarkable similarity – appropriately by men from the back – put Clough's Forest in their place."

Three days later Liverpool's 3-0 victory over Arsenal in the League Cup was followed by a decisive 3-0 defeat at the feet of Brazilian stars Flamengo in the World Club Cup final in Tokyo, a match which Liverpool later admitted they had not taken seriously.

The European Cup remained the club's first objective and an easy 7-0 second-leg win over Oulu Palloseura, followed by a much tougher one over the classy Dutchmen of AZ Alkmaar, kept them well on target.

On December 22, Ronnie Whelan, accompanied by Bob Paisley, was presented with the Young Player of the Month award by former England manager Joe Mercer. A jubilant Whelan told the *Liverpool Echo*: "I know I haven't managed to win a regular place in the first team at Anfield but I never expected to do that so soon. The fact that I've played a few times is a major bonus – and I can hardly believe I've also been picked to play for Ireland. To be honest, I feel I haven't done badly to date, but I can play better. And I hope to show that I can as I go along. The one person I admire most of all is Graeme Souness. If I could be half as good as him, I'd be happy, because the way he knocks the ball around is just great."

Whelan maintained his place in Paisley's starting XI when Manchester City visited Anfield on Boxing Day and although he scored his first Liverpool league goal of the season, he could not help prevent the Reds losing 3-1, their third home defeat of the season.

After the game, goalkeeper Bruce Grobbelaar, whose mistakes led to two of City's goals, was worried about his Liverpool future. Grobbelaar later told the *Anfield Review*: "Following the defeat against City, I thought I was going to lose my place and realised if I was left out of the next game, it may signal the end of my career. Liverpool would have wasted no time signing a new goalkeeper. Although my teammates were 'stand-offish', Bob Paisley stood by me. He picked me for the next game and he announced at the selection meeting that the moves which led to City's goals could have been broken up before they got to me. But he did give me a ticking off once about my antics. He suggested I cut out standing on my hands during a game and pick a more suitable moment – such as during the pre-match kickabout."

On December 31 it was announced that Liverpool chairman Mr. John Smith was to be awarded the CBE (Commander of the British Empire) for his service to sport. Smith, a lifelong Liverpool supporter whose father was also a very keen Red, was taken to Anfield for his first game during the 1923/24 season when he was just four.

Besides being the chairman of England's most successful football club since 1973, Smith was a member of the Sports Council and the Football Grounds Improvement Trust and chairman of the Merseyside industrial branch of the Duke of Edinburgh Award Scheme, which was run from Liverpool's training ground at Melwood, in West Derby. He was also asked to look into the problems in British tennis and the John Smith Report on Lawn Tennis, published in 1980, was well received.

Dapper John Smith, along with club secretary Peter Robinson, who joined the club in 1965, were always relentless in their pursuit for trophies. They ran the club in tandem behind the scenes with minimal fuss, providing the manager and the coaching staff with the best players and made sure everything was ticking over financially.

Smith and Robinson's contributions to Liverpool's successes on the pitch should never be overlooked. Mr. Smith told *The Times*: "Peter's responsible for everything off the field and Bob runs the playing side. I look upon myself as co-ordinator, I always know what's going on. Although I may not be at Anfield every day, Peter and I talk to each other every day of our lives. Running a football club comes down to the people inside it. There are far too many individuals in the game who are on ego trips. Football is about players and winning things. While officials at other clubs go trotting off to World Cups, disappear all summer, we are working for Liverpool. I wouldn't need two hands to count the days Bill Shankly and Bob Paisley have missed training in 17 years, whereas other managers are here, there and everywhere doing anything but their own jobs. Keeping our feet on the ground is also important. For example, after we won the European Cup the first time (1977), we finished a tour of the city at 11 at night, and by 9.15 the following morning everyone was in doing their normal job. We're modest, but highly professional. Here at Liverpool we don't like change for the sake of change. We like continuity and if there is one word in our language that depicts Liverpool Football Club, it is 'stability'."

As Liverpool approached 1982, winning another league title was seen by many as a virtually impossible task, as they ended 1981 in 12th place, 10 points behind leaders Manchester City.

Paisley's first decision of 1982 was a bold and controversial one. He decided to take the captaincy from his long serving defender Phil Thompson, the last survivor of the Bill Shankly regime, and transferred it to Graeme Souness, whose highly competitive play in midfield had so much to do with Liverpool's dominance in that area.

Paisley explained his decision to the *Anfield Review* in his programme notes: "It may have come as something of a surprise when I decided to take the captaincy off Phil Thompson. It was a difficult decision to take because Phil had been a first-class captain for the club. My reason for the decision was that I felt Phil had been going through a rough patch playing-wise and I thought the extra responsibility of leading the team was having an effect.

"Phil told me he didn't believe his job as a captain had bothered him but I believe it had. Phil accepted the decision like the true professional he is."

Souness' abrasive brand of leadership seemed to inject a new spirit of urgency. Suddenly the team were flying, hammering Swansea 4-0 away in the FA Cup, and West Ham 3-0 in the league. West Ham manager, John Lyall, gave a glowing assessment to the press after the game: "If Liverpool are a struggling team, I don't know what the rest of the league is doing. I would imagine they have designs on the championship again. They are back to their best and when Liverpool are in that mood, they are the most formidable opponents you could find."

In January, after playing 393 games for Liverpool, Ray Kennedy joined his former teammate John Toshack at Swansea for a fee of £160,000. Paisley paid tribute to Kennedy: "Ray's contribution to Liverpool's achievements was enormous and his consistency remarkable. So much so, in fact, that on the rare occasions he missed a match his absence was felt deeply simply because he was a midfield power house with tremendous vision and knowledge of the game. In my view he was one of Liverpool's greatest players and probably the most underrated."

Rush, who had been relatively subdued over the Christmas period, scored his first hat-trick for the club, in a 4-0 win over Notts County at Meadow Lane, which sent him on his way again.

There were further goals for the young Welshman against Aston Villa, Ipswich, Coventry and Leeds, taking his total to 22 for the season in 29 games and he told the *Anfield Review*: "Even though I feel more confident and much better about my general form, I still concede that I'm still learning and that there's room to improve."

By the end of February, Liverpool's league position had greatly improved as they had moved up to fourth place. Although, they were still eight points behind leaders Southampton, the Reds had played three games fewer than the Saints, Kevin Keegan's new club.

After a more than rickety start the Reds were finally moulding their season and setting themselves up for winning trophies. Despite being knocked out of the FA Cup in the fifth round at Stamford Bridge by John Neal's Chelsea, they had the League Cup final coming up as well as two mouth-watering ties against CSKA Sofia in the European Cup on the horizon.

Just as it seemed Liverpool had recovered from their early woes by winning seven of their previous eight games, on March 6, a blow was struck as the Reds suffered a 1-0 home defeat to Brighton & Hove Albion. It was Jimmy Case's first return to Anfield since signing for the Seagulls the previous August, and he was generously applauded by the Kop. This was Liverpool's fourth home league defeat of the season. The last time they were defeated four times at Anfield in the league was during the 1969/70 season, when the Reds finished fifth.

At the start of the Eighties, Merseyside was in decline, the docks and industries that once thrived had grounded to a halt, sparking doll queues, strikes and riots. In a city with 15 per cent unemployed, Liverpool saw a drastic decline in gate receipts during the 1981/82 season. The attendance at Anfield that Saturday afternoon against Brighton was a mere 28,574 and the average home attendance for the season would end up at 32,241.

It was a decrease of almost 10,000 supporters compared to the 1979/80 season and almost 14,000 less than the 1976/77 campaign, when Anfield's average attendance stood at 46,171. Even the country's most successful football club had no immunity to the traumatic and drastic changes that were seen across the country. John Smith declared to the press: "The current financial climate is eclipsing our fundamental policy of grooming reserves, which meant the first team always had two substitutes lying spare for every position. For 20 years, forty to forty-five thousand fans would come through the turnstiles; the recession has ended that, so Liverpool's playing staff will be cut from 36 to 24."

Football was the last ray of hope for many Liverpudlians with Saturday afternoon being their only outlet and enjoyment of the week. The players knew that too. Phil Neal recalls: "We were always conscious of the fact that many of our fans had fallen on hard times and we wanted to be their shining light throughout their entire year, not just at the start of the season or over Christmas. We as players always tried our absolute utmost on the pitch so that the supporters could be extremely proud of their team."

The month of March, always a busy time at Anfield, brought triumph and tribulation in equal measure. CSKA Sofia were to put Liverpool out of the European Cup. A single goal in the home tie was not sufficient to counter a bad mistake by Grobbelaar in the return, and the dismissal of Mark Lawrenson after a flare up with Tsvetanov Yonchev. The Bulgarians won 2-1 on aggregate. On the credit side, Liverpool claimed the League Cup for a second year in a row by defeating Spurs in a thrilling Wembley final. Whelan, with two goals, and Rush with one, were the heroes, although David Johnson also emerged from the shadows to make a vital contribution. Liverpool's achievement was the more meritorious because Spurs led for most of the match. At the end of normal time, Paisley refused to allow his players to sit or lie on the turf, and their apparent super-fitness seemed to dishearten the Londoners, who were well beaten in extra-time.

Liverpool ended March with an emphatic league victory over Everton, thanks to goals from Whelan, Souness and Johnston, the *Liverpool Echo* remarking: 'REDS SEW IT UP IN SECOND HALF'.

By now it was clear that in youngsters Rush and Whelan, Liverpool had unearthed something special. Rush's startling acceleration, matched by his speed of anticipation, were bringing him goals in game after game while Whelan's all-round sharpness, coupled with his ability to perform the unexpected, led shrewd judges like Joe Mercer to compare him with that great Irishman of the past, Peter Doherty.

On April 2, Notts County visited Anfield for the first time since 1957. A single Kenny Dalglish goal gave the Reds all three points and made them league leaders for the first time that season.

Craig Johnston, who had been forced to watch in frustration for most of the season, did not start his first match until the one against Manchester City on Boxing Day, but was brought in for the home game with Sunderland on March 20, and thereafter kept his place. Probably his most valuable contribution was made in the match at Old Trafford against Manchester United on April 7, when he scored the only goal to guarantee an invaluable victory over what was rapidly becoming Liverpool's bogey team.

Liverpool did not play particularly well by their standards and Johnston was rather fortunate to score with what looked like a mis-kick from close range, but there was no mistaking the merit of Grobbelaar's penalty save from Frank Stapleton, which was undoubtedly the game's turning point.

Later the goalkeeper revealed to the *Liverpool Echo* the secret of his success in guessing which way the striker would shoot: "I was reading a programme in the toilet and it had a picture of Frank scoring in a previous match. I guessed he would shoot the same way this time and I was right!"

During Liverpool's victory over Manchester United, Paisley was forced to replace Graeme Souness with Terry McDermott at half-time as his captain had failed to recover from a back injury which had kept him out of the Reds' last two fixtures. Consequently, Souness went on to miss five more league games and Phil Thompson was re-issued with the skipper's armband.

April brought six more wins in a row, including the 5-0 demolition of Manchester City at Maine Road, Liverpool's biggest league victory away from Anfield since September, 1968 when Bill Shankly's team beat Wolves at Molineux 6-0. *The Guardian* reported: "No one at Maine Road on Saturday would dispute that the championship is Liverpool's. Applying uncluttered minds to the task of beating Manchester City, they gave that club as humbling an experience as it has known since the darkest days of Malcolm Allison."

Remarkably, Paisley's team now had 66 points to second place Ipswich Town's 61, with nine more rounds of fixtures to be played. It was now clear that a new force had risen to the summit of the First Division.

Liverpool started May as they finished April, adding three more points to their tally as they edged closer to obtaining their 13th First Division title. On May 1, their victims were Nottingham Forest, a team who had recently frustrated the Reds through their disciplined approach to games. Liverpool's 2-0 win was their 11th league win in a row, which until recently remained a club record.

Two days later, Liverpool failed to make it 12 successive league victories when they drew 2-2 at White Hart Lane in a rearranged Monday night fixture. The Reds were buoyed though by the fact Graeme Souness returned to action, albeit as a second-half substitute and it was now hoped he had fully recovered from his back injury.

On May 8, Liverpool travelled to St. Andrew's to face Birmingham City and with one pass, Souness kept Liverpool on course for the championship. On a day when the Reds were below their best, matched yard for yard by a Birmingham side now even more desperately in danger of relegation, the difference between the teams was a perfect 49th-minute 40-yard ball from Souness on the right wing to Rush, unmarked beyond the far post. The young Welshman controlled the ball keenly and nearly burst the roof of the net with his ferocious volley as he scored his 29th goal of the season.

At 29, Souness was now at his peak and was regarded by many as the best and the most uncompromising midfield player in England. Liverpool's captain played with mounting authority and had become a true professional, a man willing to take endless trouble to get everything just right. Souness later told the *LFCmatchday* magazine: "I've always been extremely confident about my ability. I think that showed and maybe it upset people, but it didn't bother me. All I was concerned with was winning games. I'd be the first to say I was involved in some ridiculous challenges. But I wasn't the instigator. Yeah, I'd go out and let people know that, you know, that's the way it was going to be. Kenny was the target for all the so-called tough guys and Rushie too. That's the hardest place to play, when you've got your back to goal and defenders are trying to kick you. The outrageous tackles that people would say I was responsible for were, in fact, me responding to something else that had gone on prior with one of my teammates."

After picking up a point against Arsenal at Highbury on May 11, Bob Paisley's team now only needed three points from their two remaining fixtures to bring the championship back to Merseyside. Their next fixture the following Saturday was against Tottenham Hotspur, who had not won at Anfield for 70 years and were wholly concerned with retaining the FA Cup.

At 2pm the Kop was in full voice and the scene was set for another monumental occasion at Anfield. In the event of the league being resolved that afternoon and unknown to the players, the First Division trophy was secretly brought to Anfield. After suffering an early scare from a fantastic Glenn Hoddle strike, Liverpool went on to score three times to beat Spurs 3-1 and confirm Liverpool's 13th First Division title. Bob Paisley had stirred the foundations of his team and after an impressive 20 wins from their last 25 league games, Liverpool won the championship by four points.

Liverpool had now been confirmed First Division champions in front of their own fans for the 10th time. Proud chairman John Smith presented Graeme Souness with the trophy and Liverpool's instrumental captain made his way towards the Kop so the celebrations could really begin.

A delighted Paisley, who watched the game from the director's box, remarked: "Winning this one has been the proudest I have felt, because there was so much to do. We brought in fresh legs, not just because they were necessary, but because they were ready. There was no gamble, yet it was the hardest championship we have won with me as manager."

He was totally correct. Grobbelaar, Lawrenson, Johnston, Rush, Whelan and Lee had all done the club proud winning their first league title medal, linking up with established stars like Kenny Dalglish, Alan Hansen, Phil Neal, Terry McDermott, Graeme Souness, Alan Kennedy, Phil Thompson and David Johnson to produce a truly outstanding team.

Grobbelaar, Neal and Dalglish had played in every league game, and although 15 players had all made a major contribution to winning the title, it was the same 12 who were involved in the all-conquering run-in.

Former skipper Thompson had won his sixth League Championship medal, the only man in the 94-year history of the Football League to achieve such a feat with one club. Ray Kennedy, who joined Swansea City in January, also qualified for a fifth medal, since he had featured in 15 league games for Liverpool before his move to South Wales.

The marksmanship of Rush (17 league goals and 13 others), McDermott (14 league goals and 6 others), Dalglish (13 league goals and 9 others) and Whelan (10 league goals and 4 others) had been invaluable, but the defenders had also played their part. Neal, an England regular, was a constant inspiration at right-back and Lawrenson, while almost as elegant as the artistic Hansen, had added a touch of steel at centre-back.

Ray Clemence returned to Anfield with Spurs for the first time since he swapped Merseyside for North London and was given a warm welcome back by the Kop. After the game Clemence told the *Liverpool Echo* what he thought of his successor's first season in the Liverpool goal: "I think Bruce Grobbelaar has done very, very well. Obviously, it was difficult for him to be thrown straight into the First Division and also to play for the top club in the country. Only having limited experience was another problem for him, but on his side was the fact that he had a tremendous amount of self-confidence. At times, that has been to his disadvantage because he has tried to do more than he needs. That has cost the side a few mistakes but now he has got to grips with the job a keeper needs to do at Liverpool and he is doing that job excellently."

Liverpool had now won an incredible 13 top-flight league titles. A total unrivalled by any other club, the next best was Arsenal with eight. No wonder Bob Paisley was crowned Manager of the Year at the end of it all or that Ronnie Whelan was named Young Footballer of the Year.

Paisley, who had won his fifth First Division title in eight years as manager, summed up his time so far at Liverpool beautifully: "I don't think I could have survived at any other club. I've done it here only because I can go from the top to bottom, and get from people knowledge and comfort. This is probably why I've been able to accept the burden that's apparently on me. I do have responsibilities and that, but certainly I've been able to share them . . . it's not been as lonely a world as what it is at any other club. People really do matter at Liverpool."

1981/82: Facts and Statistics

Final league table

		P	W	D	L	F	A	W	D	L	F	A	PTS
1	Liverpool FC	42	14	3	4	39	14	12	6	3	41	18	87
2	Ipswich Town	42	17	1	3	47	25	9	4	8	28	28	83
3	Manchester United	42	12	6	3	27	9	10	6	5	32	20	78
4	Tottenham	42	12	4	5	41	26	8	7	6	26	22	71
5	Arsenal	42	13	5	3	27	15	7	6	8	21	22	71
6	Swansea City	42	13	3	5	34	16	8	3	10	24	35	69
7	Southampton	42	15	2	4	49	30	4	7	10	23	37	66
8	Everton	42	11	7	3	33	21	6	6	9	23	29	64
9	West Ham United	42	9	10	2	42	29	5	6	10	24	28	58
10	Manchester City	42	9	7	5	32	23	6	6	9	17	27	58
11	Aston Villa	42	9	6	6	28	24	6	6	9	27	29	57
12	Nottingham Forest	42	7	7	7	19	20	8	5	8	23	28	57
13	Brighton & H A	42	8	7	6	30	24	5	6	10	13	28	52
14	Coventry City	42	9	4	8	31	24	4	7	10	25	38	50
15	Notts County	42	8	5	8	32	33	5	3	13	29	36	47
16	Birmingham City	42	8	6	7	29	25	2	8	11	24	36	44
17	WBA	42	6	6	9	24	25	5	5	11	22	32	44
18	Stoke City	42	9	2	10	27	28	3	6	12	17	35	44
19	Sunderland	42	6	5	10	19	26	5	6	10	19	32	44
20	Leeds United	42	6	11	4	23	20	4	1	16	16	41	42
21	Wolves	42	8	5	8	19	20	2	5	14	13	43	40
22	Middlesbrough	42	5	9	7	20	24	3	6	12	14	28	39

Games for the 1981/1982 season

(The number after date is league position after the game)

1	29.08.1981	17	L	0-1	Wolves, Molineux, 1st Division
2	01.09.1981	15	D	1-1	Middlesbrough, Anfield, 1st Division
3	05.09.1981	10	W	2-0	Arsenal, Anfield, 1st Division
4	12.09.1981	16	L	0-2	Ipswich Town, Portman Road, 1st Division
5	16.09.1981		W	1-0	Oulu Palloseura, Raatti Stadium, European Cup 1st R 1st L
6	19.09.1981	17	D	0-0	Aston Villa, Anfield, 1st Division
7	22.09.1981	11	W	2-1	Coventry City, Highfield Road, 1st Division
8	26.09.1981	12	D	1-1	West Ham United, Upton Park, 1st Division
9	30.09.1981		W	7-0	Oulu Palloseura, Anfield, European Cup 1st R 2nd L
10	03.10.1981	13	D	2-2	Swansea City, Anfield, 1st Division
11	07.10.1981		W	5-0	Exeter City, Anfield, League Cup 2nd round 1L

12	10.10.1981	8	W	3-0	Leeds United, Anfield, 1st Division
13	17.10.1981	10	D	3-3	Brighton & H A, Goldstone Ground, 1st Division
14	21.10.1981		D	2-2	AZ 67 Alkmaar, Olympic Stadium, European Cup 2nd R 1st L
15	24.10.1981	12	L	1-2	Manchester United, Anfield, 1st Division
16	28.10.1981		W	6-0	Exeter City, St. James' Park, League Cup 2nd round 2L
17	31.10.1981	9	W	2-0	Sunderland, Roker Park, 1st Division
18	04.11.1981		W	3-2	AZ 67 Alkmaar, Anfield, European Cup 2nd R 2L
19	07.11.1981	7	W	3-1	Everton, Anfield, 1st Division
20	10.11.1981		W	4-1	Middlesbrough, Anfield, League Cup 3rd round
21	21.11.1981	9	D	1-1	West Bromwich Albion, The Hawthorns, 1st Division
22	28.11.1981	10	L	0-1	Southampton, Anfield, 1st Division
23	01.12.1981		D	0-0	Arsenal, Highbury, League Cup 4th round
24	05.12.1981	10	W	2-0	Nottingham Forest, City Ground, 1st Division
25	08.12.1981		W	3-0	Arsenal, Anfield, League Cup 4th round R
26	13.12.1981		L	0-3	Flamengo, National Stadium Tokyo, World Club Championship
27	26.12.1981	12	L	1-3	Manchester City, Anfield, 1st Division
28	02.01.1982		W	4-0	Swansea City, Vetch Field, FA Cup 3rd round
29	05.01.1982	9	W	3-0	West Ham United, Anfield, 1st Division
30	12.01.1982		D	0-0	Barnsley, Anfield, League Cup 5th round
31	16.01.1982	7	W	2-1	Wolves, Anfield, 1st Division
32	19.01.1982		W	3-1	Barnsley, Oakwell, League Cup 5th round R
33	23.01.1982		W	3-0	Sunderland, Roker Park, FA Cup 4th round
34	26.01.1982	5	W	4-0	Notts County, Meadow Lane, 1st Division
35	30.01.1982	5	W	3-0	Aston Villa, Villa Park, 1st Division
36	02.02.1982		W	2-0	Ipswich Town, Portman Road, League Cup Semi-final 1L
37	06.02.1982	3	W	4-0	Ipswich Town, Anfield, 1st Division
38	09.02.1982		D	2-2	Ipswich Town, Anfield, League Cup Semi-final 2L
39	13.02.1982		L	0-2	Chelsea, Stamford Bridge, FA Cup 5th round
40	16.02.1982	7	L	0-2	Swansea City, Vetch Field, 1st Division
41	20.02.1982	6	W	4-0	Coventry City, Anfield, 1st Division
42	27.02.1982	4	W	2-0	Leeds United, Elland Road, 1st Division
43	03.03.1982		W	1-0	CSKA Sofia, Anfield, European Cup 3rd R 1st L
44	06.03.1982	6	L	0-1	Brighton & H A, Anfield, 1st Division
45	09.03.1982	4	W	5-1	Stoke City, Victoria Ground, 1st Division
46	13.03.1982		W	3-1	Tottenham Hotspur, Wembley, League Cup Final
47	17.03.1982		L	0-2	CSKA Sofia, Vassil Levski, European Cup 3rd R 2nd L
48	20.03.1982	4	W	1-0	Sunderland, Anfield, 1st Division

49	27.03.1982	3	W	3-1	Everton, Goodison Park, 1st Division
50	30.03.1982	2	W	3-1	Birmingham City, Anfield, 1st Division
51	02.04.1982	1	W	1-0	Notts County, Anfield, 1st Division
52	07.04.1982	1	W	1-0	Manchester United, Old Trafford, 1st Division
53	10.04.1982	1	W	5-0	Manchester City, Maine Road, 1st Division
54	13.04.1982	1	W	2-0	Stoke City, Anfield, 1st Division
55	17.04.1982	1	W	1-0	West Bromwich Albion, Anfield, 1st Division
56	24.04.1982	1	W	3-2	Southampton, The Dell, 1st Division
57	01.05.1982	1	W	2-0	Nottingham Forest, Anfield, 1st Division
58	03.05.1982	1	D	2-2	Tottenham Hotspur, White Hart Lane, 1st Division
59	08.05.1982	1	W	1-0	Birmingham City, St. Andrew's, 1st Division
60	11.05.1982	1	D	1-1	Arsenal, Highbury, 1st Division
61	15.05.1982	1	W	3-1	Tottenham Hotspur, Anfield, 1st Division
62	18.05.1982	1	D	0-0	Middlesbrough, Ayresome Park, 1st Division

Friendlies

1	04.08.1981		W	2-1	Scunthorpe United, Old Show Ground, Friendly
2	09.08.1981		W	3-0	FC Zürich, Letzigrund Stadium, Friendly
3	11.08.1981		L	1-2	Servette, Charmilles Stadium, Friendly
4	13.08.1981		D	0-0	Neuchatel Xamax, La Maladiere, Friendly
5	19.08.1981		L	1-2	Atletico Madrid, Vicente Calderon, Friendly
6	22.08.1981		W	5-0	Home Farm, Tolka Park, Friendly
7	24.08.1981		W	5-0	Crusaders, Seaview, Friendly
8	13.11.1981		W	1-0	Irish International XI, Tolka Park, Friendly
9	22.12.1981		W	2-0	Rangers, Ibrox Stadium, Friendly
10	19.04.1982		D	1-1	Glentoran, The Oval, Friendly
11	19.05.1982		W	8-7	Bury Select XI, Gigg Lane, Testimonial*

* Testimonial for: Keith Kennedy (Alan Kennedy's brother)

Appearances for the 1981/1982 season

Name	League	FA Cup	LC	EC	WCC*	Total
Bruce Grobbelaar	42	3	10	6	1	62
Kenny Dalglish	42	3	10	6	1	62
Phil Neal	42	3	10	6	1	62
Mark Lawrenson	39	3	10	6	1	59
Graeme Souness	35	3	9	6	1	54
Alan Hansen	35	3	8	5	1	52
Sammy Lee	35	2	6	5	1	49
Ian Rush	32	3	10	4	0	49
Terry McDermott	29	3	10	5	1	48
Phil Thompson	34	1	7	5	1	48
Ronnie Whelan	32	3	8	4	0	47
Alan Kennedy	34	3	6	4	0	47
David Johnson	15	1	5	4	1	26
Craig Johnston	18	1	2	1	1	23
Ray Kennedy	15	0	3	4	1	23
Kevin Sheedy	2	0	2	0	0	4
Steve Nicol	0	0	0	0	0	0
Steve Ogrizovic	0	0	0	0	0	0
Richard Money	0	0	0	0	0	0
Howard Gayle	0	0	0	0	0	0

*World Club Championship

Goalscorers for the 1981/1982 season

Name	League	FA Cup	LC	EC	Total
Ian Rush	17	3	8	2	30
Kenny Dalglish	13	2	5	2	22
Terry McDermott	14	0	3	3	20
Ronnie Whelan	10	0	3	1	14
Craig Johnston	6	0	1	0	7
David Johnson	2	0	3	2	7
Graeme Souness	5	0	1	0	6
Mark Lawrenson	2	1	0	1	4
Sammy Lee	3	0	0	1	4
Phil Neal	2	0	1	0	3
Ray Kennedy	2	0	0	1	3
Alan Kennedy	3	0	0	0	3
Alan Hansen	0	1	0	1	2
Own goals	1	0	1	0	2
Kevin Sheedy	0	0	2	0	2

The squad during the 1981/1982 season

Bruce Grobbelaar, Goalkeeper
Steve Ogrizovic, Goalkeeper
Alan Kennedy, Defender
Mark Lawrenson, Defender
Phil Thompson, Defender
Phil Neal, Defender
Richard Money, Defender
Alan Hansen, Defender
Craig Johnston, Midfielder
Kevin Sheedy, Midfielder
Graeme Souness, Midfielder
Ronnie Whelan, Midfielder
Terry McDermott, Midfielder
Sammy Lee, Midfielder
Ray Kennedy, Midfielder
Steve Nicol, Midfielder
David Fairclough, Striker
Ian Rush, Striker
Kenny Dalglish, Striker
David Johnson, Striker
Howard Gayle, Striker

Transfers for the 1981/1982 season

In:
Mark Lawrenson, Brighton & Hove Albion, £900,000, August 1981
Steve Nicol, Ayr United, £300,000, 22 October 1981

Out:
Colin Irwin, Swansea City, £350,000, August 1981
Ray Clemence, Tottenham Hotspur, £300,000, 15 August 1981
Jimmy Case, Brighton & Hove Albion, £350,000, 19 August 1981
Avi Cohen, Maccabi Tel Aviv, £100,000, November 1981
Ray Kennedy, Swansea City, £160,000, January 1982
Richard Money, Luton Town, £100,000, April 1982
Kevin Sheedy, Everton, £100,000, May 1982
Colin Russell, Huddersfield Town, £25,000, 23 September 1982

A collection of statistics for the 1981/1982 season

The season in numbers:
Total games: 62
Games won: 39
Games drawn: 13
Games lost: 10
Clean sheets – League: 20
Clean sheets – Overall: 31
Total goals: 129
Average attendance at home – League: 35,213
Average attendance at home – Overall: 32,241
Average goals per game – League: 1.86
Average goals per game – Overall: 2.21
Average goal minute – League: 51
Average goal minute – Overall: 54

Goals split down to competitions:
League – 80
League Cup – 28
European Cup – 14
FA Cup – 7
World Club Championship – 0

Player debuts:
Bruce Grobbelaar against Wolves on 29.08.1981
Craig Johnston against Wolves on 29.08.1981
Mark Lawrenson against Wolves on 29.08.1981

Statistics and information provided by LFChistory.net

14 : PAISLEY BOWS OUT

1982/1983

UNKNOWN TO FANS AT THE TIME, BOB PAISLEY chose his native Durham to announce he would be spending just one more season in charge of Liverpool before passing the baton to his successor. He told a football writers' dinner at the Three Tuns Hotel, staged in his honour: "I'll give it another 12 months, which will see me complete 44 years at Liverpool and then I'll hand it over. We've come through a transitional period and once I'm certain that things are running smoothly, it will be time to go."

Throughout the last two or three seasons, something had been haunting Paisley and that had been the memory of how his predecessor had stepped down in somewhat similar circumstances. "I remember Bill going too early, and how he felt afterwards," Paisley recalled. "I begged him to stay on longer but he refused and I wouldn't have wanted to make the same mistake."

Paisley informed his players of his future plans during a pre-season tournament in Marbella in August 1982, and any niggling doubts he had about going too prematurely were firmly put to rest on the same trip. He later told Granada TV: "During a pre-season trip to Spain, I suffered a severe ear infection. I was consequently off balance for a few weeks and at the time it was quite frightening. I thought to myself, if I've been ruthless in the past to get rid of players, then I have to act the same way with myself as well and not go beyond my limits."

Liverpool's players and public found that much had changed when they returned to Anfield for the 1982/83 season. Coloured seats were installed at the Anfield Road end of the ground and three sides of the stadium were now seated, helping to generate an increase in gate revenue as the club were able to charge more for seated tickets.

However, no one would have even contemplated the sacrilege of interfering with one of football's great institutions, the Kop. The company Peter Robinson used to install the seats had presumed they would be fitting the same red seats they had installed into the Paddock area of the Main Stand two years earlier. Paisley had other ideas though and rang them up to ask what other colours they had available. His reason behind this was when he watched the reserves from the Kemlyn Road stand, the red shirts would get lost against the red seats in the Main Stand and the Paddock, so having a different array of colours put in would enable him to see the players better. Paisley chose orange, ochre, lilac, violet red, emerald green and cream, which gave Liverpool the most colourful stand in England.

In addition, the Anfield pitch was fully relaid for the first time since 1920. "The pitch has been virtually unchanged for more than fifty years and has grown old and tired," Arthur Riley, the retired groundsman said.

Riley, born a stone's throw from Anfield, is another gentleman whose work and service to the Liverpool cause should never be forgotten. He followed in his father Herbert's footsteps and joined the Anfield staff straight from school. He soon became a popular figure within the club and witnessed many changes through the years, including the installation of floodlights and undersoil heating. Riley ensured that the overall appearance of the ground was always maintained to the highest standard. Such was his reputation, Wembley officials often turned to him for advice. He took great pride in the fact that Anfield was always considered to be one of the finest playing surfaces in the country and constantly strove to keep it in as immaculate condition as possible until his retirement following the 1981/82 season.

Riley told the *Liverpool Echo* in 1977: "I was fifteen when I joined my dad at Anfield. That was in 1928, the season the Kop opened. In those days the steps were wooden railway sleepers, with ashes in between, but the general size of the place is the same today, although there is a new roof and the terraces are now concrete. There were four of us – my dad, myself, Alan Constantine and Joe Hewitt, an ex-player who eventually ran the reserve team. My dad had very strict rules about the pitch. In the early part of the season, he would only allow us to cut the grass with a hand mower to prevent damage. It took us two days. After a few weeks of the season had gone, we could use the motor mower. The Anfield pitch got much more wear and tear then because the players trained on it as well. The club did not get the training ground at Melwood until about 1950. I worked as my dad's assistant until 1940 when I joined the Army. I served during the war until 1946 and when I came home on leave had to go to Anfield to help Dad – there was regional football every Saturday and the ground had to be kept in good order. He ran the place. When I returned after the war, Dad didn't do a lot on the ground and I eventually was made head groundsman in 1950."

Although Riley got on well with everyone at Anfield. He particularly enjoyed working with Bill Shankly because they both shared the same work ethic, drive and determination needed to make the club a success. Arthur's wife Rose became Nessie Shankly's cleaner and Arthur would cut Shankly's lawn at his home in West Derby. One of Arthur's duties was to scatter the ashes of fans who had passed away, on request of their families. Arthur recalls: "There was this one time, I was laying a man's ashes over by the corner arc at the Kop end and all of a sudden Mr. Shankly came running over shouting, 'Arthur what are you doing, son? Scatter them along the goal-line, with a bit of luck he might jump up and stop the ball from going in the net'."

Despite being able to make improvements to Anfield, it was announced in August 1982 that Liverpool had made a financial loss of £154,758 after a profit of almost £60,000 in 1980/81. Their accounts also revealed that the overall annual cost of running the club hit a new peak of £3,023,839 which represented a breakdown of £60,000 a week to keep Anfield's mighty dynamo ticking over.

Liverpool chairman John Smith revealed in the annual report that plans for a new stand had now been put on hold. He told the *Daily Express*: "Unfortunately, our results on the field of play have not resulted in a corresponding improvement in financial attainments. The consequent loss of revenue, together with the declining prospects for the game as a whole, has convinced the board that it would be neither financially sensible nor justifiable to proceed with the project at the present time."

During the summer of 1982, changes to the playing staff were minimal. David Johnson re-signed for his first club Everton where he stayed for a couple of years before making his way down the league ladder. Paisley's main addition to his squad was striker David Hodgson who was signed from Middlesbrough for £450,000.

Liverpool kicked off the 1982/83 season with every reason to believe they could retain their title, but the fans were becoming increasingly worried about the club's long-term future due to the knowledge that Paisley, the most successful manager in the league's history, was considering retirement. Therefore, before their title defence got underway, he brought the matter right out into the open by declaring his intention to step down the following June.

On Tuesday, August 24, the *Liverpool Echo* ran the headline: 'PAISLEY TO QUIT - IT'S OFFICIAL' followed by Ian Harvgraves' report: "Bob Paisley is definitely to quit as Liverpool's manager. The club ended intense speculation about the future of their manager when chairman Mr. John Smith announced officially that Mr. Paisley would he stepping down at the end of the season.

"Mr. Paisley, who has been at Anfield for forty-three years and has won a record eighteen major trophies as manager during the last eight, disclosed over the weekend that he had been having talks with the club over his future. Mr. Paisley would be invited to help choose his successor and that he would also be asked to stay on in a consultative capacity. Today Mr. Smith said: 'I wish to announce officially that Mr. Paisley no longer desires to be team manager after the end of the coming season. Nevertheless, I am delighted that his association with us will continue in another capacity for years to come. The board has the situation under constant review and we hope this statement will clarify the situation before Bob's successor is named at the end of the season.' The identity of the man who will eventually succeed the most successful manager in the history of league football is bound to become the subject of intense speculation over the next eight months, but Liverpool have now made it clear they will not be saying anything further until a decision has been reached.

"The job is an unusual one, not only because Liverpool are an extraordinary family club, who rarely, if ever, bring in outsiders, but their staff is so strong and well-organised that the manager is kept almost completely clear of financial and administrative matters. leaving him free to concentrate entirely on the team. Whoever gets the job will have a formidable record to live up to, with Messrs Bill Shankly and Bob Paisley having dominated British football for the last 23 years."

For the Charity Shield against Spurs, Liverpool fielded the same team that had roared to the title during the second half of the previous season, with unlucky Craig Johnston relegated to substitute and new signing David Hodgson left to watch the action from the bench. With three international centre-backs in Phil Thompson, Alan Hansen and Mark Lawrenson all available, manager Paisley continued an experiment he had used during the pre-season tour and fielded Hansen as a Continental-style sweeper. The system looked effective enough as Liverpool cruised to a 1-0 victory. Thompson was a spare man at the back and created the winning goal for Ian Rush. However, Paisley's new system had to be abandoned immediately when Hansen then strained a thigh muscle and had to miss the season's first seven league games.

Accordingly, Lawrenson partnered Thompson in an orthodox formation in the opening league game against West Bromwich, with Dalglish dropping into an attacking midfield role and Hodgson coming in for his league debut. Paisley was presented with his fifth Manager of the Year award before the kick-off. Liverpool won easily with a goal from Sammy Lee and a penalty from Phil Neal and the Reds had returned to action with their typical champion's touch.

A drab draw with Birmingham in midweek was followed by a convincing 2-0 success at Highbury, after which manager Paisley greeted the press with the ominous words: "The best is yet to come." With Hansen still missing, Liverpool's defence did not look as solid as might have been expected and this was emphasised when the team conceded six goals in two games at Anfield against Nottingham Forest and Luton. Both provided marvellous entertainment, though the critical Paisley complained that his team's defensive play in both games hadn't been strong enough and growled: "You are allowed to tackle."

In the players' defence, before the season had started the Football Association announced that all referees had been instructed to dismiss players without prior warning for professional fouls. Consequently, while some referees stuck to the letter of the new law, others virtually ignored it, which caused a certain amount of confusion among the players.

The Forest match on September 7 was especially exciting. Liverpool twice led through goals by the lively newcomer Hodgson, only for Forest to equalise on each occasion and then take the lead five minutes before half-time. Although Forest kept their lead for most of the second half, it was Liverpool who had the last word, with a goal eight minutes from time by skipper Graeme Souness and a typical Ian Rush winner, created by Dalglish in the dying seconds, for the Reds to clinch a dramatic 4-3 win.

The Luton game was notable for the fact that the visitors were forced to employ no fewer than three goalkeepers. Jake Findlay, who started in goal for the Hatters, went off injured after pulling a stomach muscle while throwing the ball out to a defender and had to be replaced by full-back Kirk Stephens. Then, later, Mal Donaghy, another defender, replaced Stephens in goal, with Stephens returning to his position as an outfield player. Both replacement goalkeepers wore a Liverpool goalkeeping shirt as Findlay couldn't remove his Luton shirt due to his injury. Despite fielding three different goalkeepers, each of whom conceded a goal, last season's Second Division champions performed well to secure a 3-3 draw.

As well as beating Swansea City and Southampton comfortably in the league, Liverpool also beat Irish part-timers Dundalk 5-1 over two legs in the first round of the European Cup.

In the second leg at Anfield on September 28, Terry McDermott made his 329th and last appearance for Liverpool. At the start of the season, it was clear that McDermott would finally have to look elsewhere for first-team football and he returned to Newcastle United, who were now in the Second Division, for a fee of £100,000. McDermott told the press: "I'm looking forward to going back to Newcastle, although I'll miss Liverpool. Tyneside is one of the few places I would look forward to going back to. The move is not just for the money. If it was, I'd have gone for Bordeaux because they made me an offer that could never be bettered. It will be nice to play with Kevin Keegan again. He and Kenny Dalglish are the two really world class men I've played with. I'll be leaving a team who will obviously continue doing great things and I wish them the very best."

Bob Paisley paid tribute to one of his most trusted servants: "Off the field Terry was one of the biggest jokers we have had and a man who enjoyed a pint or two. But no matter how well he celebrated he was always in at training the following morning and that is all that mattered to Liverpool Football Club."

Kenny Dalglish was also a huge admirer of the departing McDermott: "What a player Terry was, blessed with unbelievable stamina. 'You've got two pairs of lungs,' I said to Terry and I'm sure he did. Terry could run and run and his mind shifted as quickly. As a footballer, Terry was a creature of instinct and intelligence, a killer mix.

"If I even hinted at darting into a particular area, Terry read my mind. The ball was waiting for me, almost smiling at me. Not only could Terry see a great pass, he could deliver it. Vision and execution are qualities found in only the very best of players and Terry had those strengths. Along with his keen eye for goal, what made Terry even more special was his full-on, committed attitude. Surrender was for cowards, not for men like Terry, who'd never give up."

Phil Thompson, who played his own part in bringing his fellow Kirkby native to Anfield back in 1974 had fine memories of McDermott too: "Terry was an unbelievable character. The lads nicknamed him 'Lege' which was short for 'Legend'. He was such a bubbly and funny character and helped to make the dressing room light-hearted and relaxed. He was like that from the day he came. I should say that he had a strange sense of humour. Terry could drink and get home at two in the morning, but he could still get through any fitness regime you could throw at him the next day. That was never a problem for him. He could go in a sauna for 20 minutes without breaking sweat! He actually hated the sauna. I remember he had a chain that he wore round his neck. I can remember him being in the sauna and the chain must have been getting hotter and hotter. He suddenly screamed in pain. It was really funny."

An unbeaten run of seven games ended with defeats at Ipswich and West Ham that coincided, rather surprisingly, with the return of the elegant Hansen. However, the side soon bounced back again with a solid victory over Brighton at Anfield to set the scene for the first big confrontation of the season with Everton.

Played at Goodison on November 6, this proved a nightmare for the Toffees and their manager Howard Kendall, who were totally humiliated in a 5-0 thrashing. Kendall gambled by fielding his new signing Glenn Keeley from Blackburn Rovers alongside newly-appointed skipper Billy Wright in central defence and the two took a terrible roasting from Kenny Dalglish and Ian Rush, who had not previously been in very good form.

A superb interception, run and pass by Hansen enabled Rush to open the scoring and after Liverpool had had another goal disallowed, and missed at least two more great chances, Everton's hopes effectively disappeared when they were reduced to 10 men. Dalglish was put clean through just outside the Everton penalty area, a despairing Keeley held him back by his shirt and under the amended laws, the referee had no option but to dismiss him. Rush, who had not scored in the previous seven games, ended up with four goals, Mark Lawrenson added another one and the Everton camp were left totally shattered.

The last player to score a hat-trick in a Merseyside derby was Liverpool striker Fred Lowe, at Anfield in September, 1935. Lowe also netted four during the Reds' biggest win over Everton to date (6-0).

Ian Rush, who matched Lowe's feat, albeit at the other end of Stanley Park, later shared his memories from that day with the *Liverpool Echo*: "I remember walking off the coach, going into the dressing room and Bob Paisley turned around and said, 'Do you know that no one has scored a hat-trick in the Merseyside derby in nearly 50 years?' I asked myself, 'What is he telling me that for?' He may have just been trying to fire me up but part of me thinks Bob being Bob had spotted something in the way Everton were going to set up that made him believe I could get at them a bit. But I don't think even he could have predicted what followed. I went out and scored four!

"To win a derby 5-0 is an incredible achievement and ever since that day I've had Evertonians tell me that the scoreline would have been different if they hadn't gone down to ten men when Glenn Keeley was sent off. But I've always joked that they are right – we probably would have won by six or seven!

"It was just one of those games when you feel you can score with every attack and I was lucky enough to get the four goals and Mark

Lawrenson got the other. What a lot of people don't remember, though, is Neville Southall was absolutely brilliant that day. He made some unbelievable saves and without him we probably would have scored even more. My favourite goal from that game was the one for my hat-trick. I can remember being put through and thinking, 'This is my big chance' but my shot hit the post, but before I knew it the ball was back at my feet and I scored the rebound. That was my favourite because I knew how important it was and also because it happened in front of the Liverpool fans in the Park End. It was a fantastic moment and something that will live with me for ever.

"After the game I had to get back home to Wales but I was banned from driving at the time so the funny thing was I had to get a lift off Kevin Ratcliffe. As we were walking back to his car none of the Evertonians were giving me stick but they were all giving him loads! We got in the car and there was me, Kevin and the match ball so you can imagine what that journey must have been like for him. I asked him if he'd get the ball signed by the Everton lads for me and I couldn't repeat what he told me to do in a family newspaper. But Kevin, being the kind of fella he is, did get it signed for me and that's a gesture I will always appreciate."

The Everton game was Liverpool's 13th in the league and they were now leaders of the First Division with 25 points, closely followed by Manchester City two points behind. West Ham, Manchester United and Nottingham Forest were also close, just three points adrift.

By early December, Liverpool had established a clear lead and begun what the *Liverpool Echo* described as "a triumphal tour of the country" which was, however, briefly interrupted by an unexpected 1-0 defeat at Norwich. Phil Thompson's legs were beginning to cause him problems that led him to miss a number of games, Craig Johnston was starting to establish himself on a regular basis and David Hodgson appeared reasonably often without scoring enough goals to clinch automatic selection. However, all that hardly mattered as Rush was proving himself the country's sharpest opportunist, even developing a certain skill with his head, and Dalglish was also enjoying a new lease of life.

On December 11, a Rush goal and two Phil Neal penalties brought an exhilarating victory over Graeme Taylor's ambitious Watford, which gave Anfield fans their first sight of John Barnes' power and grace, and that was followed by an even more spectacular performance at Aston Villa, as Hodgson, Dalglish, Rush and full-back Alan Kennedy scored on the way to a 4-2 triumph, widening the gap to five points at the top of the league.

Liverpool's impressive performance at Villa Park was followed by the welcome news that captain Graeme Souness, who had been in irresistible form in midfield, had agreed to sign a new three-year contract. Souness told the *Liverpool Echo*: "If I leave Liverpool there is only one way that I could go and that would be down the ladder. Any player in Europe would say that Liverpool is the best club in the world. I am happy here. My wife is from the city and the kids are settled in school. It couldn't be better."

On December 21, Liverpool embarked on an 8,000-mile round trip to take part in a friendly match in Sudan against a Khartoum XI in front of 40,000 spectators. After making a loss during the recession, such lucrative offers helped balance the books.

Liverpool's worldwide popularity was emphasised by an invitation from the Sudanese president himself, Mr. Gaafar Mohamed Nemeri, who flew the squad out on his private jet. In addition to cashing in on their international reputation and the recent football boom in Africa following the 1982 World Cup in Spain, the Reds did their best to entertain the crowd.

However, it was clearly visible the sweltering heat had affected their ability to put on a show and only when temperatures inside the packed stadium finally started to drop were the Reds able to up their game. Kenny Dalglish scored Liverpool's only goal of the encounter with only a few minutes to go to earn a 1-1 draw.

When Liverpool returned from their African adventure it was back to business domestically. The following week the Reds played two league games in little more than 24 hours of each other. On December 27, Dalglish's third and final hat-trick for the club saw the Reds end the year at Anfield on a suitably high note against Manchester City, beating them 5-2, but the following day they were held at Roker Park against bottom side Sunderland.

Future Liverpool player, the 18-year-old Barry Venison, was the Black Cats' most impressive player that afternoon and his mature and commanding performance didn't allow Kenny Dalglish time or space to create any of his usual threatening final-third attacks.

It was Ian Rush's turn to score a hat-trick when the Reds returned to Anfield on New Year's Day. This time their victims were Notts County as the Reds treated their home supporters to another five-star display. For the second fixture against Notts County in succession, this was all about Rush as the young Welshman had scored a hat-trick at Meadow Lane the previous season.

On the day Rush opened the scoring after 15 minutes, before Justin Fashanu equalised two minutes later for the Magpies. Kenny Dalglish restored Liverpool's lead on the half-hour mark and from then on, the result was in no doubt. Phil Neal missed a penalty but after half-time Dalglish added his second and Liverpool's third then fed Rush with a superb through ball from which he shook off the attention of two defenders and beat the goalkeeper comfortably.

Rush reached his hat-trick, his third of the season, three minutes from time after Hodgson had done the dribbling but tumbled as he shot. Final score: Liverpool 5-1 Notts County. Rush told the press after the game: "I just can't stop scoring! Kenny Dalglish is providing me with such great service by playing so brilliantly."

With half the season played, Liverpool were leading the First Division by eight points from Manchester United and Nottingham Forest and their league success had been supported by almost routine progress in both the European Cup and the Milk Cup.

Clearly, Paisley was doing his best to bow out of management in the best way possible.

Speculation about the identity of his successor was then ended when the *Liverpool Echo* revealed it was to be his loyal assistant, the long-serving Joe Fagan, but no official announcement was to be made by the club for at least three months.

Many names had been mentioned as possible Liverpool managers, including Nottingham Forest's Brian Clough, Aberdeen's Alex Ferguson and Anfield old boys John Toshack and Gordon Milne but in the end the Liverpool board stuck to their policy of continuity, having first made sure that popular 'Uncle Joe', who had been on the Anfield staff since May 1958, was prepared to take over the hot seat at 62, an age when most managers are only too happy to retire.

Chairman John Smith told the *Liverpool Echo*: "At Liverpool we are all members of one large family. Nobody is bigger than the club. Everyone works for Liverpool FC and for each other. Liverpool's thinking contrasts vividly with that of most top clubs, who have invariably suffered badly when an outstanding manager has departed. Those lessons have not been lost on the men who matter at Anfield, and help to explain why the board have been reluctant to bring in an 'outsider' like John Toshack despite his success at Swansea and his past links with the club.

"It would be almost impossible for anyone outside Anfield to come in above the heads of Fagan and Moran, who have forgotten more about successful professional football than most managers and coaches will ever learn. Even Roy Evans will probably take over the reins some day."

On January 3, Liverpool extended their lead to 10 points after seeing off Arsenal 3-1 at Anfield and the 1982/83 season was quickly turning into a one-horse race. Ian Rush was again amongst the scorers, netting his 22nd goal of the season.

Liverpool's domination of the league continued without even the suspicion of a hitch, as they won their next four games. This included Birmingham City's visit to Anfield on January 22. Birmingham's team included former Liverpool player Howard Gayle who made his debut for the Blues that afternoon, just eight days after the young Scouser swapped his native Merseyside for the Midlands.

Toxteth-born Gayle only made five first-team appearances for Liverpool after signing professional forms for his hometown club in 1977. His shining moment in a Liverpool shirt came when he ran Bayern Munich's defenders ragged in the second leg of the European Cup semi-final on April 22, 1981 at the Olympic Stadium.

Kenny Dalglish limped off early on and Gayle impressed for an hour despite being repeatedly fouled. He was then replaced by Jimmy Case for fear of getting himself sent off for retaliation. It was a performance of astonishing maturity in such a big game from the young winger and his reward was to play in three of the final four league matches of the season before the European Cup final.

With key players fit again, Gayle knew he would not make the starting line-up in Paris and had to settle for a place on the bench. Gayle never added to the games he played for Liverpool in the 1980/81 season and spent most of his time in the reserves where he scored 62 goals in 156 games. However, he will always be remembered for being the first black player who played for Liverpool, a really incredible fact considering the club had been in existence for 88 years.

Despite their impeccable league form, at the end of February and the start of March, Liverpool suffered unexpected and painful defeats in both the European and FA Cup competitions. Careless defending and a couple of slips by Bruce Grobbelaar in goal saw Liverpool eliminated from Europe in the third round by Polish side Widzew Lodz. Then came the shock of the season, if not the decade, as the hot favourites were knocked out of the FA Cup by unfancied Brighton.

At the time of the game, Liverpool were well ahead at the top of the First Division while Brighton were at the bottom. The match was televised live and millions of viewers saw Liverpool knocked out of their stride by a side who owed much to the inspiration of their manager, former Liverpool and England inside forward Jimmy Melia.

Brighton won the contest 2-1 with another former Red, Jimmy Case, scoring the winning goal for Brighton after 68 minutes. Four minutes later, the normally reliable Phil Neal missed a penalty to underline that it was not to be Liverpool's day. To make the defeat even worse, Paisley now knew that he would retire without achieving his last ambition he had left in the game, to win the FA Cup – a trophy which had eluded him his entire career since he was left out of the 1950 final during his playing days.

Brighton's matchwinner Case recalled: "As I came off the pitch this TV reporter shoved a bloody great big microphone into my face and said, 'This is Bob Paisley's last season. Do you realise you have just robbed him of his last chance to win the FA Cup, the only trophy he has never won?' I gave him a stare and then said, 'What about me? I've never won it either. Do you think Bob Paisley would have lost any sleep thinking about me if we had lost?'"

Prior to Brighton's shock victory at Anfield, Liverpool had gone an incredible 63 home cup matches without defeat. Their last loss had been against Middlesbrough in the fourth round of the League Cup on November 12, 1974.

The Brighton tie was Liverpool's first ever match at Anfield on a Sunday and that had nothing to do with it being on television. In the previous round of the cup, both Everton and Liverpool were drawn at home and consequently Everton moved their match to the Sunday. In the fifth round the same happened again, and once again, Everton requested to play on the Sunday but this time, their opponents, Tottenham, refused, so Liverpool were given the Sunday match.

At the time The Sunday Observance Act (1780) prohibited admission to a building on a Sunday for payment. Clubs sneakily got around this by allowing free admittance into their ground, on the one condition that supporters bought a teamsheet on entrance, which cost cleverly the price of a match ticket.

By the end of March, Liverpool had gone 15 league games unbeaten and hadn't suffered defeat since their trip to Carrow Road on December 12. What's more, they had extended the gap at the top to 13 points and had led the First Division since October 29.

The goals also kept coming and they had now scored 75 in 32, 50 of which were scored at Anfield. Rush was hitting the back of the net with his head and either foot, Dalglish continued to score with almost monotonous regularity and Souness contributed several piledrivers to provide a touch of variety.

One player who never grabbed any of the headlines but was

equally as important to Liverpool's success as the rest was Sammy Lee. The little Scouser with a massive heart would go on to only miss two of Liverpool's 60 games of the 1982/83 campaign. Teammate, Kenny Dalglish, later played tribute to Lee's contribution to the formidable Liverpool side of the early Eighties: "What a player Sammy was, his energy levels were fantastic, he was like a coiled-up spring and was as strong as an ox. On the pitch he was a great workhorse, pass and move and constantly closing everyone down. He was the epitome of the Liverpool way of playing. He was just a great wee player with a great wee character. He was everybody's pal and loved the club."

On March 26, Liverpool claimed their second piece of silverware for the season. A 2-1 triumph over Manchester United at Wembley handed the Reds the League (now Milk) Cup for a third consecutive time. Norman Whiteside scored the opener for Manchester United before Alan Kennedy equalised with 15 minutes to go.

The winner was then scored in the eighth minute of extra-time by Ronnie Whelan who remarkably repeated his extra-time goal from the League Cup the year before as he hit a perfect curling shot which left United's keeper Gary Bailey thrashing at fresh air.

Captain Graeme Souness insisted that Paisley went up to collect the cup, as it would be his last appearance at Wembley as manager. It was a truly fitting tribute to the departing legend.

Souness recalls: "It was all agreed beforehand that if we won the trophy, the boss would be sent up to collect it and not me. I remember telling him after the game that as we had played extra-time, he would have to go up and collect it as I was too tired! He refused at first and needed a little push at the bottom of the stairs but when he got up there, I think he enjoyed it. I thought it was a natural thing to do. After everything he had done for us and all the trophies we had lifted because of him – it was now his turn."

Despite missing the whole month of November through injury, Milk Cup matchwinner Ronnie Whelan was now into his second season as a permanent fixture in Paisley's starting XI and Bob Paisley, later spoke of his admiration for his majestic left midfielder: "I have never believed that Ronnie gets anything like the credit that he deserves. We all showered him with compliments when he first arrived on the scene, and put him on a pedestal from which it was easy to fall. Ronnie is a two-footed player.

"A lot of the football greats have been largely dependent on one foot. It's a rare gift to be able to dribble the ball with two feet, or play it comfortably whichever side it comes to you. Ronnie is a very sweet striker of a ball. It really pings off his foot like a well-timed shot in golf or tennis. No extra power is applied, but the ball zips away because it has been struck perfectly. Oddly enough, he is nothing like as effective when the ball is stationary for a free-kick.

"He prefers it when it arrives with a bit of pace on it. He may not be a prolific scorer, but his regular role out on the left of our midfield requires a lot of discipline. There are surprisingly few players who warm to the task of patrolling the touchline in the modern game. I suppose we are asking them to be winger/midfield man/full-back all rolled into one. There are times when it's difficult to force your way into a game from the flank, and yet the team needs you to stay out there to provide the width that can stretch opponents and create room for others. It's a testimony to those natural qualities in Ronnie's make-up that enables him to contribute in all facets of that multi-purpose job out on the left. He's a players' player. His biggest fans are his team mates because they know they can rely on him to do what is asked of him simply, quickly and unselfishly."

Liverpool resumed their league commitments on April 4 against Alan Durban's Sunderland in front of almost 36,000 fans at Anfield and the

Reds faced the familiar problem of having to patiently break down a packed defence. On this occasion, it took them 71 minutes before the Wearsiders' keeper, Chris Turner, was beaten.

The breakthrough came when Sammy Lee's corner was cleared as far as Souness who blasted a guided missile past Turner to give the Reds all three points and increase their lead at the top to a phenomenal 16 points with just nine games to go.

Two days later, Liverpool travelled down the East Lancs Road to face relegation-stricken Manchester City. The Citizens were completely outplayed as the Reds stormed to their fifth successive victory at Maine Road, beating them 4-0. City's newly appointed manager John Benson was realistic during his post-match interview, telling the press: "Let's face it, there is nobody who can touch Liverpool. They are still streets ahead of the rest and that includes Manchester United."

On April 9, Liverpool welcomed John Toshack's Swansea City to Anfield for a 11.30 morning kick-off. The *Liverpool Fanclub* magazine reported: "The last time Toshack visited Anfield with Swansea, his team were riding high and the atmosphere was charged with emotion following the death of Bill Shankly. This time it was Grand National morning, the sunshine found the crowd in a relaxed mood, and Swansea were in deep trouble. John had turned to youth for a relegation escape route, and although his teenagers took Liverpool the distance, their inexperience was eventually exposed. The Welshmen's offside trap and some wayward finishing from Ian Rush prevented the Reds from scoring in the first half. But within 12 minutes of the restart Rush atoned after good work by Dalglish and Whelan to score his 31st goal of the season in all competitions. There was no way back for Swansea after that. Ante Rajkovic allowed Rush to set up a cracker for Sammy Lee, and David Fairclough scored his third goal of the week after taking over from Craig Johnston in the most famous number 12 shirt in the business. It was a bit of a dash but the Liverpool players made their way to Aintree to see the big race."

On April 12, despite a midweek goalless draw at Highfield Road, Liverpool's lead at the top was increased to 17 points and were now unbeaten in 19 games.

The following weekend Liverpool travelled to face in-form Southampton, who had only lost one of their previous 11 outings. Three points at The Dell would have virtually confirmed Paisley's sixth and final league title. However, the Reds suffered their first league defeat of 1983 and were beaten 3-2.

Although Graham Taylor's Watford were currently in second place, only Manchester United could now deny Liverpool the championship as they had played three games fewer, but their hope of pulling off a miracle was short lived the following Monday when they lost 2-0 at Goodison Park.

As things now stood Manchester United had to win all seven of their remaining games and Liverpool lose their remaining five and even then, it still wouldn't be enough for Ron Atkinson's United due to Liverpool's superior goal difference.

Even though Liverpool's points total could no longer be bettered, the celebrations couldn't begin until one more point was either won by Liverpool or dropped by Manchester United. Liverpool had hoped that point would have come the following Saturday at home to Norwich. Frustratingly, the champagne had to stay uncorked as the Canaries beat the Reds 2-0 on the same day that Manchester United took all three points at Watford.

Norwich's young captain Dave Watson, a boyhood Liverpool fan and former Anfield reserve, refused to head a guard of honour before the game: "Our manager, Ken Brown, wanted us to stand in a line and clap when Liverpool came out. I told him nobody loves them more than me, but we're here to beat them, not applaud them." And beat them they did! The 2-0 victory for the visitors was Liverpool's first home league defeat for over a year and gave Norwich a rare double over the Reds.

It now felt like Liverpool were crawling to the title and the following Saturday they were beaten yet again, this time at White Hart Lane by means of a Steve Archibald double. On the same afternoon, Manchester United could only draw away at Norwich which meant they could no longer equal or better Liverpool's total of points, mathematically ending their chance of catching the Reds.

Liverpool had clinched their 14th First Division title in the most bittersweet circumstances. After their most inept performance on a London ground for years, Liverpool sat in the visitors' dressing room deflated and uninterested in the champagne that Spurs manager Keith Burkinshaw had kindly handed in for celebrations.

Burkinshaw tipped Liverpool for the title way back in October but Bob Paisley, the arch-pessimist, was not jumping for joy. The habit of winning means everything at Anfield and even though Phil Thompson was happy enough to collect his seventh League Championship medal, he stated that "the champagne tasted sour today".

Indirectly, the game provided ammunition for those who wished to reduce the size of the First Division. Surely Liverpool would not be sitting on a 14-point lead and wading through half-a-dozen largely meaningless fixtures if the league was slimmed down to a more competitive 16 or 18 clubs. After 39 games and with 81 points to their name, Paisley's men had been crowned champions with the same number of points they had earned after 36 games.

Two days later, Liverpool astonishingly lost their fourth league game in a row at the City Ground to old foes Nottingham Forest. The last time the Reds had lost four consecutive league games was

18 years earlier in the lead up to the club's first FA Cup triumph in 1965.

On May 7, a fifth straight defeat was avoided in Paisley's final home game as the Reds drew 1-1 with Aston Villa. Paisley's day of tributes started in the morning at Liverpool's Supporters' Club.

Paisley thanked the fans and admitted that retiring has been a lot harder than it should be because of their support.

He was then asked how he felt on the day of his last home game, in which he replied: "At least I know it's my last game, as there will be a few in the managerial world that won't know yet that they are going to go." As Bob wrote out the teamsheet from his office for the very last time, he enjoyed a typical pre-match lunch consisting of two pasties and a bowl of soup. There was champagne and smoked salmon upstairs, which was put on in his honour, but Bob wasn't to break the habits of a lifetime, even though it was a special occasion.

Before kick-off, the First Division trophy was awarded to Souness, who immediately handed it to Paisley to lift to the roar of the 40,000-strong crowed.

He then walked a couple metres in each direction, to the Kop chant of 'PAIS-LEY, PAIS-LEY', before heading back down the stairs and out of the limelight. Paisley was never too keen on presentations and would often refer to them as "a palaver". His personality required everything in life to be carried out with the minimum fuss possible.

The game finished in a draw and the mood in the dressing room was once again one of sheer disappointment. Not only did they fail to win, but also the players felt that they had let the manager down by not winning his final game in front of his loyal home supporters.

Bob Paisley still had time to make his 25th and final signing as manager in the form of 19-year-old Irish full-back Jim Beglin from

Shamrock Rovers for £20,000. Beglin first came under the watchful eye of Paisley the previous November when Liverpool faced Rovers in a friendly at Glenmalure Park. Beglin was destined for Arsenal when the deal mysteriously fell through but only a few days later he joined the Reds on a month's loan and only 10 days into his stay he became an official Liverpool player.

Beglin, who had just claimed his first Republic of Ireland Under-21 cap, was hoping to follow in the footsteps of Ronnie Whelan but interestingly, when Bob Paisley made his initial approach, Beglin had actually registered for a course with Aer Lingus, the airline who flew Liverpool to many of their away matches, as a back-up plan if his football career came to a dead-end.

The final game of the Paisley era came at Vicarage Road on May 14. After failing to win their previous six games surely it was now time for the champions to bow out on a high. They didn't and instead slumped to their fifth defeat in seven games, losing 2-1 to Graham Taylor's impressive Watford.

Incredibly, the last time Liverpool failed to win in seven successive games was during the 1954/55 season when Don Welsh managed an average Second Division Liverpool side.

Having gone into virtual freefall, the Reds finished the season on 82 points, 11 more than runners-up Watford and 12 more than Manchester United.

Despite, their woeful run-in, Liverpool had won the First Division by a larger points total than any of their previous 13 victories, surpassing league title number 11, won in 1979 by eight points, a season which is believed by many to have had the most complete Liverpool team of all time.

Indeed, they were so far ahead that they were able to take just two points from their final seven games and still finish as champions. It was as if the incentive to generate memorable football had vanished and enough had already been done to leave Paisley with the happiest memories, who said in his usual good-humoured way: "We thought the league was going to get cut down to eighteen teams so we thought we'd see if we could win it in 36 games."

Despite a disastrous finish, there was another Manager of the Year award for Bob Paisley, his sixth in all. The exceptional Kenny Dalglish picked up a personal double of the PFA Player and the Football Writers' Association Player of the Year. Only once before had anyone won the game's major two individual awards, Terry McDermott in 1980. A player of the talent and reputation that Dalglish possessed could be forgiven for becoming big-headed and star-struck but the man's modesty was as famous as his goalscoring record.

"Individual awards are invariably spin-offs from club success, and as such they are very welcome because the honour of winning them is a tribute to the team," Dalglish said. Ian Rush's superb goalscoring efforts were also rewarded as the Welshman was named Young Footballer of the Year.

In all matches, the side had scored 120 goals, 87 of them in the league with Rush (31) and Dalglish (20) confirming their unquestioned status as the finest pair of strikers in the business. Dalglish's keen brain and eye for an opening were matched by Rush's astonishing anticipation and speed off the mark, while both benefitted from the skill of Souness in slipping the ball through or over defences from well behind.

Sadly, Phil Thompson's future now seemed in doubt and Hodgson had yet to establish himself, while Ronnie Whelan had missed 19 games through injury. On the other hand, Grobbelaar had begun to achieve far more consistency in goal, Hansen and Lawrenson had developed one of the strongest defensive partnerships in the league, and both Lee and Johnston had done valuable work on the flanks.

No wonder that Bob Paisley was able to hand over the team to his successor with quiet confidence.

At the age of 64 and after a total of 535 games in charge, Bob Paisley retired as the most successful manager in British football.

During his nine-season tenure at Anfield, a total of 20 trophies were won, averaging over two a season and including six First Division championships and three European Cups.

Paisley summed up this time at Liverpool beautifully: "Not in my wildest dreams could I ever have imagined what happened here. When I took over I joked about it, by saying my only hope is that I'm here long enough to win as many trophies as Bill did, and then I'd be about ninety-nine. I don't know what I've won now really, but I've enjoyed every minute. People have made a lot more money out of football than me, but nobody would have enjoyed it as much I have. Liverpool is my adopted city now, they are my type of people, so humorous. Therefore, at the end of the day, if my success has provided a little bit of happiness to them, then I'm satisfied."

1982/83: Facts and Statistics

Final league table

		P	W	D	L	F	A	W	D	L	F	A	PTS
1	Liverpool FC	42	16	4	1	55	16	8	6	7	32	21	82
2	Watford	42	16	2	3	49	20	6	3	12	25	37	71
3	Manchester United	42	14	7	0	39	10	5	6	10	17	28	70
4	Tottenham	42	15	4	2	50	15	5	5	11	15	35	69
5	Nottingham Forest	42	12	5	4	34	18	8	4	9	28	32	69
6	Aston Villa	42	17	2	2	47	15	4	3	14	15	35	68
7	Everton	42	13	6	2	43	19	5	4	12	23	29	64
8	West Ham United	42	13	3	5	41	23	7	1	13	27	39	64
9	Ipswich Town	42	11	3	7	39	23	4	10	7	25	27	58
10	Arsenal	42	11	6	4	36	19	5	4	12	22	37	58
11	WBA	42	11	5	5	35	20	4	7	10	16	29	57
12	Southampton	42	11	5	5	36	22	4	7	10	18	36	57
13	Stoke City	42	13	4	4	34	21	3	5	13	19	43	57
14	Norwich City	42	10	6	5	30	18	4	6	11	22	40	54
15	Notts County	42	12	4	5	37	25	3	3	15	18	46	52
16	Sunderland	42	7	10	4	30	22	5	4	12	18	39	50
17	Birmingham City	42	9	7	5	29	24	3	7	11	11	31	50
18	Luton Town	42	7	7	7	34	33	5	6	10	31	51	49
19	Coventry City	42	10	5	6	29	17	3	4	14	19	42	48
20	Manchester City	42	9	5	7	26	23	4	3	14	21	47	47
21	Swansea City	42	10	4	7	32	29	0	7	14	19	40	41
22	Brighton & H A	42	8	7	6	25	22	1	6	14	13	30	40

Games for the 1982/1983 season

(The number after date is league position after the game)

1	21.08.1982		W	1-0	Tottenham Hotspur, Wembley, Charity Shield
2	28.08.1982	3	W	2-0	West Bromwich Albion, Anfield, 1st Division
3	31.08.1982	2	D	0-0	Birmingham City, St. Andrew's, 1st Division
4	04.09.1982	3	W	2-0	Arsenal, Highbury, 1st Division
5	07.09.1982	1	W	4-3	Nottingham Forest, Anfield, 1st Division
6	11.09.1982	4	D	3-3	Luton Town, Anfield, 1st Division
7	14.09.1982		W	4-1	Dundalk, Oriel Park, European Cup 1st R 1st L
8	18.09.1982	2	W	3-0	Swansea City, Vetch Field, 1st Division
9	25.09.1982	1	W	5-0	Southampton, Anfield, 1st Division
10	28.09.1982		W	1-0	Dundalk, Anfield, European Cup 1st R 2nd L

11	02.10.1982	1	L	0-1	Ipswich Town, Portman Road, 1st Division
12	05.10.1982		W	2-1	Ipswich Town, Portman Road, League Cup 2nd round 1L
13	09.10.1982	5	L	1-3	West Ham United, Upton Park, 1st Division
14	16.10.1982	3	D	0-0	Manchester United, Anfield, 1st Division
15	19.10.1982		L	0-1	HJK Helsinki, Olympia Stadion, European Cup 2nd R 1st L
16	23.10.1982	4	D	1-1	Stoke City, Victoria Ground, 1st Division
17	26.10.1982		W	2-0	Ipswich Town, Anfield, League Cup 2nd round 2L
18	30.10.1982	1	W	3-1	Brighton & H A, Anfield, 1st Division
19	02.11.1982		W	5-0	HJK Helsinki, Anfield, European Cup 2nd R 2L
20	06.11.1982	1	W	5-0	Everton, Goodison Park, 1st Division
21	10.11.1982		W	1- 0	Rotherham United, Anfield, League Cup 3rd round
22	13.11.1982	1	W	4-0	Coventry City, Anfield, 1st Division
23	20.11.1982	1	W	2-1	Notts County, Meadow Lane, 1st Division
24	27.11.1982	1	W	3-0	Tottenham Hotspur, Anfield, 1st Division
25	30.11.1982		W	2-0	Norwich City, Anfield, League Cup 4th round
26	04.12.1982	1	L	0-1	Norwich City, Carrow Road, 1st Division
27	11.12.1982	1	W	3-1	Watford, Anfield, 1st Division
28	18.12.1982	1	W	4-2	Aston Villa, Villa Park, 1st Division
29	27.12.1982	1	W	5-2	Manchester City, Anfield, 1st Division
30	28.12.1982	1	D	0-0	Sunderland, Roker Park, 1st Division
31	01.01.1983	1	W	5-1	Notts County, Anfield, 1st Division
32	03.01.1983	1	W	3-1	Arsena, Anfield, 1st Division
33	08.01.1983		W	2-1	Blackburn Rovers, Ewood Park, FA Cup 3rd round
34	15.01.1983	1	W	1-0	West Bromwich Albion, The Hawthorns, 1st Division
35	18.01.1983		W	2-1	West Ham United, Anfield, League Cup 5th round
36	22.01.1983	1	W	1-0	Birmingham City, Anfield, 1st Division
37	29.01.1983		W	2-0	Stoke City, Anfield, FA Cup 4th round
38	05.02.1983	1	W	3-1	Luton Town, Kenilworth Road, 1st Division
39	08.02.1983		W	3-0	Burnley, Anfield, League Cup Semi-final 1L
40	12.02.1983	1	W	1-0	Ipswich Town, Anfield, 1st Division
41	15.02.1983		L	0-1	Burnley, Turf Moor, League Cup Semi-final 2L
42	20.02.1983		L	1-2	Brighton & H A, Anfield, FA Cup 5th round
43	26.02.1983	1	D	1-1	Manchester United, Old Trafford, 1st Division
44	02.03.1983		L	0-2	Widzew Lodz, Stadion LKS, European Cup 3rd R 1st L
45	05.03.1983	1	W	5-1	Stoke City, Anfield, 1st Division
46	12.03.1983	1	W	3-0	West Ham United, Anfield, 1st Division

47	16.03.1983		W	3-2	Widzew Lodz, Anfield, European Cup 3rd R 2nd L
48	19.03.1983	1	D	0-0	Everton, Anfield, 1st Division
49	22.03.1983	1	D	2-2	Brighton & H A, Goldstone Ground, 1st Division
50	26.03.1983		W	2-1	Manchester United, Wembley, League Cup Final
51	02.04.1983	1	W	1-0	Sunderland, Anfield, 1st Division
52	04.04.1983	1	W	4-0	Manchester City, Maine Road, 1st Division
53	09.04.1983	1	W	3-0	Swansea City, Anfield, 1st Division
54	12.04.1983	1	D	0-0	Coventry City, Highfield Road, 1st Division
55	16.04.1983	1	L	2-3	Southampton, The Dell, 1st Division
56	23.04.1983	1	L	0-2	Norwich City, Anfield, 1st Division
57	30.04.1983	1	L	0-2	Tottenham Hotspur, White Hart Lane, 1st Division
58	02.05.1983	1	L	0-1	Nottingham Forest, City Ground, 1st Division
59	07.05.1983	1	D	1-1	Aston Villa, Anfield, 1st Division
60	14.05.1983	1	L	1-2	Watford, Vicarage Road, 1st Division

Friendlies

1	08.08.1982	W	3-0	Portsmouth, Fratton Park, Friendly
2	10.08.1982	D	0-0	Servette, Charmilles Stadium, Friendly
3	14.08.1982	W	2-0	Real Betis, Estadio Municipal de Utera Molina, Malaga Tournament
4	15.08.1982	D	1-1	Malaga, Estadio Municipal de Utera Molina, Malaga Tournament
5	23.11.1982	D	1-1	Shamrock Rovers, Glenmalure Park, Friendly
6	21.12.1982	D	1-1	Khartoum XI, Sudan, Friendly
7	10.01.1983	W	3-1	Tranmere Rovers, Prenton Park, Friendly
8	01.02.1983	W	6-2	Blackpool Select XI, Bloomfield Road, Friendly
9	10.05.1983	L	0-2	England XI, Anfield, Testimonial*
10	16.05.1983	L	3-4	Israel, Ramat-Gan Stadium, Friendly

*Testimonial for Phil Thompson

Appearances for the 1982/1983 season

Name	League	FA Cup	LC	EC	CS	Total
Bruce Grobbelaar	42	3	8	6	1	60
Alan Kennedy	42	3	8	6	1	60
Phil Neal	42	3	8	6	1	60
Graeme Souness	41	3	8	6	1	59
Sammy Lee	40	3	8	6	1	58
Kenny Dalglish	42	3	7	5	1	58
Mark Lawrenson	40	3	8	3	1	55
Alan Hansen	34	3	8	6	1	52
Ian Rush	34	3	8	5	1	51
Craig Johnston	33	3	6	4	0	46
Ronnie Whelan	28	1	6	5	1	41
David Hodgson	23	3	5	5	1	37
Phil Thompson	24	0	4	5	1	34
David Fairclough	8	0	2	1	0	11
Steve Nicol	4	0	0	0	0	4
Terry McDermott	2	0	0	1	0	3
Howard Gayle	0	0	0	0	0	0
John McGregor	0	0	0	0	0	0
Bob Wardle	0	0	0	0	0	0

Goalscorers for the 1982/1983 season

Name	League	FA Cup	LC	EC	CS	Total
Ian Rush	24	2	2	2	1	31
Kenny Dalglish	18	1	0	1	0	20
Phil Neal	8	0	1	2	0	11
Graeme Souness	9	0	2	0	0	11
Craig Johnston	7	1	1	1	0	10
David Hodgson	4	1	2	2	0	9
Mark Lawrenson	5	0	2	0	0	7
Ronnie Whelan	2	0	2	3	0	7
Alan Kennedy	3	0	1	2	0	6
David Fairclough	3	0	1	0	0	4
Sammy Lee	3	0	0	0	0	3
Own goals	1	0	0	0	0	1

The squad during the 1982/1983 season

Bruce Grobbelaar, Goalkeeper
Bob Wardle, Goalkeeper
Alan Kennedy, Defender
Mark Lawrenson, Defender
Phil Thompson, Defender
Phil Neal, Defender
Alan Hansen, Defender
John McGregor, Defender
Kenny Dalglish, Midfielder
Ronnie Whelan, Midfielder
Craig Johnston, Midfielder
Sammy Lee, Midfielder
Steve Nicol, Midfielder
Terry McDermott, Midfielder
Graeme Souness, Midfielder
Ian Rush, Striker
David Hodgson, Striker
David Fairclough, Striker
Howard Gayle, Striker

Transfers for the 1982/1983 season

In:
John McGregor, Queen's Park, Free, 17 May 1982
Bob Wardle, Shrewsbury Town, Player Exchange *, 11 August 1982
David Hodgson, Middlesbrough, £450,000, 12 August 1982
Jim Beglin, Shamrock Rovers, £20,000, May 1983

Out:
David Johnson, Everton, £100,000, 9 August 1982
Steve Ogrizovic, Shrewsbury Town, Player Exchange *, 11 August 1982
Terry McDermott, Newcastle United, £100,000, September 1982
Howard Gayle, Birmingham City, £75,000, 14 January 1983
David Fairclough, Lucerne, Free, 4 July 1983

A collection of statistics for the 1982/1983 season

The season in numbers:
Total games: 60
Games won: 38
Games drawn: 10
Games lost: 12
Clean sheets – League: 19
Clean sheets – Overall: 27
Total goals: 120
Average attendance at home – League: 34,836
Average attendance at home – Overall: 32,092
Average goals per game – League: 2.62
Average goals per game – Overall: 2.48
Average goal minute – League: 50
Average goal minute – Overall: 51

Goals split down to competitions:
League – 87
League Cup – 14
European Cup – 13
FA Cup – 5
Charity Shield – 1

Player debuts:
David Hodgson against Tottenham on 21.08.1982
Steve Nicol against Birmingham City on 31.08.1982

Statistics and information provided by LFChistory.net

15 : HAT-TRICK HEROES

1983/84

JOSEPH FRANCIS FAGAN WAS BORN IN WALTON Hospital, on March 12, 1921, and brought up in Smith Street, within the Kirkdale area, two miles away from Liverpool city centre. Fagan left school in 1937 and signed for the St Helens-based Earlestown Bohemians club, known as the 'Bohs', who played in the Liverpool County Combination. This was a strong amateur league in which the 'A' teams of both Everton and Liverpool competed. Liverpool were impressed by Fagan's ability and invited him to Anfield for a trial. Manager George Kay offered him a contract but Fagan, then aged 17, declined as he thought his first team opportunities at Liverpool would be limited and he would be able to stand out more if he joined a club based in a different city.

On October 8, 1938, he signed for Manchester City, where he went on to be quite a dependable centre-back. Fagan returned to Liverpool on June 30, 1958 as a coach, starting off in the youth set-up. He was put in charge of the reserves in July 1971 and following Bill Shankly's surprise departure as manager he was promoted to first team trainer in July 1974. By 1979 he had become right-hand man to Bob Paisley.

On May 23, 1983 at a press conference at Anfield, 62-year-old Joe Fagan was officially named Paisley's successor, who in turn became a paid director with special responsibility for signings.

League rules stipulated at the time that clubs could only have one paid director. Accordingly, general secretary Peter Robinson was promoted to chief executive, leaving his place on the board open for Paisley.

Fagan told the *Liverpool Echo*: "This is something I didn't expect but I'm pleased to accept. In this game of ours you do not expect anything at all. You just work at your own job and do the best you can. When the chairman and board first asked me, I wasn't too happy at first. It was really a question of my age but they decided I wasn't too old. I honestly think it will be impossible for anyone to follow Bob Paisley at this stage but at least I know the drill. He is supreme in all he has done but that doesn't worry me. I start afresh. Bob and I have worked together for many years and I've enjoyed every minute of it. The Boot Room staff here have always been very loyal and very helpful. That's not going to change, I know I can expect full support from them."

Although he was becoming a director, Paisley wouldn't be involved in the day-to-day running of the club but had a special responsibility for the vital area of recruitment and scouting. He was also available to offer his advice in other areas if required. "I'm delighted the job's staying in the family," Paisley told the *Liverpool Echo*. "There will be no break-up. Joe is a seasoned campaigner and he's well enough experienced to know he's got to get on with the job. I don't expect any drop in standards at Anfield – that's how much I respect him. Any help I can give to anyone, whether it's the groundsman or one of the office staff, I will be only too happy to give."

Liverpool chairman John Smith informed the journalists present that the new appointments would take effect on July 1 and promoting a manager from within is fundamental to Liverpool's belief in maintaining stability. He said: "We knew what Bob had done and how he worked, while Bill was here. Equally, when Bob decided to retire, without any hesitation, we appointed Joe Fagan."

The only other change to the Liverpool backroom staff ahead of the 1983/84 season was the return of Chris Lawler, who was invited back to Anfield by Joe Fagan as reserve team coach, in succession to Roy Evans who would now be mainly involved with the first team.

Liverpool's key summer transfer targets in 1983 were Charlie Nicholas of Celtic, who decided his future lay in North London and joined Arsenal for £750,000 and Brondby's Michael Laudrup.

Laudrup was reported to be on the verge of signing but the deal fell through when the club looked to make it a four-year contract, whereas the striker, represented by his father Finn, only wanted to sign for three years. Laudrup instead moved to Juventus, although it would take him two years to actually play for the club.

Fagan's first major signing as manager was 23-year-old defender Gary Gillespie from Coventry City. At 17, Gillespie made football history by becoming the youngest player to captain a Scottish League team, Falkirk.

Gillespie played six years at Coventry, making around 200 appearances until he wanted to move to a level above an annual relegation battle. He had already had talks with Arsenal in the summer of 1983 when he was informed that Liverpool had come in for him.

Joe Fagan's first signing had his work cut out for him at Liverpool to split up the successful Lawrenson and Hansen partnership in the centre of defence and Gillespie spent the 1983/84 season in the reserves apart from a solitary first team appearance in the first leg of the League Cup semi-final against Walsall on February 7, 1984.

A groin injury to Ian Rush, who was clearly going to be a key member of Fagan's side, and the departure of David Fairclough, caused so much alarm during pre-season that Fagan immediately went out and signed Michael Robinson, the big, powerful and intensely whole-hearted striker, who had shown up well against them, playing for Brighton the previous season.

Robinson later relived his dream move to Liverpool, the team he supported from the Kop from the age of six, with *LFChistory.net*: "It all started with a phone call from Brighton's chairman Mike Bamber who invited me around to his house that evening. He told me that the club had agreed a deal to sell me to another club. Mr Bamber asked me to guess where I was going. I knew Seville, Manchester United and Everton were interested in me, but he knew I would never sign for Manchester so I said, 'The Toffees?' He smiled, stood up and went over to the cupboard and came back with a bottle of Cognac and said, 'You are close, but we haven't sold you to Everton, across the park, we've sold you to Liverpool, all you have to do is agree personal terms with them'. Liverpool were currently in Holland taking part in a pre-season tournament in Rotterdam. When I got to Gatwick airport the following day to fly to Schiphol, because of all the nerves and excitement, I realised I left my passport at home. I couldn't miss this flight as it wouldn't look good for me with Liverpool Football Club waiting for me at the other end. So, my girlfriend at the time and now wife, Chris, flew down the M6 to give me my passport and I finally made the flight. It was a good job as well, as at the other end I would be greeted at a hotel by Mr. Paisley, Mr. Fagan, Mr. Smith and Mr. Robinson.

"I am now in the presence of these four great gentlemen and Bob Paisley started by revealing to me that they have been tracking my progress for a while and wanted to buy me when I was at Man City.

He told me City refused as they didn't want to sell me to a rival club and decided to sell me to Brighton, a team where if I did really well it wouldn't cause them too much controversy. This made me feel wanted as they were also talking about specific games I was involved in which also reassured me as I knew Liverpool had been tracking my progress. Mr. Smith, the chairman, then asked me how much I was earning at Brighton. I replied, 'This is Liverpool Football Club, you don't have to pay me anything, it's just my honour to come and help the team, money doesn't interest me at all, just pay me what you think is right'.

"Then Mr. Smith sent Mr. Robinson to phone Brighton to find out how much I earned there. I was one of the best paid players in the country on about £1,200 a week. I think only Bryan Robson and Peter Shilton were paid more. Brighton players had a reputation for being highly paid, that's one of the reasons they had to sell me. Anyway, we tied up all the paperwork and I signed for my boyhood club, Liverpool. I will never forget what Mr. Smith then said, 'Michael, at Liverpool we don't sign great footballers, we sign people who are great at football'. Joe Fagan then handed me a beer and said, 'Get this down you lad, you've deserved it'. By this time things were a lot more relaxed, so I asked Joe what would be expected of me and what sort of style would we be playing? He said, 'Well, Michael, we thought that we would leave that up to you, as you're the player. Regarding our style it's really quite simple, Michael lad.

"'We always put 11 out not to give them an advantage from the start. Pass it around a bit, usually to someone wearing a red shirt. Then just kick it in their net and if you can't, then give it to someone who can, and the lads at the back, just bust their bones, not allowing them to score, should it be more difficult than that, Michael?'"

At first Fagan found some difficulty in adjusting to his new role, especially the numerous press conferences expected of a Liverpool manager, but he received a lot of support from coaches Ronnie Moran and Roy Evans and from the players, with whom he had always been extremely popular, and most of his problems soon disappeared.

However, at the end of July, Liverpool's pre-season plans were disrupted by the news that Ronnie Whelan would have to undergo an operation on his pelvis which would rule him out of the start of the season. Fagan told the *Liverpool Echo*: "At the moment we have no idea just how long Ronnie will be out of action, but it does look as though he will be missing from the first few games of the season."

During the annual pre-season canter on the continent, Liverpool held both European champions Hamburg and Dutch side Feyenoord to a draw, but lost both games on penalties, prompting the *Liverpool Echo* to remark that they had been the best team in the tournament despite finishing bottom. Such confidence was visibly shaken in the Charity Shield clash with Manchester United, which revealed weaknesses in a defence from which Alan Hansen was missing, and a surprising lack of firepower considering the number of goals scored the previous season.

Great friends Sir Matt Busby and Bob Paisley were presented to two teams and then made a slow lap of honour in an open top Land Rover with the main trophies won by the two clubs the previous season on display.

The match also taught Fagan a thing or two, notably not to make a substitution immediately before a set-piece situation. While Craig Johnston and Dave Hodgson were still taking up positions, after replacing Phil Thompson and Michael Robinson, Bryan Robson profited from the confusion to score his second goal from a free-kick as United went on to win 2-0.

After a disappointing start at Wembley, Fagan gave his verdict to the *Liverpool Echo*: "I fully expected this sort of thing to happen when I took over as manager. It's the sort of thing that always happens, and Bob Paisley had similar problems when he was in my position. If everything had gone perfectly on Saturday and we had won I would have been delighted – but a bit surprised. I knew we had one or two problems, and now it's up to us to sort them out."

Fagan's style was simple and straightforward: "I'm not one for the bon mots like Bob or the abrasive quips like Shanks. What I have to offer is one word — honesty. I couldn't be devious if I tried."

Jim Beglin, the young Irish left-back who went on to make his debut under Fagan, said of him: "He was just a very genuine, nice man. He was a very humble, down to earth person. He had a lovely way about him and was very gentlemanly. Underneath that soft exterior, there was also a hardened professionalism. Joe had authority and when strong words were needed, Joe could produce them."

Like Bob Paisley, Joe Fagan had been working closely with the team long before becoming manager, so he knew that continuity was the key. While radical change is almost always necessary sooner or later, Fagan recognised that this was not yet the case at Liverpool. Above all else, Fagan had the ability to impart his considerable wisdom. He was, like Paisley, an incredibly knowledgeable football man who was able to get the best out of his players, and to inspire their loyalty.

These are key strengths. It is no good knowing a lot about the game but continually rubbing players up the wrong way, and failing to get them to play for you, either from mishandling them or through lack of respect. Equally, it is no good being likeable if the players will take advantage; the steel has to be there too, in order to be successful.

Fagan had a perfect balance of straightforward honesty, unquestionable authority and football acumen. There was nothing remarkable about him — he didn't have the incredible motivational skills of Shankly, and perhaps lacked the really sharp tactical mind of Paisley, but he had a little bit of everything needed to prosper.

By the time the opening round of league fixtures came round, Rush had recovered from his groin strain and Liverpool were further strengthened to begin their title defence at Molineux, by the return of Alan Hansen.

Craig Johnston was picked on the left of midfield, with the dependable Sammy Lee on the right, and Michael Robinson kicked off alongside Rush and Kenny Dalglish in a three-pronged attack. The champions made a terrible start, conceding a penalty within the opening 90 seconds but Ian Rush later salvaged a point for the Reds when he popped up in his usual style to hold off a challenge by two defenders and slot home an equaliser just after the restart.

The Reds clearly still had a lot of work to do and Fagan now faced the prospect of Liverpool's run without a win climbing into double figures. "That was a hell of a way to make my first appearance in the directors' box," Fagan told the press after the game. "I'm sitting up there for first time in my life and suddenly we're 1-0 down, I looked at my watch and it was only two minutes past three. I can imagine how Shanks felt in those circumstances. It was a strange, new experience but, once over the initial shock, I thoroughly enjoyed it. I decided to sit in the directors' box rather than in the dug-out, because I wanted to be more objective, to put together my thoughts for when we had the half-time meeting. There is always so much shouting going on down at the bench, so the players can't hear me anyway!"

Liverpool's first victory of the Fagan era came four days later in their midweek trip to Norwich. The Reds ruined Norwich City's big party, as they were celebrating the 48th anniversary of the opening of their Carrow Road ground. The Canaries squandered numerous early chances and were ultimately made to pay the price. Liverpool weathered the pressure well before moving up a gear with a superbly taken Graeme Souness effort, the midfielder lobbing goalkeeper Chris Woods after 29 minutes. Liverpool's victory was their first in 10 games and ample revenge for the double completed over them by Ken Brown's team the previous season.

It was becoming clear that Liverpool's longest-serving player was now thought of as a reserve to the preferred central defence pairing of Mark Lawrenson and Alan Hansen. Despite playing in the Charity Shield, Phil Thompson failed to feature on the Liverpool teamsheet for the away trips to Wolves and Norwich. Thompson, still only 29, turned down an offer to go to newly promoted Leicester City, now managed by former Liverpool player Gordon Milne, on a month's loan and vowed to stay and fight for this place in Liverpool's starting line-up: "I had a good chat with Gordon but decided that it was too early in the season to be thinking about going anywhere on loan. My allegiance is still very much with Liverpool. If I stay here, I will be in the boss's mind. Had I gone away to Leicester, even for a month, I would have been out of the way. I can still see chances for me to get back my place in the side and I still have a future at Anfield."

Four wins and two draws got the league season off to a healthy start with four of the eight goals scored coming from Ian Rush, who was already showing signs of enjoying a remarkable season.

However, the match at Old Trafford on September 24 produced what seemed to have become an annual defeat at the hands of Manchester United. This time the Reds were far from been outplayed, but were beaten by a Frank Stapleton half-volley. In spite of losing his first league encounter, Joe Fagan was upbeat in this post-match interview: "It was a great game. I'm disappointed with the result but not with the way we played. I told the lads they had nothing to be ashamed about. I couldn't fault them for effort. We talked about the goal and it would be easy to blame somebody. But let's put it down to good football by United. Let's not start looking for excuses."

Phil Neal, whose neat, constructive play from right-back had been such a feature of Liverpool's performances, played his 417th consecutive game for the Reds at Old Trafford, a Liverpool record that still stands today. Incredibly, Neal had played in every single match since October 23, 1976 but a second-half injury in the defeat at United ended his record run. After having to be replaced by Steve Nicol, Neal subsequently went on to miss Liverpool's following three games.

Neal later spoke about his phenomenal record with *LFChistory. net*: "There were two occasions when I could have missed a game. One was when I got a fractured cheekbone. Roger Davis, the centre forward at Derby, gave me an elbow (January 24, 1976). I went in for treatment on the Sunday after it occurred on the Saturday and had my cheekbone lifted in line with the rest of my face to put my face back in shape. By the way they did it, it's never recovered today. Come middle of the week I was walking around the training ground watching the players train. We were playing West Ham that Saturday, which was a good footballing team. Bob Paisley came to me on Wednesday and said, 'How are you feeling?' I said, 'I'm ok. I'm over the op and everything else'. I chose to play against the specialist's wishes who said that I shouldn't play for a month. I got away with it. The other time, was when I got over a broken toe, but I had to play for six weeks with size 8 ½ on one foot and size 7 on the other. Ronnie Moran made me a plaster cast on the little toe I had broken. It was uncomfortable with my normal size shoes. I had to find some way to be still able to kick a ball, tackle and maybe have a little injection to keep the pain away for 90 minutes. There were

LIVERPOOL FOOTBALL CLUB/19

little incidents when I could have missed a game but I was doubly determined not to. It was so exciting. I didn't miss a day's training in all those years I was there. I wouldn't ring in for a cold. Every day I had a smile on my face."

Danish outfit Odense Boldklub were the first European team to visit Anfield during the 1983/84 season. The Reds already had a one-goal cushion from the first leg, and added another five. Kenny Dalglish broke the British European Cup goalscoring record with his second goal in the game, taking his total to 15, one better than fellow Scot, Denis Law. "The first I even knew I held the record was when Kenny scored his goal in Denmark in the first leg a fortnight ago and I read that he was within one of equalling my record," commented Law. "I'm not disappointed he's done it. In fact, I'm happy it's gone to another Scot and a wonderful player."

The following Saturday, Liverpool's first league defeat of the season against Manchester United was followed by a much more surprising upset, a home reverse against unfancied Sunderland, who won through a penalty by Gary Rowell.

It was a frustrating afternoon for the Reds as they dominated much of the play, but Sunderland's defence was magnificent and even the genius of Dalglish couldn't get through.

So far Michael Robinson had failed to make much of an impression, despite considerable effort, but he got Liverpool back on the winning track again, almost single-handed, with a magnificent hat-trick at West Ham, the goals being his first in the league for the club.

The big man's first goal came direct from a long punt downfield by Bruce Grobbelaar, his second was volleyed from a weak clearance by veteran defender Billy Bonds and his third was fired home from a pass by Dalglish. West Ham legend Bonds, who played his 700th game for the Hammers that afternoon, wasn't best pleased with

Robinson's hat-trick: "He ruined my big day. He caused us endless trouble."

After the match and as the Liverpool bus was about to leave Upton Park, the door suddenly opened and off jumped Liverpool's hat-trick hero Robinson because somebody had pinched his match ball.

He frantically searched Liverpool's dressing room and the referee's room, but no ball! He asked a lot of people but nobody knew where it was. It was only when he got back on the coach that it was found hidden in the back toilet. It was a wind up. Robinson told the press: "After being in awe of this lot I'm seeing them for what they are – jokers like every other footballer, but only better."

A single goal from 21-year-old substitute Steve Nicol, his first for the club, was enough to maintain the winning momentum against QPR on their infamous plastic pitch.

After 10 matches, Liverpool were in second place just two points behind front-runners, Manchester United. At the end of October came a truly fabulous performance from Rush, who scored five times at Anfield as Liverpool thrashed Luton 6-0. His goals came in a variety of ways, including a magnificent header from a cross by Nicol. Rush became only the fourth player to score five goals in a single game for Liverpool. The last man to do so was striker John Evans in 1954 when he netted five times against Bristol Rovers.

In fact, Rush played through a pain barrier to write himself into the Liverpool record books. It was only after taking a couple of painkillers that he decided to play. Rush had been affected by a virus of his groin and said: "I came here not expecting to play, but at 5 o'clock I'd got five goals. It's unbelievable. The lads say I've got so many match balls, I can open up a sports shop but this one is a bit different as it reads, 'Five goals, no sweat, brilliant' signed by Kenny Dalglish."

Liverpool's next league match was against Everton, who were 15th in the table after only winning four of their opening 11 games. Prior to kick-off, a television show set in Liverpool called Scully, which featured cameos from Graeme Souness and Kenny Dalglish, was in production. The lead character, a working-class lad who idolised Kenny and Liverpool, fantasised of scoring a goal for the Reds in a Merseyside derby. The club agreed that the production team could film the character's dream sequence in front of the Kop on matchday, which started with actor, Andrew Schofield, running out with the players in a full Liverpool strip prior to the game. The match finished exactly as expected, with Liverpool winning 3-0 in convincing fashion.

Rush scored the first of his side's three goals and so completed a spell of seven goals in eight days, which recalled memories of Jackie Balmer's 10-goal haul in three games shortly after World War II.

In between the two league matches, Rush had also scored the winner in the second round European Cup tie against Athletic Bilbao, and was now being hailed as Europe's most outstanding striker.

By the end of November, Liverpool were generally going well, heading the First Division and progressing through the early rounds of the European and Milk Cup. In addition, Kenny Dalglish collected his 100th league goal for the club at Ipswich when the master elected to turn and bend a left-foot shot into the far top corner, becoming one of the first players to score 100 goals in Scotland and England. The game ended 1-1 and also saw the comeback of Ronnie Whelan, making his first start of the season after recovering from his pelvis operation.

On December 12, Liverpool were shocked to the core by a 4-0 thrashing at Coventry, the club's heaviest defeat since December 1976 when they lost 5-1 at Villa Park. However, in typical Liverpool fashion they immediately hit back with a 5-0 victory over Notts

County, who were now managed by former Liverpool defender Larry Lloyd.

Joe Fagan was delighted with the way his team bounced back after that disaster at Coventry but was reluctant to talk of winning the title again: "Being at the top makes no difference this early in the season. Let's see how it is after Christmas and New Year. We were awful at Coventry but we bounced back to show what we were capable of. All credit to the players, they were disappointed that they had let the club down at Coventry."

Athough Paisley had retired from football management, he was still very much involved in the game. As well as spying trips at home and abroad and helping the Liverpool scouting system, he would make appearances at supporters' clubs and functions on Merseyside as a guest speaker and take part in various press activities on television and radio. "I'm happy with my life and I'm pleased I continued my association with the club," he told the *Anfield Review*. "It's nice to know that it can't be said I left management when the team was struggling. We are doing well enough and there have not been any dire calls for assistance. I arrive at the ground between 10 and 10.30am when the players have started their training, and I usually leave my office about two in the afternoon. In the evening, there is always something to do or somewhere to go. It's at Anfield that I make my plans for the week. Part of my routine this season has included trips to Europe, vetting opponents. By early November, I'd made four trips to the Continent to check on the opposition, and I also do scouting missions in England and Scotland. Nothing would please me more than to snap up another Kenny Dalglish, or a Mark Lawrenson or Graeme Souness. Liverpool are always on the look-out for men to step into the shoes of long-serving players, but key men of the calibre of the three I've mentioned are so rare that the club would probably have to give me a 15-year contract to find them! That's how priceless they are."

After victories at West Brom on Boxing Day and at Forest on New Year's Eve, Liverpool went on to end 1983 three points clear at the top of the First Division. Joe Fagan sat down with Ken Rogers for the *Liverpool Echo* and perfectly summed up his first few months at the helm. "It's been like Tales of the Unexpected hasn't it?" claimed Fagan. "It has given me a new lease of life, it's a different job with a fresh outlook and I must admit, it's rejuvenated me a bit. It's better than taking the tablets! I suppose I had a fear at the outset that I would not be able to do the job properly. It's all right being associated with a club for 25 years, managing it is altogether different.

"One of the things on my side was that I had a good squad of players. Another thing was that the backroom staff know the job backwards. Ronnie Moran, Roy Evans, John Bennison, Chris Lawler and Tom Saunders ... they all do a hell of a job at Anfield. One of the things I realised a long time ago was that the help you get from the chairman downwards is second to none. There is no such thing as back-biting here. They have all helped me tremendously and I have a high regard for all of them for making my job so easy. I had no experience of going on TV or talking to the media. Whenever I'd been asked before, I always said no. Once I got the job, I knew there was no use hiding. I try to answer things honestly, rather than be a diplomat. If I get an awkward question, I'm not the sort of person who can come out with 1,000 words or just say nothing. That is not my way. I try to give a straight answer. People talk about being top as we go into a New Year, but as far as I'm concerned there's no New Year in football. The season goes right through and we are only at the halfway stage on Saturday. Nothing is cut and dried. We'd like to be out in front by a mile, but the Manchester Uniteds, Southamptons and Forests are still there. Who knows what will happen at the end of the day?"

Liverpool suffered another setback at the turn of the year, drawing 1-1 at home against rivals Manchester United. When Johnston gave the Reds an interval lead over Ron Atkinson's side at Anfield they seemed to be heading for a rare success over their rivals but everything was changed by an incident early in the second half. Dalglish suffered a depressed cheekbone in a heading duel with United defender Kevin Moran and had to go straight to hospital. Liverpool won a free-kick, but it was generally agreed the incident was not malicious, though manager Fagan took the precaution of dashing down to the touchline for a quick word with Graeme Souness. "Graeme is Kenny's room-mate and thinks he's the bee's knees, quite rightly, so I thought I would stop him getting too carried away," said Fagan, who had already shown himself to be just as shrewd as his distinguished predecessors.

Besides the news that Dalglish would be sidelined for the foreseeable future, the United disappointment was followed by a 1-0 defeat at home to Wolves, one of the season's major shocks, in view of the fact that the Midlands club were bottom of the First Division at the time.

Liverpool soon got back on track at Aston Villa the following Friday night, where Rush produced one of the finest second-half pieces of centre forward play ever seen on the football pitches of England.

Freezing weather meant the pitch was dangerously treacherous but Liverpool somehow kept their feet and Rush performed like a champion ice skater. He scored all three goals, the first after a burst through the middle of the defence, the second with a ferocious left-foot volley and the third with a neat chip over helpless Nigel Spink.

Rush, who had now hit six hat-tricks in two-and-a-quarter seasons at Liverpool, told the press: "The second goal gave me most satisfaction, but I could have had four. I missed a chance in the first half. I have scored five goals in a game, and one day I want to hit six."

With the players determined to do everything possible to win at least one trophy for their unassuming boss, it was becoming clear this would be a memorable season, even though it was also turning into something of a marathon.

The Milk Cup, a competition Liverpool had already won three years in a row, under various names, involved no fewer than 13 ties, with every single round needing a minimum of two games.

Lowly Fulham had taken them to a second replay in the second round, Birmingham and Sheffield Wednesday made them play twice apiece, and even little Walsall put up a tremendous fight over the two legs, before Liverpool again qualified for Wembley. Fagan gave new signing Gary Gillespie his first-team debut against the Third Division leaders Walsall in the first leg of the semi-final at Anfield.

On January 29, once more Liverpool became the unexpected victims of a prodigious giant-killing act by Brighton, who followed their success of the previous season at Anfield by winning 2-0 at the Goldstone Ground.

Brighton became the second club to knock Liverpool out of the FA Cup in successive seasons. The first was Everton in 1905 and 1906. Moreover, with the exception of FA Cup finals, this was the first time that an English second tier club had featured in a live television game.

Fortunately, Liverpool's disappointment found quick consolation in Europe. Kenny Dalglish returned to action after more than two months recovering from a broken cheekbone to help the team narrowly beat Sven Göran Eriksson's Benfica at Anfield. At the time a single Rush strike was deemed not enough to take to Portugal for the second leg but it proved more than adequate in the end. With Grobbelaar desperately determined not to repeat the slips of the last two years, and Souness helping Hansen and Lawrenson form a near impregnable defence, the Portuguese cracks suffered the shock of their lives, being outplayed 4-1 at an Estadio da Luz reduced to near silence, despite the presence of 80,000 fanatical fans.

On March 10, Joe Fagan swooped to sign Ipswich's high-scoring midfielder, 26-year-old John Wark, for £475,000. The signing was a major coup for Liverpool boss Fagan who won the race for Wark's signature in the face of stiff competition from both Manchester United and Arsenal.

The Scottish international admitted that he was so astounded at Liverpool's interest in him that he thought Fagan's first approach early on a Sunday morning was nothing more than a hoax call. Wark told the *Liverpool Echo*: "The phone rang and the caller said, 'It's Joe Fagan here'. I thought it was one of my Ipswich teammates, possibly Eric Gates, messing around. He eventually convinced me he was who he said he was. I am really glad now that I did not say what I was going to."

In the league, the champions were still occupying the top spot, but unlike the previous season they were unable to shake off the following pack. On February 11, full-backs Alan Kennedy and Phil Neal completed an unusual double by scoring Liverpool's two goals, in the home victory over Arsenal and this only emphasised the attitude of the whole team, in which every player played for his fellows rather than himself.

Many of the league games were tense, tight affairs but Rush's opportunism conferred a clear advantage and the defenders gave little away. A rare defeat against close rivals Southampton was followed by a 2-0 triumph, where new signing Wark wasted no time in scoring his first Liverpool goal on his debut. Wark, who started and finished the move, set Sammy Lee away, in a quick exchange so typical of Liverpool. Lee and Dalglish carried it through, and then the ball came back to Wark, who had raced to the edge of the area and he let fly with a solid shot that rifled past Eric Steele into the far corner. The Reds doubled their lead late on when Rush scored his 36th goal of the season.

As the month of March entered its climax, Liverpool were on track for an extraordinary treble. First up came the Milk Cup final at Wembley against Everton. The meeting of the Mersey rivals produced fantastic scenes in the capital with thousands of fans travelling down together and enjoying themselves side by side, so much so the authorities confessed afterwards that they had never handled a more enjoyable meeting. The game finished 0-0 and most went home happy. A reply was needed to settle the battle of Merseyside three days later at Maine Road, Manchester, where a superb Graeme Souness strike from just outside the box was the difference between the two clubs and handed Joe Fagan his first trophy as manager.

Although from the stands it looked like one of Souness' typical sublime finishes, after the game Liverpool's captain admitted it wasn't his greatest effort and was more charitable to Neville Southall who could have saved it. Souness told the camaras after the game: "I miscontrolled it and had my back to goal but flashed a leg at it and it just dipped in front of Neville before going in. It was more like a hit and hope moment. All in all, it has been a great occasion for the city of Liverpool to have two teams in the final, it meant a lot to people." Souness added: "We were very lucky to come away from the first game with a draw. There was a bit of havoc when we were presented with the trophy as a fan got in the way between me and Bruce Grobbelaar as I passed it down the line but it was all good fun."

Liverpool had now won the League Cup, under its various different names, for the fourth successive time. Even though Joe Fagan had been heavily involved in many of Liverpool's trophy wins, it took some time for it to sink in that he had won his first major trophy as manager. He told the *Liverpool Echo*: "My feelings have not quite arrived yet. My first thought is for the players and the coaching staff because they are the people most directly concerned. Winning a trophy is a manager's dream and I've been incredibly lucky to achieve it quicker than most people. Never forget, it was Bob Paisley's era that brought the players here. To be honest I felt a bit embarrassed when they said they wanted to win something for me. Our club has gone on for so many years that winning trophies has become a tradition, and I wouldn't like to break it."

On April 7, the Reds emulated their 6-0 home victory against Luton in October by hitting West Ham for six at Anfield. Ian Rush and Souness continued their excellent finishing form, as they both scored twice. After 34 rounds of fixtures, Liverpool led the First Division by two points to second-placed Manchester United while a seven-point gap had emerged between United and Forest who were leading the chasing pack in third. At that point it was obvious that the run-in to the 1983/84 season was going to be a two-horse race.

The two European Cup semi-finals against Dinamo Bucharest were tough, bad-tempered affairs and during the first leg at Anfield one of the Romanians had his jaw broken after a clash with Souness. A goal by Lee was Liverpool's only score and with the Romanians thirsting for revenge in the return leg, Liverpool were clearly up against it. In fact, Souness played one of the greatest games of his career, keeping his cool and refusing to be intimidated.

Dinamo Bucharest eventually lost their self-control on a wet, miserable afternoon which saw the stadium shrouded by umbrellas and it was Liverpool who cruised through to the final in Rome, thanks to two more goals from the unstoppable Rush, his 40th and 41st of the season.

Alan Hansen later recalled Joe Fagan's post-match reaction in the Liverpool dressing room after his team had just qualified for the European Cup final: "I remember when we'd gone to Romania and beaten a very good Dinamo Bucharest team 2-1 on the day and 3-1 on aggregate to reach the final in Rome. We were naturally jubilant but as we came back into the dressing room a poker-faced Joe told us to sit down, shut up and listen. He then went into the usual Liverpool mantra of, 'Don't get carried away, you've won nothing yet, you've still got the final to come and you must keep your feet on the ground'. It took the steam out of us completely – only for Joe to let out a tremendous roar, punch the air with his fist and scream, 'YOU BEAUTIES' and the whole place erupted again."

Back in the league, Liverpool suffered their third league defeat of the year at relegation-battling Stoke but despite this defeat, Fagan's team still sat on top of the First Division the following morning courtesy of Notts County beating Manchester United 1-0 at Meadow Lane.

Liverpool battled on grimly, content to draw with Leicester, Ipswich and Birmingham, while rivals United also continued to drop vital points. On May 7, Bobby Gould's Coventry City visited Anfield for a Bank Holiday Monday fixture and another four-goal blast from Ian Rush, which included a rare penalty, gave the Reds revenge for that early 4-0 drubbing at Highfield Road. Alan Hansen also added to the 5-0 scoreline to edge the Reds closer to their 15th league title.

Against the Sky Blues, Rush took his tally to 46 for the season which enabled him to surpass Roger Hunt's record, set in 1962, of 42 goals scored during a single season.

Moreover, with 31 league goals now to his name, the Welshman became the first player to reach 30 goals in a First Division campaign since Bob Latchford's achievement for Everton during the 1977/78 season. On the same day, Ipswich Town killed any remaining title hopes that the red half of Manchester held by beating United 1-0 at Old Trafford.

With a far superior goal difference Liverpool now needed just a draw from their two remaining games to clinch the First Division championship.

Following Rush's extraordinary goalscoring feat, Billy Liddell, himself one of Anfield's greatest ever goalscorers, paid tribute to Liverpool's goal machine.

Liddell, who was now 62, told the *Liverpool Echo*: "The game has changed a lot since my day and, of course, they play far more games now than we used to. However, marking has become much closer and there is a greater use of tactics, which makes scoring much more difficult. Even the present Liverpool team, one of the greatest there has ever been, score far fewer goals than quite ordinary sides used to get 20 to 30 years ago, so Rush's feat is that much more impressive. Ian is always in the right place and he proves that by rarely needing to beat more than a single player."

The title was finally won on May 12, with a solid, if unspectacular, 0-0 draw at Notts County in their penultimate game. 'REDS ARE TRIPLE CHAMPIONS' was the headline in the *Liverpool Echo*, and their scribe Ian Hargraves followed by reporting: "Liverpool are league champions again for the third time in succession and the seventh time in nine seasons. Though unable to beat Notts County, already relegated, the point they achieved was sufficient to give them the title as Manchester United could only draw at White Hart Lane."

While most other managers in Fagan's position would have milked the occasion for what it's worth, knocking back the champagne provided by Notts County, revelling in the back-slapping and basking in the media glare, Joe's only concern was leaving Meadow Lane as he had found it. Fagan looked around at the mess that laid before him. With a resigned yet happy shrug he picked up the nearest brush and began sweeping the dressing room floor. Someone had to do it and it may as well be him, he thought. It was polite to leave a visiting dressing room as spick and span as you found it and Notts County's had been very tidy just a few hours earlier.

It had always been a basic tenet of the Boot Room philosophy that if a job needed doing, no matter how small, then it should be done and done properly.

Three days later, the newly crowned champions returned to Anfield for a Tuesday night match against Norwich City. Souness and his men were presented with the brand-new Canon League trophy by league president Jack Dunnett. Unlike the previous year, the Reds were applauded on to the pitch by their opponents and manager Ken Brown.

However, the players were unable to provide the farewell performance the Anfield faithful were hoping for. Had it not been for Ian Rush appearing from nowhere to head home Alan Kennedy's curling centre after 30 minutes Liverpool might easily have lost.

The game ended 1-1 and, although it wasn't the perfect season finale, the Kop took it all in good spirits, inviting the players and staff to give them a wave, urging Bruce Grobbelaar to entertain them with a handstand and reminding all and sundry that they were watching the champions in action. Yet, still, that wasn't enough to satisfy thousands of diehards who stayed on the Kop for 40 minutes after the final whistle, demanding an encore from the men who were going to Rome on May 30 to try and win the European Cup and bring their haul of major trophies to three. The supporters' sit-in finally brought its reward as the players and manager came back on the pitch, now in their suits, to pay their respects and show their appreciation to their loyal following.

Fagan was clearly moved by the fans' gesture: "It was very emotional and something I didn't expect. But this isn't about me, it's about the players, the lads downstairs, the directors and the fans. Becoming league champions once again, it is just beginning to sink in and I am glad the issue has been settled now. I thought it would go down to today's game, the final one. I was nearly right but thank God we wrapped things up at Notts County. We haven't always played the free-flowing football that I would have liked, but I could never fault any of the lads for lack of effort. They have battled away in every game and what has pleased me has been the way they have coped with all kinds of conditions."

Liverpool finished the campaign on 80 points, two less than the previous season, and three more than eventual runners-up Southampton.

Lawrie McMenemy's Saints went unbeaten in their last nine games to pip Manchester United and Nottingham Forest to the runners-up spot, their highest top-flight finish to date.

Three times throughout history Liverpool had been close to achieving three consecutive First Division titles. After winning back-to-back titles in 1922 and 1923 the Reds ended the following season finishing a disappointing 12th. On two occasions, Bob Paisley won the league two seasons in a row, but failed to complete a hat-trick in 1978 and 1981, finishing second and fifth respectively.

Indeed, the clock had to be turned back almost 50 years to discover the last time a side managed a title hat-trick. That was when the legendary Arsenal side of the Thirties emulated the record of Huddersfield Town set in the Twenties.

Kenny Dalglish, who picked up his fifth League Championship medal gave his take on the season's proceedings: "We are champions again for the third consecutive season! We had to graft for it and fight off Manchester United. I honestly believe that the best team in England won the highest honour in the professional game. How do we do it? Well, it's about wanting to win, wanting to sustain your standards, playing good, simple and straightforward football with all members of the team attacking and defending when necessary.

"It's about team-work, sweating to make 10 yards to cover for a teammate, 20 yards to decoy a defender and 30 yards to knock a potentially dangerous ball into touch. It's about us responding to the greatest fans in the land and working for a managerial staff who treat pros like men and get their perfect response. There are no favourites at Anfield, just members of the club.

"The ground staff, turnstile operators, clerical staff, stewards, players and management have all played their parts of varying degrees in winning a title. The day we sit back and reckon ourselves will be the day we come in for a terrible fall. I don't see that happening under this regime. Not if we want to keep wearing a Liverpool shirt that is."

Grobbelaar – who had now played 185 consecutive games for the Reds – Kennedy, Hansen and Lee had not missed a single league match when the season ended while Neal and Rush had missed only one each.

Souness had made 37 appearances and Dalglish 33, while Johnston (28), Robinson (23), Whelan (20) and Nicol (19) all made valuable contributions. As far as goalscoring was concerned, Rush had been in a class of his own, with 32 league goals and 47 in all, plus two more for Wales. Souness and Dalglish had also reached double figures, but neither Hodgson nor Robinson had shown themselves to be significant marksmen.

Meanwhile, Phil Thompson, apart from the Charity Shield, played no further part in the campaign. Lawrenson and Hansen were settling down at the heart of a defence while Thompson had featured in a central midfield role for Liverpool's reserves, now managed by Chris Lawler, as they won their 13th title in 16 years, an incredible achievement in itself.

On an individual level, Rush achieved his own personal treble of awards, coming from home and abroad. He emulated former team-mates Terry McDermott and Kenny Dalglish by being awarded the FWA Footballer of the Year and the PFA Player of the Year in the same season.

Liverpool's top marksman was also presented with the European Golden Boot, the first British player to win the prestigious award, which had been won by past legends of the game such as Eusébio and Gerd Müller.

Furthermore, Joe Fagan was acclaimed Manager of the Year after his first season in command. Alan Hansen, who like Dalglish had won his fifth League Championship, told the *Liverpool Echo*: "Perhaps in many people's minds Joe Fagan won't go down as an obvious managerial great, even though he has just become the first manager in the English game to complete the treble of major trophies.

"However, people should not forget the part he played behind the scenes in the previous two decades, especially when he was number two to Bob Paisley between 1974 and 1983. While Bob picked the team and ultimately took the final decision as manager, they worked very much as a team and Joe virtually ran the show.

"Like Paisley, Joe is something of a reluctant manager. I don't think he enjoys the high profile and media attention that goes with the job.

Joe feels for every player and that's why players are never afraid to seek him out for advice. I remember early in my Liverpool career I was struggling to get into matches in the first 15 to 20 minutes. He noticed this and told me, 'You'll have to start looking after yourself better'. I told him, 'I'm doing just that, I'm not going out, I haven't touched a drink for weeks, I'm watching what I eat and I'm training hard.' He replied in an instant, 'Well then, that's your answer. You need a good night out'. Joe is like that, one of the old school who doesn't mind players enjoying themselves, as long as it is at the right time and things are going well.

"Despite his genial nature and popularity, you dare not get on his wrong side. If he thinks anyone is taking liberties, he will come down on you like a ton of bricks. He always strikes the right balance between when to take things seriously and when the time was right for a joke."

There was no rest for the league champions as just two days later they faced Newcastle United at St. James' Park in a farewell tribute to Kevin Keegan who was to retire from the game as a player.

Fagan took a full-strength squad to Tyneside, with the exception of Ian Rush, who was receiving the Football Writers' Association Footballer of the Year award at the Cafe Royal in London. And while the night undoubtedly belonged to Keegan and his 36,722 Geordie fans, Liverpool were given just the sort of game they were looking for in preparation for their European Cup final in Rome.

Fagan fielded his likely cup final team, apart from leading scorer Rush, and they had to work hard for their 2-2 draw, with goals coming from Robinson and Souness.

Appropriately, the two Newcastle goals were scored by the former Liverpool favourites Keegan and McDermott. The emotion spilled down from the terraces as Keegan was whisked away by helicopter, which landed perfectly in the centre circle after the final whistle. Keegan, who had refused a testimonial fund from Newcastle, did not receive a financial award from the night. Consequently, the £80,000 proceeds raised from the match went towards helping to buy Keegan's successor.

While Liverpool's European Cup opponents Roma were preparing for the final in a training camp in the Dolomite mountains, where their every move was closely monitored, Joe Fagan's men visited Tel Aviv in Israel.

The Reds warmed up for their upcoming test in Rome with a convincing 4-1 victory over the national Israel side at Bloomfield Stadium. It was a convincing performance as Israel had thrashed the Republic of Ireland only a month or so earlier and the English champions were without their leading scorer, Ian Rush, who was on duty for Wales. The temperatures were up into the eighties which meant the players had to sweat it out but they responded well with Ronnie Whelan, in particular, looking most impressive. Whelan scored two goals, one in each half, with Michael Robinson, deputising for Rush, and skipper Graeme Souness getting the others.

Despite performing well on the pitch, some of Liverpool's players let the club down off it as they indulged in some rather inadequate behaviour involving large quantities of alcohol.

Italian newspapers sent journalists to cover Liverpool's build-up and what they saw shocked them. David Hodgson recalls one particular incident: "In Israel just before the European Cup final, we'd been playing fizzbuzz, one of those drinking games. There was Alan Hansen, Alan Kennedy, Bruce Grobbelaar, Stevie Nicol, myself, Ronnie Whelan, Ian Rush, Sammy Lee, all drinking in the square in Tel Aviv. Things got said and a fight started. Me and Rushie were quite close so it's us back to back against everybody else. Somehow it calmed down and I went back to the hotel with Rushie and Alan Kennedy, who fell on the ground and couldn't get up. The old Liverpool director Mr. Moss was coming out of the hotel just at that moment. So, I've got down to pick up Alan and I couldn't get up either. And Mr. Moss is stood above us frowning. He says, 'Gentlemen, this is Liverpool Football Club'. So, I grabbed hold of his trousers and pulled myself up his body. And I put my arm around him and said, 'Mossy, you old bugger, you might be a director but I think you're a great fella'. After breakfast the next morning, they call this big meeting upstairs and around the table there's Bob, Joe Fagan, Moran, Evo and Mr Moss, who stands up and says, 'I've been at this club for over 20 years and I've never witnessed anything like last night in my life. I've had many accolades passed on to me, but never have I received one so touching than from David Hodgson'. Then they lift the tablecloth and underneath it's piled high with beer! After that meeting, Bob Paisley turned to me and said, 'You're a good Geordie, son. That's what you are'."

The Liverpool management's tactics were second to none. Now, before a European Cup final, was not the time to punish the team and the idea was to bring them back together again. Souness, as captain, was delighted. "It was masterful psychology," he said. "No one fell out and no grudges were held."

On May 30 came the grand climax in Rome, scene of Liverpool's first European Cup triumph back in 1977. This time they even had to tackle a Roma side who were playing on their own ground and boasted five members of Italy's 1982 World Cup-winning team.

Unlike 1977, there were a lot fewer Liverpool fans present and the atmosphere felt a lot more intimating than seven years previously. Despite that, Liverpool captain Souness had his own ideas to fill the players with confidence. Robinson recalls: "When we arrived in the Stadio Olympico, we had a ghetto blaster with us and we were playing this one song by Chris Rea – 'I don't know what it is but I love it'. We weren't nervous and we wanted to show them, we went directly outside the home team's dressing room playing this ghetto blaster at full blast. Roberto Falcao opened the door with a rather bewildered expression on his face realising it was us making all the noise. Then Graeme took the ghetto blaster and took it out into the stadium. I asked him, 'Graeme what you doing? You're just going to antagonize them'. 'No, Michael,' he said, 'I'm just tiring them out'."

Phil Neal scored Liverpool's only goal after 14 minutes before Roberto Pruzzo equalised for the hosts just before half-time. The score remained 1-1 after extra-time and the match went to a penalty shoot-out.

Robinson, who replaced Kenny Dalglish in the first half of extra-time, later shared his memories with *LFChistory.net*: "I must say in extra-time everyone was playing for the winner, neither teams wanted the shootout, apart from Bruce that is, who was time wasting! When the final whistle went after extra-time Joe Fagan called us all in and said, 'Lads you've been fantastic tonight, you've fought like gladiators been fed to the lions in the Roman Amphitheatre'. He then just walked off and one of us shouted, 'Joe, who is taking the penalties?' He turned round lighting up a cigarette and just said, 'Well I wouldn't fancy one'. It was as if whatever happened from here didn't matter to Joe, he was more than proud and satisfied with our performance that everything else would just be a bonus. So, it was down to Graeme. Alan Kennedy was first to put himself forward to take one but Graeme wasn't so keen.

"Steve Nicol also offered, as long as he was the first up. I supposed he felt that if he missed, it wouldn't be as disastrous as if it was a decisive one. Souness, the captain, put himself down for one and

Phil Neal and Ian Rush were the two other obvious choices, leaving number five. Graeme turns to me and says, 'Michael, do you want it?' Although I was a forward player and should have fancied it, I really didn't. I was honest with Graeme, 'I really didn't want to take it, but if you want me to I would'. Graeme knew me and he would have known I was feeling extremely uncomfortable. Therefore, he chose Alan Kennedy, as he preferred someone who was willing to take one have it. Graeme then said, 'Don't worry, we will need an attacking player for sudden death'. I didn't know if that made me feel better or worse. With the five players and order decided, Steve Nicol stepped up and blasted it over the bar. Although obviously I was disappointed he missed I felt a sense of relief because now if I ended up taken a penalty and missing, I wouldn't be the only one crying on the plane on the way home. Phil, Graeme and Ian all scored and Grobbelaar's wobbly-legged antics in goal caused two Roma misses. Then it came to Alan Kennedy for our number five.

"If he scored Liverpool would be crowned European champions for the fourth time in eight years and if he missed then more than likely it would have come down to me. I was a bag of nerves. Alan scored I was a European champion, but the relief I was feeling, however, was difficult to describe."

Liverpool's backroom team that night consisted of Fagan, Ronnie Moran, Roy Evans and Chris Lawler. An all-Scouse Boot Room had conquered Europe, an achievement which is unlikely to ever be repeated. Alan Hansen exquisitely summed up the occasion after picking up his third European Cup medal: "It wasn't the greatest game in the world but it certainly is the greatest victory ever."

Souness was the epitome of Liverpool's unflinchable and unbreak-able spirit that night in Rome and showed sheer courage and grit to inspire his teammates in a hostile atmosphere. He deservedly became the third player to lift the European Cup for Liverpool. At the team's subsequent open top bus parade on their return to Liverpool he said: "Lifting the European Cup was the biggest thrill I've ever had in football and I actually cried after the game. It was the first time I've ever been emotional after a game of football."

Joe Fagan had won a historical treble at the first time of asking and made a fairytale start to his managerial career. The prospect of following in the footsteps of Bob Paisley, whose record of honours was second to none, must have been daunting to say the least. But Joe had not only shown his own brand of management, but his thirst for success. First came the Milk Cup final at Wembley with neighbours Everton which ended all square. But his team maintained the incredible League/Milk Cup record with victory in the replay.

Then came the trophy, considered the hardest in the world to win, the English First Division title and then Joe was the mastermind behind the club's fourth European Cup triumph, beating Roma in their own back garden. His team's victories on the field made him the first British manager to win three major trophies in one season.

The 1983/84 season can justifiably be judged to be the finest in Liverpool's history, but it's perhaps not a great surprise that Fagan's achievements are not more obviously celebrated at Anfield, especially given the brief nature of his reign and the success of his predecessors, Shankly and Paisley.

However, when Liverpool fans look at the all-time greats of Liverpool, Joe Fagan is certainly up there. A vital and long serving member of the Boot Room, the glue that held everything together during Liverpool's golden era. From Graeme Souness, who attributes much of his success as a player to Fagan, came perhaps the greatest tribute: "Joe's contribution to Liverpool Football Club should never be allowed to fade from the memory."

1983/84: Facts and Statistics

Final league table

		P	W	D	L	F	A	W	D	L	F	A	GD	PTS
1	Liverpool FC	42	14	5	2	50	12	8	9	4	23	20	41	80
2	Southampton	42	15	4	2	44	17	7	7	7	22	21	28	77
3	Nottingham Forest	42	14	4	3	47	17	8	4	9	29	28	31	74
4	Manchester United	42	14	3	4	43	18	6	11	4	28	23	30	74
5	QPR	42	14	4	3	37	12	8	3	10	30	25	30	73
6	Arsenal	42	10	5	6	41	29	8	4	9	33	31	14	63
7	Everton	42	9	9	3	21	12	7	5	9	23	30	2	62
8	Tottenham	42	11	4	6	31	24	6	6	9	33	41	-1	61
9	West Ham United	42	10	4	7	39	24	7	5	9	21	31	5	60
10	Aston Villa	42	14	3	4	34	22	3	6	12	25	39	-2	60
11	Watford	42	9	7	5	36	31	7	2	12	32	46	-9	57
12	Ipswich Town	42	11	4	6	34	23	4	4	13	21	34	-2	53
13	Sunderland	42	8	9	4	26	18	5	4	12	16	35	-11	52
14	Norwich City	42	9	8	4	34	20	3	7	11	14	29	-1	51
15	Leicester City	42	11	5	5	40	30	2	7	12	25	38	-3	51
16	Luton Town	42	7	5	9	30	33	7	4	10	23	33	-13	51
17	WBA	42	10	4	7	30	25	4	5	12	18	37	-14	51
18	Stoke City	42	11	4	6	30	23	2	7	12	14	40	-19	50
19	Coventry City	42	8	5	8	33	33	5	6	10	24	44	-20	50
20	Birmingham City	42	7	7	7	19	18	5	5	11	20	32	-11	48
21	Notts County	42	6	7	8	31	36	4	4	13	19	36	-22	41
22	Wolves	42	4	8	9	15	28	2	3	16	12	52	-53	29

Games for the 1983/1984 season

(The number after date is league position after the game)

1	20.08.1983		L	0-2	Manchester United, Wembley, Charity Shield
2	27.08.1983	10	D	1-1	Wolves, Molineux, 1st Division
3	31.08.1983	7	W	1-0	Norwich City, Carrow Road, 1st Division
4	03.09.1983	3	W	1-0	Nottingham Forest, Anfield, 1st Division
5	06.09.1983	5	D	1-1	Southampton, Anfield, 1st Division
6	10.09.1983	4	W	2-0	Arsenal, Highbury, 1st Division
7	14.09.1983		W	1-0	Odense Boldklub, Odense Stadion, European Cup 1st R 1st L
8	17.09.1983	3	W	2-1	Aston Villa, Anfield, 1st Division
9	24.09.1983	4	L	0-1	Manchester United, Old Trafford, 1st Division
10	28.09.1983		W	5-0	Odense Boldklub, Anfield, European Cup 1st R 2nd L
11	01.10.1983	6	L	0-1	Sunderland, Anfield, 1st Division

12	05.10.1983		W	4-1	Brentford, Griffin Park, League Cup 2nd round 1L
13	15.10.1983	5	W	3-1	West Ham United, Upton Park, 1st Division
14	19.10.1983		D	0-0	Athletic Bilbao, Anfield, European Cup 2nd R 1st L
15	22.10.1983	2	W	1-0	Queens Park Rangers, Loftus Road, 1st Division
16	25.10.1983		W	4-0	Brentford, Anfield, League Cup 2nd round 2L
17	29.10.1983	2	W	6-0	Luton Town, Anfield, 1st Division
18	02.11.1983		W	1-0	Athletic Bilbao, San Mames, European Cup 2nd R 2L
19	06.11.1983	1	W	3-0	Everton, Anfield, 1st Division
20	08.11.1983		D	1-1	Fulham, Craven Cottage, League Cup 3rd round
21	12.11.1983	1	D	2-2	Tottenham Hotspur, White Hart Lane, 1st Division
22	19.11.1983	1	W	1-0	Stoke City, Anfield, 1st Division
23	22.11.1983		D	1-1	Fulham, Anfield, League Cup 3rd round replay
24	26.11.1983	1	D	1-1	Ipswich Town, Portman Road, 1st Division
25	29.11.1983		W	1-0	Fulham, Craven Cottage, League Cup 3rd R. 2nd replay
26	03.12.1983	1	W	1-0	Birmingham City, Anfield, 1st Division
27	10.12.1983	1	L	0-4	Coventry City, Highfield Road, 1st Division
28	17.12.1983	1	W	5-0	Notts County, Anfield, 1st Division
29	20.12.1983		D	1-1	Birmingham City, St. Andrew's, League Cup 4th round
30	22.12.1983		W	3-0	Birmingham City, Anfield, League Cup 4th round R
31	26.12.1983	1	W	2-1	West Bromwich Albion, The Hawthorns, 1st Division
32	27.12.1983	1	D	2-2	Leicester City, Anfield, 1st Division
33	31.12.1983	1	W	1-0	Nottingham Forest, City Ground, 1st Division
34	02.01.1984	1	D	1-1	Manchester United, Anfield, 1st Division
35	06.01.1984		W	4-0	Newcastle United, Anfield, FA Cup 3rd round
36	14.01.1984	1	L	0-1	Wolves, Anfield, 1st Division
37	17.01.1984		D	2-2	Sheffield Wednesday, Hillsborough, League Cup 5th round
38	20.01.1984	1	W	3-1	Aston Villa, Villa Park, 1st Division
39	25.01.1984		W	3-0	Sheffield Wednesday, Anfield, League Cup 5th round R
40	29.01.1984		L	0-2	Brighton & Hove Albion, Goldstone Ground, FA Cup 4th round
41	01.02.1984	1	W	3-0	Watford, Anfield, 1st Division
42	04.02.1984	1	D	0-0	Sunderland, Roker Park, 1st Division
43	07.02.1984		D	2-2	Walsall, Anfield, League Cup Semi-final 1L
44	11.02.1984	1	W	2-1	Arsenal, Anfield, 1st Division

45	14.02.1984		W	2-0	Walsall, Fellows Park, League Cup Semi-final 2L
46	18.02.1984	1	D	0-0	Luton Town, Kenilworth Road, 1st Division
47	25.02.1984	1	W	2-0	Queens Park Rangers, Anfield, 1st Division
48	03.03.1984	1	D	1-1	Everton, Goodison Park, 1st Division
49	07.03.1984		W	1-0	Benfica, Anfield, European Cup 3rd R 1st L
50	10.03.1984	1	W	3-1	Tottenham Hotspur, Anfield, 1st Division
51	16.03.1984	1	L	0-2	Southampton, The Dell, 1st Division
52	21.03.1984		W	4-1	Benfica, Estadio da Luz, European Cup 3rd R 2nd L
53	25.03.1984		D	0-0	Everton, Wembley, League Cup Final
54	28.03.1984		W	1-0	Everton, Maine Road, League Cup Final replay
55	31.03.1984	1	W	2-0	Watford, Vicarage Road, 1st Division
56	07.04.1984	1	W	6-0	West Ham United, Anfield, 1st Division
57	11.04.1984		W	1-0	Dinamo Bucharest, Anfield, Eur. Cup Semi Final 1st L
58	14.04.1984	1	L	0-2	Stoke City, Victoria Ground, 1st Division
59	18.04.1984	1	D	3-3	Leicester City, Filbert Street, 1st Division
60	21.04.1984	1	W	3-0	West Bromwich Albion, Anfield, 1st Division
61	25.04.1984		W	2-1	Dinamo Bucharest, 23 August Stadium, Eur. Cup Semi Final 2nd L
62	28.04.1984	1	D	2-2	Ipswich Town, Anfield, 1st Division
63	05.05.1984	1	D	0-0	Birmingham City, St. Andrew's, 1st Division
64	07.05.1984	1	W	5-0	Coventry City, Anfield, 1st Division
65	12.05.1984	1	D	0-0	Notts County, Meadow Lane, 1st Division
66	15.05.1984	1	D	1-1	Norwich City, Anfield, 1st Division
67	30.05.1984		D	1-1	Roma, Stadio Olimpico, European Cup Final

Friendlies

1	03.08.1983	L	3-4	Manchester United, Windsor Park, Testimonial*
2	05.08.1983	D	0-0	Hamburg SV, Rotterdam, Rotterdam Tournament
3	07.08.1983	D	3-3	Feyenoord, Rotterdam, Rotterdam Tournament
4	10.08.1983	W	3-1	WAC Morocco, Stade Mohamed V, Testimonial**
5	12.08.1983	L	1-2	Atletico Madrid, Estadio Municipal, La Linea Tournament
6	14.08.1983	W	3-2	Dinamo Bucharest, Estadio Municipal, La Linea Tournament
7	17.05.1984	D	2-2	Newcastle United, St. James' Park, Testimonial***
8	22.05.1984	W	4-1	Israel, Bloomfield Stadium, Friendly

*Testimonial for long serving Irish FA officer Billy Drennan
**Testimonial for former Moroccan international Larbi Aherdane
***Farewell match for Kevin Keegan

Appearances for the 1983/1984 season

Name	League	FA Cup	LC	EC	Other	Total
Bruce Grobbelaar	42	2	13	9	1	67
Alan Hansen	42	2	13	9	1	67
Alan Kennedy	42	2	13	9	1	67
Sammy Lee	42	2	13	9	1	67
Mark Lawrenson	42	2	12	9	1	66
Ian Rush	41	2	12	9	1	65
Phil Neal	41	2	12	8	1	64
Graeme Souness	37	2	12	9	1	61
Craig Johnston	29	2	12	8	1	52
Kenny Dalglish	33	0	8	9	1	51
Michael Robinson	24	2	9	6	1	42
Steve Nicol	23	2	9	4	0	38
Ronnie Whelan	23	1	5	5	0	34
David Hodgson	5	0	4	2	1	12
John Wark	9	0	0	0	0	9
Gary Gillespie	0	0	1	0	0	1
Phil Thompson	0	0	0	0	1	1
John McGregor	0	0	0	0	0	0
Bob Bolder	0	0	0	0	0	0
David West	0	0	0	0	0	0
Jim Beglin	0	0	0	0	0	0

Goalscorers for the 1983/1984 season

Name	League	FA Cup	LC	EC	Total
Ian Rush	32	2	8	5	47
Graeme Souness	7	0	5	0	12
Kenny Dalglish	7	0	2	3	12
Michael Robinson	6	1	3	2	12
Ronnie Whelan	4	0	3	2	9
Steve Nicol	5	0	2	0	7
Craig Johnston	2	1	0	1	4
Own goals	2	0	0	1	3
Phil Neal	1	0	1	1	3
Sammy Lee	2	0	0	1	3
John Wark	2	0	0	0	2
Alan Kennedy	2	0	0	0	2
Alan Hansen	1	0	0	0	1
David Hodgson	0	0	1	0	1

The squad during the 1983/1984 season

Bruce Grobbelaar, Goalkeeper
Bob Bolder, Goalkeeper
Alan Kennedy, Defender
Mark Lawrenson, Defender
Phil Thompson, Defender
Phil Neal, Defender
Alan Hansen, Defender
Gary Gillespie, Defender
John McGregor, Defender
Jim Beglin, Defender
John Wark, Midfielder
Kenny Dalglish, Midfielder
Ronnie Whelan, Midfielder
Sammy Lee, Midfielder
Graeme Souness, Midfielder
Steve Nicol, Midfielder
Craig Johnston, Midfielder
David Hodgson, Striker
Michael Robinson, Striker
Ian Rush, Striker
David West, Striker

Transfers for the 1983/1984 season

In:
David West, Dorchester Town, £15,000, 1983
Gary Gillespie, Coventry City, £325,000, 8 July 1983
Bob Bolder, Sheffield Wednesday, £125,000, 8 August 1983
Michael Robinson, Brighton & Hove Albion, £200,000, 8 August 1983
Ken De Mange, Home Farm, Unknown, 8 August 1983
Brian Mooney, Home Farm, £20,000, 15 August 1983
John Wark, Ipswich Town, £475,000, 10 March 1984
Paul Walsh, Luton Town, £700,000, 17 May 1984

Out:
Alan Harper, Everton, £100,000, 1 June 1983

A collection of statistics for the 1983/1984 season

The season in numbers:
Total games: 67
Games won: 37
Games drawn: 22
Games lost: 8
Clean sheets – League: 20
Clean sheets – Overall: 34
Total goals: 118
Average attendance at home – League: 32,021
Average attendance at home – Overall: 30,290
Average goals per game – League: 2.38
Average goals per game – Overall: 2.39
Average goal minute – League: 46
Average goal minute – Overall: 47

Goals split down to competitions:
League – 73
League Cup – 25
European Cup – 16
FA Cup – 4
Charity Shield – 0

Player debuts:
Michael Robinson against Manchester United on 20.08.1983
Gary Gillespie against Walsall on 07.02.1984
John Wark against Watford on 31.03.1984

Statistics and information provided by LFChistory.net

16 : DOUBLE DELIGHT

1985/86

FAGAN NOW FACED THE PROSPECT OF HAVING TO live up to expectations – both his own and the fans' – after such a dream start to his managerial career.

However, the omens were not good as his skipper and one of the strongest characters in the side, Graeme Souness, had left for Italy. When Souness joined Sampdoria in June 1984, Michael Robinson noted "it was as if we'd lost three players". Souness was now gone and with Dalglish's effectiveness starting to wane, Liverpool were approaching a crossroads, especially as Souness had not been adequately replaced and nobody had been brought in who could eventually take over from Dalglish. Players of their worth, their sheer quality, are not easily discovered and if they were not such rarities, their names wouldn't be mentioned in such awed tones decades later.

In the summer of 1984, midfield maestro Jan Mølby was signed from Ajax for £200,000 and Kevin MacDonald joined ranks from Leicester in November. As well as Souness, David Hodgson and Michael Robinson moved on to seek pastures new at Sunderland and Queens Park Rangers respectively.

Phil Thompson, now 31, eventually brought the curtain down on

438

a wonderful playing career at Anfield by agreeing to join Sheffield United in March 1985 after being on loan at Bramall Lane for four months. Thompson left his beloved Reds as one of the greatest characters who has graced Liverpool's shirt and as one of the most decorated players in English football history.

Bob Paisley's first signing, Phil Neal, took over captaincy duties as Liverpool made a terrible start to the 1984/85 season. As if Souness' absence from midfield wasn't bad enough, goal machine Ian Rush didn't feature until October because of injury. At the end of October, the European champions were in 20th place, only two places from rock bottom (two wins, five draws, four losses). By December, Liverpool had moved to 10th, but in the end couldn't catch Everton who won the title by a country mile and the Reds finished runners-up. On a brighter note, Fagan's purchase from the previous season, John Wark, had come into his own and finished as Liverpool's top scorer with 27 goals in all competitions from midfield.

Three months before the 1985 European Cup final in Brussels, Fagan, at the time of his 64th birthday, had announced to members of the club's hierarchy that he was contemplating retirement. He was tired, and the job had taken its toll.

He would make a final decision at the end of the season but it was widely accepted that he would be stepping down. In a Brussels hotel room, on the eve of that ill-fated game, chairman John Smith called a board meeting. The directors were informed that Fagan would be retiring after the game and that 34-year-old Dalglish would be taking over as the club's first player-manager with Bob Paisley as his advisor. Fagan told his players before the game that after the match they could call him just 'Joe' instead of 'Boss'.

The week before the European Cup final against Juventus, Dalglish received a phone call from Peter Robinson who asked if he and John

Smith could pay him a visit. Dalglish describes what then happened in his autobiography: "I thought the conversation was going to finish then but Peter added, 'Don't you want to know what we want to see you for?' 'Yes,' I replied, 'If you want to tell me'. 'Well, we'd like to offer you the manager's job'. 'That's no problem, Peter, you can still come to the house'."

On the flight back to Liverpool from Brussels, Dalglish informed Ronnie Moran and Roy Evans that he wanted them to carry on with their jobs. It wasn't a difficult decision for Dalglish to make as he had been under their tutelage for eight years: "I trusted Ronnie and Roy implicitly. They were totally honest, loyal men who'd never be stool-pigeons in the dressing room. Ronnie and Roy watched us like hawks, scrutinising every move and word. I know modern day clubs use technology to chart performances in training but I'd back the eyes of Ronnie and Roy ahead of anyone's computer."

Hooliganism destroyed the 1985 European Cup final and it was heartbreaking for Joe Fagan to retire under such tragic circumstances. Fagan's sadness was for everyone to see, weeping on Roy Evans' shoulder as he disembarked from the team's plane at Speke airport.

It was a great pity that one of the Boot Room's original members had had the chance to bow out at the top but then suffered a fate far worse than he could have expected. In his mind, as the plane touched down in Belgium, defeat would have been the worst conceivable outcome but the far more significant loss of 39 opposing fans turned the whole experience in an evening that was about as sour as it could possibly get.

Liverpool returned to England in the middle of a media frenzy and held a press conference later that day presenting Dalglish as the new boss. John Smith told the gathering: "Kenny is entering the managerial side for the first time and we have every reason to believe he will have a successful period in office. We feel we have a man of great ability on the field who has got an old head on young shoulders."

Dalglish's appointment was a popular one amongst the players. Danish midfielder Mølby said: "I think a lot of people within the club once Joe Fagan announced he was going to leave thought his natural successor was going to be Phil Neal. Dalglish's appointment was a masterstroke by the club. We were all a bit wary because Kenny was one of those players who you never got to know and he always kept you at a little bit of a distance. But I have to say, from my own point of view, Kenny becoming manager, was great for me."

Peter Robinson later told the *Daily Express* how the decision was made to appoint Fagan's successor: "When Joe told us he wanted to finish, the chairman (John Smith) appointed a sub-committee of four people – I don't think this has ever been said – comprising himself, myself, Bob Paisley and Tom Saunders. Tom was little-known but had made a tremendous contribution over the years and was youth development officer. We had a situation with that little committee where we all knew Kenny Dalglish in different ways, we had all dealt with him in different ways. We did discuss it at length, it wasn't an immediate decision and at the end of the day we came down unanimously in favour of Kenny. In life you either get decisions right or wrong and that was one we got right."

In August 1985, the world of football was still in a state of shock following events at Heysel Stadium three months earlier. The tragedy which struck the European Cup final between Liverpool and Italian giants Juventus resulted in an indefinite ban on English clubs playing in Europe with the Reds being ordered to serve at least an extra three years before being re-admitted.

Dalglish had a hard task facing him. Not only did he have to follow in the footsteps of another successful Anfield boss, he also needed to win back the League Championship Liverpool had lost to Everton the previous season, which had been barren in terms of trophies won.

On the eve of the opening game of the 1985/86 campaign Dalglish refused to make predictions on the forthcoming campaign. "It's an important season, but it's always an important season," he said. "This is no different from any other. I've been reasonably happy with the way things have gone and the lads have certainly worked very hard. How will we do? We'll just have to wait and see."

Arsenal were the first team to put his managerial qualities to the test on August 17. The Scot picked himself and selected full-back Jim Beglin for a left midfield role. After 36 minutes the Irishman played his part in the first goal, crossing accurately for Ronnie Whelan to head home. Soon after the hour mark, Steve Nicol converted Dalglish's low cross, and although the Reds were grateful to goalkeeper Bruce Grobbelaar for two spectacular saves, their new player-manager had begun his new job with a home win.

Mark Lawrenson recalls Liverpool's first game of the new season: "It was our first competitive outing since Heysel and it felt like the whole world press had turned up. I remember coming back in after that game and just feeling completely drained. Press who had turned up from places like Japan had made us feel like the proverbial goldfish. Yet, after that game it did get better, but certainly leading up to it, I don't think I have ever been more nervous before a game before, and that's including European Cups, league title deciders and FA Cup finals."

Ronnie Moran was delighted to have been kept on and had to make the adjustment of stopping shouting at Kenny in training to calling him 'boss'. "Myself and Roy just carried on as normal and Kenny was great to get on with," Moran said. "As Kenny was still a player, he still went through the mill every day with all the other players and did everything the other players did. And we just carried on with our same training routines. Kenny took the team meetings and we helped him pick the team, but Kenny would always have the final say. Regarding making subs when Kenny was on the pitch – Roy and I had a thing going with him. If he wanted someone substituted, he would give us a signal. And if we from the bench thought somebody needed to come off, we would have a word with him on the quiet at half-time or get a message to him during the second half.

"Even with himself, if we ever thought he needed to come off, we'd tell him and we wouldn't have to worry about anything."

Dalglish was equally happy with Moran's work, who was now in his 36th year at the club: "The contribution and help Bugsy gave me was enormous and I am eternally grateful for him, both as a player and as a manager. I don't think anybody that worked with him during his spell at Liverpool will have anything but total admiration, respect and gratitude for what he did for them. I don't think it's a coincidence that in the most successful spell in the club's history, Ronnie Moran was of great importance."

Liverpool's first away game of the 1985/86 season ended in a 2-2 midweek draw at Villa Park with Ian Rush missing an 88th-minute penalty to deny Dalglish maximum points from his opening two games in charge.

Unlike the Arsenal game, Dalglish left himself out of the squad altogether and in his place selected Paul Walsh. Dalglish believed that a team built for the future must learn to operate without him. However, former Liverpool striker Ian St John was of the opinion that Kenny should continue for as long as he could: "I believe he should keep playing, until his legs give up, because he will find that his playing days were his best days in the game and once a player stops playing altogether – that's when the worries start." St John added: "What Kenny will have to come to terms with is criticism, simply because he has been such a good player that he hasn't received any, but as a manager you can't avoid it. Criticism comes from various quarters and it's something that nobody likes and can be very difficult to accept, especially as a young manager."

The following Saturday, Dalglish and his players suffered their first defeat of the season at St. James' Park. Dalglish was replaced in the 35th minute after a nasty leg gash, which needed four stitches. He was clearly downhearted and he seemed to require a major physical effort to speak when asked about the game. Someone inquired whether anyone else was injured and his brief reply – "only their pride" – summed up his thoughts.

After tricky away trips at Villa and Newcastle, Liverpool returned to Anfield to face Ipswich Town for a Monday afternoon fixture.

The home crowd knew that nothing but a win was needed as early league leaders Manchester United were already five points ahead of the Reds after taking nine points from their first three games. The Anfield faithful weren't disappointed as their team ran out rampant 5-0 winners. Roy Hayes of the *Liverpool Daily Post* wrote: "Kenny Dalglish's call for an improved performance from his players was answered in tremendous style as Liverpool went on an Anfield goal romp against Ipswich. He didn't hide his disappointment after Liverpool's lacklustre defeat at Newcastle, on Saturday, but the Reds put 'a Cheshire cat' smile back on his face with as ruthless a display as you're likely to see this season."

On September 12, former Everton hard man Steve McMahon became Dalglish's first signing as the Scot wanted to bolster his midfield with a player of similar qualities to Graeme Souness.

Liverpool paid Aston Villa £350,000 for McMahon's services,

their second attempt at securing the Scouser's signature. When neighbours Everton sold McMahon in 1983 in a £300,000 deal, the Halewood-born midfielder admitted that he turned down a double-your-money offer from Liverpool. He recalls: "I had already agreed to go to Villa and I was ready to sign the contract when I got a call from Liverpool telling me they wanted to sign me. People say I was greedy and left Everton for the money. I didn't because Liverpool offered me more. They actually said, 'What have Villa offered you?' I told them the package, which at the time was a lot of dough, and they said, 'We'll double that, no problem'." McMahon politely declined their offer and told them that for personal and family reasons he didn't dare do the virtually impossible and move straight from the blue half of Liverpool to the red.

McMahon made his debut in Liverpool's following game at Oxford which was to be Alan Kennedy's 359th and last game for the club.

Unfortunately, Kennedy scored an own goal with his last touch for the club. Kennedy later shared with *LFChistory.net* his memories from that afternoon at the Manor Ground: "Oxford United in those days had some good players, John Aldridge and Ray Houghton to name a couple. I've never been able to forget the own goal I scored during my last game. The ball was played down the middle and Aldo, who scored their first goal, was chasing after me and the ball. I got to it first and instead of putting it wide of the goal, I put it towards the middle of the goal. Well, Bruce expected that I was going to play it wide, so he left his goal to collect it and it goes in the back of the net. Two apiece, a minute to go, no chance of recovery. Kenny wasn't happy and came into the dressing room to have a go at me, and while he was there, he had a go at Paul Walsh for whatever reason. That was my last ever game for Liverpool. I knew I had to go as I knew it was going to be impossible to keep my place in the team. The youngster will always win against the older player. It's never nice when it happens, when somebody says to you that, 'You aren't good enough anymore'. Jim Beglin was coming in to take my position and I had to accept it. I ended up going to Sunderland and my career went downhill after that I'm afraid."

Liverpool had made a steady start to the season and after eight games they lay in fourth place, one point behind Everton and Arsenal. Top of the table were Ron Atkinson's Manchester United, who were taking the First Division by storm with some attractive and entertaining football. They had taken maximum points from their eight fixtures, and eight points already separated them from the Toffees and the Gunners.

After English clubs were banned from European competitions early in the year, the Football League created a consolation competition for them named the ScreenSport Super Cup as a form of financial and sporting compensation.

Six clubs, including Liverpool, had qualified for Europe for the 1985/86 season. Everton would have been in the European Cup, Liverpool, Southampton and Tottenham had qualified for the UEFA Cup via the league, Norwich as League Cup winners, while Manchester United would have been in the Cup Winners' Cup.

The teams were split into two groups of three with each side playing each other twice, before the top two from each group went through to a two-leg semi-final, followed by a two-leg final. Rumour had it that Everton and Liverpool were kept apart in the draw, meaning that Group One consisted of Everton, United and Norwich and Liverpool, Southampton and Tottenham made up Group Two. The Reds were comfortable throughout the group stages.

Liverpool's first game in the newly created competition was on September 17 when they beat Southampton 2-1 and then Tottenham 2-0 in front of minuscule crowds at Anfield, and their only dropped points came away to Saints, who held them to a 1-1 draw in early December.

On September 21, Dalglish's men featured in one of the most thrilling derby matches for years at Goodison Park. Dalglish opted to recall himself to the Reds' line-up after an absence of five league games, skipper Phil Neal was relegated to substitute and Alan Hansen took over as captain.

With just 20 seconds on the clock, Dalglish justified his selection by hitting a vicious curling shot into the corner of the net to send the 51,509 fans present into two differing types of extreme emotion. After 17 minutes, Liverpool increased their lead when Ian Rush and Ronnie Whelan interchanged passes on a counter attack. Whelan slipped the ball back and the lethal Welsh striker netted comfortably.

Just before half-time, the rampant Reds struck yet again, with a goal which particularly hurt Evertonians because it was scored by Steve McMahon, a former Blues favourite. McMahon began the move himself which led to his goal with a crossfield ball to Whelan. Jim Beglin and Dalglish continued the attack, the manager dragging the ball back from near the corner flag for McMahon to hammer past Neville Southall from 30 yards.

Everton clearly had problems and manager Howard Kendall made a bold decision to replace inexperienced centre-back Ian Marshall with forward Adrian Heath at the interval. Everton almost achieved the impossible, as Graeme Sharp and Gary Lineker replied, but time ran out for a third Everton goal and the game ended 3-2, handing Dalglish his first away win of the season.

A week after the Everton success, Mølby struck two penalties, adding to goals by Mark Lawrenson and Ian Rush, as Liverpool beat Tottenham Hotspur 4-1 at Anfield. Seven days later the Reds set off for London, searching for their third consecutive win on Queens Park Rangers' controversial artificial pitch. After nine minutes it looked as if it would come their way when Paul Walsh, in for Dalglish, gave them the lead but goals from Terry Fenwick and Gary Bannister brought the home side all the points.

On the same day, table-toppers Manchester United, already being proclaimed champions by the media, drew at Luton, thus failing to equal Tottenham's First Division record of 11 straight victories.

By October 19, United were 10 points clear with Chelsea, Arsenal, Sheffield Wednesday and Everton all closing in on Liverpool's second place. That day more than 54,000 packed Old Trafford to witness the clash between the league's highest-placed teams. The Reds were deprived of Dalglish and Walsh, who had both suffered training injuries, and so fielded only one recognised striker in Ian Rush. After a goalless first half, Craig Johnston put Liverpool ahead 18 seconds into the restart, a deserved reward for their early dominance and for a man who won the man-of-the-match award with tenacity in midfield and adventurous forward play. It was the first home league goal conceded at Old Trafford that season and more seemed set to follow. The few chances created in a fiercely contested game fell primarily to Liverpool. Then after 64 minutes came United's salvation.

Mark Lawrenson, Liverpool's stylish defender, got a bad bouncing ball in the way of an attempted clearance. McGrath saw the chance before most and as the ball broke, he thundered in to almost crack an upright as he drove in the equaliser. Liverpool proved their point that the title race was far from over in dramatic fashion.

A few months into his first season as player-manager, Dalglish told Scottish television about how he had adapted to his new position: "I think it was easier for the players to adjust than me as I had always enjoyed the dressing room banter and being one of the lads. But unfortunately, when you become manager the lads put up an invisible barrier between themselves and the manager. It was just to be expected, because I did the same when I was a player with the managers I had. Although I was always friendly and corporative with them, there was always that little barrier that never came down.

"I'm just going to try my very best and if I'm not good enough, I'm not good enough, and I'll be the first to judge myself if I'm good enough or not. I've got the same attitude to this job that I had as a player; give the club my very best and hope that I become successful."

On October 25, Dalglish paid £40,000 for 6ft 3in goalkeeper Mike Hooper to replace reserve Bob Bolder, who had been sold to Sunderland earlier in the month. After impressing with Fourth Division Wrexham, as well as receiving a degree in English Literature at Swansea University, Hooper joined ranks as Bruce Grobbelaar's understudy who hadn't missed a game for four years.

Dalglish featured 10 times in Liverpool's opening 20 games and scored three goals but Mark Lawrenson later revealed that he encountered some awkward moments whilst playing alongside his manager: "Me and Alan Hansen used to have rows with Kenny on the pitch, terrible rows, really personal attacks on each other. When we played the ball up to him and he didn't receive it exactly where he wanted it then he would slaughter us. Hansen and I would slaughter him back to protect each other. After the final whistle I would be slightly worried about what Kenny was going to be thinking, as he's the manager. However, he would say, 'Whatever happens on the pitch, as long as we get the right result then it doesn't matter'. That's the way he was and that's how he endeared himself to everybody."

Five successive league wins, plus a 2-1 home Milk Cup triumph over Manchester United, followed for Liverpool as the Reds entered

November. Jan Mølby scored both Liverpool goals against rivals United that night. The Great Dane's first was a magnificent solo effort 10 minutes into the second half, which is considered as one of the greatest goals ever scored at the Kop end. Mølby's devasting run started on the halfway line and ended with a thumping drive of such ferocity that goalkeeper Gary Bailey could hardly have seen it whistle past. However, nobody outside the ground would have been able to witness his masterpiece. Financial disagreements between the Football League hierarchy and the broadcasters had led to no televised football been shown in England during the first few months of the season.

After the game, Mølby admitted he had made a bet with his good friend and fellow Dane, Jesper Olsen, on the season's outcome: "At full time, as we were coming off the pitch, he was giving me some stick. He was saying that the league was already over to which I replied, 'We will see'. So, we had a little bet, it was only a few pounds, but I said, 'I don't know if we will win the league, but we'll definitely finish above you'. And he said, 'No chance'."

The gap at the top of the First Division was starting to close and while Liverpool were winning 3-0 at Coventry City on November 9, the Mancunians were crashing to their first league defeat − 1-0 away to improving Sheffield Wednesday. By the end of the month, United were only two points ahead of the Reds, with West Ham emerging as serious title contenders, lying only three points behind the Merseysiders.

The coaching staff at Liverpool always had plenty of goals to savour but on one occasion they had to keep their celebrations to a minimum. The Reds were looking to expand their unbeaten run to 10 games at St. Andrew's on November 23. Prior to the game, the Liverpool bench had been asked by the police not to come out of the dugout if they scored because away team staff had had objects thrown at them in previous games.

In the 10th minute, Craig Johnston burst into the box on the right side and crossed hard and low for Ian Rush to make it 1-0; cue the celebrations! Ronnie Moran couldn't get up and celebrate so he joyfully punched Roy Evans on the thigh and gave him a dead leg instead. Sixteen minutes later, Mølby's free-kick on the left found its way to Paul Walsh who headed in from close range. A big scuffle seemed to break out on the bench as staff tried to hit each other on the legs.

Dalglish's men maintained their championship challenge with a 3-0 home win over Aston Villa on December 7 but they then suddenly hit a bad patch and went five league matches without a victory.

On December 18, loyal servant Phil Neal, whose last senior league outing was from the bench on November 9 at Highfield Road, joined Third Division strugglers Bolton Wanderers, as player-manager. Neal had made an incredible 650 appearances, nearly all at right-back, before losing his place to the younger Steve Nicol.

Neal, who was called 'Zico' by supporters because of the number of goals he scored as a defender, won a League Championship medal in his first full season at Anfield in 1975/76, something he would achieve on no less than eight occasions. He also played in six European club finals for Liverpool and was the only member of the 1977 European Cup-winning side in Rome to return there seven years later for a similar but much sterner test against the Italian champions.

Liverpool's final game of 1985 came against Nottingham Forest in a 1-1 draw at the City Ground and Dalglish summed up a festive period that had only given his team three points from 15: "When we lost to Arsenal at Highbury on December 14, we played badly, we started badly and we lost two bad goals. Against Man City, at Maine Road, on Boxing Day, their manager, Billy McNeill, had to introduce his players to the ball at half-time. We had so much of the play but we couldn't score. Over Christmas, we were playing well enough, but we weren't getting the results we obviously would have liked."

Liverpool's sticky period ended on January 12, 1986, when they beat Watford 3-2 at Vicarage Road. However, they were still five points behind Manchester United, having played a game more, and level on points and matches with second-placed Everton. But Chelsea and West Ham, who were also right up there, had two games in hand. The Hammers were the visitors to Anfield on January 19, knowing that striker Ian Rush needed just one goal to register his 100th in the league for the Reds.

Gary Gillespie and John Wark replaced the injured Kevin Mac-Donald and Steve McMahon for the crunch fixture, and helped the home side take a controversial lead in the 58th minute. Alvin Martin tussled with Paul Walsh just inside the box and referee George Tyson awarded a penalty, which Mølby tucked away to Phil Parkes' right. Nine minutes later, after Craig Johnston had showed good skill on the right side of the area, Rush knocked in the goal he had been looking for and became the ninth player to score 100 league goals for the Reds. Soon after, the Welshman combined with Wark to set up the in-form Walsh and he banged in the third. Dickens' reply for West Ham was purely academic.

At the beginning of February, with well over half of the season gone, Bob Paisley, Dalglish's mentor, reflected on the Scot's time so far as player-manager: "Kenny is Kenny and he has got his own thoughts about the game. I'm just on the sidelines, for whenever he wants to talk about anything, but he's running the show and picking the teams and if there's anything that I might think that could be an obstacle for him, I'll give him a little warning. But he's certainly his own man. The great players have not got a great record as managers," Paisley added. "Let's hope that isn't the case with Kenny. Things can go adrift; you get a couple of injuries and then you are suddenly struggling. But Kenny has certainly got the knowledge to persevere with players, as I think that's the failing many other players have suffered when they became a manager – they didn't have the patience."

February proved to be a disappointing month for the Reds and doubts about their ability to challenge for the title began to increase. After losing 2-1 at Ipswich they played host to Manchester United in a Sunday fixture. Liverpool hadn't beaten Untied in the league at Anfield since Boxing Day, 1979. Colin Gibson put the visitors ahead but John Wark capped a fine game with an equaliser, five minutes before half-time. Safe keeping by Chris Turner and Liverpool's inability to cash in on their chances meant they had to settle for a draw. After 31 minutes Paul Walsh was substituted due to a Kevin Moran tackle which ruptured his ankle ligaments and consequently ruined his season. It was a crying shame for Walsh who had firmly established himself in the first team and had already scored 18 goals in 30 games.

Two weeks later, on February 22, the Reds entertained Everton, in a match which was billed as a title decider. More than 45,000 spectators crammed into Anfield to see the Blues gain a 2-0 revenge for their September derby defeat. Fifteen minutes from time they opened the scoring through captain Kevin Ratcliffe, who saw his tame, long-range shot sneak under Bruce Grobbelaar's body. Gary Lineker added a second and Liverpool's title aspirations were all but over. The defending champions thus went three points ahead of Manchester United, who had a game in hand. Liverpool lay third, eight points adrift of Everton and level on points with Chelsea, though the Londoners had played three matches less. West Ham, with four games in hand on Everton, were nine points behind.

It was rough luck on Grobbelaar, who was nursing an elbow injury, and had made two superb saves to keep his side in the match. But the extrovert Zimbabwean was going through a dodgy spell, having fumbled a shot from York City's Tony Canham earlier that week, pushing the Reds' fifth round FA Cup tie into extra-time. But Grobbelaar was not the only one to receive criticism. One critic of Dalglish's team was none other than his newly appointed captain Alan Hansen, who later proclaimed: "At the end of February, there were 12 games to go and we were a long way behind Everton, who had just beat us and we went for dinner that night and I said to Kenny, 'This is the worst Liverpool side I've ever played in', to which he replied, 'The team spirit is still good and if we can go on a run then I think we can win something'. I said, 'You've got to be joking, this team won't win anything'."

Dalglish was right and Hansen was wrong as from March, Liverpool silenced their critics by winning 11 and drawing one of their final 12 league games, conceding only four goals in the process. It all started at Tottenham on Sunday, March 2, after it seemed they were going to fall further behind in the Championship race. Another Grobbelaar error, where he misjudged Glenn Hoddle's corner, palming the ball in the air, allowed Chris Waddle to give Spurs the lead. But as the contest wore on, the Reds became stronger. Mølby rifled in an equaliser in the 66th minute and Ian Rush then scored a typical goal in the dying seconds. Rush was delighted to score the winning goal, not only to give the team maximum points, but also for his flustered goalkeeper: "Bruce was the most relieved man in the ground when I scored the goal. I'm glad for him that I got the winner."

Three days later, Liverpool crashed out of the Milk Cup semi-final, drawing at home to Queens Park Rangers and so failing to reverse the one-goal handicap suffered in the first leg. This loss deprived Liverpool of a place in the final and a possible clean sweep of the three domestic titles. During the first leg at Loftus Road, 19-year-old, Bootle-born defender, Mark Seagraves deputised for the injured Gary Gillespie. Three days after that, Anfield was again the stage as the two teams met in the league. This time Dalglish wore the number seven shirt and the Reds made no mistake, trouncing the London side 4-1.

Other home wins in Liverpool's run-in included a 6-0 thrashing of Oxford United and a 5-0 defeat of Coventry, where Ronnie Whelan scored a hat-trick. After that encounter the Reds found themselves sitting on top of the table, level on points with Everton, who had played a match less. Chelsea, with a game in hand, were six points behind and Manchester United five. But on paper the biggest threat came from West Ham United. They trailed Liverpool by seven points but knew that if they won their three matches in hand, they could overtake them. The battle for the First Division crown was now wide open but Everton and Liverpool, lying neck and neck in the table while also trying to set up the first all-Merseyside FA Cup final, were both chasing their first Double, proving once again that the city was dominating English football.

Liverpool scored three or more goals on 23 occasions during the 1985/86 season, as happened on April 26, as Birmingham visited Anfield. The *Football Echo* reported: "Liverpool made sure of going into the last week of the championship on top of the First Division by giving relegated Birmingham a real hammering at Anfield before a near full house this afternoon. Defender Gary Gillespie had an afternoon to remember. Brought back after injury at the expense of Mark Lawrenson, the tall defender scored two goals in less than 15 minutes at the start of the second half, to put Liverpool's victory beyond doubt. Gillespie completed his hat-trick from the penalty spot, by popular request after Rush had been brought down."

By the evening of April 26, Manchester United and Chelsea were no longer Championship contenders, leaving the Reds, Blues and Hammers to fight it out. Liverpool had two games remaining, Everton three, and West Ham four. It was on Wednesday, April 30 when the title was practically won, and lost. Goals from Ian Rush and Ronnie Whelan gave Liverpool a 2-0 win at Leicester, as Everton went down 1-0 at lowly Oxford United.

Kenny Dalglish's troops needed a last-match victory over Chelsea, three days later, to clinch the League Championship. Everton and West Ham, meanwhile, were ready to take advantage of any slip-up in a dramatic finale to the season.

But it was to be Liverpool's day.

On May 3, Liverpool's title rivals hoped that Stamford Bridge would prove a bridge too far in Liverpool's assault on their eighth league title in 11 seasons. They were sorely disappointed. A 23rd-minute Roy of the Rovers goal, from who else but Kenny Dalglish, who chested down Jim Beglin's clever dink down the inside-left channel and guided it past goalkeeper Tony Godden settled things.

In front of 43,900 paying customers at Stamford Bridge, the 1985/86 season was finally decided as the Reds won 1-0 to clinch their 16th League Championship and also ended a bleak run of not winning in the league at Chelsea for 12 years. "Ah, it could easily have gone in the enclosure," Dalglish told the press after his league-winning goal but Dalglish cannot kid the fans or the record books. He became the first player-manager to win the championship. Thousands of delighted Liverpool fans saluted their heroes, who had regained a title they lost to neighbours Everton only 12 months ago.

Liverpool's season was not finished there either.

Back on February 5, Liverpool drew 1-1 at Norwich in the first leg of their Screensport Super Cup semi-final. Due to heavy fixture congestion, the second leg wasn't played at Anfield until May 6, three days after their title-clinching trip to Stamford Bridge. Prior to the encounter 26,696 fans witnessed the league trophy presentation, which for the first time in football history was handed to a player-manager. After receiving the trophy, Dalglish handed it immediately over to skipper Alan Hansen, who in turn passed it along the awaiting line of players. The biggest roar from the Kop was when Dalglish's 'right hand man', Bob Paisley, who celebrated this 47th year with the club that week, received the trophy at the end of the line.

There was no suggestion that Liverpool would take their eye off the ball against Norwich with the all-Merseyside FA Cup final just five days away, and goals from Kevin MacDonald, Jan Mølby and Craig Johnston secured a 3-1 win and their place in the final. Because of the fixture pile-up and the English season having to finish early due to the 1986 World Cup in Mexico, the final of the Super Cup had to be played at the start of the following season when Liverpool beat Everton by an emphatic 7-2 aggregate scoreline.

All 17 of the players who had taken part in the 1985/86 campaign joined in a lap of honour at the final whistle. But the fans refused to leave until Dalglish stepped out again to take his own bow. "The fans were tremendous. If the Kop had not been too packed, I would have been up there alongside them," Dalglish told the press. "They've been great to me ever since I came here. There's been a few times I've tried to jump over those railings after I've scored, but I've never made it yet. It was a very emotional moment, but enjoyable as well. The lads were proud to have won the title and I think the fans were proud to come along here tonight."

The following Saturday, the newly-crowned champions rubbed more salt into Everton's wounds by defeating the Blues 3-1 in the FA Cup final, becoming only the third English team in the 20th century to achieve the 'double'. When Gary Lineker fired Howard Kendall's side ahead in the first half, Wembley glory looked a million miles away for Liverpool, who had fielded no-one eligible to play for England in their line-up. But second-half efforts from Ian Rush, twice, and Craig Johnston, put the club in the history books.

Despite being the first player-manager to lead a club to a league and FA Cup 'double', Dalglish told the press that the triumph was won collectively, rather than individually: "The lads have put in a great deal of effort this season and have done everything that has been asked of them. They deserve so much credit for what they've achieved. I am delighted as much for them as I am for myself and I'm so fortunate and proud to be associated with them."

It was said that in truth it was the supporters who won the 1986 FA Cup final. Both Reds and Blues travelled to and from the capital together harmoniously, in good humour and with no segregation.

What's more, after the final whistle the united chant of "Merseyside" bellowed around Wembley from both sets of supporters. "It was a great advert for football in Britain after the bad press the game had been receiving over the years," declared Dalglish. The following day Liverpool and Everton players shared a flight back to Liverpool Airport together. During the flight, there was a light-hearted disagreement between the players about the amount of room on the plane. Jan Mølby recalls: "'Move your fat arse,' Everton full-back Pat Van Den Hauwe shouted at little Sammy Lee. 'Sorry,' replied Sammy, 'but what do you expect? I've got two medals in my back pocket!'"

Liverpool had become the first northern club to win the 'double' since Preston North End in 1889 and subsequently Dalglish became the first player-manager to be awarded the Bells Whiskey Manager of the Year trophy.

As a player, Kenny Dalglish featured 31 times from Liverpool's 63 games scoring on seven occasions. As a manager, he guided his team to 41 victories in all competitions, losing just seven games, the fewest amount of games a Liverpool side had ever lost during a single top-flight season.

Since that painful defeat against Everton on February 22, their only home defeat of the season, the Reds went on a remarkable 18-game unbeaten run in all competitions.

Dalglish and his double-winning heroes scored an incredible 138 goals during the course of the season, which today remains a club record. For the fourth time in five seasons Ian Rush was the club's top marksman with 33 goals, followed by notable contributions from Jan Mølby and Paul Walsh who notched up 21 and 18 respectively. Dalglish had more than silenced the critics, who had originally questioned his appointment, but for the phenomenal Scot this was only the start…

1985/86: Facts and Statistics

Final league table

		P	W	D	L	F	A	W	D	L	F	A	GD	PTS
1	Liverpool FC	42	16	4	1	58	14	10	6	5	31	23	52	88
2	Everton	42	16	3	2	54	18	10	5	6	33	23	46	86
3	West Ham United	42	17	2	2	48	16	9	4	8	26	24	34	84
4	Manchester United	42	12	5	4	35	12	10	5	6	35	24	34	76
5	Sheffield Wednesday	42	13	6	2	36	23	8	4	9	27	31	9	73
6	Chelsea	42	12	4	5	32	27	8	7	6	25	29	1	71
7	Arsenal	42	13	5	3	29	15	7	4	10	20	32	2	69
8	Nottingham Forest	42	11	5	5	38	25	8	6	7	31	28	16	68
9	Luton Town	42	12	6	3	37	15	6	6	9	24	29	17	66
10	Tottenham	42	12	2	7	47	25	7	6	8	27	27	22	65
11	Newcastle United	42	12	5	4	46	31	5	7	9	21	41	-5	63
12	Watford	42	11	6	4	40	22	5	5	11	29	40	7	59
13	QPR	42	12	3	6	33	20	3	4	14	20	44	-11	52
14	Southampton	42	10	6	5	32	18	2	4	15	19	44	-11	46
15	Manchester City	42	7	7	7	25	26	4	5	12	18	31	-14	45
16	Aston Villa	42	7	6	8	27	28	3	8	10	24	39	-16	44
17	Coventry City	42	6	5	10	31	35	5	5	11	17	36	-23	43
18	Oxford United	42	7	7	7	34	27	3	5	13	28	53	-18	42
19	Leicester City	42	7	8	6	35	35	3	4	14	19	41	-22	42
20	Ipswich Town	42	8	5	8	20	24	3	3	15	12	31	-23	41
21	Birmingham City	42	5	2	14	13	25	3	3	15	17	48	-43	29
22	WBA	42	3	8	10	21	36	1	4	16	14	53	-54	24

Games for the 1985/1986 season

(The number after date is league position after the game)

1	17.08.1985	4	W	2-0	Arsenal, Anfield, 1st Division
2	21.08.1985	3	D	2-2	Aston Villa, Villa Park, 1st Division
3	24.08.1985	10	L	0-1	Newcastle United, St. James' Park, 1st Division
4	26.08.1985	4	W	5-0	Ipswich Town, Anfield, 1st Division
5	31.08.1985	8	D	2-2	West Ham United, Upton Park, 1st Division
6	03.09.1985	4	W	2-0	Nottingham Forest, Anfield, 1st Division
7	07.09.1985	2	W	3-1	Watford, Anfield, 1st Division
8	14.09.1985	4	D	2-2	Oxford United, Manor Ground, 1st Division
9	17.09.1985		W	2-1	Southampton, Anfield, SSSC Group Phase
10	21.09.1985	2	W	3-2	Everton, Goodison Park, 1st Division

11	24.09.1985		W	3-0	Oldham Athletic, Anfield, League Cup 2nd round 1L
12	28.09.1985	2	W	4-1	Tottenham Hotspur, Anfield, 1st Division
13	05.10.1985	2	L	1-2	Queens Park Rangers, Loftus Road, 1st Division
14	09.10.1985		W	5-2	Oldham Athletic, Boundary Park, League Cup 2nd round 2L
15	12.10.1985	2	W	1-0	Southampton, Anfield, 1st Division
16	19.10.1985	2	D	1-1	Manchester United, Old Trafford, 1st Division
17	22.10.1985		D	1-1	Southampton, The Dell, SSSC Group Phase
18	26.10.1985	2	W	3-2	Luton Town, Anfield, 1st Division
19	29.10.1985		W	4-0	Brighton & Hove Albion, Anfield, League Cup 3rd round
20	02.11.1985	2	W	1-0	Leicester City, Anfield, 1st Division
21	09.11.1985	2	W	3-0	Coventry City, Highfield Road, 1st Division
22	16.11.1985	2	W	4-1	West Bromwich Albion, Anfield, 1st Division
23	23.11.1985	2	W	2-0	Birmingham City, St. Andrew's, 1st Division
24	26.11.1985		W	2-1	Manchester United, Anfield, League Cup 4th round
25	30.11.1985	2	D	1-1	Chelsea, Anfield, 1st Division
26	03.12.1985		W	2-0	Tottenham Hotspur, Anfield, SSSC Group Phase
27	07.12.1985	2	W	3-0	Aston Villa, Anfield, 1st Division
28	14.12.1985	2	L	0-2	Arsenal, Highbury, 1st Division
29	21.12.1985	2	D	1-1	Newcastle United, Anfield, 1st Division
30	26.12.1985	2	L	0-1	Manchester City, Maine Road, 1st Division
31	28.12.1985	4	D	1-1	Nottingham Forest, City Ground, 1st Division
32	01.01.1986	3	D	2-2	Sheffield Wednesday, Anfield, 1st Division
33	04.01.1986		W	5-0	Norwich City, Anfield, FA Cup 3rd round
34	12.01.1986	3	W	3-2	Watford, Vicarage Road, 1st Division
35	14.01.1986		W	3-0	Tottenham Hotspur, White Hart Lane, SSSC Group Phase
36	18.01.1986	3	W	3-1	West Ham United, Anfield, 1st Division
37	21.01.1986		W	3-0	Ipswich Town, Anfield, League Cup 5th round
38	26.01.1986		W	2-1	Chelsea, Stamford Bridge, FA Cup 4th round
39	01.02.1986	4	L	1-2	Ipswich Town, Portman Road, 1st Division
40	05.02.1986		D	1-1	Norwich City, Carrow Road, SSSC Semi-final 1st leg
41	09.02.1986	3	D	1-1	Manchester United, Anfield, 1st Division
42	12.02.1986		L	0-1	Queens Park Rangers, Loftus Road, League Cup Semi-final 1L
43	15.02.1986		D	1-1	York City, Bootham Crescent, FA Cup 5th round
44	18.02.1986		W	3-1	York City, Anfield, FA Cup 5th round replay
45	22.02.1986	3	L	0-2	Everton, Anfield, 1st Division
46	02.03.1986	3	W	2-1	Tottenham Hotspur, White Hart Lane, 1st Division

47	05.03.1986		D	2-2	Queens Park Rangers, Anfield, League Cup Semi-final 2L
48	08.03.1986	2	W	4-1	Queens Park Rangers, Anfield, 1st Division
49	11.03.1986		D	0-0	Watford, Anfield, FA Cup 6th round
50	15.03.1986	2	W	2-1	Southampton, The Dell, 1st Division
51	17.03.1986		W	2-1	Watford, Vicarage Road, FA Cup 6th round replay
52	22.03.1986	2	W	6-0	Oxford United, Anfield, 1st Division
53	29.03.1986	2	D	0-0	Sheffield Wednesday, Hillsborough, 1st Division
54	31.03.1986	1	W	2-0	Manchester City, Anfield, 1st Division
55	05.04.1986		W	2-0	Southampton, White Hart Lane, FA Cup Semi-final
56	12.04.1986	1	W	5-0	Coventry City, Anfield, 1st Division
57	16.04.1986	1	W	1-0	Luton Town, Kenilworth Road, 1st Division
58	19.04.1986	1	W	2-1	West Bromwich Albion, The Hawthorns, 1st Division
59	26.04.1986	1	W	5-0	Birmingham City, Anfield, 1st Division
60	30.04.1986	1	W	2-0	Leicester City, Filbert Street, 1st Division
61	03.05.1986	1	W	1-0	Chelsea, Stamford Bridge, 1st Division
62	06.05.1986		W	3-1	Norwich City, Anfield, SSSC Semi-final 2nd leg
63	10.05.1986		W	3-1	Everton, Wembley, FA Cup Final

Friendlies

1	27.07.1985	W	5-1	Burnley, Turf Moor, Friendly
2	30.07.1985	D	2-2	Crewe Alexandra, Gresty Road, Friendly
3	02.08.1985	L	0-1	Oldham Athletic, Boundary Park, Friendly
4	05.08.1985	W	4-1	Brighton & Hove Albion, Goldstone Ground, Friendly
5	07.08.1985	W	2-1	Charlton Athletic, The Valley, Friendly
6	10.08.1985	D	3-3	Bristol City, Ashton Gate, Friendly
7	12.08.1985	L	2-3	Everton, Anfield, Testimonial*

*Testimonial for Phil Neal

Appearances for the 1985/1986 season

Name	League	FA Cup	LC	Other	Total
Bruce Grobbelaar	42	8	7	6	63
Craig Johnston	41	8	7	5	61
Alan Hansen	41	8	7	4	60
Mark Lawrenson	38	7	7	6	58
Jan Mølby	39	8	5	6	58
Ronnie Whelan	39	7	7	4	57
Ian Rush	40	8	6	2	56
Jim Beglin	34	7	7	5	53
Steve Nicol	34	4	3	6	47
Steve McMahon	23	4	5	4	36
Paul Walsh	20	2	4	6	32
Kenny Dalglish	21	6	2	2	31
Sammy Lee	15	3	3	5	26
Kevin MacDonald	17	2	2	4	25
Gary Gillespie	14	5	2	3	24
John Wark	9	4	3	2	18
Phil Neal	13	0	2	1	16
Alan Kennedy	8	0	0	0	8
Mark Seagraves	0	1	1	0	2
Gary Ablett	0	0	0	0	0

Goalscorers for the 1985/1986 season

Name	League	FA Cup	LC	EC	Total
Ian Rush	22	6	3	2	33
Jan Mølby	14	3	2	2	21
Paul Walsh	11	1	4	2	18
Ronnie Whelan	10	1	3	0	14
Steve McMahon	6	1	3	0	10
Craig Johnston	7	1	1	1	10
Kenny Dalglish	3	1	1	2	7
John Wark	3	2	1	0	6
Kevin MacDonald	1	1	1	2	5
Mark Lawrenson	3	1	0	1	5
Steve Nicol	4	0	0	0	4
Gary Gillespie	3	0	0	0	3
Jim Beglin	1	0	0	0	1
Phil Neal	1	0	0	0	1

The squad during the 1985/1986 season

Bruce Grobbelaar, Goalkeeper
Bob Bolder, Goalkeeper
Jim Beglin, Defender
Alan Kennedy, Defender
Gary Gillespie, Defender
Mark Lawrenson, Defender
Steve Nicol, Defender
Alan Hansen, Defender
Phil Neal, Defender
John McGregor, Defender
Gary Ablett, Defender
Kenny Dalglish, Midfielder
Ronnie Whelan, Midfielder
John Wark, Midfielder
Kevin MacDonald, Midfielder
Jan Mølby, Midfielder
Mark Seagraves, Midfielder
Craig Johnston, Midfielder
Sammy Lee, Midfielder
Steve McMahon, Midfielder
Paul Walsh, Striker
Ian Rush, Striker

Transfers for the 1985/1986 season

In:
Steve McMahon, Aston Villa, £350,000, 12 September 1985
Mike Hooper, Wrexham, £40,000, 25 October 1985
John Durnin, Waterloo Dock, £500, 29 March 1986

Out:
Alan Kennedy, Sunderland, £100,000, September 1985
Phil Neal, Bolton Wanderers, Free, December 1985

A collection of statistics for the 1985/1986 season

The season in numbers:
Total games: 63
Games won: 41
Games drawn: 15
Games lost: 7
Clean sheets – League: 16
Clean sheets – Overall: 24
Total goals: 138
Average attendance at home – League: 35,316
Average attendance at home – Overall: 31,592
Average goals per game – League: 2.76
Average goals per game – Overall: 2.72
Average goal minute – League: 50
Average goal minute – Overall: 52

Goals split down to competitions:
League – 73
League Cup – 25
European Cup – 16
FA Cup – 4
Charity Shield – 0

Player debuts:
Steve McMahon against Oxford United on 14.09.1985
Mark Seagraves against QPR on 12.02.1986

Statistics and information provided by LFChistory.net

17 : WONDERFUL TO WATCH

1987/88

THE FIRST DIVISION TROPHY REMAINED ON Merseyside for a sixth consecutive season as Everton came from behind to pip Liverpool at the post in the closing stages of the 1986/87 season. Following Liverpool's magnificent 'double' success of 1986, Dalglish was bitterly disappointed to not have won anything the following season. He was determined not to relive that experience again despite losing the considerable services of Europe's deadliest striker, Ian Rush.

Liverpool's European ban had left the club suffering financially and they were forced to part with their greatest asset for a record fee for a British footballer, £3.2million. Rush was supposed to join Juventus in the summer of 1986 but their president Giampiero Boniperti said, to Rush's great surprise during contract negotiations, that he was going to be loaned out to Lazio in Serie B for the 1986/87 season as Michel Platini had decided to play on one more year.

The French maestro and Michael Laudrup would occupy the two places allowed for foreigners at the Italian club so Rush suggested he be loaned straight back to Liverpool, to which Boniperti obliged.

Those who feared Rush wouldn't give 100 per cent for the club in his final season soon calmed down as he found the back of the net 21 times in his first 21 games and ended the season top scorer with 40 goals to his name.

Critics had said that without Rush, Liverpool were simply an ordinary team but they had said that after the departures of Kevin Keegan and Graeme Souness and were proved wrong. By the start of the 1987/88 campaign, Dalglish had assembled a squad capable of producing attractive, effective football.

The Reds' manager had shown he was not afraid to spend money when he splashed out £750,000 on Oxford United's Scouser, John Aldridge, in January 1987. The Garston-born striker was a passionate Liverpool fan from a very early age and frequently cheered on Bill Shankly's team from the Boys' Pen, before graduating on to the Kop. At the age of 28, Aldridge thought his chance of playing for his boyhood heroes had passed him by as he plied his trade with Newport County and Oxford but the imminent departure of Rush to Turin resulted in Dalglish needing to strengthen his attacking force and Aldridge needed no second invitation when he finally made his dream move to Anfield.

Succeeding a legend like Rush was a considerable task and the prolific goalscorer had nothing but admiration for the man he was replacing: "I'd settle right now on being just half the player Rushie was at Anfield and if people give me that kind of recognition when my Liverpool career is over, I'll remember it as the greatest compliment of my life. Obviously, I'd love to be as good as he is, but I can't get anywhere near him. Nobody can. Granted there is a similarity in the way we look, but that is where the similarity ends."

During the summer of 1987, Aldridge was joined by two big-money England internationals. First to arrive on June 9 was winger

John Barnes, a £900,000 buy from Watford. A month later, Dalglish paid Newcastle United a staggering £1.9 million, a British transfer record, for the services of their wondrous forward Peter Beardsley.

Beardsley recalled: "I was eventually given permission to talk to Kenny Dalglish, at what was supposed to be a secret rendezvous, a small hotel in Wigan. It only had six bedrooms and Kenny had booked one where we could talk in private along with both the Liverpool chairman and chief executive. Kenny was convinced that no-one would find us, but somehow the news leaked out and a couple of press men arrived. After Kenny gave them the slip, we were on our way to complete the negotiations in Southport. The talks went so smoothly that we agreed terms within an hour."

Both new recruits had undisputed ability with the Geordie described as the best player in the world by chairman John Smith: "I think it's true to say that in life, patience is a virtue, and Peter is worth waiting for. Not only is he one of the best players in this country, but without any doubt in my book, is the leading player in Europe and the world.

"This is the first time in the history of Liverpool – maybe in the history of any club – that two current England players have been signed in such quick succession. Liverpool FC can count themselves very fortunate in signing him."

Repair work on a collapsed sewer underneath the Kop prevented Liverpool fans from seeing their new-look team in action until the fourth match of the season as the famous terrace looked like a building site. Friendly matches were arranged to fill the gaps in the fixture list so that the players could maintain their fitness and sharpness. Liverpool won both games, beating an Irish Olympic XI, 5-0 at Lansdowne Road and then securing a 1-0 victory over Atlético Madrid in front of 25,000 onlookers in the Estadio Vicente Calderón.

Liverpool had not lost an opening league fixture since 1981 when they went down 1-0 to Wolves at Molineux and they extended that run against Arsenal on August 15, 1987, after the Reds won 2-1 at Highbury. Dalglish, who celebrated 10 years at Liverpool five days before the Arsenal match, didn't appear on Liverpool's teamsheet as his appearances on the pitch were getting less and less frequent. When asked why he was not playing himself, Dalglish bluntly said: "The reason why I don't pick myself is simply because I can't get in the team."

Bruce Grobbelaar started his seventh campaign as first-choice goalkeeper and Gary Gillespie continued to partner captain Alan Hansen at centre-back, as Mark Lawrenson was still recovering from a ruptured Achilles tendon that he suffered at Wimbledon the previous March.

Barry Venison and Nigel Spackman, who arrived during the previous season, were also included on Dalglish's first teamsheet of the season, although Spackman was a substitute. The team's newest arrivals, Beardsley, Barnes and Aldridge all played their part in Liverpool's first goal against the Gunners as Aldridge headed home superbly in the ninth minute after good work down the left-hand side from Beardsley and Barnes. Paul Davis equalised for the North Londoners eight minutes later but just before the end Steve Nicol popped up to score the winner with a marvellous header from outside the area.

Dalglish was delighted with Steve Nicol's performance, as the Scot played at left-back for his first competitive match since December 1986: "When you welcome back someone after so long out of action it is almost akin to having a new player. It was certainly great from our viewpoint to have Steve available again because he can fill a number of positions and do a good job in each one."

Matchwinner Nicol gave his verdict on Liverpool's opening fixture at Highbury: "It was probably the hottest day for football I have ever known in Britain. But it was Arsenal who seemed to wilt in the sunshine as we went from strength to strength to record a heartening win. I enjoyed my new role as left-back. I can't recall having been picked to play there in the First Division before, although it was quite common for me to fill that position for my previous club Ayr United. It is very easy playing behind John Barnes. He has such a tremendous control that you feel sure that nothing is going to go wrong once he is in possession, even when there are two or three defenders around him. I ended up enjoying the thrill of scoring. It followed a free-kick on the goal line. I was on the edge of the penalty area standing behind Barnes and shouting for him to roll it back to me. But instead he floated it into the middle. Craig Johnston went in and almost got a vital touch, but instead it was cleared out towards me. It didn't come out very quickly and I thought about trying to lob it back in towards the heads, but it came more naturally onto my head, and I just concentrated on trying to get some power behind it and getting it on target. I was only just inside the box and with the angle I guess the ball must have flown twenty yards, dead straight, beyond the keeper into the top corner."

In their second game, away to FA Cup holders and First Division dark horses Coventry City, the Reds turned on the style to win 4-1, thanks to a brace from Nicol, an Aldridge penalty and Beardsley's first goal for the club. Coventry manager John Sillett was full of praise for Dalglish's new-look team: "It was the best football in the First Division that I've seen for 18 months. It was an absolute joy to watch, it was just annoying that they have to come here to Highfield Road and do that!"

After a 1-1 draw at West Ham, Liverpool could, at last, play their first match in front of their own spectators on September 12. Unfashionable Oxford were the visitors to Anfield and returned home with a 2-0 defeat, thanks to first-half strikes from Aldridge, against his old team, and Barnes.

The winger proved to be an instant hit with the home crowd, making the first goal and scoring with a tremendous free-kick. Dalglish was content about Barnes' Anfield debut: "He did what we expected him to do. He made a goal, scored one, and entertained. You remember that."

Liverpool first showed interest in Barnes in January 1987 but the Jamaica-born multi-talented winger didn't make a decision about his future until June, when he decided that heading north was the direction he wanted to take after spending six years at Vicarage Road. Due to the time it took Barnes to make his decision, a situation made worse by some of the coverage in the tabloids, some Liverpool fans had to be convinced he would be a good fit at Anfield and Barnes was left feeling quite nervous about how he would be received by the supporters.

The fact that Liverpool's first three fixtures were away from home, helped Barnes' initial relationship with the people who he was soon to be adored by: "I suppose if the first game would have been at Anfield I would have been very nervous, as I wouldn't have known how the fans would have taken me. This was because there were a lot of reports in the newspapers that I didn't want to come to Liverpool in the first place, which were totally untrue, which caused a negative attitude towards me before I even got there. I even had to phone Peter Robinson to put the record straight. However, as we started away from Anfield, the team and myself played quite well and the travelling supporters told the home supporters that, 'That boy Barnes can play a bit'."

Towards the end of August, Dalglish signed 18-year-old Mike Marsh on a free transfer. Previously, Marsh was playing for Kirkby Town on a Saturday and the Railway Pub on Sundays, the latter being sponsored by Kirkby native and Liverpool's reserve team coach, Phil Thompson, who had returned to the club in 1986 as reserve team manager.

Tommo was advised to take a closer look at Marsh and Liverpool signed him up. Marsh was a reserve at Liverpool for four years and later admitted that he did not feel worthy of being in such exclusive company. The players had been his heroes one minute and team-mates the next.

After a home victory over Charlton Athletic, in which Mark Lawrenson made his long-awaited comeback, the Reds travelled north to face Newcastle United on Sunday, September 20. At the time Tyneside was buzzing because of the arrival of the first Brazilian player in the First Division, nippy striker Mirandinha. A 24,000 crowd plus millions of television viewers saw Liverpool produce a super show to run out 4-1 winners.

Again, the star of the show was the versatile Nicol, this time operating on the right of midfield, who scored his first hat-trick in senior football. Aldridge grabbed the other goal as Liverpool moved into third place, three points behind leaders Queens Park Rangers with two matches in hand.

Nicol was a great defender, but also a superb attacking player. He was quite adept at taking on defenders and an accurate crosser of the ball. After scoring six goals in his first six league games, Nicol topped the goalscoring charts at the beginning of the 1987/88 season and Ronnie Moran later told *LFChistory.net*: "Shanks always preached that we had eleven captains. He wanted to see players think things out and rectify things if they were going wrong. I remember Steve

Nicol getting a hat-trick once at Newcastle. Nobody told him where he had to go and what to do, he just worked it out himself. He got the match ball and I told him it was probably the only one he'd ever get, but nobody told him off for joining in the attack."

In their next league clash, at home nine days later to a Derby County team reinforced by the arrivals of England stars Peter Shilton and Mark Wright, the Anfield men again blasted four goals, which included a John Aldridge hat-trick, in a stylish display. 'SIMPLY TOTAL SUPREMACY' was the *Liverpool Echo* headline with Ian Hargraves writing: "It did not matter who had the ball, for although John Barnes and Steve Nicol inevitably took the eye with their speed and trickery, everyone else looked perfectly capable of either creating a goal or scoring himself. Liverpool were playing 'total football,' the style made famous by the great Ajax and Dutch national team of the Seventies, and it was a joy to behold."

Once on top of the First Division perch, Liverpool were impossible to dislodge. They assumed that position on October 17 with an emphatic Anfield victory over Queens Park Rangers. Craig Johnston, John Aldridge's penalty and two late strikes from John Barnes were more than enough to earn the win. Barnes' second goal was particularly superb. He robbed Kevin Brock on the halfway line and set off on a dazzling run which left two defenders in his wake and goalkeeper David Seaman mesmerised by the finish. Liverpool went top of the table on goal difference, with still two games in hand on their nearest challengers.

Aldridge had taken over the responsibility of leading the attack with devastating effect, scoring in each of the first nine league matches in the 1987/88 season. He had also scored in the last league game of the previous season and his club record of scoring in 10 consecutive league games still stands today. Rush was in no doubt after watching his successor in action in October 1987 that Aldridge was the right man for the job: "I always felt that John was the main man to take over from me. He is scoring goals at a faster rate than I ever did, and Liverpool look a better side than they did last year. There are not many strikers around like John, and by playing with wingers Liverpool have so many more options this season."

On October 19, Dalglish spent even more of the Ian Rush money, bringing Republic of Ireland midfielder Ray Houghton to Anfield for £825,000 in one of the quickest transfer deals concluded by the club. Following the Reds' first home game of the season against Oxford back in September Kenny Dalglish wrote in his diary: "I was impressed, and not for the first time, by Ray Houghton's performance in Oxford's midfield. He looks a fine player and is a good competitor."

Houghton was the last player in Dalglish's new jigsaw and after securing his dream move to Liverpool, he told the *Liverpool Echo*: "It never entered my head that Liverpool wouldn't come in with a bid for me. They had made one bid earlier in the season but it wasn't considered high enough by the Board. My contract was up at the end of the season so Oxford knew that any interested club would get me on the cheap. There was no pressure on me while I was playing at Oxford. In fact, all the press speculation about my future made it easier for me to play for Oxford. I never felt I was in the shop window because it was obvious that a lot of clubs had been watching me for a long time. They knew exactly what I could do and I was really pleased that Liverpool came in for me again. I've fulfilled an ambition in getting to Anfield but the biggest challenge is still to come; getting into Liverpool's first team won't be easy, but I'm prepared to wait."

It was not until October 28 that the Reds first tasted defeat during the 1987/88 season. That came in a Littlewoods League Cup tie at home to Everton but four days later at the same venue, they avenged that reversal in the televised 137th league Merseyside derby.

Steve McMahon, who had developed a habit of scoring against his old club, finished off a move started by Barnes and in the second half Peter Beardsley rifled a loose ball high into the net past Neville Southall. In the next match, Houghton, on his debut as a substitute, scored his first goal for Liverpool in a tough 1-1 draw against Wimbledon at Plough Lane, a result which gave his new club their best start to a league programme in terms of points for 20 years.

Two more consecutive draws followed against Manchester United at Old Trafford and Norwich City at Anfield resulted in them losing pole position of the First Division to Arsenal, although the Gunners had played two more games than the Reds.

Drawing at United meant Liverpool had gone 11 league fixtures without defeating their Mancunians rivals. However, by the end of November convincing victories over Watford and Tottenham saw Liverpool return to the top of the First Division. Spurs were forced to play 72 minutes with a man less after the dismissal of midfielder Steve Hodge for an elbow on Houghton.

It was Terry Venables' first game as manager of Tottenham and future Liverpool defender Neil Ruddock was delighted to be named in Venables' first starting XI but the game turned out to be a disaster for him. Ruddock told *LFChistory.net*: "It was the first time I had ever played against Liverpool and I was only 19 at the time. Gary Gillespie stamped on my leg in the second half and I had to go off. I went off but I didn't know it was broken for about a week, so I was hobbling about with a broken leg all week!"

The team remained unbeaten into 1988 and the Reds enjoyed one of their greatest festive periods on record, winning all four games, scoring 12 goals without conceding. Liverpool's Boxing Day encounter was at Oxford, where the Reds cruised to a 3-0 victory thanks to efforts from Aldridge, Barnes and McMahon.

That win gave the side a new club record start to the season of 20 unbeaten league matches, which surpassed the efforts of George Kay's team and their long-standing record of 19 matches achieved at the beginning of the 1949/50 season.

On New Year's Day 1988, Coventry came to Anfield in search of their first league points at the ground since November, 1975.

However, the Sky Blues would have to wait a little bit more as the Reds put another four past Steve Ogrizovic like they had done back in August. *The Times* reported: "Liverpool showed the form that has set them apart this season. The Football League's engraver could confidently cut the club's name on the base of the new Barclays Trophy this morning and not lose a moment's sleep worrying about whether he would be called to change it at a later stage. It was the eighth occasion since mid-August that Kenny Dalglish's side had plundered four goals in a match, and with Nottingham Forest – who must face Everton at Goodison Park tomorrow – surprisingly losing at home to Newcastle United, they have extended their advantage at the top to 13 points while stretching their unbeaten league run to 22 games."

Skipper Alan Hansen was more enthusiastic and confident about the Liverpool team of the 1987/88 season than he was of the Liverpool team of two years prior: "This team, I'd say, is more attacking than most Liverpool teams I've played in. We have always based our game on attack, but certainly with Barnes and Beardsley, they are doing things individually that other players in other teams didn't do. It's a pleasure to sit behind them and watch them play from the halfway line."

On January 16, 1988, a worldwide audience of 250 million and an Anfield attendance of 44,294 watched the Reds demolish Arsenal

2-0 and open up a mammoth 15-point gap at the top of the division. Compared to other performances that season, this did not rank among Liverpool's very best and the match had a touch of sadness about it as it was Mark Lawrenson's last for the club. He suffered a recurrence of an Achilles tendon injury that forced him to retire from football before moving to Oxford as manager at the start of April.

On the plus side, what impressed that afternoon was the quality of Liverpool's goals. A minute before the break, McMahon maintained pressure on Arsenal by retrieving the ball heroically on the touchline before passing to Beardsley and after John Lukic had parried his shot, Aldridge pounced to score his 20th goal of the season from close range. Former France captain and three-time European Footballer of the Year, Michel Platini, who was at Anfield commentating for French television, said afterwards: "They (Liverpool) have the quality to make teams suffer. They don't play like a British side. They have the flair of a French or Italian side the way they keep the ball on the ground, rather than in the air."

During the early stages of 1988, Dalglish trimmed his squad. First to leave was John Wark, who had been playing in the reserves and had only started one game during the 1987/88 season against Blackburn Rovers in the League Cup.

Wark moved back to Ipwich and said: "Hard as it was to depart Anfield, I knew it was the right thing to do. I could have stayed in the reserves and played the odd game, but I love playing football and I don't like sitting on the bench. That was the reason I left. Actually, I went back to Ipswich, because my wife is from Ipswich and she was a bit homesick as well. I dropped a division, don't forget that."

Striker Paul Walsh was next to go after making 112 outings and netting 37 goals for the Reds, as the striker accepted an offer to join Tottenham. However, Walsh later revealed to LFC TV that he may have left Liverpool rather prematurely: "Kenny had just signed Peter Beardsley and Roy Evans came to me and asked how would I fancy playing right midfield. I said no because I wanted to play up front but looking back in hindsight I should have stayed at Liverpool and taken that on because I could have done a decent job there."

Before Liverpool's 2-0 victory at Charlton on January 23, which enhanced their lead at the top to 17 points, Bob Paisley had commented to the press that Liverpool were leading the poorest First Division that he can remember. After increasing their league run to 24 games without defeat, Dalglish told the press: "I've no thoughts on Bob Paisley's comments. There is nothing we can do about the standard of the First Division. We just concentrate on our own ability taking each day as it comes, and hope that we'll be good enough to win something at the end of the season."

Tommy Smith agreed with his former manager's viewpoint referring to the competition offered by Liverpool's current rivals: "There were far more good players knocking about in the Sixties than there is now which obviously made more teams stronger. Liverpool's situation this season has been downgraded by the opposition. In my day you could predict the winners out of the top 12 to 13 teams, but nowadays you can only pick about three or four clubs at the most to go past the post."

On February 6, the Reds suffered a shock 0-0 home draw with West Ham, which was the second time the Hammers had taken points from Liverpool that season and the first time they had done so at Anfield in 11 years. Even though Liverpool's lead was reduced to 15 points, they stretched their own defensive record to not conceding a single goal in 10 games in all competitions. Against West Ham, Aigburth native Gary Ablett made his first league start of the season in place of the injured Gary Gillespie. Ablett was a hard-working defender dedicated to Liverpool's cause who played either at left-back or centre-back. Ablett came through the ranks at Liverpool and made his debut for the reserves on 23 November 1982. Four years later the 21-year-old finally took his bow for the first team.

The West Ham score draw was followed by a sparkling performance against Watford on a rain-soaked Vicarage Road pitch as the Anfield aces charged on to a 4-1 triumph, which put them 12 points clear of second-placed Manchester United with two matches in hand.

As Liverpool were still unable to compete in official European competitions, a frequent talking point was how that Liverpool team would have faired against the top teams in Europe.

Ric George, the scribe for the *Liverpool Echo*, gave his opinion on the hotly-debated topic: "Comparisons throughout the Continent between the Reds and Real Madrid are unceasing. It is hard to determine who is the stronger except to say that on a Vicarage Road surface where there was arguably more water than grass, there is no way the skilful Spanish side would have coped the way Liverpool did."

The in-form Peter Beardsley scored twice at Watford with John Aldridge and John Barnes, on his old ground, the other marksmen. With full-back Jim Beglin still recovering from the broken leg he suffered in January 1987, and Ronnie Whelan also injured, Nigel Spackman, in his first full season for the Reds, was proving more than an able replacement.

Ian St John, who was one of the country's leading commentators at the time, thought that Spackman had a paramount role in Liverpool's starting XI: "Although Spackman does have a very quiet job in this Liverpool side he's one of the unsung heroes. I've never seen him have a bad game, he just works away in the middle of the field and is a very good professional."

Liverpool's total domination of Watford earned them a tribute from another Frenchman, Monaco boss Arsène Wenger, who had brought his title-chasing team to England on a tour during their winter break. A known admirer of Kenny Dalglish's men, he said: "Everything they do on the field is geared to success and winning. They are a strong all-round team with good individuals such as Beardsley, Nicol, Hansen and Barnes. What impressed me was how everyone worked for each other when defending and their eagerness to win back the ball was absolutely fantastic."

Liverpool started March with a trip to Spain to take part in Sammy Lee's testimonial against his current club, Osasuna. Unfortunately, Lee was injured and unable to feature, as was former Liverpool striker Michael Robinson who was also playing for the Spanish club at the time. Liverpool won the match 2-0.

Lee, the little energetic midfielder with a big heart who wore the red shirt with such pride before moving on to Queens Park Rangers and then Osasuna, told the *Liverpool Echo*: "Liverpool remain the greatest club in the world for me. There is no doubt about that what-soever. I am thrilled and grateful that they have found the time to come over to Spain to support me. It's an honour to have them here and I'm really disappointed that I can't play myself, but that's football. I'm just happy to see the lads again."

Liverpool's next league encounter was at Loftus Road where 19-year-old defender Alex Watson, the younger brother of Everton defender Dave, was told only an hour before kick-off that he was about to make his debut partnering Alan Hansen in the heart on the defence. Dalglish, who turned 37 the previous day and named himself as a substitute for the first time of the season in an official game, was thrilled with Watson's efforts: "He was magnificent and surpassed all our expectations." Barnes scored the only goal of the game after 34 minutes, side-footing home after Seaman had pushed out to him Aldridge's low shot.

On March 13, Liverpool qualified for the FA Cup semi-final for the third time in four seasons as the Reds turned the tie into an exhibition match beating Manchester City 4-0, the 10th time they had scored four goals that season.

At Derby three days later, the Reds equalled Leeds United's record start to a season of 29 unbeaten games in Division One, set in 1973/74. The record nearly remained intact as Derby bolstered their chances of retaining First Division status as Mike Forsyth's 85th-minute equaliser for the Rams cancelled out Craig Johnston's first-half drive from close range.

The following Sunday, Liverpool attempted to break Leeds' 14-year record at Everton, the only side to have tarnished their invincible tag this season in the third round of the Littlewoods Cup at Anfield in October.

However, by the sound of Dalglish's pre-match comments, breaking records was far from his priority: "We are still going flat out, not chasing records but to pick up points. We have to get all the points we can as quickly as we can. Whether there is a record at stake or not at Everton, it won't make any difference."

Bets were taken that Liverpool would complete their league programme without losing a match but those punters who had had a flutter saw their winnings disappear at Goodison Park that afternoon. A shot from Everton's Wayne Clarke made the rest of the First Division sigh with relief and made sure their neighbours didn't surpass the record set by Don Revie's team.

Despite the setback at Everton, Liverpool boasted a 14-point lead with two games in hand over Manchester United and the following weekend they achieved a 2-1 victory over Bobby Gould's Wimbledon, where player-manager Kenny Dalglish made his first appearance of the season as a late second-half substitute.

Liverpool's April fixtures began with an away visit to Nottingham Forest in the league. The Reds were yet to face Clough's Forest so far that season and as things turned out, both league games and the small matter of an FA Cup semi-final were all going to be disputed within 12 days of each other.

The Reds lost the first of the three meetings between the two sides by means of a 2-1 league defeat at the City Ground, their second loss in 32 league games. The Reds gained part one of their revenge with a 2-1 FA Cup semi-final victory at Hillsborough, both goals being scored by John Aldridge, taking his goal tally to 25 for the season.

The revenge was completed on April 13 with a 5-0 romp at Anfield, a display so impressive that the whole 90 minutes were featured in the Liverpool Championship Video which went on general sale. 'THE MASTERS OF DEVASTATION' was how the *Liverpool Echo* headline described the defeat of Brian Clough's talented young side.

Ray Houghton, John Aldridge (twice), Gary Gillespie and Peter Beardsley were the scorers and local scribe Ian Hargraves wrote: "Some of the football was unbelievable in its pace, in its accuracy and its imagination. On this performance, no other side in the land could hope to live with them, and the April Fool joke about giving them a two-goal handicap in all three games seemed almost credible."

Although he didn't get on the scoresheet that night, Barnes was heavily involved in the majority of Liverpool's attacks and later admitted that the 5-0 demolition of Nottingham Forest was one of his most memorable games in a Liverpool shirt: "One of the big lessons I had learned at Liverpool and Watford is that we play in a team sport and it's not about the individual. "The Nottingham Forest game was the best team performance during my time at Liverpool and some critics commented that it was the best performance they had ever seen from a football team. We won 5-0 and we played breathtaking football for 90 minutes against a good side who were the third-best in the country."

One of those critics who was at Anfield that evening was the legendary Sir Tom Finney who certainly enjoyed Liverpool's performance: "It was the finest exhibition I've seen the whole time I've played and watched the game. You couldn't see it bettered anywhere, not even in Brazil. The moves they put together were fantastic."

Amid the three Forest games, Liverpool shared a six-goal Anfield thriller with Manchester United. Second-placed United came back from 3-1 down to earn a point. Both teams conceded three goals for the first time that season, the pick of Liverpool's three being Steve McMahon's 20-yard tremendous right-footed shot which went well beyond the despairing Chris Turner at the Anfield Road end.

Following his post-match comments, United manager Alex Ferguson, faced disciplinary action from the Football Association. He had said: "I can now understand why a lot of managers have to leave here choking on their own sick, afraid to tell the truth because they've been beaten. We've got a draw today and so I can speak the truth. To win here you have to surmount a lot of pressure, a lot of obstacles and if you want to blame the referee, you can't say so. The provocation and intimidation they are under is incredible. I don't know what the referee's assessor thought of that today.

"The referees here are forced into making decisions that are not correct. These are facts. Every manager who comes here knows about them but has to leave the ground biting his tongue, afraid to say anything because his team have been beaten. I've been here a few times and seen it."

While Ferguson was giving interviews, Dalglish walked past, heard what was being said and returned holding his new baby daughter, Lauren. He indicated that the media would get more sense from his little girl than Ferguson.

"Kenny's a young lad," responded the United manager. "He heard me talking to the press and interrupted to make his point of view. As I said to him, he's got a platform for the press himself. . . the press like to hear what Kenny Dalglish has to say if they can understand him."

After 34 games played, Liverpool's lead remained at 11 points and the Reds were now mathematically two points away from collecting their 10th English crown in 15 years. They could have achieved those points with victory at Norwich on April 20, but the Canaries delayed Liverpool's 17th League Championship with a well-deserved goalless draw at Carrow Road and they ended up being the only First Division side that Liverpool failed to score against during the 1987/88 season.

Despite only picking up that one point, for anybody other than the mathematical pendants Liverpool were now First Division champions once again.

Liverpool supporters didn't have to wait much longer as three days later, their team secured the title with a 1-0 home win over Tottenham, thanks to Beardsley's 16th goal of the season.

It wasn't Liverpool's greatest performance of the campaign and apart from a moment of magic from Beardsley the event was otherwise too much of a formality to be a shining attraction. Barnes, who had played such a huge part in Liverpool's success, missed the occasion through injury, but joined his teammates on this pitch after the final whistle when the post-match celebrations began.

Skipper Alan Hansen, who had been immaculate since August, claimed his seventh League Championship medal at the club in his own testimonial year and warned: "We've got three or four players who are only in their first season here and so the team can go from strength to strength. We've won it in style. Throughout the season we've scored lots of goals, packed grounds wherever we've played and given people a lot of entertainment."

Dalglish, who had figured only twice all season, both as a substitute, also claimed his seventh League Championship medal and added: "You can't condense the championship into one afternoon. We've enjoyed the season; we've played well and deserved what we've got. You can't dispute that."

Paul Walsh didn't qualify for a medal and although he was on the losing side, he took fond memories away from his first trip to Anfield as a Spurs player. "I remember coming back to Anfield with Tottenham in 1988," said Walsh. "The day Liverpool won the league. I didn't come out for a warm-up but when we came out onto the pitch, I got a fantastic reception from the Kop. They were singing my name and it left me a bit emotional. I've got to say I will never forget that."

The Reds were home and dry with four games to spare, but in typical Liverpool fashion, Dalglish declared his team wouldn't be taking their foot off the pedal, even though the FA Cup final was looming. Moreover, the Reds required seven more points to take over Everton's 90-point record total, which they achieved during the 1984/85 season.

On April 30, the Reds took on Chelsea at Stamford Bridge, where the Blues and their caretaker manager, Scotland Road native and former Liverpool player Bobby Campbell, held the league champions to a one-all draw. Gordon Durie's 71st-minute penalty was cancelled out just four minutes later by a superbly taken free-kick from the fit-again John Barnes that flew high into the right-hand corner of the net. The same 1-1 result followed two days later against Southampton when Dalglish, his players and staff were presented with the new Barclays Division One trophy as well as the traditional First Division trophy, which had made the short journey from Goodison Park. Alan Hansen lifted the trophy and made his first slip of the season as the top part fell off and landed on the Anfield turf.

On May 7, just a week before the FA Cup final, the Reds went to Hillsborough and thrashed Sheffield Wednesday 5-1, giving Wembley opponents Wimbledon a clear demonstration of their intention.

Liverpool's final league game of the campaign also finished one apiece against Luton Town at Anfield, with Liverpool's goal coming from a John Aldridge spectacular bicycle-kick after 17 minutes.

Anfield rose as one in the 62nd minute when Dalglish climbed out of the dugout to replace Craig Johnston. At the age of 37, and with a magnificent managerial career already unfolding, it was expected to be the great Scot's last appearance in the red shirt of Liverpool.

The Reds were then forced to finish their 4000th competitive game with 10 men after Nigel Spackman and Gary Gillespie went off after a clash of heads in the 75th minute, having only one substitution left to make.

Although Lawrie Sanchez's header and Dave Beasant's penalty save from John Aldridge, who sadly became the first player to miss a penalty in an FA Cup final at Wembley, prevented the newly-crowned champions from achieving the 'double' as Wimbledon won the FA Cup final, the Liverpool players from the 1987/88 season can without a doubt look back, knowing they produced some of the greatest football ever witnessed in any league in the world.

Aldridge, who was devastated at the time, later admitted: "To be honest, it wasn't a penalty, I've gone over the ball and Clive Goodyear made a great tackle. Maybe that was in the back of my mind, but it shouldn't have made a difference. I should have put it away. It was just not meant to be for whatever reason and if ever a team deserved to win a 'double', that team did."

Dalglish's exciting new side finished nine points ahead of runners-up Manchester United with 90 points, which equalled Everton's 1985 record. In taking their 17th First Division title the Reds moved alongside the Leeds United team of 1968/69 as one recording the fewest league defeats in a top-flight season (two). Leeds, though, had played 42 times as opposed to Liverpool's 40. Statisticians could point out that in 1888/89 Preston North End lost none of their 22 league matches but in those days, of course, there was just one division, not four.

The 1987/88 season also saw the Reds win the Professional Footballers' Association's Fair Play trophy for being the team with the fewest disciplinary points from all four divisions, providing proof, if any was needed, that their success was down to skill rather than brute force or rough tactics.

John Barnes was voted the PFA's and Football Writers' Footballer of the Year. Alan Hansen was runner-up in the latter poll as Liverpool players collected 98 per cent of the votes! Dalglish also collected his second Manager of the Year award in three seasons and John Aldridge finished as the First Division's top scorer with 26 league goals, an incredible feat to achieve during his first full season with his boyhood club. Peter Beardsley and John Barnes added another 30 league goals between them, also in their debut season at Anfield.

The club were also the biggest crowd-pullers in the land, averaging almost 40,000 for every home league game, beating Manchester United's attendance for the first time since winning promotion to the First Division 1962. The paying Anfield supporter had more than their value for money; not only did their team go the whole season unbeaten at home in the league for the first time in eight seasons, but also the football on show and the attacking prowess of Kenny's new front three was arguably the best and most exhilarating they had ever witnessed.

In the eyes of many Kopites after Rush's departure to Serie A and losing the league to Everton, 1987/88 was a season they truly hadn't seen coming. In the centenary year of the Football League, there could have been no more appropriate winners than Liverpool who had won it a record 17 times, eight more than their nearest rivals Everton. Liverpool, despite all their glorious triumphs, never rested on their laurels and one had the feeling that their latest League Championship success would not be their last...

1987/88: Facts and Statistics

Final league table

		P	W	D	L	F	A	W	D	L	F	A	GD	PTS
1	Liverpool FC	40	15	5	0	49	9	11	7	2	38	15	63	90
2	Manchester United	40	14	5	1	41	17	9	7	4	30	21	33	81
3	Nottingham Forest	40	11	7	2	40	17	9	6	5	27	22	28	73
4	Everton	40	14	4	2	34	11	5	9	6	19	16	26	70
5	QPR	40	12	4	4	30	14	7	6	7	18	24	10	67
6	Arsenal	40	11	4	5	35	16	7	8	5	23	23	19	66
7	Wimbledon	40	8	9	3	32	20	6	6	8	26	27	11	57
8	Newcastle United	40	9	6	5	32	23	5	8	7	23	30	2	56
9	Luton Town	40	11	6	3	40	21	3	5	12	17	37	-1	53
10	Coventry City	40	6	8	6	23	25	7	6	7	23	28	-7	53
11	Sheffield Wednesday	40	10	2	8	27	30	5	6	9	25	36	-14	53
12	Southampton	40	6	8	6	27	26	6	6	8	22	27	-4	50
13	Tottenham	40	9	5	6	26	23	3	6	11	12	25	-10	47
14	Norwich City	40	7	5	8	26	26	5	4	11	14	26	-12	45
15	Derby	40	6	7	7	18	17	4	6	10	17	28	-10	43
16	West Ham United	40	6	9	5	23	21	3	6	11	17	31	-12	42
17	Charlton Athletic	40	7	7	6	23	21	2	8	10	15	31	-14	42
18	Chelsea	40	7	11	2	24	17	2	4	14	26	51	-18	42
19	Portsmouth	40	4	8	8	21	27	3	6	11	15	39	-30	35
20	Watford	40	4	5	11	15	24	3	6	11	12	27	-24	32
21	Oxford United	40	5	7	8	24	34	1	6	13	20	46	-36	31

Games for the 1987/1988 season

(The number after date is league position after the game)

1	15.08.1987	3	W	2-1	Arsenal, Highbury, 1st Division
2	29.08.1987	7	W	4-1	Coventry City, Highfield Road, 1st Division
3	05.09.1987	9	D	1-1	West Ham United, Upton Park, 1st Division
4	12.09.1987	7	W	2-0	Oxford United, Anfield, 1st Division
5	15.09.1987	3	W	3-2	Charlton Athletic, Anfield, 1st Division
6	20.09.1987	3	W	4-1	Newcastle United, St. James' Park, 1st Division
7	23.09.1987		D	1-1	Blackburn Rovers, Ewood Park, League Cup 2nd round 1L
8	29.09.1987	2	W	4-0	Derby County, Anfield, 1st Division
9	03.10.1987	2	W	4-0	Portsmouth, Anfield, 1st Division
10	06.10.1987		W	1-0	Blackburn Rovers, Anfield, League Cup 2nd round 2L

11	17.10.1987	1	W	4-0	Queens Park Rangers, Anfield, 1st Division
12	24.10.1987	1	W	1-0	Luton Town, Kenilworth Road, 1st Division
13	28.10.1987		L	0-1	Everton, Anfield, League Cup 3rd round
14	01.11.1987	1	W	2-0	Everton, Anfield, 1st Division
15	04.11.1987	1	D	1-1	Wimbledon, Plough Lane, 1st Division
16	15.11.1987	2	D	1-1	Manchester United, Old Trafford, 1st Division
17	21.11.1987	2	D	0-0	Norwich City, Anfield, 1st Division
18	24.11.1987	1	W	4-0	Watford, Anfield, 1st Division
19	28.11.1987	1	W	2-0	Tottenham Hotspur, White Hart Lane, 1st Division
20	06.12.1987	1	W	2-1	Chelsea, Anfield, 1st Division
21	12.12.1987	1	D	2-2	Southampton, The Dell, 1st Division
22	19.12.1987	1	W	1-0	Sheffield Wednesday, Anfield, 1st Division
23	26.12.1987	1	W	3-0	Oxford United, Manor Ground, 1st Division
24	28.12.1987	1	W	4-0	Newcastle United, Anfield, 1st Division
25	01.01.1988	1	W	4-0	Coventry City, Anfield, 1st Division
26	09.01.1988		D	0-0	Stoke City, Victoria Ground, FA Cup 3rd round
27	12.01.1988		W	1-0	Stoke City, Anfield, FA Cup 3rd round replay
28	16.01.1988	1	W	2-0	Arsenal, Anfield, 1st Division
29	23.01.1988	1	W	2-0	Charlton Athletic, Selhurst Park, 1st Division
30	31.01.1988		W	2-0	Aston Villa, Villa Park, FA Cup 4th round
31	06.02.1988	1	D	0-0	West Ham United, Anfield, 1st Division
32	13.02.1988	1	W	4-1	Watford, Vicarage Road, 1st Division
33	21.02.1988		W	1-0	Everton, Goodison Park, FA Cup 5th round
34	27.02.1988	1	W	2-0	Portsmouth, Fratton Park, 1st Division
35	05.03.1988	1	W	1-0	Queens Park Rangers, Loftus Road, 1st Division
36	13.03.1988		W	4-0	Manchester City, Maine Road, FA Cup 6th round
37	16.03.1988	1	D	1-1	Derby County, Baseball Ground, 1st Division
38	20.03.1988	1	L	0-1	Everton, Goodison Park, 1st Division
39	26.03.1988	1	W	2-1	Wimbledon, Anfield, 1st Division
40	02.04.1988	1	L	1-2	Nottingham Forest, City Ground, 1st Division
41	04.04.1988	1	D	3-3	Manchester United, Anfield, 1st Division
42	09.04.1988		W	2-1	Nottingham Forest, Hillsborough, FA Cup Semi-final
43	13.04.1988	1	W	5-0	Nottingham Forest, Anfield, 1st Division
44	20.04.1988	1	D	0-0	Norwich City, Carrow Road, 1st Division
45	23.04.1988	1	W	1-0	Tottenham Hotspur, Anfield, 1st Division
46	30.04.1988	1	D	1-1	Chelsea, Stamford Bridge, 1st Division
47	02.05.1988	1	D	1-1	Southampton, Anfield, 1st Division
48	07.05.1988	1	W	5-1	Sheffield Wednesday, Hillsborough, 1st Division
49	09.05.1988	1	D	1-1	Luton Town, Anfield, 1st Division
50	14.05.1988		L	0-1	Wimbledon, Wembley, FA Cup Final

Friendlies

1	23.07.1987	L	2-3	Bayern Munich, Olympia Stadion, Testimonial
2	26.07.1987	W	4-0	Aalborg Chang, Aalborg Stadion, Friendly
3	28.07.1987	D	1-1	Brønshøj BK, Ringsted Stadion, Friendly
4	01.08.1987	W	3-0	Vejle, Spjald Stadion, Friendly
5	03.08.1987	W	3-0	Karlstad BK, Tingvalla IP, Friendly
6	06.08.1987	W	4-1	Vålerenga, Bislett, Friendly
7	09.08.1987	W	1-0	Celtic, Parkhead Stadium, Testimonial
8	19.08.1987	W	5-0	Irish Olympic XI, Lansdowne Road, Friendly
9	23.08.1987	W	1-0	Atletico Madrid, Vicente Calderon, Villa De Madrid Trophy
10	19.10.1987	W	4-0	Dundee, Dens Park Stadium, Testimonial
11	01.03.1988	W	2-0	Osasuna, El Sadar, Testimonial
12	16.05.1988	W	3-2	England XI, Anfield, Testimonial

Appearances for the 1987/1988 season

Name	League	FA Cup	LC	Total
Steve Nicol	40	7	3	50
Steve McMahon	40	7	2	49
Alan Hansen	39	7	3	49
John Barnes	38	7	3	48
Peter Beardsley	38	7	3	48
Bruce Grobbelaar	38	5	3	46
John Aldridge	36	6	3	45
Gary Gillespie	35	5	2	42
Ray Houghton	28	7	0	35
Craig Johnston	30	3	2	35
Nigel Spackman	27	5	1	33
Ronnie Whelan	28	2	3	33
Barry Venison	18	2	2	22
Gary Ablett	17	5	0	22
Mark Lawrenson	14	2	3	19
Paul Walsh	8	0	1	9
Jan Mølby	7	1	0	8
Mike Hooper	2	2	0	4
Kenny Dalglish	2	0	0	2
John Wark	1	0	1	2
Alex Watson	2	0	0	2
Kevin MacDonald	1	0	0	1
Steve Staunton	0	0	0	0

Goalscorers for the 1987/1988 season

Name	League	FA Cup	LC	Total
John Aldridge	26	2	1	29
Peter Beardsley	15	3	0	18
John Barnes	15	2	0	17
Steve McMahon	9	0	0	9
Steve Nicol	6	0	1	7
Ray Houghton	5	2	0	7
Craig Johnston	5	1	0	6
Gary Gillespie	4	0	0	4
Ronnie Whelan	1	0	0	1
Alan Hansen	1	0	0	1

The squad during the 1987/1988 season

Bruce Grobbelaar, Goalkeeper
Mike Hooper, Goalkeeper
Gary Gillespie, Defender
Alex Watson, Defender
Mark Lawrenson, Defender
Steve Nicol, Defender
Steve Staunton, Defender
Alan Hansen, Defender
Barry Venison, Defender
Gary Ablett, Defender
John Barnes, Midfielder
John Wark, Midfielder
Ray Houghton, Midfielder
Craig Johnston, Midfielder
Mike Marsh, Midfielder
Ronnie Whelan, Midfielder
Steve McMahon, Midfielder
Kevin MacDonald, Midfielder
Mark Seagraves, Midfielder
Nigel Spackman, Midfielder
Jan Mølby, Midfielder
Kenny Dalglish, Midfielder
Peter Beardsley, Striker
Paul Walsh, Striker
John Aldridge, Striker
John Durnin, Striker

Transfers for the 1987/1988 season

In:
John Barnes, Watford, £900,000, 9 June 1987
Peter Beardsley, Newcastle United, £1,900,000, 14 July 1987
Mike Marsh, Kirkby Town, Free, 21 August 1987
Ray Houghton, Oxford United, £825,000, 19 October 1987

Out:
John McGregor, Rangers, £70,000, June 1987
Ken De Mange, Leeds United, £65,000, September 1987
Mark Seagraves, Manchester City, £100,000, 25 September 1987
Brian Mooney, Preston North End, £82,000, 9 October 1987
John Wark, Ipswich Town, £100,000, 4 January 1988
Paul Walsh, Tottenham Hotspur, £500,000, 16 February 1988

A collection of statistics for the 1987/1988 season

The season in numbers:
Total games: 50
Games won: 32
Games drawn: 14
Games lost: 4
Clean sheets – League: 21
Clean sheets – Overall: 27
Total goals: 99
Average attendance at home – League: 39,682
Average attendance at home – Overall: 39,429
Average goals per game – League: 2.45
Average goals per game – Overall: 2.22
Average goal minute – League: 53
Average goal minute – Overall: 53

Goals split down to competitions:
League – 87
FA Cup – 10
League Cup – 2

Player debuts:
John Barnes against Arsenal on 15.08.1987
Peter Beardsley against Arsenal on 15.08.1987
Ray Houghton against Luton Town on 24.10.1987
Alex Watson against QPR on 05.03.1988

Statistics and information provided by LFChistory.net

18 : TAKEN FOR GRANTED?

1989/90

BY THE END OF THE 1988/89 SEASON, THE REDS
and their manager were left exhausted. The Hillsborough
disaster that cruelly and unlawfully took the lives of 96
innocent men, women and children had almost broken the team,
the management and the city. The press and the supporters saw
a new side to Dalglish as he united the club and city in its grief.
The harrowing scenes Dalglish witnessed at Hillsborough and in its
aftermath, and the care he showed to the victims' families without
seeking help to deal with the mental anguish he was experiencing
himself, was a testament to the Scot's true character.

Despite winning the 1989 FA Cup final, symbolically, against
Everton, the Reds lost the league to Arsenal in the most painstaking
way possible. The last league game was between the two top teams
at Anfield and only victory by a two-goal margin in favour of the
Gunners would win them the League Championship. In the final
minute, Michael Thomas scored Arsenal's second that grabbed the
title away from the hosts. Liverpool had literally been 45 seconds
away from a second 'double'. If ever Liverpool needed an extra
incentive to win a League Championship, it was then and the Reds

entered into the 1989/90 season with a clear message to their rivals: we're going to win it back!

Jim Beglin left on a free transfer in the summer of 1989 to rebuild his career at Leeds United. Only a few days into the pre-season, Beglin's right knee gave way. Another operation followed and then he was loaned out to Plymouth Argyle. The only other departure that summer was Kevin MacDonald who by then was out of the first-team picture due to his lengthy lay-off caused by a double leg fracture suffered at The Dell in September 1986. The midfielder signed for Coventry City, also on a free, in July 1989, where he went on to play 44 games in two seasons.

Dalglish strengthened his defence by adding Swedish international Glenn Hysén (pronounced Hussain) from Fiorentina for £600,000. The Swede had earned rave reviews for his displays against England in two 1990 World Cup qualification matches that inspired great interest in him from English clubs. Liverpool stole him right from under the nose of Alex Ferguson at Manchester United who thought they had his transfer signed, sealed... but forgot the deliver bit. Ferguson and United chairman Martin Edwards flew out to Florence to conclude the transfer but were then told by Hysén's agent that his client had already signed for Liverpool. By the time of his arrival on Merseyside, Hysén had been captain of the Swedish national team for many years and voted one of the 10 best players in Europe when France Football announced their Golden Ball winner in 1987, so this was a big coup for Liverpool. "When I first joined Liverpool from Fiorentina, I was star-struck," Hysén later recalled. "I remember sitting in the dressing room at Melwood for the first time alongside Bruce Grobbelaar, Steve Nicol, Alan Hansen, Ian Rush and John Barnes, thinking to myself how privileged I was to be with some of the best players in Europe."

Dalglish's only other purchase that summer was 17-year-old Steve

Harkness from Carlisle United. Harkness was a centre forward at Carlisle when he impressed Kenny Dalglish in a youth cup tie against Liverpool and had only played 13 games for their first team when Liverpool snapped him up. Harkness was a big prospect and was appointed captain of the England Under-18s team. Peter Beardsley, who also started his career at the Cumbrians and was Harkness' boyhood hero, soon took the teenager under his wing. "Peter had obviously heard about my background," Harkness recalled. "When I started training with the lads at the beginning of the season, he came straight up to me for a chat. He told me how much he had enjoyed his own time at Carlisle and what a friendly club it was."

The Charity Shield trophy at Wembley was a great way to start the season, especially when Arsenal were the victims. Peter Beardsley scored the only goal of the game on the half-hour mark, converting brilliantly from a superb Barry Venison cross. Alan Hansen was restored as captain, after having missed all but the closing eight fixtures of the previous season through a knee injury. Hysén on his debut was immaculate and was named Man of the Match. Dalglish preferred his old strike partner Ian Rush, who returned from Italy in August 1988, to John Aldridge to lead the Liverpool attack against the league champions. Aldridge had been Liverpool's most prolific scorer for the previous two seasons, netting an incredible 60 goals in 92 games, and he was unfortunate to be an unused substitute as the Reds retained the Tennent's Charity Shield.

The real business of the new season started on August 19, with a visit to Anfield from First Division new boys Manchester City. It took Liverpool just seven minutes to break the deadlock as John Barnes uncompromisingly converted from the penalty spot with his left foot after City defender Brian Gayle was judged to have handled a Peter Beardsley strike. City's equaliser after 23 minutes was fortuitously gained, following a confusing ricochet off the Liverpool wall from Andy Hinchcliffe's free-kick. Second-half goals from Beardsley and Nicol assured the Reds of all three points from their league opener. Yet again, Aldridge was an unused substitute.

A winning start at Anfield was followed by two frustrating draws away at Aston Villa and Luton Town. On August 30, the Reds took a midweek break from their domestic duties and travelled to the Spanish capital to take on Real Madrid in the annual Santiago Bernabéu Trophy.

With no European football, and a reduced league programme of 38 games, four fewer than three seasons earlier, First Division clubs were finding these lucrative friendlies hard to resist. It was the first time Liverpool had played the Spanish giants in their iconic stadium and judging by the match report in the *Liverpool Echo*, the Reds failed to impress: "Liverpool discovered last night exactly what awaits English clubs when the European door is finally re-opened. Any thoughts that our teams will immediately reconquer the continent should be cast aside in the light of a Real Madrid performance which augurs well for the coming season and new coach and former Liverpool marksman John Toshack. True, defensive lapses contributed to the Reds downfall, but their 2-0 defeat was an accurate reflection of a match in which they were always struggling and at times outclassed."

On September 9, Liverpool faced Derby County in their third consecutive away fixture in the league. Dalglish's side turned it up a notch and left the Baseball Ground with a 3-0 victory with all three Liverpool goals coming in the second half. Ian Rush stabbed home from close range to get the Reds off the mark and claimed his first goal of the season. This must have come as a relief for Liverpool's predatory Welshman who also contributed hugely to Liverpool's two late goals scored by Barnes from the penalty spot and Beardsley. A great weight had been lifted from Rush's shoulders which would put him in good stead for the rest of the season.

As Rush began to find the back of the net, it was now becoming apparent that goal machine Aldridge was no longer in Dalglish's plans after making only one appearance from the bench in Liverpool's first five competitive games.

The club were taking offers for his services and with a £1,250,000 move to Real Sociedad looming, Aldridge was allowed to come off the bench when a penalty was awarded during the Tuesday night 9-0 massacre of Crystal Palace at Anfield on September 12.

Beardsley graciously made way for Aldridge who tucked the spotkick away with efficiency and at the end of an emotional farewell appearance, he threw his shirt and boots into the Kop. The Scouser became the first non-Basque player to sign for Real Sociedad and was also a big hit with their fans, scoring more than a goal every other game.

Aldridge described his goal against Crystal Palace as the most bittersweet experience of his career: "I wouldn't describe it as an altogether happy memory for me because I was leaving the club I loved and the club I had always dreamt of playing for. But to get the chance to score at the Kop end in my last game was special. It was a very poignant moment for me. Everyone knew I didn't want to leave. I'd have stayed there for the rest of my career if I could and I told Kenny I wouldn't go unless he gave me a chance. But he made it clear that Ian Rush and Peter Beardsley were his preferred front two and with a World Cup coming up the following summer, I realised I couldn't hang around and just sit on the bench. I remember when we got the penalty against Palace and the Kop suddenly started singing my name. They clearly wanted me to come on to take it and

I was a bit surprised when Kenny went along with their wishes. If I had to leave the club then this was the best way to do it, scoring a goal at the Kop end and having the crowd show their appreciation for what I had given the club over the years. At the end of the game I was all over the place emotionally and it's really difficult to put into words exactly how I was feeling at that time. It was a real mix of emotions, that's for sure."

Following Liverpool's biggest ever top-flight victory, in which no less than eight players managed to get their name of the scoresheet, Dalglish told the press: "Aldo is our most popular player here. He's achieved a lifetime's ambition by playing for the club and contributing so much to it. We're only selling him because we can't give him what he deserves here. Maybe, like Rush, he will be back one day. But as Rush knows, players may come and players may go from Anfield, but Liverpool go on for ever."

After five rounds played, Liverpool sat unbeaten at the top of the First Division, level on points but with a superior goal difference over early front runners, Millwall. Following a score draw against Norwich City at Anfield, Liverpool turned their attentions to a two-legged Littlewoods League Cup tie with Wigan Athletic. During the first leg at Anfield the Reds were 2-1 down but they saved themselves from embarrassment and scored four times in 24 minutes to win through 5-2.

Strangely, the second leg was also played at Anfield as Springfield Park did not meet the required safety standards with the away terrace having had its capacity cut to just 378. Stand-in striker, 20-year-old Steve Staunton, who replaced the injured Ian Rush at half-time, became the first Liverpool player to score a hat-trick after coming on as a substitute as the Reds beat the Latics 3-0 on the night and 8-2 on aggregate.

Staunton arrived from Irish club Dundalk for a fee of £20,000 in 1986 as a 17-year-old and made his breakthrough into the first team two years later. The Irishman's versatility proved useful for Liverpool as he could play in a number of different positions.

Although "Stan" played as a left-back more often than not, Barry Venison and David Burrows had earlier featured in that position during the 1988/89 season, but through solid performances and his attacking flair, Staunton ousted his teammates and made the left-back position his own during the last three months of the previous season.

By the time the Reds crossed Stanley Park on September 23 for the first Merseyside derby of the season, Everton were the division's new leaders. Liverpool allowed their rivals a goal start as striker Mike Newell, who spent five years playing in Liverpool's youth sides, put the Toffees ahead after just 18 minutes.

The Reds then found their stride and nudged Everton off the top spot with an excellent 3-1 victory. Barnes scored his first derby goal from a well taken header after a pinpoint cross by Beardsley. Ian Rush finished the afternoon off by netting twice in two minutes. Rush's 23rd goal in 24 Merseyside derby games, well past the record of Dixie Dean, was the ultimate answer to those who had criticised his manager for having sold Aldridge to Sociedad.

At the time it had been said that Rush would never be the same again as Dalglish was no longer on the field providing him with the majestic service he was used to before his move to Juventus. But Beardsley had always been brought in to replace Dalglish and against Everton he came as close as he ever had done to recreating the previous telepathic partnership Rush shared with Dalglish.

On October 14, the Reds came away from Wimbledon with maximum points after Ronnie Whelan's winner kept them at the top of the table after eight games. However, the same wasn't to be said following their next fixture as the unbeaten league leaders crashed to a devasting 4-1 defeat at The Dell against Chris Nicholl's young emerging Southampton side.

The Reds slipped down to second after suffering their biggest league defeat in almost three years and their biggest ever top-flight league defeat at The Dell. Dalglish couldn't find a single good word to say about his players, claiming that the supporters in the stands did a better job than those on the pitch.

Four days later, things got worse for the Reds as they crashed out of the Littlewoods Cup thanks to a late Alan Smith goal as George Graham's team took revenge for their Charity Shield defeat at the start of the campaign. Despite beating Spurs 1-0 at Anfield the following Sunday, the fans knew that their team's form was far from the vintage Reds they were used to and the next two games brought two more defeats. Cyrille Regis' second-half headed goal gave Coventry their first win in 23 attempts at Anfield, which was followed by a 3-2 reversal at Loftus Road against 17th-placed QPR.

Liverpool were far away from producing championship winning form, only managing three points from 12 and despite struggling with defensive injuries, in their previous four league fixtures they were giving away an average of two goals a match. Although no-one would dispute that Liverpool were going through a sticky patch, judging by Dalglish's post-match interview after defeat to QPR, the Scot didn't sound too deflated: "No one likes to lose, even less when you're wearing a red shirt. The important thing is that we continue to believe in what we're doing. We'll just have to take our chances with the bounce of the ball and add a little bit of thought and we'll be perfectly happy. It's still early and the commitment and attitude of the players is right."

In spite of their poor form the Reds were holding on to third place, just four points behind new league leaders Chelsea. After getting back to winning ways with a 2-1 victory at Millwall, Liverpool met their old foes Arsenal for the third time of the season. Thirty minutes in, Rush set up Liverpool's opener by cushioning the ball down for Steve McMahon to unleash a precise drive to score his second goal of the season. In the second half, Liverpool were given a two-goal cushion from Barnes, who ignored Arsenal's substantial wall and the imposing height of their 6ft 4inch goalkeeper to curl his free-kick around the obstacle and over John Lukic into the top corner of the Anfield Road end net. Although Alan Smith halved Liverpool's lead 10 minutes from the end, it was the Reds who finished the game taking all three points as the fierce encounter ended 2-1.

The Times summed up the physical nature of the game, writing: "At the end of yesterday's clash between the nation's two heavy-weights, Anfield had been transformed into 'Emergency Ward 10'. The description was uttered by George Graham, Arsenal's manager, after he had left with casualties which included O'Leary and the bloodied Niall Quinn. His defeated side finished in comparatively healthy condition. Liverpool suffered various head injuries. Hysén and Hansen were both cut and Venison, dazed with concussion, was lying in hospital."

Before their midweek trip to Sheffield Wednesday on November 29, Liverpool had regained their place at the top, albeit on goal difference. The title race was really starting to hot up. Liverpool, Arsenal, Aston Villa and Chelsea all had 27 points each, however, the Reds had played a game less than their rivals. Liverpool's visit to Hillsborough was an emotional return to the scene of the previous season's tragedy. The Reds suffered a 2-0 defeat in what was their first game at that ground since 1964. Before the game, as the players stood in silence, club captain Alan Hansen and Sheffield keeper Chris Turner, laid a wreath on the empty Leppings Lane End terrace. In the stand above, 4500 Liverpool supporters had thrown scarves, flowers and banners onto the stone steps. It was an atmosphere in which a football match seemed like a terrible intrusion.

Liverpool started December with a 4-1 victory at bottom-placed Manchester City, where the gap in class was simply too great. Nick Tanner made his first-team debut that afternoon at Maine Road, replacing Gillespie after 16 minutes who went off with hamstring trouble. Tanner joined Liverpool from Bristol City for £20,000 in July 1988.

He was used mainly as a midfield player by Rovers and had made over 100 appearances for the Pirates. Like so many other new arrivals at Anfield, Tanner had to be patient, especially as Liverpool felt he might be a better central defender than a midfielder. Central defence was a position in which the Liverpool team was still strong and the Bristolian waited patiently for his chance while turning out for Phil Thompson's reserves.

In December, the club mourned the death of one of the original members of the Boot Room, Reuben Bennett, who passed away quietly in his sleep in a Liverpool hospital after suffering a long illness, one week short of his 76th birthday.

Bennett dedicated more than half a century to the sport of football and stayed at the club well into his 70s. Bennett's son Michael explained how Kenny Dalglish would keep his dad busy: "Kenny was very good to my dad. We used to say, 'For heaven's sake, will you retire? Is Kenny going to have your death on his hands?!' But he'd say, 'Kenny said I've got a job for as long as I want it'. They allowed him to make a contribution, and that's all he wanted to do in the later years."

Tommy Smith, one of the players who was brought up on Bennett's tough stewardship during the Sixties, told the *Liverpool Echo* at the time of his death: "Reuben Bennett was Bill Shankly's original right-hand, a fellow Scot and a really strong individual, who used to say to us, 'Get some fire in your bellies and get out there and get the job done'. I can still see him out on the training field, socks down and hard as they come. If you picked up an injury and said you needed treatment, Reuben would look at you and say, 'Just rub it down with a kipper'. You might have a nasty cut, but it was just a pin-prick to him, 'Clean it up with a wire brush', he would say with a glint in his eye. One of his traits was that he never seemed to eat, but he enjoyed a drop of Scotch like most people north of the border. We would laugh and say to him, 'Having chips and a drop of Scotch for dinner today, Reuben?' I suppose he was one of the lesser known figures at Anfield, in some respects, but he still did a tremendous job for the club, first as a coach and then as the man who used to spy on the opposition. It's always sad when you lose one of the old brigade, one of the men who helped put Liverpool on the road to the top. Reuben Bennett played his part and will be missed."

Injuries to players, which over the past 20 years or more had seemed to have afflicted all clubs bar Liverpool, had finally caught up with the Merseysiders. With up to eight players injured at any one time during the previous seven weeks, Liverpool's efforts to bring the title back to Anfield were being seriously frustrated. "Injuries are part of professional football," Dalglish observed. "The important thing is having the right depth of quality in the squad."

The disruption to Liverpool's form, however, had not been caused by the scale of the injury problem, but by the damage done to continuity. In the first 10 games of the season, none of which Liverpool had lost, the team was virtually unchanged. In the last 10, not a game had gone by without the team being tinkered with in some department as 19 players had been called upon.

The month of December, though, could have been Liverpool's salvation, with four of their six games at home and even in their present state of comparative disarray, Liverpool would prove too much for most teams.

On December 16, Liverpool took on Chelsea at Stamford Bridge without the multi-talented John Barnes. The England international had to be carried off the field during the Reds' previous game at home to Aston Villa after his hamstring gave way in the 37th minute.

Liverpool beat the Blues 5-2 as the Reds produced one of their most iconic performances of recent times. *The Guardian* reported: "Viewers from 61 countries will have enjoyed the goal highlights at least of a match parading the English game at its best. Those fans abroad who videoed the entire Worldwide Soccer transmission will no doubt re-run Liverpool's finest moments at Stamford Bridge many times before the year is out. Chelsea's manager Bobby Campbell will also watch the contest repeatedly via the club's own tape because he knows it tells almost as much about his team's frailties as Liverpool's strengths. Campbell, Scouser and former Anfield player, after praising the 'best team in the country', made an interesting predication: 'Liverpool have a hell of a chance to win the World Cup next year, and I don't jest!'"

By the time the Reds faced Charlton Athletic at Anfield on December 30, their final game of the infamous Eighties, they were sat two points clear at the top after picking up 11 points from 15 since their defeat at Hillsborough. Liverpool's only goal against the Addicks came from fit-again John Barnes, who scored his 12th goal of the season, ensuring that Liverpool would begin the new decade as they did the last, on top of the First Division.

Rush had the chance to double Liverpool's lead in the second half, but his penalty kick was saved by former Liverpool reserve goalkeeper Bob Bolder. The reaction of Kenny Dalglish was to lavish praise on his players, which was not usually his style: "If any club deserves to go into the new year on top, it is this one. Liverpool have been the best club for longer than two decades and in the one that is about to finish it has been the club's most successful."

Liverpool ended the decade on a high note off the pitch as well. The club's elegant long-serving chairman John Smith, was included in the Queen's New Year's Honours List and received a knighthood for services to sport. "You can call me, Sir John", he said in his charming and well-spoken way. Smith retired at the end of the 1989/90 season after 17 years of service as chairman, overseeing the most successful era in Liverpool's history.

Liverpool began the Nineties on New Year's Day with a 2-2 draw against Brian Clough's Nottingham Forest at the City Ground. The Reds then came up against Third Division Swansea City in the third round of the FA Cup. A goalless draw at Vetch Field was fought out in the first game, with the home side's 21-year old goalkeeper Lee Bracey pulling off at least five memorable saves to give his side a lucrative replay at Anfield three days later.

Bracey and Swansea, who were 55 league places behind the hosts, crumbled in front of an Anfield crowd as the FA Cup holders simply blew the Swans away 8-0. It was the Reds' biggest FA Cup win since 1892, the year of their birth when they put nine past Newton in their second-ever game in the competition, and the first at Anfield.

Ian Rush grabbed a hat-trick, his first since his return from Italy, Barnes scored a brace plus a goal apiece from Ronnie Whelan and Peter Beardsley, whose finish was scored so quickly after the restart, it was missed by the cameras. Steve Nicol ended proceedings with a wonderful chip which had class written all over it. In January, 1990 the Taylor Report was published, which looked into the Hillsborough disaster. The report was an enquiry which was overseen by Lord Justice Taylor, into the causes of the tragic events that took place in Sheffield on April 15, 1989, as a result of which, at the time of the report, 95 Liverpool fans had died (Tony Bland remained in a coma at this point).

The Taylor Report found that the main reason for the disaster was the failure of police control. It recommended that all major stadiums convert to an all-seater model, and that all ticketed spectators should have seats, as opposed to some or all being obliged to stand. Although the report exonerated the fans and laid the blame for the catastrophe at the feet of the authorities, the bereaved and the survivors would still face a 30-year struggle for truth and justice.

During the first few days of February, the sad news reached the club that former manager Don Welsh had died at the age of 78 in Stevenage after a period of ill health. Welsh took over the Anfield reins in 1951, replacing George Kay, and managed the Reds for 232 games until 1956 when he was replaced by former club captain, Phil Taylor.

The former Charlton inside forward was no stranger to Merseyside at the time he was made manager. Welsh scored 43 goals in 40 games as a guest for the Reds during World War II. He was a prolific goalscorer and even hit a double hat-trick for the Reds in a 12-1 win over Southport in December, 1944. For many Liverpudlians it had been sad to hear of his death. None more so than Ronnie Moran: "I liked Don a lot. He was always passionate about the game. He inherited a lot of players in their thirties when he arrived, but I'll never forget him because he gave me my first team debut at Derby in 1952."

In footballing terms, Liverpool begun February level at the top of the First Division with Graham Taylor's Aston Villa who had played a game less. No slip ups could be permitted in the second Merseyside derby of the season on February 3, in which this time it was Everton's turn to make the short journey across Stanley Park.

Liverpool put in a superb first-half display, which was typified by the power of McMahon, who demonstrated magnificent individual skills welded to a team performance, which if Everton had not themselves been in top form, might have answered the Kop's chant for 10 goals.

The game ended 2-1 thanks to first-half strikes from Barnes and Beardsley from the spot. The victory not only provided the red half of the city with Merseyside derby bragging rights, but also put their team three points clear at the top of the table.

Liverpool's only other league fixture during the month of February was a goalless draw at Carrow Road. Liverpool were rather unfortunate though as referee Lester Shapter had judged Beardsley's cross at the dead-ball line to have gone out of play, before the England forward had squared it for Rush to slot home from close range.

However, the TV camaras showed that the ball never went out and a worldwide audience sat watching on in judgement. It was also an afternoon to forget for Glenn Hysén who became the first Liverpool player to be sent off in three years for two bookable offences on Norwich's Scottish striker, Robert Fleck.

Before visiting Old Trafford on March 18, a single Gary Gillespie's headed goal from a Beardsley corner was enough for the Reds to take maximum points against Millwall at Anfield. Liverpool were looking for their first win at Old Trafford in almost eight years and would have fancied their chances more than ever as their Mancunian rivals were struggling in the bottom half of the table fighting a relegation battle. Liverpool had seemed to have timed to perfection the unleashing of their true form, by convincingly defeating and outplaying Alex Ferguson's below-par team.

After Liverpool had established a two-goal advantage early in the second half, both their goals coming from Barnes, they played with such enterprise that a rout seemed inevitable. Although no more goals followed at the Liverpool end, an unmarked Whelan chipped a backpass from 30 yards over Grobbelaar into his own net, to give United a lifeline with eight minutes to go. To date, Whelan's moment of madness is considered by many to be one of the most bizarre and comical own goals in top-flight history.

Liverpool's 20-match unbeaten run came to an abrupt end on March 21 in a midweek fixture against Tottenham at White Hart Lane. It was Liverpool's first reversal in all competitions since November 29 at Hillsborough and at the end of the night the Reds found themselves in second place, three points behind Villa. In a largely disappointing game, Paul Stewart's well directed header from Paul Gascoigne's cross seven minutes from time gave Tottenham the victory their more persistent aggression deserved.

A 10-day break in the domestic fixture list due to internationals meant that Liverpool couldn't put their defeat at White Hart Lane immediately behind them. On March 31, Southampton, who in October had inflicted a 4-1 defeat on the Reds, visited Anfield.

Twenty minutes from the end of a pacy and enthralling match, Liverpool found themselves 2-1 down to their enterprising visitors from the south coast and they could not complain. The 35-year-old Jimmy Case, who learnt his trade at Anfield, made the first goal and scored the second. Case fired home a stunning drive from outside the area, struck with so much venom that Grobbelaar hardly saw it go past him. The Reds showed the winning resilience that champions are made of and fought back to win 3-2 after Rush's powerful, low winner eight minutes from time. Victory over the Saints prompted a huge feeling of relief amongst the Anfield faithful as their team survived a mini crisis.

Liverpool followed up their victory against Southampton with a 2-1 win over Wimbledon at Anfield on April 3, thanks to first-half goals from Rush and Gillespie. The Reds now found themselves on top of the pile again, three points clear and a game in hand over the Villans, who had lost their previous two games. The First Division title was now a two-horse race and the Reds were in pole position with seven games to go to claim their eighteenth league title.

With the Reds leading the First Division, there was talk of another 'double' being on the cards. After battling through the previous rounds of the FA Cup, a semi-final clash with Crystal Palace was waiting for Dalglish's men at Villa Park. Liverpool had already put 11 goals past Steve Coppell's side in the two league meetings between the clubs that season. Palace were also fighting for First Division survival.

Therefore, on these grounds the Reds were overwhelming favourites to progress to the final. It was the first time the FA Cup semi-finals had been split for television, as until then the matches had started simultaneously at 3pm on a Saturday, available only on radio.

In one of the greatest FA Cup semi-finals of all time, Palace were trailing 3-2 in the closing stages, when in the 89th minute Andy Gray scored a dramatic equaliser, before Alan Pardew's goal in extra-time sealed the upset and a shock victory for the Eagles.

Liverpool were comfortably controlling the tie and at the interval, captain Alan Hansen thought his side would be coasting to the final. "If it was a boxing match, it would have been stopped," said Hansen. "We were so far in front it was untrue. The one thing you were taught to avoid at all times at Liverpool was complacency. I must admit it was probably me to blame, because I went into that dressing room at half-time thinking 'there is no way in the world we can get beaten here'. It just seemed to me it would end up four or five, or even another nine, by the way it was going."

Following that astounding defeat to Palace, Liverpool's ingenious forward, Peter Beardsley was diagnosed with a stress fracture to his knee, which deprived him of playing any further part in the 1989/90 season. Despite being without Beardsley's abilities for the season's run-in, Dalglish had a secret weapon up his sleeve.

Towards the end of March, the Scot had added a different dimension to his strike force in the form of Ronny Rosenthal. The Israel international became an instant cult hero with his explosive start to his Liverpool career. He had been on trial at First Division Luton Town where he scored two goals in three games but they couldn't broker a deal with Liege.

The asking price was £500,000. Liverpool asked Liege if they could have a look and after only one reserve appearance he was signed on loan. Rosenthal's full debut for the first team was against Charlton on April 11 where he scored three times in Liverpool's 4-0 win at Selhurst Park. "Kenny told me an hour before the game I'd be playing," said Rosenthal. "After 10 minutes I scored with my right foot, then again immediately after half-time with my left and finally with my head after combining with John Barnes. The perfect hat-trick, I believe they call it."

After a fairytale start to his Liverpool career, Rosenthal was soon becoming the Kop's new idol, but his fourth goal in two games against Nottingham Forest three day later could not disguise Liverpool's continuing uncertainty as they allowed Forest to recover from a two-goal deficit.

The League Championship race had some life left in it after all. Dalglish's summing up of his side's performance against Forest would be impossible to better: "We got what we deserved. If you give them away at one end and don't put them away when they are presented to you at the other end, you pay the price."

Although Arsenal were no longer seriously involved in the title race, they did enough to deny their rivals three points in a Wednesday night televised encounter at Highbury. Again, Rosenthal was the difference, the Israeli's introduction after 64 minutes injected some breathtaking speed and he was responsible for Barnes' equaliser four minutes from time.

In the opinion of George Graham, the destiny of the First Division trophy had now been decided: "Without question Liverpool will win it." Dalglish was more restrained and said: "We have a better chance than Arsenal, but even if we had lost tonight, we would still have been in the best position. The fewer games there are to play, the harder it is for us to be caught."

Prior to the Chelsea game on April 21, just over a year on from the Hillsborough disaster, Liverpool unveiled a memorial next to the Shankly gates at Anfield which featured the names of those who lost their lives and an eternal flame. Rosenthal's belated contribution to Liverpool's season continued to be decisive as he netted the Reds' first in a 4-1 victory over the Londoners. Liverpool were now within touching distance of winning their 10th league title in 15 seasons.

The Reds now needed four points from their last three games to clinch the title. QPR were next in line and if Liverpool were able to beat Don Howe's side and Aston Villa failed to win at home to Norwich, the league title would be returning to the Anfield trophy cabinet. *The Football Echo* reported: "Liverpool collected their 18th Championship crown at Anfield this afternoon coming from behind to beat Queens Park Rangers, while rivals Aston Villa were being held to a home draw by Norwich. There was a sense of eager anticipation in the air at Anfield, the home fans banking on a powerful performance from a side hoping to turn the title screw. The only problem was that the visitors were full of running early on, and they rocked the Reds after 14 minutes when Roy Wegerle scored. The Reds lost David Burrows through injury, but when the going gets tough, the answer is to rely on pure class. Rush, not for the first time in his career, conjured up a crucial goal to level matters before the break. And England international Barnes secured the lead with a penalty in the 63rd minute. Liverpool were now champions of England and only then were they ready to talk about it."

Steve McMahon, who wore the captain's armband for most of the second half as Hansen was unable to complete the game through injury, told the awaiting cameras: "It was unbelievable, I was the proudest man on the pitch today, we lost the league at home before the home supporters last season, so what a tremendous boost that is for them. It was incredible, apart from being the only Scouser on the Liverpool team, I just can't believe it really."

By the time the players had done a lap of honour and retreated back to the dressing room, the champagne celebrations were well and truly underway and the mood was jubilant and light-hearted. When Dalglish was fulfilling his media commitments he was suddenly lifted up by Bruce Grobbelaar and Jan Mølby and thrown fully clothed into the Anfield bath to join his fully naked countryman Gary Gillespie for a post-match soaking.

In their final home game of the season on Tuesday, May 1, after defeating Derby County 1-0 through a Gary Gillespie goal, Liverpool were presented with the First Division trophy. The match was originally scheduled for February 27, but was called off due to dangerous high winds. After missing the game itself through injury, Alan Hansen joined his teammates on the pitch and lifted the trophy for the third time as club captain in front of a strong crowd of 38,038.

Against the Rams, Kenny Dalglish made his first appearance as a player in two years and at 39, it was his 515th and last appearance for the club. Ian Rush told the press after the game: "We've missed out on the double again and of course that is disappointing. But as everyone knows, the championship is the hardest trophy to win and the one we want the most. And we kept smiling when we heard that Kenny had put himself in the squad for the match against Derby on the night we were to receive the trophy. He hadn't been doing too well in the five-a-sides so he got some real stick from the lads when he announced the decision."

Hansen had now matched Phil Neal's record of eight championship medals and was delighted after coming back from an eight-month absence due to a knee injury: "The players had battled on throughout the season. People had been knocking the team left, right and centre, but we've had one league defeat since November and that speaks for itself and we won the championship with two games to go. Personally, I'll be seeing my contract out until 1992 and then we'll just have to see. I'd like to do the double again in fact we've just made a record called, 'We're forever blowing doubles'.

"There's a famous saying at Liverpool that goes, 'Never look back, because if you do, you'll just be looking at your last lap of honour'. I have eight championship medals now, the same as Nealy and my only aim now is to be able to play nine games next season, which will give me another championship medal and take the record."

The Reds finished the 1989/90 season in style, beating Coventry 6-1 at Highfield Road, their biggest ever finish to a season. John Barnes scored his first hat-trick for the club, Rosenthal scored a brace, his seventh goal in five starts and Rush joined the goal-fest with a rare goal from outside the penalty area.

Barnes finished the club's top scorer for the season and he was the second-highest goalscorer in the league behind Gary Lineker. He was also voted the 1990 Player of the Year by the Football Writers' Association and joined legends such as Danny Blanchflower, Kenny Dalglish, Stanley Matthews and Tom Finney as a two-time winner of the award.

Despite winning their 18th title by a nine-point margin, there were signs that Liverpool had fallen away from the peak they reached two years earlier and it would not have been too critical to have said that the Reds had not been as consistently convincing as they were in 1988.

It was Dalglish's third league title in five years, which earned him his third Manger of the Year award. "The lads should be applauded for the way they picked themselves up after what happened last year against Arsenal," Dalglish said. "Later on, in the season, when we lost to Crystal Palace in the FA Cup semi-final, three days later we went to Charlton and won 4-0. That was due to the character and attitude as well as the ability of the players. They managed to get themselves in such a strong position and in the end, they went on to win the league quite comfortably.

"We had to use over 20 players over the course of the season, not including me. So, it just shows that injuries are part and parcel of football and we were stretched to the limit. Every single player that played made a contribution. If they hadn't, we wouldn't have won it. It's the lads who need to take all the credit, I can only do my best to steer them in the right direction."

A somewhat spoilt set of Liverpool fans had now witnessed their team win no less than 18 league titles. The Anfield faithful had now taken for granted that if the Reds didn't win the League Championship they weren't far away from doing so.

Although the supporters felt incredibly proud of each title win, there was maybe a sense of complacency creeping in and the celebrations on the Kop were starting to become less and less flamboyant, less joyous and less theatrical.

As Dalglish and his side celebrated the club's continued dominance, the very idea that Liverpool would now have to wait three decades before they again won English football's top prize would have felt unthinkable.

Yet the club was about to enter one of its most barren periods as far as winning the League Championship was concerned. The Anfield crowd, always loyal no matter what position in the table they found their team, were about to painfully watch on as Manchester United, Arsenal, Chelsea and Manchester City became the pre-eminent sides in the country.

Thirty years of hurt awaited Liverpool, until a man named Jürgen Klopp changed everything...

1989/90: Facts and Statistics

Final league table

		P	W	D	L	F	A	W	D	L	F	A	GD	PTS
1	Liverpool FC	38	13	5	1	38	15	10	5	4	40	22	41	79
2	Aston Villa	38	13	3	3	36	20	8	4	7	21	18	19	70
3	Tottenham	38	12	1	6	35	24	7	5	7	24	23	12	63
4	Arsenal	38	14	3	2	38	11	4	5	10	16	27	16	62
5	Chelsea	38	8	7	4	31	24	8	5	6	27	26	8	60
6	Everton	38	14	3	2	40	16	3	5	11	17	30	11	59
7	Southampton	38	10	5	4	40	27	5	5	9	31	36	8	55
8	Wimbledon	38	5	8	6	22	23	8	8	3	25	17	7	55
9	Nottingham Forest	38	9	4	6	31	21	6	5	8	24	26	8	54
10	Norwich City	38	7	10	2	24	14	6	4	9	20	28	2	53
11	QPR	38	9	4	6	27	22	4	7	8	18	22	1	50
12	Coventry City	38	11	2	6	24	25	3	5	11	15	34	-20	49
13	Manchester United	38	8	6	5	26	14	5	3	11	20	33	-1	48
14	Manchester City	38	9	4	6	26	21	3	8	8	17	31	-9	48
15	Crystal Palace	38	8	7	4	27	23	5	2	12	15	43	-24	48
16	Derby	38	9	1	9	29	21	4	6	9	14	19	3	46
17	Luton Town	38	8	8	3	24	18	2	5	12	19	39	-14	43
18	Sheffield Wednesday	38	8	6	5	21	17	3	4	12	14	34	-16	43
19	Charlton Athletic	38	4	6	9	18	25	3	3	13	13	32	-26	30
20	Millwall	38	4	6	9	23	25	1	5	13	16	40	-26	26

Games for the 1989/1990 season

(The number after date is league position after the game)

1	12.08.1989		W	1-0	Arsenal, Wembley, Charity Shield
2	19.08.1989	2	W	3-1	Manchester City, Anfield, 1st Division
3	23.08.1989	2	D	1-1	Aston Villa, Villa Park, 1st Division
4	26.08.1989	5	D	0-0	Luton Town, Kenilworth Road, 1st Division
5	09.09.1989	5	W	3-0	Derby County, Baseball Ground, 1st Division
6	12.09.1989	1	W	9-0	Crystal Palace, Anfield, 1st Division
7	16.09.1989	2	D	0-0	Norwich City, Anfield, 1st Division
8	19.09.1989		W	5-2	Wigan Athletic, Anfield, League Cup 2nd round 1L
9	23.09.1989	1	W	3-1	Everton, Goodison Park, 1st Division
10	04.10.1989		W	3-0	Wigan Athletic, Anfield, League Cup 2nd round 2L

11	14.10.1989	1	W	2-1	Wimbledon, Plough Lane, 1st Division
12	21.10.1989	2	L	1-4	Southampton, The Dell, 1st Division
13	25.10.1989		L	0-1	Arsenal, Highbury, League Cup 3rd round
14	29.10.1989	1	W	1-0	Tottenham Hotspur, Anfield, 1st Division
15	04.11.1989	2	L	0-1	Coventry City, Anfield, 1st Division
16	11.11.1989	3	L	2-3	Queens Park Rangers, Loftus Road, 1st Division
17	19.11.1989	3	W	2-1	Millwall, The Den, 1st Division
18	26.11.1989	1	W	2-1	Arsenal, Anfield, 1st Division
19	29.11.1989	1	L	0-2	Sheffield Wednesday, Hillsborough, 1st Division
20	02.12.1989	1	W	4-1	Manchester City, Maine Road, 1st Division
21	09.12.1989	2	D	1-1	Aston Villa, Anfield, 1st Division
22	16.12.1989	2	W	5-2	Chelsea, Stamford Bridge, 1st Division
23	23.12.1989	2	D	0-0	Manchester United, Anfield, 1st Division
24	26.12.1989	1	W	2-1	Sheffield Wednesday, Anfield, 1st Division
25	30.12.1989	1	W	1-0	Charlton Athletic, Anfield, 1st Division
26	01.01.1990	1	D	2-2	Nottingham Forest, City Ground, 1st Division
27	06.01.1990		D	0-0	Swansea City, Vetch Field, FA Cup 3rd round
28	09.01.1990		W	8-0	Swansea City, Anfield, FA Cup 3rd round replay
29	13.01.1990	1	D	2-2	Luton Town, Anfield, 1st Division
30	20.01.1990	1	W	2-0	Crystal Palace, Selhurst Park, 1st Division
31	28.01.1990		D	0-0	Norwich City, Carrow Road, FA Cup 4th round
32	31.01.1990		W	3-1	Norwich City, Anfield, FA Cup 4th round replay
33	03.02.1990	1	W	2-1	Everton, Anfield, 1st Division
34	10.02.1990	1	D	0-0	Norwich City, Carrow Road, 1st Division
35	17.02.1990		W	3-0	Southampton, Anfield, FA Cup 5th round
36	03.03.1990	1	W	1-0	Millwall, Anfield, 1st Division
37	11.03.1990		D	2-2	Queens Park Rangers, Loftus Road, FA Cup 6th round
38	14.03.1990		W	1-0	Queens Park Rangers, Anfield, FA Cup 6th round replay
39	18.03.1990	2	W	2-1	Manchester United, Old Trafford, 1st Division
40	21.03.1990	2	L	0-1	Tottenham Hotspur, White Hart Lane, 1st Division
41	31.03.1990	1	W	3-2	Southampton, Anfield, 1st Division
42	03.04.1990	1	W	2-1	Wimbledon, Anfield, 1st Division
43	08.04.1990		L	3-4	Crystal Palace, Villa Park, FA Cup Semi-final
44	11.04.1990	1	W	4-0	Charlton Athletic, Selhurst Park, 1st Division
45	14.04.1990	1	D	2-2	Nottingham Forest, Anfield, 1st Division
46	18.04.1990	1	D	1-1	Arsenal, Highbury, 1st Division
47	21.04.1990	1	W	4-1	Chelsea, Anfield, 1st Division
48	28.04.1990	1	W	2-1	Queens Park Rangers, Anfield, 1st Division
49	01.05.1990	1	W	1-0	Derby County, Anfield, 1st Division
50	05.05.1990	1	W	6-1	Coventry City, Highfield Road, 1st Division

Friendlies

1	29.07.1989	W	2-0	Dynamo Kiev, Wembley, Makita Tournament
2	30.07.1989	L	0-1	Arsenal, Wembley, Makita Tournament
3	01.08.1989	W	2-1	Malmo, Malmo Stadion, Friendly
4	03.08.1989	D	1-1	Vasalunds IF, Skytteholms IP, Friendly
5	05.08.1989	W	1-0	Halmstads BK, Halmstad, Friendly
6	07.08.1989	D	0-0	HJK Helsinki, Olympic, Friendly
7	30.08.1989	L	0-2	Real Madrid, Bernabeu Stadium, Bernabeu Trophy

Appearances for the 1989/1990 season

Name	League	FA Cup	LC	CS	Total
Bruce Grobbelaar	38	8	3	1	50
Steve McMahon	38	8	2	1	49
Ian Rush	36	8	3	1	48
Ronnie Whelan	34	8	3	1	46
Glenn Hysén	35	8	2	1	46
John Barnes	34	8	2	1	45
Alan Hansen	31	8	2	1	42
Peter Beardsley	29	8	3	1	41
Barry Venison	25	8	3	1	37
David Burrows	26	3	3	1	33
Steve Nicol	23	7	2	1	33
Steve Staunton	20	6	2	0	28
Ray Houghton	19	4	2	0	25
Jan Mølby	17	0	3	0	20
Gary Gillespie	13	2	1	0	16
Gary Ablett	15	0	1	0	16
Ronny Rosenthal	8	0	0	0	8
Nick Tanner	4	0	0	0	4
Mike Marsh	2	0	0	0	2
John Aldridge	2	0	0	0	2
Kenny Dalglish	1	0	0	0	1
Alex Watson	0	0	1	0	1

Goalscorers for the 1989/1990 season

Name	League	FA Cup	LC	CS	Total
John Barnes	22	5	1	0	28
Ian Rush	18	6	2	0	26
Peter Beardsley	10	4	1	1	16
Steve Nicol	6	3	0	0	9
Ronny Rosenthal	7	0	0	0	7
Steve McMahon	5	1	0	0	6
Gary Gillespie	4	0	0	0	4
Steve Staunton	0	0	3	0	3
Ronnie Whelan	1	1	0	0	2
Glenn Hysén	1	0	1	0	2
Jan Mølby	1	0	0	0	1
John Aldridge	1	0	0	0	1
Ray Houghton	1	0	0	0	1
Own goals	1	0	0	0	1

The squad during the 1989/1990 season

Bruce Grobbelaar, Goalkeeper
Mike Hooper, Goalkeeper
Gary Ablett, Defender
Jim Beglin, Defender
David Burrows, Defender
Gary Gillespie, Defender
Alex Watson, Defender
Steve Staunton, Defender
Glenn Hysén, Defender
Steve Nicol, Defender
Barry Venison, Defender
Alan Hansen, Defender
Nick Tanner, Defender
Kenny Dalglish, Midfielder
Ronnie Whelan, Midfielder
Ray Houghton, Midfielder
Mike Marsh, Midfielder
Jan Mølby, Midfielder
Steve McMahon, Midfielder
Jim Magilton, Midfielder
Peter Beardsley, Striker
John Aldridge, Striker
Ronny Rosenthal, Striker
Ian Rush, Striker
John Barnes, Striker

Transfers for the 1989/1990 season

In:
Glenn Hysén, Fiorentina, £600,000, 1 June 1989
Steve Harkness, Carlisle United, £75,000, 17 July 1989

Out:
Jim Beglin, Leeds United, Free, June 1989
Kevin MacDonald, Coventry City, Free, 13 July 1989
John Aldridge, Real Sociedad, £1,250,000, 13 September 1989

A collection of statistics for the 1989/1990 season

The season in numbers:
Total games: 50
Games won: 30
Games drawn: 13
Games lost: 7
Clean sheets – League: 12
Clean sheets – Overall: 19
Total goals: 107
Average attendance at home – League: 36,873
Average attendance at home – Overall: 34,814
Average goals per game – League: 2.00
Average goals per game – Overall: 2.44
Average goal minute – League: 47
Average goal minute – Overall: 49

Goals split down to competitions:
League – 78
FA Cup – 20
League Cup – 8

Player debuts:
Glenn Hysén against Arsenal on 12.08.1989
Nick Tanner against Manchester City on 02.12.1989
Ronny Rosenthal against Southampton on 31.03.1990

Statistics and information provided by LFChistory.net

19 THE WAIT IS OVER!

2019/20

I N FEBRUARY 1991, LIVERPOOL FANS WERE LEFT heartbroken by the departure of Kenny Dalglish, after leading the club to three league titles and two FA Cups in five years.

Subsequent managers couldn't emulate or get anywhere near the successes Dalglish and his predecessors enjoyed. Graeme Souness followed Dalglish in the managerial hot seat at Anfield in April 1991 after a successful five-year spell at Glasgow Rangers and he himself later admitted that he wanted to change things too quickly.

Established stars like Beardsley, McMahon, Venison and Houghton were on their way and replaced with players of much lesser talent. A 1-1 draw away to Bristol City in the FA Cup third round in January 1994 caused concern which changed to panic when Liverpool lost the replay at Anfield 1-0. This was totally unacceptable, Souness knew it and handed in his resignation the following week.

Roy Evans was finally chosen as Liverpool manager after 28 years at the club. His man-management ethos replaced Souness' auto-cratic style and Liverpool were playing entertaining football again. Evans was not as far from bringing the League Championship back to Anfield as some think. His best chance came in the 1996/97 season when the Reds were in a very strong position after winning at Southampton in the final match of the calendar year but were gradually overhauled by Manchester United.

During the summer of 1998, it was announced that Evans' responsibility would be shared by Frenchman Gérard Houllier. It would not be a happy partnership nor one that would last long. The Gérard Houllier reign started for real with a home defeat by Leeds United on November 14, the club's third loss at Anfield in a week.

It was in the cup competitions that Liverpool took their place in the history books under Houllier with an unprecedented treble success in 2001. The following season Liverpool mounted a serious challenge for the championship and 80 points might have won the title in other seasons but it wasn't enough to beat a very good Arsenal team as the Reds finished runners-up. A lack of success in the following seasons eventually led to Houllier's departure from Liverpool on May 24, 2004.

On June 16, 2004, Rafael Benítez was appointed manager, becoming the first Spaniard to manage in the Premier League. During his first season, Benítez was unable to improve Liverpool's form in the Premiership, but gave the fans the most incredible night in the club's history in Istanbul and made sure the European Cup was a permanent fixture at Anfield. The team's league form remained inconsistent, certainly not good enough for any sort of serious challenge. Events off the pitch did not help matters either, especially in 2007 when the American partnership of Tom Hicks and George Gillett arrived on the scene.

Their arrival seemed a significant watershed in the club's fortunes as well as the manager's aspirations. Liverpool ran Manchester

United very close for the 2009 Premier League title, but again finished runners-up. Benítez's reign ended after six seasons on June 3, 2010, an era that had begun with the hope and belief that the glory days really were returning to Anfield.

Roy Hodgson succeeded Benítez from the first day of July 2010, after he signed a three-year deal with the club. The following autumn, New England Sports Ventures, later known as Fenway Sports Group, agreed to buy the club. Although the supporters were overjoyed to see the back of Hicks and Gillett, there was certainly an attitude of once bitten, twice shy among the Anfield faithful.

After a wretched first half of the league season under Hodgson that saw seven victories and nine defeats from the opening 20 matches, the pressure piling up on the new boss reached breaking point. Three days after a miserable defeat at Blackburn Rovers on January 5, 2011, Roy Hodgson left Liverpool 'by mutual consent'.

To the supporters' delight, Kenny Dalglish returned to replace Hodgson until the end of the season. John Henry, Liverpool's new principal owner, thankfully recognised Dalglish's importance to the club: "Kenny is a legendary Liverpool figure both as a supremely gifted footballer and successful manager. Since returning in January he has shown extraordinary leadership and the ability to bring the best out of so many people associated with the club."

Despite winning the League Cup, Liverpool's first trophy for six years, Dalglish was replaced by Brendan Rodgers on June 1, 2012. The 39-year-old Ulsterman knew he had joined a special club and he came close to ending Liverpool's wait for a top-flight title.

A run of 11 straight wins towards the end of the 2013/14 season left the Reds five points clear at the top of the Premier League with just three matches to go. However, Rodgers' team, to the dismay of everyone connected to the club, ended the season as Premier League runners-up, two points behind champions Manchester City. A terrible 2014/15 season and dismal performances at the start of the next eventually cost him his job in October 2015.

Enter Jürgen Norbert Klopp.

The former Borussia Dortmund manager was coaxed out of his self-imposed sabbatical as a replacement for Rodgers in October 2015. At his opening press conference, the German described himself as 'The Normal One' and said being at Liverpool was the biggest honour that he could ever have imagined.

He also stated that everyone connected to the club needed to change from doubters to believers. His impact was instant and he led Liverpool to both the League Cup and Europa League finals in 2016, but both ended in defeat. With FSG president Mike Gordon managing the day-to-day operations, and the appointment of sporting director and hidden genius, Michael Edwards, taking care of the buying and selling of players, the foundations were finally in place for a long-term project that demonstrated the experience and knowhow the owners had acquired over their first five years in control.

The 2017/18 season saw the football world sit up and take notice as it became clear that Klopp was returning Liverpool to the big stage.

Klopp led the Reds on a glorious run to the Champions League final in Kiev but were defeated 3-1 by Real Madrid, with two of the goals down to disastrous goalkeeping errors by Loris Karius. Under Klopp's leadership, Anfield had once more become a cauldron and a place visiting teams feared. The atmosphere for European games resembled those of the late Seventies and early Eighties and in the

Premier League, Liverpool remained unbeaten at home in both 2017/18 and 2018/19.

For Klopp it is about the group and the team and doing things together, not as individuals. Melwood had always been a place of work but under Klopp it became an incredibly happy one. After missing out on the Premier League on the final day on the 2018/19 season to Manchester City despite achieving an astonishing club record of 97 points, the Reds went on to lift their sixth European Cup by beating Tottenham Hotspur 2-0 in the Champions League final in Madrid.

The Premier League bar was set ridiculously high and Klopp knew that to bring the league title back to Anfield after 30 years, 'The Normal One' would have to conjure up something special to go that one step further.

Liverpool's first signing of the 2019 summer transfer window was 17-year-old Dutch central defender Sepp van den Berg from PEC Zwolle for a fee which could rise to £4.4million depending on various clauses being met. At the end of July, the reigning European champions announced the arrival of Harvey Elliott from Fulham after the 16-year-old Englishman's youth contract expired with Scott Parker's side. Elliott had been the youngest player to play in the Premier League, aged 16 years and 30 days, when he made his league debut for Fulham in a 1–0 away defeat to Wolves on May 4, 2019.

After Simon Mignolet moved to his homeland and joined Club Brugge on 5 August 2019 after six eventful years at Liverpool and Adam Bogdan's contract wasn't renewed, Klopp signed two goal-keepers in a week to add stern competition to Alisson Becker's position. Free agent Adrián San Miguel was first to be snapped up after impressing with West Ham in the Premier League and was followed by 35-year-old Andy Lonergan, who was drafted in as Liverpool were short on goalkeeping options for their US tour.

After failing to make the bench for the Champions League final, Danny Ings requested a move to gain more playing time and Klopp reluctantly agreed to the request on transfer deadline day. Other notable departures that summer were Daniel Sturridge and Alberto Moreno, whose contracts had expired. They joined Trabzonspor and Villarreal respectively.

Liverpool began the 2019/20 campaign on August 4, with a disappointing penalty shootout defeat by Manchester City in the FA Community Shield at Wembley. The Reds bounced back immediately and beat Norwich City 4-1 at Anfield in their opening league fixture. An own goal by Grant Hanley and strikes from Mohamed Salah, Divock Origi and Virgil van Dijk saw Jürgen Klopp's side surge into a four-goal, half-time lead. An eventful first 45 minutes also saw Adrián make his debut for the club just four days after signing, as Golden Glove holder Alisson Becker was helped off the pitch shortly before the end of the first half with a calf injury.

After their convincing opening-day victory over the Canaries, attentions were turned to the European Super Cup in Istanbul against Premier League rivals Chelsea. With Alisson facing a spell on the sidelines, Adrián made his full debut. It was his first competitive start since January, but the Spaniard showed few signs of nerves or rustiness. Following a 2-2 draw after extra-time, the Reds overcame Chelsea on penalties to win the 2019 Super Cup. Adrián saved decisively from Tammy Abraham during the shootout. "Adrián, like Rocky, what a story!" Klopp bellowed during this post-match interview with BT Sport, referencing the film when the underdog fighter cries out to his girlfriend Adrian after going 15 rounds with heavy-weight champion Apollo Creed. "I don't know where he was two weeks ago when we were playing Manchester City," Klopp added. "When I spoke to him the first time, it was clear he would take time to get fit. But he has to be fit now and he is. He has already shown me he is a proper personality in the dressing room as well – he was maybe even louder than I was at half-time."

Fewer than 72 hours on from playing 120 minutes in Turkey, Liverpool battled their way to a hard-fought 2-1 victory at South-ampton, thanks to Mane's emphatic opener and Roberto Firmino's clinical finish after 71 minutes. The full-time whistle came as a relief after a nervy finale prompted by the otherwise solid Adrián care-lessly blasting a clearance against former Reds striker Danny Ings that flew into the net.

It had not been a dull week for Liverpool or Adrián, who was left with an ankle "swollen like an elephant's" as Klopp put it, after a pitch invader ran on to join the Super Cup celebrations in Istanbul. Victory at St Mary's meant Jürgen Klopp had reached 300 points in his 146th game in charge. Kenny Dalglish, the previous quickest, did it after 150 games.

On August 24, Unai Emery's Arsenal were overwhelmed at Anfield with Klopp, who would later be named Manager of the Month, stating after an authoritative 3-1 win: "I loved the desire, the passion, the power and the energy that we put into this game." Mohamed Salah enjoyed one of his most effective games for a while, netting his first brace of the season in a victory that ensured that Liv-erpool were the only team with their 100 percent Premier League record intact.

The Reds sat two points clear at the top of the table, were unbeaten in 42 games at Anfield and achieved a 12th successive top-flight win, matching a 29-year club record. A week later, the Reds rounded off the month of August by making it 12 points from four league outings, and set a club record of 13 successive top-flight victories, as Burnley were brushed aside 3-0 at Turf Moor.

Klopp and his players were really starting to rewrite the club's history books, since not even the great sides assembled by Shankly, Fagan, Paisley or Dalglish had ever managed a run like that.

On August 29, in Monaco, Virgil van Dijk was named UEFA Men's Player of the Year, pipping Lionel Messi and Cristiano Ronaldo to the prestigious award. Upon receiving the accolade, the 28-year-old said: "First of all, I think I need to thank all of my teammates. Without all of them and without the staff, I wouldn't have achieved what I've achieved over the last year. It's been a long road but that's part of my journey, it's part of who I am. I needed it like this, I'm not a player who was 18 years old and had that rise straight away. I had to work hard for every step of the way, that's part of me and I'm very happy about that. I'm very proud to get this trophy and it's all credit to everyone that's helped me along the way."

Klopp's players returned from the first international break of the season with a lunchtime kick-off against Steve Bruce's Newcastle United at Anfield and after just seven minutes found themselves behind due to Jetro Willems' unstoppable rocket with his weaker right foot.

Sadio Mane equalised for the Reds with a sumptuous curler before Roberto Firmino, on as a substitute, laid on goals for Mane to score his second and Mohamed Salah to secure a 3-1 win. The latter effort, created by an inventive piece of footwork from Firmino and finished in nerveless fashion by Salah, was later recognised as the club's Goal of the Month. Liverpool now found themselves five points clear of Manchester City, the biggest advantage any side had ever had after the first five games of a Premier League season. Alex Oxlade-Chamberlain made his milestone 50th appearance for the Reds against the Magpies which was a fantastic feat for a player who had shown impressive determination to recover from serious injuries.

On September 17, Liverpool began their defence of the Champions League in Italy. Klopp's men suffered their first reversal of the season as they were beaten at Napoli for the second year in a row, this time going down 2-0 at Stadio San Paolo. The following Sunday, Klopp's team clawed out a battling 2-1 victory at Stamford Bridge and became the first team in the history of the Premier League to win their first six games of the season two years running.

Winning without playing particularly well has been a trait of potential champions and ruthless goals from Trent Alexander-Arnold and Roberto Firmino were enough for Liverpool to restore their five-point lead over Manchester City in testing circumstances.

After a 2-0 midweek victory against MK Dons in the Carabao Cup, the relentless Red machine rolled on, winning again in the Premier League at Sheffield United, albeit by a slice of luck. Georginio Wijnaldum's strike went through the grasp of Dean Henderson with 20 minutes left to play at Bramall Lane. Matchwinner Wijnaldum acknowledged Liverpool were not at their fluent best but felt they could take satisfaction in clinching maximum points against a spirited Sheffield United. He said: "At the beginning of the season it's good if you collect as many points as possible because normally during the season you progress, so hopefully we're not at our best now but at the end of the season we will be. We didn't start the game well. But another win, that's the most important thing. A few years ago, we were struggling to win games like this. This season and last season also, it's going quite well."

On September 23, Alisson Becker, Virgil van Dijk and Jürgen Klopp returned to Italy for the glamour of the annual FIFA Best Awards in Milan.

Alisson was named Best Men's Goalkeeper and Klopp the Best Men's Coach for 2019, while Alisson and Van Dijk were announced in the FIFA FIFPro Men's World11. After receiving his award, an emotional Klopp told FIFA.com: "I prefer team rather than individual recognition, therefore in terms of football I'd like to share this award with my players, I am who I am because of them."

Having lost their Group E opener to Napoli, Liverpool got their Champions League defence back on track after a 4-3 victory over Red Bull Salzburg at Anfield. The Reds raced into a three-goal lead, before Jesse Marsch's team, who were inspired by a certain Takumi Minamino, staged a fightback to level the score in the second half.

However, a calm Kop end finish by Salah, in the club's 100th European Cup fixture played at Anfield, secured all three points. On October 5, there was more drama at Anfield as James Milner's 95th-minute penalty defeated Brendan Rodgers' Leicester City and made it eight consecutive league victories to open the season, equalling the club record set at the start of the 1990/91 campaign. Mane had earlier slotted in his 50th top-flight goal for the club during a 2-1 win that preceded the fourth anniversary of Klopp's appointment as Liverpool manager.

Following the second international break of the season, Alisson returned from injury as the Reds dropped Premier League points for the first time in a 1-1 draw with Manchester United before Oxlade-Chamberlain scored twice in a comprehensive Champions League

4-1 victory in Genk, including a breathtaking outside-of-the-boot strike.

Salah was also amongst the scorers at the Luminus Arena and entered the prestigious Liverpool top 25 all-time goalscorers' list with 78 goals in 117 games.

On October 27, Klopp's team returned to winning ways in the league as Salah's 50th goal at Anfield, scored in just 58 appearances, sealed a 2-1 success over Tottenham Hotspur.

The Reds ended the month defeating Arsenal on penalties following an incredible 5-5 draw in the Carabao Cup at Anfield, the first time an Anfield crowd had witnessed such a scoreline. Harvey Elliott became the youngest ever player to feature for the first team at Anfield at the age of 16 years and 209 days old, taking over from Ben Woodburn's previous record when he appeared against Sunderland in November 2016.

James Milner, who lined up alongside Elliot as captain, was exactly 17 years and three months older than his young teammate and was playing Premier League football for Leeds United before Elliot was even born. Caoimhin Kelleher saved from Dani Ceballos in the shootout, and Curtis Jones subsequently stepped up to convert the winning spotkick in front of the Kop. Jones was in dreamland: "Being a local lad, it's always been my dream to get an appearance at Anfield. To get an assist to give us a chance and then to score a penalty is just a dream come true. This is just the beginning; I'm just a young lad and I've still got a long way to go. Any opportunities I'll take with both hands. This is what you play football for."

The following Saturday, Klopp's men were trailing Aston Villa with 87 minutes on the clock but somehow conjured up a comeback and snatched a 2-1 victory from right under Villa's noses.

Under the headline: 'VAR, FIRMINO'S ARMPIT AND STUBBORN ASTON VILLA CAN'T STOP KLOPP'S MENTALITY MONSTERS' the *Liverpool Echo* correspondent, Paul Gorst, wrote: "The Reds thought they had frittered away points here at Villa Park thanks to Roberto Firmino's errant armpit. The Brazilian striker's 'goal' in the first half, in every season of professional football prior to this one, would have stood. However, the intricacies of VAR – laws that are threatening to leave an ugly mark on the game supporters so love – ruled that Firmino was in fact, offside. Liverpool's leveller arrived on 87 minutes when Mane's cross to the back post was met by Andy Robertson, of all players. The Scot nodded past Heaton to restore parity, but the visitors sensed a late winner. They usually do, these days. The stage was set for Trent Alexander-Arnold on his 100th senior appearance to steal the show but his well-struck free-kick took a deflection over the bar before the resulting corner, also taken by Alexander-Arnold, was dramatically turned home by Mane's darting header in the fourth minute of stoppage time. The smell of pyrotechnics filled the air as the away supporters celebrated wildly."

On Sunday, November 10, everyone's focus turned to Liverpool versus Manchester City as the two best teams in England, and possibly Europe, did battle at Anfield. City had not won at Anfield since 2003 when Nicolas Anelka netted a brace for the Citizens.

Liverpool duly produced an outstanding performance to best their closest rivals, beating Pep Guardiola's team 3-1 as they went eight points clear of second-placed Leicester City.

A powerful long-ranger from Fabinho and Salah's header put the Reds 2-0 up inside the opening 13 minutes at a raucous Anfield, with Mane's diving header extending their lead further in the second half. Bernardo Silva pulled one back for the visitors late on but the European champions withstood late pressure to secure a huge win.

Liverpool's majestic full-back Alexander-Arnold spoke to Sky Sports immediately after the game: "We're on a good run of form and still unbeaten, which is what we want to do. We want to be picking up the three points.

"We know at home we've got the advantage with the fans and that, so every time we're here we want to pick up the three points and feel as though we should. For us it's about keeping that momentum up, it's not about how other teams feel."

After almost a third of the fixtures played, Guardiola's team were nine points adrift. It was simply Liverpool's title to lose and they looked in no mood to slip up any time soon as they stretched their unbeaten record to 28 games dating back to January's loss at the Etihad.

In between the hustle and bustle of the Premier League, there was Champions League business to attend to. Goals from Wijnaldum and Oxlade-Chamberlain saw off Genk at Anfield to ensure the holders won their third-straight Group E match. Dejan Lovren's Kop end leveller, three weeks later, earned the Reds a 1-1 draw with Napoli at Anfield, a game in which Fabinho sustained an ankle injury that would rule him out until mid-January. The result meant that the Reds needed to avoid defeat in Salzburg to progress to the last 16.

Liverpool's season resumed at Selhurst Park following the November international break and another feat of escapology was required to secure all three points. An 82nd-minute equaliser by Wilfried Zaha, which cancelled out Mane's opener, looked set to snatch a draw for Crystal Palace but Roberto Firmino had other ideas and just three minutes later, he rammed home a winner from close range.

The Reds concluded the month with another 2-1 success in the Premier League, achieved by two precise assists from Alexander-Arnold and two immaculate Van Dijk headers, which ultimately proved to be decisive against Brighton and Hove Albion.

Liverpool endured a nervy final 12 minutes or so after Alisson was dismissed for handling outside his area and Lewis Dunk converted the resulting free-kick. But the 10 men held firm to extend their lead to a remarkable 11 points. "Brighton are a very good side, you have to give them credit," Van Dijk told Liverpoolfc.com at Anfield. "They played well, brave and tried to get out of our press and at times it worked. But we wanted the three points and got them. We had to show character and we have to fight. It was not an easy game, especially at the end. We had to dig deep and we did."

The month of December was another successful, even historic, month for Liverpool. Alisson scooped up the Yashin Trophy for the best men's goalkeeper in world football, while Virgil van Dijk finished second to Lionel Messi in the 2019 Ballon d'Or. On the pitch, the Reds faced their local rivals Everton in the 234th Merseyside derby. Divock Origi (twice), Xherdan Shaqiri and Sadio Mane all netted in the first half before Georginio Wijnaldum made it 5-2 in the closing moments. It was the highest scoring Merseyside derby at Anfield in over 86 years when the Reds beat the Toffees 7-4 in 1933.

The emphatic victory extended Liverpool's unbeaten league run to a club-record 32 games. Klopp, who became the fastest manager in Liverpool's history to 100 league wins, said: "All the goals were incredible, outstanding. Wonderful goals, sensational passes, super pieces of football. I loved it a lot."

The Reds then extended their lead at the top of the Premier League to 11 points with an assured 3-0 display away at Bournemouth. A trip to Austria in the Champions League was up next, with Klopp's side reaching the last 16 as Group E winners, after a 2-0 victory over Red Bull Salzburg. Watford's visit to Anfield on December 14, followed the good news that Klopp and James Milner both committed their futures to the club by penning contract extensions on the same day. "This club is in such a good place, I couldn't contemplate leaving," Klopp said.

On December 14, Liverpool strengthened their position at the top of the Premier League with a 2-0 win over Watford at Anfield.

Mohamed Salah scored twice to make it 16 wins from 17 for the Reds in the top-flight so far this season. Astonishingly, Liverpool's first clean sheet of the season at Anfield came against The Hornets at the 13th time of trying. The previous longest start to a season without keeping a clean sheet at Anfield came at the start of the 1964/65 campaign, when Bill Shankly's Liverpool went 11 games without achieving a single shutout.

As the first team were settling into their new surroundings in Qatar for the FIFA Club World Cup, at home, Neil Critchley led a youthful side in the Carabao Cup quarter-final at Aston Villa. More than four years after making his Liverpool debut, Pedro Chirivella became the 104th player to captain the club.

The youngest team in the club's history at that time performed valiantly in the 5-0 defeat as Klopp and Co. watched on from the Middle East.

The following day, Liverpool entered the Club World Cup at the semi-final stage, where they met Mexican side CF Monterrey at Khalifa International Stadium. An injury-time Firmino finish from

Alexander-Arnold's whipped cross secured a 2-1 victory, booking the Reds' spot in the tournament's showpiece. A busy week continued as the following day saw the club confirm an agreement had been reached with Salzburg for the transfer of Takumi Minamino for £7.25m.

The 24-year-old Japanese international, who impressed in his two appearances against the Reds in the Champions League, officially joined on January 1, 2020. On December 21, Liverpool lifted the FIFA Club World Cup for the very first time. Firmino was the match-winner again when he struck in extra-time to net the only goal of a tense finale with Brazilian side Flamengo. "We've written a chapter in Liverpool's long history and it's a fantastic feeling, nobody can take that away from us," Andy Robertson said afterwards. The Reds had become the first English club to win the European Cup, the UEFA Super Cup and the FIFA Club World Cup in the same year, with the three trophies being won in exactly 29 weeks.

Although, the Reds were now European and world champions, there was no time to bask in the glory of their achievements. Five days later a trip to second-placed Leicester City awaited them as their quest to win the prize that had eluded them for 30 years continued. However, Klopp's men showed no signs of fatigue at the King Power Stadium on Boxing Day, producing an incredible all-round performance in a 4-0 win, and they went 13 points clear of their closest title challengers. Alexander-Arnold laid on two incredible assists during his Man-of-the-Match display and bagged the fourth goal with a powerful low effort. "To get four goals at a place like this is something to be proud of," the Scouser stressed.

Liverpool finished off an eventful year at the club with a hard-fought 1-0 victory against Wolverhampton Wanderers at Anfield.

Mane's finish shortly before half-time was enough to land the three points, with the goal initially ruled out for handball in the build-up before VAR's intervention.

The Reds ended the decade 13 points clear with a game in hand over Leicester City and after half of the season now been played, the Reds had won 96 percent of the total points available.

Liverpool began 2020 on January 2 with a disciplined 2-0 home win over Sheffield United that left Blades boss Chris Wilder in awe of Klopp's team. "They won every first ball, every second ball, ran forward and ran back and they did that better than us. I love everything about them. The physical and mental part of it is amazing," Wilder said afterwards. Goals from Salah and Mane ensured Liverpool would go an entire year unbeaten in the top-flight. Attention then quickly turned to the FA Cup and a third-round meeting with Everton at Anfield. The Kop got their first look at Takumi Minamino in a Liverpool shirt and the tie was won thanks to Curtis Jones' sublime second-half goal, his first for the club. "I'm not surprised he scored that sort of goal," Klopp said. "He has made big steps, he will be a Liverpool player if nothing strange happens, 100 percent."

On January 11, the Reds made their maiden visit to the Tottenham Hotspur Stadium, where Firmino's first-half goal ensured the European champions opened up a 16-point lead over Leicester City at the top of the table with a game in hand. With 20 wins and one draw from 21 league games so far and with a points total of 61, Liverpool had made the best start to a league season in the history of the big five European leagues.

Victory against José Mourinho's side also made it 38 league games unbeaten for the Reds, breaking a club record set over 125 years ago when Liverpool went 37 games unbeaten, from February 1893 to September 1894, spanning three different seasons in three different divisions.

Further January league victories over Manchester United at home and Wolves away and a 2-2 draw at Shrewsbury Town in the FA Cup was followed by a midweek trip to West Ham United. Liverpool emerged victorious at the London Stadium to go an incredible 19 points clear at the top of the Premier League table, dispatching West Ham 2-0. The records kept on coming as victory over the Hammers meant a Liverpool side had beaten every other team in a single top-flight league campaign for the first time in their history.

On February 1, the Reds moved 22 points clear at the top of the Premier League after putting four goals past Southampton at Anfield. Mohamed Salah's 17th and 18th goals of the season meant that the Egyptian had now scored the same amount of league goals than Kevin Keegan did during his entire tenure at the club.

Keegan scored his 68 league goals in 230 games, whereas Salah managed it in just 97. "And now you're gonna believe us," the Kop sang over and over, as seven more wins from their 14 remaining fixtures would guarantee Liverpool the League Championship.

Jordan Henderson, led by example against the Saints and when he was substituted for Adam Lallana, two minutes from time, the skipper left to a well-deserved standing ovation. "I'm enjoying this season," Henderson said. "Everybody is enjoying their football, but it's about the work ethic and giving everything for each other, that's the most important thing to me. Just give everything you can for your teammates. If you do that then you get your rewards at the end."

As Klopp and the senior squad observed their Premier League

midseason break, Neil Critchley took charge of the squad for the FA Cup fourth-round replay against Shrewsbury Town. The young Reds gave a fearless display in front of a sold-out Anfield, which saw Liverpool book a place in the next round, as an own goal by Ro-Shaun Williams settled the contest.

At the age of 19 years and five days, Toxteth-born Curtis Jones became Liverpool's youngest ever captain – a record which had existed since Alex Raisbeck captained the Reds in a 3-0 win over Blackburn Rovers at Anfield in 1900 at the age of 20 years and 250 days.

After beating Norwich 1-0 in the league, the Reds were 25 points clear at the summit and now boasted the second longest unbeaten top-flight run in the history of English football. Klopp's side then made a return to an emotional venue – but this time it was an unhappy visit to the Estadio Metropolitano, the scene of the club's sixth European Cup triumph in 2019.

Atlético Madrid took charge of their Champions League last-16 tie as Saul Niguez's early finish secured a 1-0 first-leg lead. The following Monday night the Reds returned to beat David Moyes' West Ham 3-2 at Anfield and equalled the English top-flight record of 18 successive wins set by Manchester City in 2017.

The Hammers went 2-1 up on the night after Wijnaldum's opener. However, the hosts fought back as Salah equalised before Mane netted the winner in the 81st minute, meaning the Reds had taken 106 points from a possible 108.

Many of Liverpool's record-breaking runs came to an abrupt end the following weekend as Watford handed the Reds their first league defeat of the campaign with a 3-0 scoreline at Vicarage Road. Liverpool's momentum was briefly halted as the Reds crashed to their first league defeat in 44 games. "We were not good enough, simple as that," Klopp said. "Watford did exactly what they wanted to do; we didn't do exactly what we should have done. We didn't cross at the right moment, didn't pass at the right moment, because positioning was not like it should have been."

March started disastrously for the Reds, suffering elimination from the FA Cup and then from the Champions League at the hands of Chelsea and Atlético Madrid respectively. However, yet again, the Reds bounced back with a hard-fought 2-1 home win at Anfield against Eddie Howe's Bournemouth.

The history books would once again have to be updated as Liverpool's all-time record for the most consecutive home league victories in English top-flight football was set with 22 games. The previous record of 21 successive home league wins was set by Bill Shankly's Liverpool in 1972. After the game Klopp told the BBC: "I would never compare myself to Shankly. We never thought about that number before the game, but after we could. It's nice and it's special."

As Liverpool were set to receive Atlético Madrid in the Champions League, there were reports emerging that the domestic league was going to have to be halted because of the increasing dangers posed by Covid-19.

It was initially thought that all football matches in England would be played behind closed doors under government plans to combat the virus but more drastic and needed measures were to be taken. On March 13, the club announced through its official website: "Liverpool Football Club continues to implement the government's advice on the Corona-Virus outbreak and welcomes today's Premier League statement to postpone all games, including Premier League,

FA Cup, academy and Women's Super League fixtures in the best interests of players, staff and supporters."

At the time of the postponement, Liverpool were 25 points clear and just two wins away from ending a 30-year wait to become league champions. "The Friday after the Atlético game, when we arrived at Melwood, it was already clear this is not a session," Klopp said. "Yes, we trained, but it was more of a meeting. We had a lot of things to talk about, a lot of things to think about, things I never thought before in my life about."

In the following weeks, the Reds' back-room team hosted sessions for the players via online video links, with a variety of workouts taking place each day to maintain their fitness and physical conditioning during the suspension of football.

Despite not being at Melwood, the tradition of singing 'Happy Birthday' to teammates in the different native languages of the squad continued with Jürgen Klopp acting as the conductor via Zoom as he strived to maintain the team's morale under the most unpredictable circumstances.

On the April 12, after previously testing positive for Covid-19, Sir Kenny Dalglish issued the following message to supporters: "Thank you for all of your well wishes over the last few days. I'm delighted to be back home with the family after receiving brilliant care from the NHS, which we appreciate now more than ever. Marina and I would like to express our immense gratitude to the medical staff who cared for me and who continue to treat countless others throughout the country during an incredibly challenging period."

During the lockdown period, everyone connected with Liverpool Football Club was deeply saddened by the passing of former player Michael Robinson, aged 61 after losing his battle with skin cancer.

A boyhood Red who lived his dreams with the team he supported from the Kop from the age of six, Robinson was very much looking forward to seeing his team be crowned Premier League champions for the first time. Before his death he gave his thoughts on Liverpool's current team: "I'm a great admirer of Jürgen Klopp's style of football. He is an architect of the game and has created 'the perfect storm'. His team produces wave after wave of free-flowing intense football. They give the opposition no time to breathe; I wouldn't have liked to have played against a team like this – I'd be constantly out of breath! Klopp's system is very much a collaborative team effort, starting from the centre-backs bringing out the ball and the full-backs bombing forward – transforming into wingers. Then onto the midfield – what I particularly admire about Liverpool's middle three, is whoever Klopp chooses, they don't slow the play down and just 'nudge' the ball forward to the world's most fierce striking trio. It really is astonishing to watch!"

After fears that Liverpool's record breaking season would become 'null and void', the Reds welcomed the news that the Premier League would return to action and that the remainder of the 2019/20 season would be played out behind closed doors.

Intending to help players return to action from a three-month break, the number of substitutes permitted during a match increased from three to five players and two short water breaks were introduced. In addition, midfielder Adam Lallana agreed a short-term extension to his Liverpool contract that enabled him to complete the remainder of the 2019/20 season.

On June 11, Liverpool took the opportunity to test themselves against Championship side Blackburn Rovers at Anfield to step up their preparations for the return of competitive football. The Reds convincingly won 6-0 in the behind-closed-doors game and showed signs that they were ready for their remaining Premier League fixtures.

One-hundred-and-six days since they last took to the field for competitive action, Liverpool resumed the 2019/20 season against who else, but local rivals Everton at Goodison Park. Prior to kick-off, both teams observed a minute's silence in memory of those who had lost their lives during the pandemic. Liverpool, along with the other 19 Premier League clubs, wore an NHS badge on the front of their shirts to demonstrate their gratitude to the NHS workers up and down the country who had battled heroically to keep the virus at bay. The game finished goalless and Klopp's team took another small step towards league title number 19.

Three days later, goals from Alexander-Arnold, Salah, Fabinho and Mane brushed aside Roy Hodgson's Crystal Palace 4-0 at Anfield. The victory put the Reds 23 points clear and they had now scored more than 100 goals across all competitions for a third consecutive season, the first time they achieved such a feat since 1986/87. After achieving four points from six since the restart, the title could now be clinched the following night if rivals Manchester City failed to win at Chelsea.

Thursday, June 25, 2020, is a date that will be forever embedded in the memory of every Liverpool supporter.

Manchester City lost 2-1 to Chelsea at Stamford Bridge, meaning the Reds could no longer be mathematically caught in the table. The 30-year wait was finally over as Liverpool secured their 19th top-flight title and they did so with a record seven games to spare.

Shortly after it was confirmed that Liverpool were the Premier League champions, club captain Jordan Henderson – holding back the tears and emotions at Formby Hall where the team had gathered to watch the game together in their bubble – spoke to Sky Sports: "I didn't want to talk about winning the title until this moment. I'm so happy for all the boys. I'm just a bit overwhelmed and it's an amazing feeling. I'm so proud of what we have achieved. There was a lot of emotion and it was a different experience watching the game, and then to be with everyone and all the staff at the final whistle. It was a moment we will never forget."

Liverpool's first game as champions came on July 2 at the Etihad against the previous season's Premier League winners, Manchester City. After the City players gave a customary guard of honour to the newly crowned champions, the Reds crashed to a 4-0 defeat, the heaviest loss of the calendar year. Consequent victories followed against relegation battling Aston Villa at Anfield and away at Brighton & Hove Albion.

Following the Reds' victory over the Seagulls, Henderson had a scan at Melwood on a knee injury picked up in a collision with Yves Bissouma. It was a downbeat end to an otherwise good week for the new champions as the scan revealed Henderson wouldn't be able to play any part in Liverpool's final four games, in which the Reds needed three victories to surpass Manchester City's 100-point record tally for a top-flight season.

Interestingly, the last time Liverpool won the league in 1990, captain Alan Hansen was also unable to see out the remaining fixtures, also because of a knee injury. However, the Scot went on to lift the trophy in Kenny Dalglish's full number seven kit.

On July 11, Liverpool dropped their first points at Anfield since February 2019 and ended their run of 24 consecutive home league wins after they were held to a 1-1 draw by Burnley. Four days later, the Reds visited the Emirates where they suffered their third and final league reversal of the campaign as the Gunners ended the champions' hopes of exceeding City's record points tally.

In their final home game of the season, Liverpool beat Chelsea 5-3 in a pulsating clash that showed Klopp's team at its attacking best. Alexander-Arnold broke his own record for the most assists by a defender in a single Premier League season with a 13th against Frank Lampard's side and Liverpool's third goal against the Blues certified that Klopp's team had scored 50 league goals at home for a second successive season, a feat no Liverpool team had achieved since Joe Fagan's 1983/84 treble-winning season.

Then, shortly after the final whistle, the moment arrived that every Liverpool fan had long dreamed about.

Jürgen Klopp, along with his players and staff, gathered on a uniquely-built podium on the Kop for a special ceremony surrounded by fan banners and Kenny Dalglish, the last manager to guide Liverpool to championship glory back in 1990, was on hand to help deliver the silverware in n historic, long-awaited moment for the club.

Club captain Jordan Henderson was last to climb the steps on to the podium and after embracing Dalglish, the man who brought him to the club in 2011, he collected his medal from Richard Masters, chief executive of the Premier League.

Surrounded by his teammates, over a year on from lifting the European Cup in Madrid, Henderson became the first Liverpool captain to lift the Premier League trophy and 'The Hendo Shuffle' will certainly go down in Liverpool history.

It was Virgil van Dijk's fourth major honour as a Liverpool player since arriving in January 2018 and this latest piece of silverware was the one he couldn't wait to get hold of. "We finally get our hands on the Premier League trophy and it's a dream come true for all of us," the defender told Sky Sports. "It has been quite a long wait for all the Liverpool fans around the world and for us obviously. It's a fantastic feeling to say that I'm a Premier League champion and the rest of the boys as well."

Four days later, after coming back from a goal down to beat Newcastle 3-1 at St. James' Park, the Reds ended a memorable season on 99 points, 18 ahead of runners-up Manchester City.

Liverpool's title-winning 2019/20 campaign was also a record-breaking one in many regards. The Reds picked up 87 per cent of the points available throughout the season, setting a new record for their 19 top-flight title-winning seasons, surpassing the club's previous record of 81 per cent won during the 1978/79 multiple record-breaking campaign.

A total of 52 different names made it on to the Liverpool team-sheet, 45 played for the first team and 22 players made their first-team debut; numbers that were all new club records. Liverpool became the first team in history to win the league title in an eighth different decade, beating Arsenal, Everton and Manchester United's seven and Klopp's men became the first team to hold the European Cup, European Super Cup, FIFA Club World Cup and Premier League title simultaneously.

Klopp, whose name can now be mentioned in the same breath as Liverpool greats Shankly, Paisley, Fagan and Dalglish, became the new owner of the LMA Manager of the Year award.

The German, thanked Liverpool fans through the *Liverpool Echo*: "I have the great privilege of being manager of Liverpool Football Club. It is a privilege that I carry with me every single day because I know that I am working for you. I knew that Liverpool was a special place before I came here almost five years ago but it is only when you get to know the people that you feel the city's heartbeat and then you are able to realise just how special it is. For now, I would like to thank the supporters of Liverpool and the people of this city who have helped to make us champions. This is our moment. It is a special time in all of our lives and you are the ones who have made it possible. Each one of you is a champion in your own right and we cannot wait until we get the chance to celebrate what you have achieved."

Finally, Klopp and his sensational squad had given Liverpool fans what they craved more than anything else: a return to the summit of English football. Not only had Klopp's side ended a nearly unthinkable 30-year wait for the title, they had won it in the kind of breathtaking way that did justice to the memory of all the fantastic Liverpool players and teams throughout history.

Liverpool Football Club has always had a keen sense of its own history, its own magnificence, and in Klopp and his class of 2020, they had a side that was more than worthy of adding its own name to the proud roll call down the ages.

The future, of course, is still to be written and Liverpool fans across the globe will now be hoping that a 20th chapter will not be too long in the writing.

2019/2020: Facts and Statistics

Final league table

		P	W	D	L	F	A	W	D	L	F	A	GD	PTS
1	Liverpool FC	38	18	1	0	52	16	14	2	3	33	17	52	99
2	Manchester City	38	15	2	2	57	13	11	1	7	45	22	67	81
3	Manchester United	38	10	7	2	40	17	8	5	6	26	19	30	66
4	Chelsea	38	11	3	5	30	16	9	3	7	39	38	15	66
5	Leicester City	38	11	4	4	35	17	7	4	8	32	24	26	62
6	Tottenham	38	12	3	4	36	17	4	8	7	25	30	14	59
7	Wolves	38	8	7	4	27	19	7	7	5	24	21	11	59
8	Arsenal	38	10	6	3	36	24	4	8	7	20	24	8	56
9	Sheffield United	38	10	3	6	24	15	4	9	6	15	24	0	54
10	Burnley	38	8	4	7	24	23	7	5	7	19	27	-7	54
11	Southampton	38	6	3	10	21	35	9	4	6	30	25	-9	52
12	Everton	38	8	7	4	24	21	5	3	11	20	35	-12	49
13	Newcastle United	38	6	8	5	20	21	5	3	11	18	37	-20	44
14	Crystal Palace	38	6	5	8	15	20	5	5	9	16	30	-19	43
15	Brighton & H A	38	5	7	7	20	27	4	7	8	19	27	-15	41
16	West Ham United	38	6	4	9	30	33	4	5	10	19	29	-13	39
17	Aston Villa	38	7	3	9	22	30	2	5	12	19	37	-26	35
18	Bournemouth	38	5	6	8	22	30	4	1	14	18	35	-25	34
19	Watford	38	6	6	7	22	27	2	4	13	14	37	-28	34
20	Norwich City	38	4	3	12	19	37	1	3	15	7	38	-49	21

Games for the 2019/2020 season

(The number after date is league position after the game)

1	04.08.2019		D	1-1	Manchester City, Wembley, Community Shield
2	09.08.2019	1	W	4-1	Norwich City, Anfield, Premier League
3	14.08.2019		D	2-2	Chelsea, Beşiktaş Park, European Super Cup
4	17.08.2019	1	W	2-1	Southampton, St Mary's, Premier League
5	24.08.2019	1	W	3-1	Arsenal, Anfield, Premier League
6	31.08.2019	1	W	3-0	Burnley, Turf Moor, Premier League
7	14.09.2019	1	W	3-1	Newcastle United, Anfield, Premier League
8	17.09.2019		L	0-2	Napoli, Stadio San Paolo, Champions L. 1st Group Ph.
9	22.09.2019	1	W	2-1	Chelsea, Stamford Bridge, Premier League
10	25.09.2019		W	2-0	MK Dons, Stadium MK, League Cup 3rd round
11	28.09.2019	1	W	1-0	Sheffield United, Bramall Lane, Premier League

12	02.10.2019		W	4-3	Red Bull Salzburg, Anfield, Champions L. 1st Group Ph.
13	05.10.2019	1	W	2-1	Leicester City, Anfield, Premier League
14	20.10.2019	1	D	1-1	Manchester United, Old Trafford, Premier League
15	23.10.2019		W	4-1	KRC Genk, Luminus Arena, Champions L. 1st Group Ph.
16	27.10.2019	1	W	2-1	Tottenham Hotspur, Anfield, Premier League
17	30.10.2019		D	5-5	Arsenal, Anfield, League Cup 4th round
18	02.11.2019	1	W	2-1	Aston Villa, Villa Park, Premier League
19	05.11.2019		W	2-1	KRC Genk, Anfield, Champions L. 1st Group Ph.
20	10.11.2019	1	W	3-1	Manchester City, Anfield, Premier League
21	23.11.2019	1	W	2-1	Crystal Palace, Selhurst Park, Premier League
22	27.11.2019		D	1-1	Napoli, Anfield, Champions L. 1st Group Ph.
23	30.11.2019	1	W	2-1	Brighton & Hove Albion, Anfield, Premier League
24	04.12.2019	1	W	5-2	Everton, Anfield, Premier League
25	07.12.2019	1	W	3-0	Bournemouth, Dean Court, Premier League
26	10.12.2019		W	2-0	Red Bull Salzburg, Stadion Salzburg, Champions L. 1st Group Ph.
27	14.12.2019	1	W	2-0	Watford, Anfield, Premier League
28	17.12.2019		L	0-5	Aston Villa, Villa Park, League Cup 5th round
29	18.12.2019		W	2-1	Club de Fútbol Monterrey, Khalifa International Stadium, WCC Semi-final
30	21.12.2019		W	1-0	Flamengo, Khalifa International Stadium, WCC Final
31	26.12.2019	1	W	4-0	Leicester City, Leicester City Stadium, Premier League
32	29.12.2019	1	W	1-0	Wolves, Anfield, Premier League
33	02.01.2020	1	W	2-0	Sheffield United, Anfield, Premier League
34	05.01.2020		W	1-0	Everton, Anfield, FA Cup 3rd round
35	11.01.2020	1	W	1-0	Tottenham Hotspur, Tottenham Hotspur Stadium, Premier League
36	19.01.2020	1	W	2-0	Manchester United, Anfield, Premier League
37	23.01.2020	1	W	2-1	Wolves, Molineux, Premier League
38	26.01.2020		D	2-2	Shrewsbury Town, New Meadow, FA Cup 4th round
39	29.01.2020	1	W	2-0	West Ham United, London Stadium, Premier League
40	01.02.2020	1	W	4-0	Southampton, Anfield, Premier League
41	04.02.2020		W	1-0	Shrewsbury Town, Anfield, FA Cup 4th round replay
42	15.02.2020	1	W	1-0	Norwich City, Carrow Road, Premier League

43	18.02.2020		L	0-1	Atletico Madrid, Metropolitano Stadium, Champions League, 1st knockout r. 1st leg
44	24.02.2020	1	W	3-2	West Ham United, Anfield, Premier League
45	29.02.2020	1	L	0-3	Watford, Vicarage Road, Premier League
46	03.03.2020		L	0-2	Chelsea, Stamford Bridge, FA Cup 5th round
47	07.03.2020	1	W	2-1	Bournemouth, Anfield, Premier League
48	11.03.2020		L	2-3	Atletico Madrid, Anfield, Champions League, 1st knockout r. 2nd leg
49	21.06.2020	1	D	0-0	Everton, Goodison Park, Premier League
50	24.06.2020	1	W	4-0	Crystal Palace, Anfield, Premier League
51	02.07.2020	1	L	0-4	Manchester City, Etihad Stadium, Premier League
52	05.07.2020	1	W	2-0	Aston Villa, Anfield, Premier League
53	08.07.2020	1	W	3-1	Brighton & Hove Albion, American Express Community Stadium, Premier League
54	11.07.2020	1	D	1-1	Burnley, Anfield, Premier League
55	15.07.2020	1	L	1-2	Arsenal, Emirates Stadium, Premier League
56	22.07.2020	1	W	5-3	Chelsea, Anfield, Premier League
57	26.07.2020	1	W	3-1	Newcastle United, St. James' Park, Premier League

Friendlies

1	11.07.2019		W	6-0	Tranmere Rovers, Prenton Park, Friendly
2	14.07.2019		W	3-1	Bradford City, Valley Parade, Friendly
3	19.07.2019		L	2-3	Borussia Dortmund, Notre Dame Stadium, Friendly
4	21.07.2019		L	1-2	Sevilla, Fenway Park, Friendly
5	24.07.2019		D	2-2	Sporting Lisbon, Yankee Stadium, Western Union Cup
6	28.07.2019		L	0-3	Napol, Murrayfield, Friendly
7	31.07.2019		W	3-1	Olympique Lyonnais, Stade de Genève, Friendly
8	11.06.2020		W	6-0	Blackburn Rovers, Anfield, Friendly

Appearances for the 2019/2020 season

Name	League	FA Cup	LC	CS	Other	Total
Roberto Firmino	38	2	0	9	3	52
Virgil Van Dijk	38	1	0	9	2	50
Trent Alexander-Arnold	38	0	0	8	3	49
Andy Robertson	36	1	0	9	3	49
Mohamed Salah	34	2	0	9	3	48
Sadio Mané	35	1	0	9	2	47
Georginio Wijnaldum	37	0	0	9	1	47
Alex Oxlade-Chamberlain	30	2	2	6	3	43
Joe Gomez	28	2	2	8	3	43
Divock Origi	28	3	1	7	3	42
Jordan Henderson	30	0	0	7	3	40
Fabinho Tavarez	28	2	0	8	1	39
Alisson Becker	29	0	0	5	3	37
James Milner	22	2	2	9	2	37
Naby Keita	18	0	2	4	3	27
Adam Lallana	15	2	2	0	3	22
Adrián San Miguel	11	3	0	4	0	18
Dejan Lovren	10	1	1	3	0	15
Takumi Minamino	10	3	0	1	0	14
Joël Matip	9	1	0	2	1	13
Curtis Jones	6	4	2	0	0	12
Xherdan Shaqiri	7	0	0	1	3	11
Neco Williams	6	4	1	0	0	11
Harvey Elliott	2	3	3	0	0	8
Pedro Chirivella	0	3	3	0	0	6
Caoimhin Kelleher	0	1	3	0	0	4
Sepp van den Berg	0	1	3	0	0	4
Ki-Jana Hoever	0	1	2	0	0	3
Rhian Brewster	0	1	2	0	0	3
Herbie Kane	0	0	2	0	0	2
Yasser Larouci	0	2	0	0	0	2
Leighton Clarkson	0	1	1	0	0	2
Morgan Boyes	0	1	1	0	0	2
Tony Gallacher	0	0	1	0	0	1
Elijah Dixon-Bonner	0	1	0	0	0	1
Jack Bearne	0	0	1	0	0	1
James Norris	0	0	1	0	0	1
Thomas Hill	0	0	1	0	0	1
Nathaniel Phillips	0	1	0	0	0	1
Liam Millar	0	1	0	0	0	1
Joe Hardy	0	1	0	0	0	1

Jake Cain	0	1	0	0	0	1
Adam Lewis	0	1	0	0	0	1
Luis Longstaff	0	0	1	0	0	1
Isaac Christie-Davies	0	0	1	0	0	1

Goalscorers for the 2019/2020 season

Name	League	FA Cup	LC	CS	Other	Total
Mohamed Salah	19	0	0	4	0	23
Sadio Mané	18	0	0	4	0	22
Roberto Firmino	9	0	0	1	2	12
Alex Oxlade-Chamberlain	4	0	1	3	0	8
Divock Origi	4	0	2	0	0	6
Georginio Wijnaldum	4	0	0	2	0	6
Own goals	2	2	1	0	0	5
Virgil Van Dijk	5	0	0	0	0	5
Trent Alexander-Arnold	4	0	0	0	0	4
Naby Keita	2	0	0	1	1	4
Jordan Henderson	4	0	0	0	0	4
James Milner	2	0	2	0	0	4
Andy Robertson	2	0	0	1	0	3
Curtis Jones	1	2	0	0	0	3
Joël Matip	1	0	0	0	1	2
Fabinho Tavarez	2	0	0	0	0	2
Dejan Lovren	0	0	0	1	0	1
Ki-Jana Hoever	0	0	1	0	0	1
Adam Lallana	1	0	0	0	0	1
Xherdan Shaqiri	1	0	0	0	0	1

The squad during the 2019/2020 season

1	Alisson Becker, Goalkeeper
22	Simon Mignolet, Goalkeeper
13	Adrián San Miguel, Goalkeeper
62	Caoimhin Kelleher, Goalkeeper
22	Andy Lonergan, Goalkeeper
63	Ben Winterbottom, Goalkeeper
78	Vitezslav Jaros, Goalkeeper
66	Trent Alexander-Arnold, Defender
2	Nathaniel Clyne, Defender
12	Joe Gomez, Defender
6	Dejan Lovren, Defender
32	Joël Matip, Defender
26	Andy Robertson, Defender
4	Virgil Van Dijk, Defender
51	Ki-Jana Hoever, Defender
72	Sepp van den Berg, Defender
46	Adam Lewis, Defender
70	Yasser Larouci, Defender
76	Neco Williams, Defender
89	Billy Koumetio, Defender
77	Morgan Boyes, Defender
65	Tom Clayton, Defender
93	James Norris, Defender
54	Tony Gallacher, Defender
47	Nathaniel Phillips, Defender
14	Jordan Henderson, Midfielder
8	Naby Keita, Midfielder
20	Adam Lallana, Midfielder
7	James Milner, Midfielder
15	Alex Oxlade-Chamberlain, Midfielder
23	Xherdan Shaqiri, Midfielder
3	Fabinho Tavarez, Midfielder
5	Georginio Wijnaldum, Midfielder
67	Harvey Elliott, Midfielder
68	Pedro Chirivella, Midfielder
55	Herbie Kane, Midfielder
75	Luis Longstaff, Midfielder
84	Leighton Clarkson, Midfielder
48	Curtis Jones, Midfielder
57	Isaac Christie-Davies, Midfielder
99	Thomas Hill, Midfielder
69	Elijah Dixon-Bonner, Midfielder

80 Jake Cain, Midfielder
18 Takumi Minamino, Midfielder
24 Rhian Brewster, Striker
9   Roberto Firmino, Striker
10 Sadio Mané, Striker
27 Divock Origi, Striker
11 Mohamed Salah, Striker
81 Jack Bearne, Striker
97 Layton Stewart, Striker
49 Liam Millar, Striker
53 Joe Hardy, Striker

Transfers for the 2019/2020 season

In:
Sepp van den Berg, PEC Zwolle, £4,400,000*, 27 June 2019
Harvey Elliott, Fulham, £0*, 28 July 2019
Adrián San Miguel, Free Transfer, 5 August 2019
Andy Lonergan, Free Transfer, 12 August 2019
Takumi Minamino, Red Bull Salzburg, £7,250,000, 1 January 2020

Out:
Rafael Camacho, Sporting Lisbon, £7,000,000*, 27 June 2019
Daniel Sturridge, Free Transfer, 1 July 2019
Alberto Moreno, Free Transfer, 1 July 2019
Adam Bogdan, Free Transfer, 1 July 2019
Connor Randall, Free Transfer, 1 July 2019
Danny Ings, Southampton, £20,000,000*, 1 July 2019
Simon Mignolet, Club Brugge, £8,200,000*, 5 August 2019
Ryan Kent, Rangers, £7,500,000*, 2 September 2019
Bobby Duncan, Fiorentina, £1,800,000, 2 September 2019
Allan Rodrigues de Souza, Atletico Mineiro, £3,200,000, 9 January 2020
Pedro Chirivella, Nantes, Free*, 1 July 2020

A collection of statistics for the 2019/2020 season

The season in numbers:
Total games: 57
Games won: 41
Games drawn: 8
Games lost: 8
Clean sheets – League: 15
Clean sheets – Overall: 20
Total goals: 117
Average attendance at home – League: 42,054
Average attendance at home – Overall: 44,844
Average goals per game – League: 2.74
Average goals per game – Overall: 2.62
Average goal minute – League: 48
Average goal minute – Overall: 50

Goals split down to competitions:
Premier League – 85
Champions League – 15
League Cup – 7
FA Cup – 4
World Club Championship – 3
European Super Cup – 2
Community Shield – 1

Player debuts:
Adrián San Miguel against Norwich City on 09.08.2019
Herbie Kane against MK Dons on 25.09.2019
Rhian Brewster against MK Dons on 25.09.2019
Caoimhin Kelleher against MK Dons on 25.09.2019
Sepp van den Berg against MK Dons on 25.09.2019
Harvey Elliott against MK Dons on 25.09.2019
Neco Williams against Arsenal on 30.10.2019
Morgan Boyes against Aston Villa on 17.12.2019
Tony Gallacher against Aston Villa on 17.12.2019
Leighton Clarkson against Aston Villa on 17.12.2019
Isaac Christie-Davies against Aston Villa on 17.12.2019
Luis Longstaff against Aston Villa on 17.12.2019
Jack Bearne against Aston Villa on 17.12.2019
James Norris against Aston Villa on 17.12.2019
Thomas Hill against Aston Villa on 17.12.2019
Nathaniel Phillips against Everton on 05.01.2020
Takumi Minamino against Everton on 05.01.2020

Yasser Larouci against Everton on 05.01.2020
Elijah Dixon-Bonner against Shrewsbury Town on 04.02.2020
Liam Millar against Shrewsbury Town on 04.02.2020
Joe Hardy against Shrewsbury Town on 04.02.2020
Jake Cain against Shrewsbury Town on 04.02.2020
Adam Lewis against Shrewsbury Town on 04.02.2020

Statistics and information provided by LFChistory.net

Bibliography

Books:

Billy Liddell, My Soccer Story, Stanley Paul, 1960.

Shankly: My Story By Bill Shankly, 1976.

Bob Paisley, An Autobiography, Littlehampton Book Services Ltd, 1983.

Personal View of the Liverpool First Team Squad of 1986-87, Cablestar Ltd, 1987.

Stephen F. Kelly, The Kop: Liverpool's Twelfth Man, Mandarin Paperbacks, 1993.

Kenny Dalglish My Autobiography, Hodder Paperbacks, 1997.

Club of the Century Liverpool F.C, Liverpool Daily Post and Echo Ltd, 1998.

Phil Thompson, Stand Up Pinocchio, Trinity Mirror Sport Media, 2005.

Dynasty: Fifty Years of Shankly's Liverpool, GPRF, 2008.

Kenny Dalglish and Henry Winter, My Liverpool Home, 2010.

Mark Platt and Andrew Fagan, Joe Fagan: Reluctant Champion: The Authorised Biography, Aurum Press Ltd, 2011.

Liverpool Encyclopedia, De Coubertin Books, 2013.

Liverpool: The Complete Record, De Coubertin Books, 2014.

Mr Liverpool, Trinity Mirror Sport Media, 2017.

Newspapers and publications:

British Soccer Week, Daily Mirror, Telegraph, Guardian, Liverpool Courier, Liverpool Daily Post, Liverpool Echo, Liverpool Evening Express, Liverpool Football Echo, Liverpool Mercury, The Sunday Times, The Times, The Anfield Review, Lancashire Evening Post, The Yorkshire Post and Leeds Intelligencer, LFC Magazine, Liverpool Fanclub magazine, Sunderland Daily Echo, Birmingham Daily Gazette, Daily Express, Daily Mail, Match Magazine.

Websites:

www.lfchistory.net, www.liverpoolfc.com, www.playupliverpool.com, www.thisisanfield.com, www.skysports.com, www.shankly.com.

19